West Academic Publishing's Emeritus Advisory Board

JESSE H. CHOPER
Professor of Law and Dean Emeritus
University of California, Berkeley

LARRY D. KRAMER
President, William and Flora Hewlett Foundation

JAMES J. WHITE
Robert A. Sullivan Emeritus Professor of Law
University of Michigan

WEST ACADEMIC PUBLISHING'S
LAW SCHOOL ADVISORY BOARD

MARK C. ALEXANDER
Arthur J. Kania Dean and Professor of Law
Villanova University Charles Widger School of Law

JOSHUA DRESSLER
Distinguished University Professor Emeritus
Michael E. Moritz College of Law, The Ohio State University

MEREDITH J. DUNCAN
Professor of Law
University of Houston Law Center

RENÉE McDONALD HUTCHINS
Dean & Professor of Law
University of Maryland Carey School of Law

RENEE KNAKE JEFFERSON
Joanne and Larry Doherty Chair in Legal Ethics &
Professor of Law, University of Houston Law Center

ORIN S. KERR
William G. Simon Professor of Law
University of California, Berkeley

JONATHAN R. MACEY
Professor of Law,
Yale Law School

DEBORAH JONES MERRITT
Distinguished University Professor,
John Deaver Drinko/Baker & Hostetler Chair in Law Emerita
Michael E. Moritz College of Law, The Ohio State University

ARTHUR R. MILLER
University Professor and Chief Justice Warren E. Burger Professor of
Constitutional Law and the Courts, New York University

GRANT S. NELSON
Professor of Law Emeritus, Pepperdine University
Professor of Law Emeritus, University of California, Los Angeles

A. BENJAMIN SPENCER
Dean & Trustee Professor of Law
William & Mary Law School

HAPPINESS AND PEAK PERFORMANCE IN LAW SCHOOL

Cutting-Edge Science to Promote Emotional Thriving and Cognitive Greatness in Law School and Beyond

Jarrett Green, Esq., M.A.

Rebecca Simon Green, Esq.

The publisher is not engaged in rendering legal or other professional advice, and this publication is not a substitute for the advice of an attorney. If you require legal or other expert advice, you should seek the services of a competent attorney or other professional.

© 2023 LEG, Inc. d/b/a West Academic
    860 Blue Gentian Road, Suite 350
    Eagan, MN 55121
    1-877-888-1330

West, West Academic Publishing, and West Academic are trademarks of West Publishing Corporation, used under license.

Printed in the United States of America

ISBN: 978-1-68467-856-3

This book is dedicated to our six greatest teachers, who have filled our lives with profound wisdom, growth, and love: Victoria Allen, Luca Bosurgi, Sadhviji, Swami Mukundananda, Neem Karoli Baba, and our daughter Jaya Green.

Preface

"I wish I learned this stuff when I was in law school!"

We often hear this feedback from lawyers after we present to their law firms or legal organizations. They frequently add statements such as, "I would have been so much healthier and happier in law school," or "I would have been far more focused and productive in law school," or "I would have become a more resilient and successful lawyer."

Since 2014 we have been teaching the science-based tools contained in this book to lawyers at many of the largest law firms in the world, in law departments of many Fortune 500 companies, at federal and state governmental agencies, and in public interest legal organizations. Each year we present to thousands of lawyers across the United States, Asia, Europe, and South America.

And now we get to share these tools with you.

We have the greatest job in the world. We get to help people become happier, more resilient, and more successful at what they do. We get to help them transcend the legal industry's ever-present stressors and challenges so they can experience increased emotional freedom and personal power. We get to help them modulate and reduce symptoms of depression and anxiety. We get to help them optimize their thinking and behavioral patterns. We get to help them laugh and express their true self more. We get to help them enhance their focus, productivity and overall cognitive performance. We get to help them rewire their brains. We get to help them build the lives they are meant to have.

Our shared passion for positively impacting other humans and alleviating suffering drew us towards this work, and in fact, towards each other. We both struggled with intense stress, overwhelm, and emotional volatility during law school and in our respective legal careers as a law professor (Rebecca) and commercial litigator (Jarrett). We both yearned for tools that would allow us to navigate all of the stress and pressure in healthier and more effective ways. So we each embarked upon our own decade-plus journey of education and growth, which eventually led to personal transformation for each of us, as well as a calling for this work. At that point in time, we met. Our mutual love for this work was immediately palpable; our love for each other revealed itself more than a year later. We now get to do this important work together as a husband-and-wife team.

About three and a half years before this book was published, our baby Jaya was born. She is a true gift to this world and has electrified our lives with joy, silliness, and grace (*and* constant mini-challenges).

We would now like to introduce you to our second baby: this book. Unlike our first born, the baby you now hold in your hands took far longer than nine months to gestate. This book could not have been written had we not experienced the years of stress, self-doubt, and overwhelm that ultimately catalyzed a decision to change our lives, not to mention the 25 combined years of study and growth that followed. This book also could not have been written had we not been fortunate enough to work with and learn from a large collection of wise teachers and mentors, especially the ones identified on the Dedication Page. We send our profound and humble gratitude to all those invaluable sources of education and inspiration.

We sincerely hope this book positively impacts your law school experience and life.

With gratitude and warmth,

Rebecca & Jarrett

We would love to hear from you! If you have any questions, suggestions, or feedback about the book, please email us at: info@jarrett-green.com. Both of us will read every email that is received.

Summary of Contents

Preface v

The Pursuit of Happiness 1

Introduction to Happiness and Peak Performance in Law School 3

SECTION I. UNDERSTANDING & TRANSFORMING STRESS

Chapter 1. Stress 101 9

Chapter 2. What Causes Stress *Today*? 13

Chapter 3. The Need for the Stress Response in This Day and Age 17

Chapter 4. The Stress-Cognition Loop 19

Chapter 5. A Mantra for Law School Success and Happiness 27

Chapter 6. Two Core Questions 31

SECTION II. MINDSETS FOR LAW SCHOOL SUCCESS & THRIVING

Chapter 7. The Two Different Types of Thinking 49

Chapter 8. The Great Smuggler of Ancient Persia 53

Chapter 9. Is That a Doorknob or an Alligator?! 57

Chapter 10. He Cut You off on the Freeway?! 61

Chapter 11. A Symbol of Peace or Genocide? 67

Chapter 12. That Is *So* Disgusting! 71

Chapter 13. What Is a Mindset? 75

Chapter 14. Housekeepers Who Exercise (That's a Redundancy!) 77

Chapter 15. Feeling out of Place Is *Normal* 81

Chapter 16. When Should I Shift My Mindset? 83

Chapter 17. Shifting Is Not Suppressing 85

Chapter 18. The 5 Mindset Shifts 89

SECTION III. TANGIBLE TOOLS FOR LAW SCHOOL SUCCESS & THRIVING

Tool 1. Face: Chopsticks Will De-Stress You 167

Tool 2. Body: The "90-Degree Rule" 175

Tool 3. Movement: Micro-Exercise Every 3–4 Hours 181

Tool 4. Study Breaks: Make Sure They Are *Non-Intellectual* 187

Tool 5. Phone: Is Your Smart Phone Making You Dumb? 197

Tool 6. Tech Buffer: Build a "Perimeter of Protection" Around the Beginning and End of Your Day 209

Tool 7. Micro-Decisions: Eliminate and Shorten Some 219

Tool 8. Impulsivity: Act Opposite to the Stressor 237

Tool 9. Procrastination: Apply the 10-Minute Rule 243

Tool 10. Goals & Habits: Achieve What You Seek 255

Tool 11. Meditation: It's *Super* Annoying! (Yet Life-Changing) 279

Tool 12. Visualization: Trick Your Brain into Resilient Greatness 297

Tool 13. Verbalization: Neither Vent Nor Suppress 305

Tool 14. Emotional Granularity: Specifically Label Your Emotions 313

SUMMARY OF CONTENTS

Tool 15. Second-Hand Stress: Strengthen Your "No Ninja" 321

Tool 16. Nature: Purposefully Connect to Nature and Awe 327

Tool 17. Time Boxing: A Crest Jewel of Time Management 341

Tool 18. Time of Day Discernment: When Does *Your* Brain Excel on Which Tasks? 349

Tool 19. Laughter: The Underrated Superpower for Boosting Well-Being and Cognition 361

Tool 20. Kindness: Small Altruistic Acts Increase Y*our Own* Happiness 369

Final Thoughts 375

Endnotes 379

TABLE OF CONTENTS

PREFACE V

The Pursuit of Happiness 1

Introduction to Happiness and Peak Performance in Law
    School.. 3

SECTION I. UNDERSTANDING & TRANSFORMING STRESS

Chapter 1. Stress 101 9

Chapter 2. What Causes Stress *Today*? 13

Chapter 3. The Need for the Stress Response in This Day
    and Age 17

Chapter 4. The Stress-Cognition Loop 19

Chapter 5. A Mantra for Law School Success and
    Happiness 27

Chapter 6. Two Core Questions 31
Can I Change My Brain's Current Propensity for Intense
    Stress? 31
    Hiking in the Forest 33
    The Tetris Effect 34
    The Brain's Malleability 36
Do I Have Time to Rewire My Brain for Improved Happiness and
    Cognition? 38

SECTION II. MINDSETS FOR LAW SCHOOL SUCCESS & THRIVING

Chapter 7. The Two Different Types of Thinking 49

Chapter 8. The Great Smuggler of Ancient Persia 53

Chapter 9. Is That a Doorknob or an Alligator?! 57

TABLE OF CONTENTS

Chapter 10. He Cut You off on the Freeway?!..................... 61

Chapter 11. A Symbol of Peace or Genocide? 67

Chapter 12. That Is *So* Disgusting!..................................... 71

Chapter 13. What Is a Mindset?... 75

Chapter 14. Housekeepers Who Exercise (That's a Redundancy!).. 77

Chapter 15. Feeling out of Place Is *Normal* 81

Chapter 16. When Should I Shift My Mindset? 83

Chapter 17. Shifting Is Not Suppressing 85

Chapter 18. The 5 Mindset Shifts...................................... 89
- 1. Threat to Opportunity... 92
  - Bricklayers and Higher Purpose 101
- 2. Judgment to Compassion 105
- 3. Pessimism to Optimism 120
  - An Optimistic Mindset Can Be Cultivated 127
- 4. Fixed to Growth... 136
  - Lightbulbs and Babies 139
  - What if You Fall into the Lake? No Problem, You Can Swim!... 143
  - The Key Question to Ask Yourself Whenever You Fail or Fall.. 146
- 5. External Control to Internal Control 150
  - Beware of Self-Handicapping 158

SECTION III. TANGIBLE TOOLS FOR LAW SCHOOL SUCCESS & THRIVING

Tool 1. Face: Chopsticks Will De-Stress You 167

Tool 2. Body: The "90-Degree Rule" 175

Tool 3. Movement: Micro-Exercise Every 3–4 Hours....... 181

Tool 4. Study Breaks: Make Sure They Are *Non-Intellectual* 187
Examples of Cognitively Rejuvenating Activities 190
Boredom Is Electrifying!... 191

TABLE OF CONTENTS xiii

Tool 5. Phone: Is Your Smart Phone Making You Dumb? 197
Task-Switching Hinders Our Cognitive Performance 198
The Sound and Sight Are *Irresistible!* 202
The Solution: Silence-Stow-Set 206

Tool 6. Tech Buffer: Build a "Perimeter of Protection" Around the Beginning and End of Your Day 209
Rise and Shine with Your Smart Phone? 209
Smart Phone Lullaby? 212

Tool 7. Micro-Decisions: Eliminate and Shorten Some 219
Judges and Doctors Plagued by Willpower Depletion 225
Why Do They Wear the Same Outfit Every Day?! 230

Tool 8. Impulsivity: Act Opposite to the Stressor 237

Tool 9. Procrastination: Apply the 10-Minute Rule 243
Should I Work on That Paper . . .? Nah! 249

Tool 10. Goals & Habits: Achieve What You Seek 255
1. Pick Just One Major Behavioral Goal at a Time 256
2. Break the Goal into Baby Steps 258
3. Make the Goal Specific, Tangible, and Measurable 263
4. Tie the Goal to a Pre-Existing Cue 265
5. Set up the Goal 268
6. Reward Yourself for the Goal 272
7. Track Your Progress 275
Summary 277

Tool 11. Meditation: It's *Super* Annoying! (Yet Life-Changing) 279
Closing 294

Tool 12. Visualization: Trick Your Brain into Resilient Greatness 297

Tool 13. Verbalization: Neither Vent Nor Suppress 305

Tool 14. Emotional Granularity: Specifically Label Your Emotions 313

Tool 15. Second-Hand Stress: Strengthen Your "No Ninja" 321

Tool 16. Nature: Purposefully Connect to Nature and Awe 327
Can I Receive Some of the Benefits of Nature from the Comforts of My Desk? 332
Green Is the New Black 339

Tool 17. Time Boxing: A Crest Jewel of Time Management 341

Tool 18. Time of Day Discernment: When Does *Your* Brain Excel on Which Tasks? 349

Tool 19. Laughter: The Underrated Superpower for Boosting Well-Being and Cognition 361

Tool 20. Kindness: Small Altruistic Acts Increase Y*our* *Own* Happiness 369

Final Thoughts 375

Endnotes 379

HAPPINESS AND PEAK PERFORMANCE IN LAW SCHOOL

Cutting-Edge Science to Promote Emotional Thriving and Cognitive Greatness in Law School and Beyond

The Pursuit of Happiness

As a human being in the United States, you possess an inalienable constitutional right to "life, liberty and the pursuit of happiness." While law school appropriately harps on important legal questions relating to "life" and "liberty," the concept of "happiness" is mysteriously absent from the law school curriculum.

Nobody wants to be subjected to an unreasonable search and seizure; that would hamper our happiness. Similarly, to be incarcerated without due process of law would reduce our happiness. And to be denied the right of freedom of speech would also impair our happiness.

However, assuming we are not unreasonably searched, incarcerated, or censored, and further assuming our various other constitutional and legal rights are not violated, does this mean we will experience happiness in life? Of course not. Happiness is not just the absence of legal violations; it is the presence of something sacred and sublime that enhances the quality of our relationship to life. Happiness allows us to not just experience life, but to flourish in life.

So how do we actually exercise our constitutional right to pursue happiness? On this, the framers were silent. No constitutional interpretation – whether originalist, textualist, or pragmatist – will provide the answer. Law school will teach you many invaluable lessons, but this is not one of them.

Until now.

INTRODUCTION TO HAPPINESS AND PEAK PERFORMANCE IN LAW SCHOOL

Wouldn't it be amazing if you could enhance your happiness and cognitive firepower? If you could reduce your law school stress and anxiety, and expand your resilience, self-confidence, and overall joyfulness? What if your mind could be clearer, more focused, and flat-out better at learning, reading, outlining, memorizing, public speaking, exam-taking, decision making, and various other law school competencies?

If this interests you, then keep reading!

No matter who we are, or how successful we are, or how intelligent we may be, or what our cultural background is, or what our political views are, or whether we want to go into corporate law or public interest law, or whether we want to be a criminal defense attorney or a prosecutor, all law students – *and all humans* – have two things in common: we all want to be happier in life and we all want our brains to work even better.

Regarding happiness, irrespective of our unique emotional makeup, we all want to experience even greater or more frequent joy, mental well-being, internal peace, emotional balance, resiliency, and bliss. There is not a person on the planet (*and certainly not in law school!*) who can say they have achieved complete and ever-lasting happiness. Realistically, the overwhelming majority of us are miles away from this unachievable standard.

And law school certainly doesn't help this issue, as evidenced by the plethora of studies revealing the widespread mental and emotional suffering that is plaguing both our law schools and the legal profession generally.* This quote from

---

* Any basic Google search will reveal the fundamental mental and emotional challenges facing our industry, but if you'd like some targeted resources, please see: Eaton, W. W., Anthony, J. C., Mandel, W., & Garrison, R. (1990). Occupations and the prevalence of major depressive disorder. *Journal of Occupational Medicine, 32*(11), 1079–1087. DOI: 10.1097/00043764-199011000-00006; Krill, P. R., Johnson, R., & Albert, L. (2016). The prevalence of substance use and other mental health concerns

Nitya Prakash seems apropos: "Law school is like looking both ways before crossing the street and then getting hit by an airplane."*

Regarding our brains, irrespective of how intelligent we are or how vast our cognitive gifts, we all want to experience even better sustained attention, focus, reading comprehension, information absorption, memorization, verbal and written expression, creativity, decision making, and overall discretionary judgment. Again, there is not a person on the planet (*although some law school "gunners" may pretend otherwise*) who can say they possess perfect cognitive functioning.

In reality, the vast majority of us, if fully honest with ourselves, would delightedly welcome improvements to several aspects of our cognition if given the opportunity. Yet, such improvements elude us, for reasons we'll explain later in this book. Law school's constant and overwhelming academic challenges, combined with its population of highly intellectual students, can expose an even deeper yearning in us for improved cognition.

So, just as the old adage states "the two guarantees in life" are taxes and the sun rising each morning, we can say with equal confidence that the "two guarantees in law school" are the desire for greater happiness and the desire for improved cognition.

Nevertheless, very few law students make a concerted or strategic effort to satisfy these desires. Instead, their grueling efforts are dedicated almost exclusively to such matters as reading and briefing for class, outlining for finals, and memorizing the elements of a prima facie case for malicious sandal-weaving (*if that's not a real tort, it should be*).

---

among American attorneys. *Journal of Addiction Medicine, 10*(1), 46–52. DOI: 10.1097/ADM.0000000000000182. See also Benjamin, G. A., Darling, E. J., & Sales, B. (1990). The prevalence of depression, alcohol abuse, and cocaine abuse among United States lawyers, *International Journal of Law and Psychology, 13*(3), 233–46 (1990). DOI: 10.1016/0160-2527(90)90019-y; Flores, R. & Arce, R. M. (2014, January 20). Why are lawyers killing themselves? *CNN.* https://www.cnn.com/2014/01/19/us/lawyer-suicides/index.html.

* Confession: the actual quote is identical to the above version, except the word "Adulting" was used instead of "Law school." But we believe that Mr. Prakash's words are especially applicable to adulting *in law school.*

INTRODUCTION TO HAPPINESS AND PEAK PERFORMANCE IN LAW SCHOOL

The purpose of this book is two-fold:

(1) to convince you that it is worth your time to make a consistent (yet minimally demanding) effort to improve your happiness and your cognition; and

(2) to provide you with a collection of simple techniques that have been scientifically proven to enhance one's happiness and cognition without a significant time commitment.

There is arguably a third purpose of this book: to give you a much-deserved piece of law school reading that is not painfully complex and stressful. (Have you noticed that law school reading tends to leave you feeling like Muhammed Ali punched you in the brain – or is that just us?) It is our sincerest hope that as you read this book, you will find yourself feeling entertained, energized, uplifted, and empowered.

The book is broken up into three parts. Section I explores the stress response and how the human brain is capable of being rewired in ways that lead to greater resilience, happiness, and cognitive functioning. Section II provides a framework for shifting your mindsets or high-level attitudes in order to improve your emotional well-being and cognitive performance in law school. Section III offers 20 practical "brain hacks" you can use to achieve these same results. So, Section I provides the scientific foundation, Section II provides guidance on how to optimize your high-level thinking and framing of law school challenges, and Section III provides tangible behavioral tools for enhancing your well-being and performance in law school.

If we are successful as authors, then you will finish this book with an intention to gradually improve your happiness and cognitive functioning, as well as a clear roadmap and collection of science-based techniques for becoming an even happier and brainier version of yourself. That would be a beautiful, life-altering result – because there is *nothing* more important in life than dedicating oneself to becoming a happier and more fulfilled human being whose brain and thinking function even more powerfully. (Not even IRAC'ing the landmark case on malicious sandal-weaving!)

Section I

Understanding & Transforming Stress

In order to change our relationship to stress – and its control over us – we first must understand the nature of stress. "You cannot change what you cannot see," as they say. So let's take a clear look at what stress is, why we have it, and how it impacts our neurological functioning and our law school performance. From there, we will be able to take tangible actions to begin controlling and reducing our stress, as well as unlocking our brain's higher functioning.

Chapter 1

Stress 101

If we were to ask you, "Why do we humans have the stress response?" You would likely say something to the effect of, "for survival," or "for protection," or "to stay alive." And you'd be correct. Yet most people's understanding of the stress response (aka the "fight-or-flight response") ends right there, so we want to take you a little deeper.

Imagine yourself back in caveperson days. You were at the local river when you caught a fresh salmon. Talking had not yet been invented, so you expressed your glee with a series of guttural groans and squawks. (You were especially giddy because the last time you ate was nine days ago, since they didn't have Chipotle on every corner back then.)

You are triumphantly making your way back to your cave or hut (depending on your housing preference and socioeconomic class), when out of the blue a tiger pops out of the bushes from 20 feet away, simultaneously uttering a vicious roar and staring you dead in the eyes. In less than *one tenth of a second*, your entire physiological system goes into overdrive – in order to somehow survive this sudden threat of death.

Your respiratory system goes into overdrive, causing you to breathe fast and shallow. Your endocrine system goes into overdrive, causing cortisol, adrenaline, and noradrenaline (the three primary stress hormones) to flood your system and get you all "jacked up" energetically. Your cardiovascular system goes into overdrive, causing your heart to beat hard and fast. Your circulatory system goes into overdrive, causing your blood to rush to your four limbs, so your limbs are as nimble and responsive as humanly possible. Finally, your muscular system goes into overdrive, causing the muscles throughout your body to involuntarily contract, so that you can instantaneously punch or run without a moment's delay. All of this occurs in less than one-tenth of a second after seeing or hearing the tiger – long before you can even comprehend what is happening, and long before your analytical thinking begins to evaluate the species or specific risk at issue.

That is a lightning-fast physiological reaction! And, what's more, during that same tenth of a second, not only do all of the physiological systems that will increase your chances of survival go into overdrive, each of the physiological systems that will decrease your chances of survival goes into underdrive, so your limited resources are diverted exclusively to survival.

So which systems go into underdrive? Your reproductive system goes into underdrive, because your brain knows that the ability to procreate nine months from now is irrelevant if the tiger kills you today. Your urinary system goes into underdrive, because expelling toxins from the blood and body are important for long-term health, but if you die today your long-term health will have become a moot issue. Your digestive system goes into underdrive, because digesting and processing nutrients, minerals, and proteins are, similarly, necessary for long-term health, but dead people don't do much digesting. And finally, your immune system goes into underdrive, because fighting off long-term disease and illness is extremely important generally, but not if you are already dead.*

Your primitive brain regions know the only thing that matters in this moment is surviving this lethal threat. So physiological systems that would ordinarily ceaselessly advance your long-term survival temporarily de-activate to allow their vast resources to be instantly diverted to the small collection of systems that will increase your chances of punching or running your way to survival. The brain is keenly aware that nothing matters in this moment other than surviving this lethal threat.

---

* This is why five of the top six causes of death in the U.S. (heart disease, cancer, chronic lower respiratory diseases, stroke and cerebrovascular diseases, and Alzheimer's disease) are strongly tied to chronic stress. Each time we experience a jolt of stress, our immune system goes into underdrive and various short-term biochemical reactions occur that gradually increase our susceptibility to those illnesses over time. It truly is the quintessence of "death by a thousand cuts," or more specifically, "death by a thousand stressors." (The only cause of death in the top six that is not directly tied to chronic stress, accidental injuries, is an umbrella category that includes everything from car accidents to unintentional gun deaths to slip-and-falls. While chronic stress is not a contributing factor to this entire category of deaths, the evidence shows that many of the individual deaths in this category occur when individuals are under heightened acute stress.)

STRESS 101

There is one other fascinating physiological reaction that should be mentioned. Sticky platelets begin forming in your blood within milliseconds of noticing the tiger. Why might that be? So that your blood thickens – or coagulates – in the event you are cut open. That's right, even before your conceptual or analytical thinking can comprehend what is occurring, your primitive brain is already clotting your blood in case those tiger teeth penetrate your skin.

That is a very sophisticated and finely tuned system.

CHAPTER 2

WHAT CAUSES STRESS *TODAY*?

Since the fight-or-flight response is designed to protect us from dying at the hands (or paws) of an aggressive predator, wouldn't that suggest that the only moments you feel stress in life are when you are facing an imminent threat of death?

As intense as law school can be, you are not facing a continual threat of death in performing your law school duties. Hopefully you are not being chased by a lion each time you read your Torts textbook or evading a leaping jaguar when your Civil Procedure professor is explaining the burden of persuasion on a motion for summary judgment.

So we can safely assume that since you are never facing an imminent threat of death in law school, you must never be stressed out. Safe assumption? Obviously, that's ridiculous. So why is it that you feel so much stress in law school and life — even when you are not facing an imminent threat of death?

It's because, while our stress response is innate, many of the events that trigger it are learned over the course of our life. Infants are born with the stress response, but it is only triggered by physically threatening events. But from our very early childhood, our brains slowly become wired to interpret non-lethal challenges identically to lethal challenges. This is actually a learned physiological behavior, not an innate physiological tendency.

If you're not convinced by this, we'd like to invite you to try a simple experiment. Next time you are in the presence of an infant, go ahead and bring a live tiger into the room with the infant. You can feel free to leave the room for a couple minutes to get a cup of coffee or catch up on emails. After two minutes, return to the room and see what the infant is doing. Assuming she is still in one piece, we guarantee you she will be crying. Why? Because her innate stress response was triggered by the presence of this dangerous predator, despite the fact that this infant has never seen a tiger before (depending, of course, on the unique parenting style of her parents). Without ever having seen a tiger, her brain will go into immediate stress the moment the tiger flashes its teeth or makes an aggressive gesture or sound.*

Now move onto the second stage of the experiment. Remove the tiger from the room, and once the infant has returned to a state of calm, hand the infant your most stressful reading assignment from law school. You can even place before her a Practice Final Exam from your least favorite class. Go ahead and leave the room again for a couple minutes, and then return to check on her emotional state. You'll notice something very interesting: while merely thinking about this very reading assignment (and Practice Final Exam) triggers the stress response in you, it has no such effect on the infant. She is unphased by it. For similar reasons, you will never see an infant go into the stress response upon learning the Dow Jones plummeted by 500 points that day.

Yet over the course of this infant's childhood, she will slowly begin responding neurologically and physiologically to non-lethal events or goals as if they are critically important to her life. Her brain will begin to go into stress whenever those events or goals do not unfold as she wishes, and eventually, whenever she even thinks about that mere possibility. She will ultimately become like the rest of us: stressed from the routine obstacles of life, such as failures and mistakes she makes, unexpected traffic jams on the way to important outings, emails containing undesirable updates, personal or professional rejections, long checkout lines while shopping, judgmental text messages from friends or family members, login problems as she tries to access one of her many accounts, and countless other "bumps" that will inevitably arise throughout the typical week.

And if she ends up going to law school, her brain will also get triggered into stress by the customary challenges of law school, such as lengthy reading assignments, legal writing deadlines, challenges with outlining, falling behind on calling back grandma or other loved ones, thoughts of final exams, and

---

* The authors of this book hereby waive any and all liability for any baby maulings that occur as a result of or in furtherance of the very reasonable scientific experiment we have suggested.

WHAT CAUSES STRESS TODAY? 15

of course getting cold-called by that professor who eternally loves the Socratic Method.

Importantly, anytime we feel a jolt of stress from these standard law school and life difficulties, the full set of physiological reactions we previously outlined goes into effect. Yes, that's right, when you are feeling nervous about being called on in class or stressing about final exams, ***your blood is coagulating***. Your brain is confused; it literally thinks you are about to be sliced open by the teeth of a predator. So we are living life constantly overwhelmed by stress for no valid reason, simply because our brain is misconstruing the situation and inducing an inappropriate physiological response that makes us less happy.

In light of the brain's continual state of confusion over deadly versus non-deadly threats, and the fact that most of us never face attacks from lethal predators in this day and age, it's only natural to wonder whether we even need the stress response at this point in human history. Would we be better off without the stress response in this day and age? If we could waive a magic wand to eliminate it, would we be wise to do so?

CHAPTER 3

THE NEED FOR THE STRESS RESPONSE IN THIS DAY AND AGE

Even though the stress response is the cause of so much unnecessary emotional suffering throughout our days, it still does keep us alive – even in this modern time. It is true that we are not facing a regular threat of death from predators these days, but we do face periodic threats of death from other sources. Every time we drive a car, walk across a busy intersection, or hike along a scenic view, our stress response is keeping us alive.

For example, say you are driving your car while enjoying a lovely conversation with your friend located in the passenger seat, when suddenly a car from the next lane over springs across the line towards your car. Your split-second stress response, and all the physiological reactions it involves, causes you to yank the steering wheel with just enough time to avoid disaster. Or, have you ever been emailing or texting on your phone while walking along a hallway or sidewalk only to suddenly jerk your head up at the last second before running face-first into someone or something? *(Come on, don't lie to us!)* Well, it was your stress response that sparked your rapid, face-salvaging reflex.

Say, instead, that you are hiking along a steep overhang. You are able to focus your conscious attention on the beauty of the wilderness and the view because your stress response will unequivocally alert you whenever you get too close to the edge. Or, you are walking down a flight of stairs when your foot slips on a wet spot, causing you to begin an inevitable tumble down the stairs. Before your misguided foot even clears the slippery step, though, your stress response intervenes – causing you to instinctively flail towards the railing and grasp it with lightning-fast reflexes, sparing you an atrocious fall.

So the reality is that we undoubtedly need the stress response in this day and age. The problem is that we only need it very rarely – compared to how frequently we ignite it. So the question becomes: Can we preserve our ability to unleash the stress response in the rare instances of physical danger, while reducing our tendency to continually default to the stress response from the various challenges and difficulties that routinely occur in law school and life?

As you will see below, the answer is a definitive "yes." But before we explain why that is so, we first want to get your buy-in on a critically important threshold question: If you succeeded in reducing your tendency to continually stress over law school matters, would your cognition and academic performance improve?

CHAPTER 4

THE STRESS-COGNITION LOOP

We have been sold a book of lies. In law school, in our undergraduate education, and in life. There is this "badge of honor" illusion pervading society that proclaims: If we are a *chaotic ball of stressed-out misery* as we work for something, or towards our goal, it means we are maximally dedicated to it, passionate about it, and treating it with the reverence it deserves. In order to demonstrate – to myself and others – that I care deeply about the goal and am trying my absolute best, I must experience emotional turmoil. I must be stressed out and miserable inside.

If I want to be the best possible employee, I have to sacrifice my well-being and grind myself into the ground for the company. If I want to be the best possible lawyer, I have to inundate myself with inordinate amounts of stress as I zealously fight for the best interests of the client or the cause, regardless of the effect on my own wellness. And if I want to be the best possible law student, I have to continually push myself beyond my emotional limits and experience a perpetual state of angst as I desperately push for law school "success." Law school is deeply important after all, so constantly being overwhelmed is just the cost I have to pay for my dedication and ultimate success.

This is all an illusion.

And one that is contradicted by very basic neuroscience. Here's why: law school (and all academic or intellectual endeavors) involve the interplay between two primary brain regions – the prefrontal cortex (aka the "PFC") and the amygdala.* Our PFC is primarily responsible for our executive functioning, i.e., our highest-level of cognition, such as focus, attention control, impulse inhibition, logical reasoning, strategy, planning, goal selection and monitoring, behavioral implementation and adaptability, regulation of aspects of speech

---

* Many other brain regions are obviously implicated by law school and any such endeavor, but these are the two primary ones that are disproportionately and most directly responsible for our academic success and emotional well-being along the way.

and language, emotional regulation, working memory, cognitive flexibility, problem solving, decision making, and discretionary judgment. Sounds important.*

Our amygdala, on the other hand, is the fear or emotion center of our brain, and it is primarily responsible for regulating our stress response and sympathetic nervous system. In furtherance of these important functions, its job is to keep us alive by guarding against and responding to threats, dangers, and problems.

So our PFC is primarily responsible for our highest-level thinking, while our amygdala is primarily responsible for our lowest-level, survival thinking. As a matter of simple neuroscience, whenever we are experiencing a jolt of stress, our PFC goes into underdrive and our amygdala goes into overdrive. This means that our PFC has significantly reduced neural activation (i.e., brain cell activity) and our amygdala has significantly increased neural activation. Our highest and most sophisticated levels of thinking thus become impaired in favor of the lower-level, survival thinking that is now in charge. This interplay between the PFC and the amygdala is often referred to as "amygdala hijacking" because our highest and best thinking has been highjacked by our subordinate, base thinking.

What effect does this have on law school performance? We doubt you need us to tell you the answer, but it can be summarized in one word: plummet. When we are experiencing a jolt of stress in connection with law school, it means our highest level "law school brain" is under-functioning and our lowest level "survival brain" is over-functioning. If a neuroscientist or doctor connected you to a live brain scan, such as an electroencephalogram (EEG), for an entire week and then monitored the results, you would learn that every time you felt a stress jolt during the week, your PFC went into under-activation and your amygdala went into over-activation. You

---

* An extraordinarily evolved prefrontal cortex is what separates us humans from the rest of the animals. Even though the remaining regions of our brains are proportionately sized to theirs, our prefrontal cortex is far larger and more elaborate than their prefrontal cortexes. This is why your dog or cat would not be as good a law student as you.

THE STRESS-COGNITION LOOP   21

would literally be able to see the difference in neural activity on the screen.*

    This neurological shift would affect various aspects of your cognitive functioning while you are feeling that stress jolt. Indeed, the many cognitive faculties governed by the PFC outlined above would each be impaired, since the PFC, itself, is under-activated. Your brain is confused and falsely believes your physical survival is threatened, so it deactivates your high-level cognitive functioning (which, if left undisturbed, will only impede physical survival) in favor of the low-level cognitive functioning that will advance physical survival. It is therefore not surprising that most of the cognitive faculties that are most central to law school success are diminished while we are experiencing a stream of stress.

    What's more, after an initial spike for a couple minutes, our focus and attention plummet for up to an hour after a stress jolt, which is why you may notice yourself reaching for social media, web-browsing, and other distractions when you are shaken by stress. This experience often is not a focus or attention problem *per se*, but rather a stress management problem that secondarily manifests as a focus or attention problem. And, logically, when we have chronic, unmanaged stress, we generally suffer from chronic problems with focus and attention.

    Here's how it can play out: You are dedicatedly reading your assignment for the night when you receive an unexpected text message from a law school friend saying they heard the Property final exam is likely to ask about the rule against perpetuities. Your focus and attention instantly (*and involuntarily*) divert from your reading assignment to the Final Exam, still two months away, and you spiral into stress due to your deep-seated contempt for the rule against perpetuities. After a few minutes of being roiled by stress, you try your best to return to your reading but find yourself struggling to focus and unable to resist reaching for a distraction, like Twitter or your favorite website. After twenty minutes of this numbing distraction, you try to convince yourself to return to the reading that was so

---

    * Being connected to an EEG or functional MRI for an entire week of law school would obviously pose some logistical challenges, but the assessment would confirm your brain's regional activation differences, assuming you overcame those challenges.

unceremoniously sabotaged by your stress jolt.* You can see how focus and attention problems that result from chronic, unmanaged stress can significantly impair your law school performance.†

The stress jolt also impairs your comprehension abilities. Have you ever noticed yourself reading a particularly complex and dense case while under a wave of stress, and when you get to the end of the paragraph, you realize you have *no idea* what that paragraph meant? You anxiously return to the top of the paragraph and re-read it, only to realize again that you have *zero idea* what it meant.

What was happening in your brain during that experience? It is not as if you became instantly illiterate. What occurred is actually quite simple and predictable: Your brain interpreted the stress as a sign that you were under physical attack, so it deactivated your high-level comprehension abilities, since high-level comprehension is a hinderance to survival while under a sudden physical attack. Indeed, there's no need for sophisticated comprehension or hair-splitting interpretations of what occurred while facing a violent attack: You are being attacked and you need to run or hit ASAP. It's pretty simple! So your fancy law school comprehension abilities are temporarily reduced, manifesting in reading comprehension problems – or auditory

---

* It is actually a wonderful thing that your focus and attention get instantaneously and fully diverted to the stressor the moment it arises because if a tiger popped out of the bushes along your path, you would want 100% of your focus and attention instantaneously and fully diverted to it, and away from whatever less important matter you happened to be thinking of at that moment. Split attention would substantially increase the likelihood of death. Unsurprisingly, this tidal wave of focus and attention lasts for a couple of minutes, which is the typical time it takes to survive (*or succumb to*) the dangerous predator. Once you have survived the predator, thanks in part to the short-term spike of focus and attention, your brain needs to recover, since this heightened level focus and attention is not sustainable in the long run. During the recovery process, your focus and attention are appropriately deactivated as they rejuvenate, leading to reduced focus and attention and increased distractibility over the subsequent period. Also known as: "Instagram time."

† Relatedly, our stress jolts cause a disproportionate depletion of energy and will power. Because our brain believes our survival is at stake, large quantities of energy are justifiably expended during the stress response. Subsequent fatigue is a very reasonable price to pay for surviving a deadly attack. But if our system is regularly going into the stress response during the non-lethal challenges of law school, then we are bleeding away our precious and limited energy, causing our baseline energy levels to lower. If you find yourself regularly fatigued or exhausted, even when you get decent sleep, your unmanaged stress is the likely culprit. Of course, depleted energy and will power translate to impaired productivity, concentration and overall academic performance.

THE STRESS-COGNITION LOOP 23

comprehension problems if you are gripped by stress while the professor is lecturing during class.

The stress jolt also reduces several facets of your memory, such as working memory, short-term memory, and memory retrieval. Have you ever read and briefed for class, feeling very prepared and confident, only to notice your brain suddenly seize up upon getting unexpectedly called on by the professor? As the professor's gaze – and all of your peers' eyes – descend upon you, your stomach swirls and your throat tightens. As the professor asks you a series of irritatingly probing questions, you suddenly cannot remember the details of the fact pattern or the analytical nuances of the case, even though you knew them seconds before being called on. It can feel like brain fog or some inexplicable memory loss.

Importantly, you are not suffering from memory problems *per se*, but rather stress management problems that are impairing your ability to access the collection of memories you previously formed when you briefed the case. This cognitive faculty is called memory retrieval, and it is materially compromised when we are stressed. Memory retrieval impairments can also devastate our final exam performance, as the unmanaged stress of the exam weakens our ability to retrieve or access information on "game day" even though we effectively stored the information in our hippocampus (the long-term memory center of the brain) while studying for the exam.

The stress jolt also impairs our verbal and written expression or fluency. It is one thing to have something valuable to say; it is an entirely different thing to be able to express it in an effective and eloquent manner. Both verbal and written fluency are hindered by stress because the brain knows that tapping into our sophisticated language skills will only get us killed when facing a predator in the wild. What if, instead of frantically running or wildly hitting when the tiger pops out of the bushes, you utilized your highfalutin law school talk to try to convince the tiger not to attack you? How would that work out for you? Perhaps you demonstrate your rhetorical prowess by reciting an *ad hoc* Shakespearean soliloquy to the tiger:

To be or not to be,
Depends on whether thou shall eat me,

Devour my flesh or set me free,
My fate kneels beneath thee on its knee,
The moral decision thou shall see,
Will be to release me full of glee.*

You are now tiger food. To prevent this from occurring, your verbal and written expression goes into underdrive the moment the stress floods in, and those preserved resources are diverted to surviving the tiger. In the modern-day setting, this reaction causes us to get tongue-tied or stumble on our words when called on in class or when doing other forms of public speaking, whether in moot court or eventually "real court," and in countless other situations as a lawyer, such as negotiations, client presentations, and team updates. Similarly, our impaired written expression manifests as "writer's block": We struggle to eloquently express the nuanced concepts we have in our mind – something that becomes an issue not only during the briefing and outlining process throughout the semester, but also during the essay section of any law school exam.

Finally, the stress jolt impairs our problem solving, decision making, and discretionary judgment. Neuroscientists often describe this phenomenon as "perceptual narrowing," where our capacity to observe and balance the multi-dimensional factors that influence our discernment and decision making is minimized. Have you ever sent an insta-reply to an upsetting text from a friend or family member in the midst of stressfully slogging your way through an avalanche of reading? If so, then you know all about "perceptual narrowing"! In that split second, it felt irresistibly tempting to zing them with a slightly harsh reply, so you *let 'er rip*, as they say. But just a few minutes later, the guilt and regret began to set in. You realize you should not have sent that text, and you wish you could fish it back.

We call it "The Other DUI": "Deciding Under the Influence" *of stress*. When we are in the shackles of stress, the quality of our perception, discernment, and decision making is objectively

---

* For any thespians or Shakespearean commentators out there, please resist the urge to write us a letter informing us that this is *not* a soliloquy, since it is a unilateral communication to the tiger, not a self-directed inner dialogue outwardly spoken. Now that you are in law school, we want to congratulate you on your newfound ability to annoy your friends and family in two completely different ways: (1) correcting their Shakespeare references; and (2) always talking about the law.

THE STRESS-COGNITION LOOP

reduced. This reduction has manifold effects on law school performance, including on all four components of IRAC – i.e. – issue-spotting, rule analysis, application of rule, and conclusion – not to mention the critical decisions you make on a daily basis regarding time allocation and task prioritization.

For all of the foregoing reasons (*see what we did there?**), we can all agree that unmanaged stress impairs our cognitive and academic performance in law school.

---

* According to research, over 90% of U.S. Supreme Court cases begin the Conclusion section of the Majority Opinion with "For all of the foregoing reasons,". (OK, we don't have any research to support that claim. It's just a hunch.)

CHAPTER 5

A MANTRA FOR LAW SCHOOL SUCCESS AND HAPPINESS

In light of this conclusive neuroscience, we would like to offer a mantra (or affirmation) that you can recite to remind you of the truth and disconnect you from the illusion. Here it is: *"Stress minimization equals cognitive maximization."**

We don't believe it is an exaggeration to state that if you truly accept this foundational reality, your entire law school experience (and legal career) can transform. We wish that you would be motivated to prioritize your emotional well-being, mental health, and stress resiliency just because you care about being happy and healthy. But if you are like most law students (and lawyers), it can be easy to feel you must sacrifice these things in favor of academic success.

But that feeling hinges upon the illusion that emotional well-being and academic success are in tension with each other. As you now fully understand, whenever you invest time and effort in minimizing your stress or maximizing your well-being, you are simultaneously – *and by necessity* – investing in maximizing your cognition and academic success.

Our hope is that this mantra helps you concretize the reality that stress resiliency and emotional well-being are core competencies and drivers of academic success. Even if you are unwilling to invest in your emotional well-being and stress resiliency so you can lead a happier and healthier life, perhaps you are willing to do so in order to get better grades. It is the ultimate "win-win" situation.

In his landmark book, *The Happiness Advantage*, Harvard psychologist and happiness expert Shawn Anchor outlines the scientific interplay between happiness and success.[1] He likens this relationship to the orbiting of the earth and the sun.

---

* Here's an alternative mantra to consider, but we invite you to select whichever one most resonates with you: *"Stress resilience equals cognitive excellence."*

Throughout much of human history, it was believed that the earth was the center of the universe and that the sun revolved around the earth. Then, in 1543, Nicholas Copernicus published *De Revolutionibus Orbium Coelestium*, in which he argued that the exact opposite was true, i.e., the earth orbits the sun. Copernicus' then-controversial argument was, of course, later proven to be correct. Anchor explains that a similar misconception has governed our view of the relationship between happiness and success throughout history – which is now being corrected:

> Today a similar fundamental shift in the field of psychology is underway. For untold generations, we have been led to believe that happiness orbited around success. That if we work hard enough, we will be successful, and only if we are successful will we become happy. Success was thought to be the fixed point of the work universe, with happiness revolving around it. Now, thanks to breakthroughs in the burgeoning field of positive psychology, we are learning that the opposite is true. When we are happy – when our mindset and mood are positive – we are smarter, more motivated, and thus more successful. Happiness is the center, and success revolves around it.

Anchor's book is laden with scientific studies supporting the principle that happier and more emotionally healthy people are far more successful academically and professionally. Happiness is the pathway to success, not vice versa. In the 13 years since Anchor first published his book, the scientific research supporting this principle has exploded. We will reference many of these cutting-edge studies in this book. In fact, this book cites over 350 scientific studies throughout its chapters – and takes a quintessentially science-based approach. (Due to the sheer volume of studies cited, we have mostly listed the studies in endnotes, rather than footnotes, in order to not disrupt the continuity of your reading and to reduce the total length of the book by nearly 20 pages. But we encourage you to flip to the endnotes to locate the specific studies we reference whenever it suits you. Moreover, we have used footnotes throughout the book to address substantive points, as opposed to mere citations.)

A MANTRA FOR LAW SCHOOL
SUCCESS AND HAPPINESS

As you read on, we invite you to let go of the antiquated myths that have plagued law school and society for generations, and to instead live your life according to scientific truth. If you prioritize minimizing your stress and maximizing your happiness as you navigate law school, the science says your brain will function better and you will be more successful.*

---

* Throughout this book, we will be discussing the concepts of happiness, stress resilience, mental health, and emotional well-being. Although there are technical differences between each of these concepts, we have elected not to get caught up in the various technical definitions in this book. In his Concurring Opinion in the 1964 case of *Jacobellis v. Ohio*, Supreme Court Justice Potter Stewart famously quipped that he might not be able to adequately define the contours of "indecency," but "I know it when I see it." 378 U.S. 184, 197 (1964). Similarly, we believe that when it comes to happiness, stress resilience, mental health, and emotional well-being, the technical definition of each is of little importance to you because "you know it when you see it." Or more accurately, "you know it when you *feel* it." That being said, we want to provide a very basic (and admittedly oversimplified) definition of each concept that likely comports with your intuitive knowing. Happiness is the experience of joy and contentment combined with a sense that one's life is good and worthwhile. Resilience is the ability to navigate or adapt to difficult or unwanted life events and experiences without excessive mental or emotional impairments. Mental health is one's state of mind about oneself and life that influences one's thoughts, feelings, and actions throughout the day, as well as the absence or effective regulation of psychological conditions. Emotional well-being is an overall positive state of one's emotions and ability to process unpleasant emotions and life difficulties in healthy and adaptive ways.

CHAPTER 6

TWO CORE QUESTIONS

In light of everything we have discussed thus far, two core questions naturally arise: (1) Can we change the way our brain functions so the constant law school challenges do not overwhelm us with intense stress? And, assuming the answer to the first question is "yes," (2) Do we have time to do so in the midst of all of the law school chaos?

The answer to both questions, of course, is "<u>no</u>." Thanks for reading this book – we hope you enjoyed it! Please write a good review on Amazon. We wish you luck with that constant influx of debilitating stress that is unchangeable and that you have no time to address!

We are joking! Of course the answer to both questions is "yes." We will now address them one at a time.

CAN I CHANGE MY BRAIN'S CURRENT PROPENSITY FOR INTENSE STRESS?

The bad news, which we laid out previously, is that your brain has become wired over the course of your life to go into stress from routine academic and life challenges. The good news, however, is that the science proves you can rewire your brain – so the same challenges that currently trigger you into stress either will not trigger you or will trigger you far less.

One of the great discoveries of modern science is neuroplasticity, i.e., the ability of the human brain to modify, change and adapt its neural wiring, structure, and functioning throughout life in response to our actions, thoughts, and emotions.* As recently as the early 2000s, it was believed that our brain structures, wiring, and patterns were essentially fixed by the time of early adulthood. Now we know that is not true –

---

* Neurogenesis is the related ability of the brain to grow new neurons. Although neurogenesis is technically different than neuroplasticity, mainstream discussions of brain optimization often use the term "neuroplasticity" to refer to both neuroplasticity and neurogenesis.

the human brain is inherently dynamic and fluid, and constantly evolving, shifting, and reformatting.

What causes the brain to evolve, shift, and reformat? The unique experiences we subject the brain to – in the form of our actions, thoughts, and emotions. In this sense, there is a feedback loop between the structure of the brain and our individual experiences. Certainly our brain's structure influences our actions, thoughts, and emotions in response to life events; but the opposite is also true – the actions, thoughts, and emotions we experience in response to life events influence our brain's structure.

Think of a person's morning coffee routine. We will call this person Connie. For the first 17 years of Connie's life, she never tasted coffee. As a result, her brain was not wired for coffee in any way, and she had no urges or yearnings for coffee. Coffee was a non-factor in her life. Then one day when she was 17 years old, Connie said to herself, "I'm going to try coffee today! Everyone seems to drink it, so it must be delicious." She then had a cup and found it decent, but it wasn't her favorite thing. She then continued to drink coffee each morning, and little by little began to enjoy it more and more.

After a few weeks, Connie has a busy morning trying to finish her homework for the day and doesn't find time to have her cup of coffee. Her brain starts reacting: "Give me my coffee!!" She tries to focus on her homework, but her brain constantly yanks her attention away from her homework to the rich aroma and flavor of coffee. She notices herself feeling a bit fatigued and irritable, and she senses that she'll feel better and more alert if she has her coffee. She hurriedly gets up from the desk and makes and drinks a cup of coffee, causing her brain to feel relieved and satiated.

What has happened is that through her consistent actions over time, Connie's brain has gotten wired for coffee. Now that her brain is wired for coffee, her brain wiring dictates her current emotions, thoughts, and actions. When she doesn't have her morning coffee these days, she experiences *thoughts* (i.e., visual fantasies of coffee and inner reflections that she'll feel better after drinking coffee) and *emotions* (i.e., irritability and yearning), and she takes *actions* (i.e., hurriedly making and drinking a cup of coffee) that she would not have taken but for her neural wiring. If she had never begun drinking coffee, she would not experience this set of thoughts, emotions, and actions. But now that she has consumed enough coffee, her brain has become wired to auto-generate them.

Now say Connie decides to quit drinking coffee. She does not like the feelings of irritability and pining she experiences when she is delayed in getting her morning coffee, so she elects to cease this habit. Her brain will initially resist this decision by generating intense waves of intrusive thoughts and visceral emotions demanding that she drink coffee. But eventually, when she resists the impulse to drink coffee for enough days or weeks, the intrusive thoughts and visceral emotions will begin to fade. And if she resists the impulse for long enough, those thoughts and emotions will disappear entirely. What has occurred is that her voluntary and consistent action (i.e., not drinking coffee) has again rewired her brain, causing her brain to cease generating the very thoughts, emotions, and behavioral impulses that it was generating just weeks or months ago.

This is neuroplasticity. The brain is constantly evolving, re-structuring, and rewiring based on the real-time experiences it goes through. As we begin to understand our brain's neuroplasticity, we can begin to deliberately subject our brain to real-time experiences that will rewire it in ways that will benefit our happiness and our academic success. We can provide it with specific thoughts, immerse it with specific emotions, and commit specific actions that, together, will rewire it, causing it to begin auto-generating these very thoughts, emotions, and behavioral impulses on its own.

Hiking in the Forest

Neuroscientists like to use the image of a hiking path in the forest as a metaphor for the brain's rewiring process. Imagine yourself on a hike. You see a clear, well-worn path that cuts through the middle of bushes and shrubs for the next 100 feet. Which way will you walk? Along the path, obviously.

How did that path get there in the first place? Has it always been there? The path was not always there; it began because *someone* (whether an animal or a hiker) chose to walk across the bushes and shrubs. That action was repeated several times. Then more beings walked along that same path, and eventually the path started to deepen as the bushes and shrubs thinned out. Over time, a well-worn path formed.

But what would happen if a blockade were erected that prevented any human or animal from walking along that path for three years? Moreover, what would happen if cones were set up to guide every human and animal for the next three years to walk along a new path that runs parallel to the original path, but 10 feet to the left?

Walking along the new path will be challenging at the beginning. Travelers will stumble along the bushes and shrubs, and it will require much greater focus and effort to traverse the path. However, over time, the original path will start to fill in, or grow over, with bushes and shrubs. And the new path will begin to manifest and deepen. Eventually the original path will have disappeared, and the new path will look identical to how the original path appeared at the outset (apart from being 10 feet away). Now a random hiker will default to walking along the new path, as opposed to the old path.

This is how the brain gets rewired. As we subject our brain to specific actions, thoughts, and emotions over time, the brain becomes reconfigured with new pathways (referred to as "neural pathways"), and the old pathways in the brain begin to fill in or weaken from reduced usage. As the new pathway deepens and solidifies over time, we are able to traverse that pathway more easily, and we eventually begin defaulting to that pathway.

The Tetris Effect

In 1984, a new video game called Tetris swept the globe. As many of you probably know (due to Tetris' recent three-dimensional comeback), the game challenged players to strategically arrange each shape that dropped into the screen in a way that maximally and efficiently fit into the available empty slots. The faster and better the players filled in the empty spaces, the more points they earned and the more they advanced in the game. Tetris became a nationwide sensation in the United

TWO CORE QUESTIONS 35

States. Then, after a few months, something fascinating occurred.

Individuals who had been playing hours and hours of Tetris every day for a couple of straight months began rushing into psychologist and psychiatrist offices across the country, desperately reporting that they were suffering from hallucinations and feeling like they were "losing their minds." They explained that when they were not playing Tetris and, instead, interacting in society, they would see "dropping Tetris shapes" everywhere they looked. If they saw two buildings next to each other with a space in between, their brain would instantly concoct a giant building-sized shape to drop into the open gap. If they were having a conversation with two people, their brain would manufacture a shape to fill in the gap between the two heads. Wherever they looked in the real world, their brain would uncontrollably hone in on all the empty spaces and automatically fill them in with perfectly shaped pieces created by their minds. They couldn't concentrate on anything, and they couldn't get anything done. Their ever-present hallucinations were eroding their functionality in life. No wonder they felt like they were losing their minds! These individuals frantically pleaded for help from mental health professionals, begging for anything that could help eliminate their maddening hallucinations.

So what brilliant therapeutic intervention did the mental health experts recommend for this debilitating psychological condition, which later became known as the Tetris Effect (or Tetris Syndrome)? Did they prescribe anti-hallucination medication? Did they recommend a prolonged course of electroconvulsive therapy? Did they suggest in-depth psychoanalysis to uncover possible childhood trauma?

No. Their entire therapeutic intervention can be captured in three words: "Stop. Playing. Tetris."

After a couple of days of not playing any Tetris, the players found that their hallucinations began to reduce noticeably. After a week, even greater reductions occurred. And within a few weeks, the hallucinations had vanished completely.

So what had happened in the players' brains? By continually exposing their brains to the experience of seeing and fitting shapes into open spaces, their brains got wired to auto-generate these very images even when they were not playing the game. In effect, they *voluntarily* engaged in their own "brainwashing," first forcing their brains to engage in a very specific neural activity, and then, as a result, training their brains to engage in that neural activity on their own – without prompting and without intentionality. And finally, once they stopped forcing their brains to engage in that neural activity, their brains eventually stopped auto-engaging in the activity.

It's a classic case of neuroplasticity. In a matter of months, these high-volume Tetris players rewired their brains to see Tetris everywhere they looked, and then rewired their brains again, this time to eliminate the original rewiring. In other words, they built a new set of neural pathways from scratch in their neurological forest and then eliminated these neural pathways from that forest.

The Brain's Malleability

There are many cutting-edge studies revealing the human brain's remarkable ability to adapt, restructure, and rewire based on the unique experiences to which it is exposed. One of the most famous was a study of London taxi drivers by University College London (UCL). Before GPS, the drivers were required to navigate London's uniquely complex topography of 25,000 interconnected streets and thousands of places of interest using their own maps and memories. The UCL study found that even after only a couple of years in the profession, the drivers had a materially larger hippocampus (the long-term memory center of the brain) than did the average non-taxi driver.[2]

By exposing their brains to London's dizzying, maze-like topography, they had enabled their long-term memory center to restructure and build new neurons. "The human brain remains 'plastic,' even in adult life, allowing it to adapt when we learn new tasks," explained Professor Eleanor Maguire, the leading researcher on the study from the Wellcome Trust Center for Neuroimaging at UCL. "[W]e have seen directly and within individuals how the structure of the hippocampus can change with external stimulation." She then added an appropriately understated, very British summary of the implications, "This offers encouragement for adults who want to learn new skills later in life."

A Harvard Medical School study found that an 8-week introductory course in "Mindfulness-Based Stress Reduction" led to significant changes in the brains of the participants as compared to those of a control group that did not participate in the course.[3] The participants experienced thickening and restructuring in the following four regions of the brain: (1) the posterior cingulate (which modulates mind-wandering and self-perception); (2) the temporo parietal junction (which is responsible for perspective-taking, empathy, and compassion); (3) the left hippocampus (which controls learning and memory and assists with emotional regulation); and (4) the Pons (an area of the brain stem where many regulatory neurotransmitters are produced). Furthermore, the participants experienced shrinking in the size of the amygdala, which, as you know, is the fear (and fight-or-flight) center of the brain. The control group, in contrast, experienced no changes in any regions of their brains in the eight-week period. So several different regions of the brain can reformat and restructure in only eight weeks just from an introductory stress reduction course.

Another fascinating study found that when individuals wore blindfolds for five days, the region of their brain responsible for vision (the visual cortex) began assisting with sound and touch (something the visual cortex never does when vision is intact).[4] Not only did their visual cortex activate when listening or touching, but the sensitivity of their listening and touching also increased during the temporary period they wore blindfolds — and the functions all returned to baseline when the blindfolds were removed. That's right, within just a few days of wearing blindfolds, our brain begins converting brain cells typically used for sight to senses that are actually available, such as listening and touching, which then strengthen beyond their normal potency.

Another study assessed people's capacity to rewire their brain to be more resilient to stress and to perform better cognitively under stress, also known as "stress inoculation." In order to capture the consensus of the scientific data in this area, the study evaluated 37 prior studies in peer-reviewed journals. Based on its thorough analysis of the large collection of studies, the study concluded that "stress inoculation training was shown to be effective in reducing performance anxiety, reducing state anxiety, and enhancing performance under stress."[5]

The human brain truly is mind-boggling (*pun intended*) in its ability to adapt, restructure, and rewire based on the unique experiences it goes through. This is why the tools and techniques we will be sharing for the remainder of the book have the potential to significantly improve your life: your brain is highly malleable and trainable, and these tools and techniques will allow you to exploit this reality for your benefit.

But we must address one final question that may have been nagging at you before we turn to those tools and techniques: In light of your overloaded schedule and the time scarcity you likely feel on a daily basis, do you, in fact, have time to make these changes?

DO I HAVE TIME TO REWIRE MY BRAIN FOR IMPROVED HAPPINESS AND COGNITION?

If we were to ask you and the rest of your law school class whether you brush your teeth each morning, we believe well over 90% of you would say "yes." Why do you do it? Because you know that a minute or two of tooth brushing in the morning leads to vast benefits, from preventing cavities, to fighting gingivitis, and to improving breath, among others. You don't have to brush your teeth for two hours per day to receive these benefits. Rather, when you consistently spend a minute or two each morning (and perhaps at night) brushing your teeth, the incremental benefits of each session compound and lead to good oral hygiene. This consistent, preventative care precludes tartar and plaque from ever building up in the first place.

But if we asked how many of you spend one to two minutes each morning doing a practice that is exclusively dedicated to advancing your mental, emotional, or cognitive well-being, how many of you would say "yes"? We suspect a much smaller

TWO CORE QUESTIONS   39

percentage of you. We work with law students and lawyers across the country and globe, and when we ask these two questions side-by-side, there is always a huge disparity in answers across the two questions.* We similarly sense you do a pretty good job of showering – despite all of your law school obligations – and that we would get similar results if we were to substitute showering for toothbrushing in our questioning.

So the next question becomes: How did it become so normal for us to find time in our busy schedules to brush our teeth and clean our bodies, but not to find similar amounts of time to brush our minds or clean our brains? Why do we prioritize the well-being of our teeth and skin so far above the well-being of our heart and brain? And do we want to continue living this way?

The truth is that we *do* have time to care for our mental, emotional, and cognitive well-being. We just have chosen not to. For the remainder of this book, we are going to share tools that take about the same time as brushing your teeth – and that have been scientifically proven to significantly reduce stress, improve emotional well-being, and enhance cognitive functioning. Moreover, the more we apply these tools over time, the more our brain becomes wired to function this way on its own – without intention or effort. Our baseline levels of resiliency, happiness, and cognitive performance begin to elevate.

We will not ask you to meditate for three hours per day on the top of a mountain. You definitely don't have time for that (and, most likely, not the gear to get there). But you do have time to practice rewiring your brain for enhanced well-being and cognition for 1–2 minutes in the morning, 1–2 minutes in the afternoon, and 1–2 minutes in the evening. If you dedicate yourself to this simple practice, you will spend a maximum of 6 minutes per day, or 42 total minutes per week, on it. That still gives you 167 hours and 18 minutes per week to read and brief for class! (There are 168 hours in a week, in case you ever wondered.) Importantly, many of the tools and reframing

---

* We recently asked these two questions during a webinar to a sub-group of lawyers at a global law firm. 100% of the participants answered "yes" (via a "thumbs-up" emoji) to the toothbrushing question, but only **one** thumbs-up emoji appeared in response to the second question. So we asked that person if they would be willing to share what their morning well-being practice was. The individual unmuted and responded, "My hand had slipped, and I accidentally hit the thumbs-up emoji. I'm sorry about that."

techniques we share with you actually take the same amount of time that you are already spending emotionally reacting to the challenges of law school. You will just transfer the time spent impulsively reacting into time spent purposefully responding. So much of what we are suggesting doesn't actually require any additional time commitment.

But regarding the tools and techniques that do require small additional time commitments, remember that every minute you spend applying or practicing these tools and techniques, you are not only working to improve your resiliency and well-being, but also to optimize your cognitive functioning and academic prowess. "*Stress minimization equals cognitive maximization.*" (We thought it was a good moment to repeat the mantra.) Seems like a wonderful use of your time.

Interestingly, carving out small windows of time to enhance your resiliency, happiness, and cognitive performance is something every one of you is *already* doing every single day – but in very large quantities of time. To what are we referring? Sleep. That's right, sleep.

Let's assume for the moment you sleep an average of seven hours per night. (We'll stop with the math after this point, we promise!) Now let's assume we just excitedly proclaimed that we have a brilliant idea for optimizing your law school performance: *reduce* your nightly sleep from seven hours to three hours. You can create *four additional hours* every day to do your reading, briefing, and outlining! Ingenious! With these extra four hours every day, you will undoubtedly get way more accomplished and position yourself for maximal law school success, right?

Wrong. You know this idea is horrible. It would undoubtedly reduce your law school productivity and success. And why is that? Because you know that in order to maximize your law school performance, you need to get adequate sleep at night. You don't sleep (or aim to sleep) seven hours per night because you are lazy; you do it because it's necessary for maximizing your cognitive and academic performance (and for securing your emotional well-being and resiliency throughout the day).

Sleep is the quintessential example of the link between well-being and cognitive performance. If you reduced your sleep to

TWO CORE QUESTIONS 41

three hours per night, the academic benefits from having four extra hours of time would be far outweighed by the academic problems that would arise from your constant state of exhaustion. You would be delirious at all times, unfocused, nodding off during class and while reading, and you would be in a general state of brain fog and impaired cognition throughout life that would translate to lower academic performance and worse grades. And simultaneously, your stress and emotional turmoil would skyrocket: You would be agitated, impatient, and reactive on a daily basis.

Anyone who has ever had a few straight nights of very little sleep (can we see some raised hands, law students?) can attest to its detrimental impact on their emotional resiliency and overall mental state. So you willingly sacrifice many hours each day that could be spent on law school performance in exchange for lying on a bed, unconscious, so you can optimize your mind, emotions, and cognition – knowing that this self-care time will optimize your chances of law school success.

Now all you need to do is apply that same reasoning to your waking hours. We don't mean you should carve out four of your waking hours each day and dedicate them to emotional and cognitive optimization, but certainly you can carve out the 6 minutes per day we referenced earlier, or even more time if you are willing. Once you understand – *and truly believe* – that this self-care* time is not a detriment to your law school success, but an asset, you will use it without guilt or shame, and you will increase the amount of time you do it.

Stephen Covey, the author of the landmark 1989 book, *The 7 Habits of Highly Effective People*, spent years studying and analyzing the most successful professionals across various industries, looking for the one habit that most commonly separates the supremely successful from the merely successful. He ultimately determined it was a habit he termed "production

---

* Even the term "self-care" can have a negative connotation in high-performance realms such as law school, business school, and medical school. As if self-care is a frivolous act of self-indulgence for the weak and less committed. If you have any of these (false) associations, it's certainly not your fault, but the fault of misguided social conditioning. You may consider instead using the term "self-optimization" (in your own mind and when communicating with others) in order to evade the stigma and tap into the scientific truths that automatically justify the behavior. "I am going to take a few minute break to practice self-optimization, and then I'm going to return to my reading."

capability." The vast majority of merely successful professionals spent 100% of their working time on "production," i.e., drafting documents, writing letters (they didn't have email back then), brainstorming strategy, executing strategy, preparing for meetings, etc. But the supremely successful ones regularly carved out time for "production capability," the act of consciously evaluating and seeking ways of improving one's *capacity to produce*.

Those individuals who regularly pull away from "production" in order to spend a few minutes on "production capability" inevitably end up discovering ways to improve the quality of their production, the efficiency of their production, and their overall relationship to their work. They not only end up more productive and successful, but also more satisfied and fulfilled.

But the vast majority of professionals are stuck on the hamster wheel, mindlessly producing *at all times* – without having the wisdom or courage to regularly step off the hamster wheel to assess whether there are ways of optimizing their production. They are so overwhelmed by all of their work and deadlines that they unconsciously – and wrongly – assume that the way to maximize their production is to white-knuckle their way through their work, one day at a time. They don't understand the reality that if they build short but regular experiences of production capability into their routine, they will end up producing far more and far better in the long-term.

This exclusive focus on production at the expense of production capability is one of the biggest problems facing law students. Because of the overwhelming amount of reading and other tasks that are in the queue at every moment, most law students get stuck spending 100% of their law school time on production: reading, briefing, outlining, attending office hours, taking practice tests, etc. And then weeks, months, and the entire semester (and eventually their entire law school career) pass without them engaging in regular, thoughtful analysis of how to optimize their production. As a result, they end up producing far less and performing far worse than they would have if they had had the wisdom and courage to regularly take

TWO CORE QUESTIONS

a few moments to step off the hamster wheel of production and onto the ramp of production capability.

Section II

Mindsets for Law School Success & Thriving

Take a look at the figure below and see if you can solve the problem. Your goal is to connect all nine dots. There are three and <u>only</u> three instructions: (1) connect all nine dots; (2) by drawing only four straight lines; and (3) not lifting your pen or pencil up while drawing those lines.

Give yourself five minutes to see if you can figure it out. (Feel free to draw the same configuration of nine dots on a few different pieces of paper. This way you can make several different attempts.)

● ● ●

● ● ●

● ● ●

Instructions

1. Connect all 9 dots
2. By drawing only 4 straight lines
3. And not lifting your pen/pencil up while drawing those lines

How did that go? If you are like 96–97% of undergraduate students, then you failed to solve it. That's right, on average, less than 5% of university students are able to solve the problem. (Both of your authors epically failed when we first tried, for the record.)

On the next page (hidden from your current view), we have provided the solution.

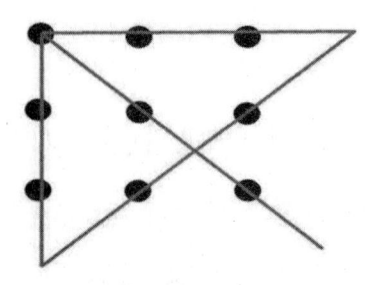

Now that you have seen the solution, what would you say is the key to solving the problem? If you said, *"Thinking outside the box,"* you'd be correct. The over 95% of people who are unable to solve the problem frantically draw all of their lines within the box and never consider drawing outside the box. Why is that? Because they have unconsciously added one more instruction to the three given instructions: *Stay within the box.* None of them was aware of thinking it, but it's the reason for failure for all of us who failed. In fact, if you look back, you'll see that there isn't even a box pictured, just nine dots configured in a formation that resembles a box. But this formation triggers our unconscious thought that a box exists, and then a secondary unconscious thought that we must stay within that box follows.

We have all been conditioned throughout our lives to stay within the box, to *not* draw outside the lines, to follow rules, and to "comply." So this simple configuration triggers our unconscious conditioning, which in turn derails our conscious thinking – unbeknownst to us.

Importantly, had we included a fourth instruction, "You can draw outside the box," probably 95% of you would have solved it – because your unconscious thinking would have been superseded by your conscious awareness. Yet because we did not utter this instruction, and instead remained silent on the issue of drawing within or outside the box, your unconscious thinking intervened and sabotaged your conscious thinking.*

This exercise is a microcosm of how our thinking works throughout the day – in law school and in life. We are continually engaged in conscious thinking activities, but we don't realize

---

* We mentioned twice that there were "only three instructions" and even underlined the word "only." Yet your unconscious thinking nevertheless overrode these clear signals. That is some powerful unconscious thinking!

that our unconscious thinking is constantly dictating or shaping our conscious thinking. So in order to optimize our conscious thinking (i.e., what we think of as our "cognition"), we must learn how to detect – and optimize – our unconscious thinking.

Modern science shows that unconscious thinking is not only critical to conscious thinking, but also to stress levels, resiliency, emotional well-being, and overall happiness. It would not be an exaggeration to say that if we want to unlock our happiest, most resilient, best-thinking, and most successful self, we *must* master our unconscious thinking.* This mastery involves a three-step process that we can wire our brain to perform: (1) noticing our unconscious thinking (i.e., converting unconscious thoughts into conscious thoughts); (2) assessing whether those previously unconscious, but now conscious, thoughts are impeding our happiness and cognitive performance [*hint: they often are!*]; and if they are, (3) replacing, modifying, or reframing those thoughts with thoughts that improve our happiness and cognitive performance.

---

* To clarify, we are not referring to what Sigmond Freud termed the "unconscious mind," which he described as a reservoir of feelings, urges, thoughts, and memories outside our conscious awareness that arise from our primal impulses. We are referring to the unconscious thinking that is recognized as valid and critically important by all the "hard sciences," such as neuroscience, economics, physiology, and biology.

CHAPTER 7

THE TWO DIFFERENT TYPES OF THINKING

Only one person in history has won the Nobel Prize in Economics despite not being a trained economist. He is a psychologist named Daniel Kahneman, and he won it in 2002. How did he possibly do that, you wonder? Well, he used his cutting-edge psychological research about the way the human brain functions to rebut (i.e., *annihilate*) several principles of traditional economic theory, such as that people provided with appropriate information make rational decisions in their self-interest and that economic systems reliant upon rational actors are inherently reliable. He is also the author of *Thinking Fast and Slow*, widely recognized as one the most, if not the most, profound books about human cognition of the last 100 years.[6]

Kahneman's ground-breaking findings about human thinking are now black-letter principles of economics, neuroscience, psychology, physiology, and biology. Perhaps his most critical discovery was that the human mind generates two different types of thinking – what he termed "System 1" thinking and "System 2" thinking.

First look at the image below and notice what your brain does the moment it sees the image:

Thomas M. Perkins/Shutterstock.com

Your brain likely generated a series of unconscious thoughts and emotions within milliseconds – e.g., thoughts about his personality, his aggression, his reasons for being upset, etc., as well as emotions such as angst, fear, defensiveness, or perplexity. In fact, the research shows you reached some of these core thoughts and emotions within one tenth of a second after seeing the image, and several others in the milliseconds that followed. You did not have to purposefully construct these thoughts and emotions; they manifested on their own. This is System 1 thinking, which is automatic, fast, and unconscious thinking.

Now look at the image below and notice whether your brain responds differently to it:

$$17 \times 24$$

Does it feel like your brain is in molasses? Your brain likely responded with a vacuous pause and then labored to figure out the answer. This is System 2 thinking, which is deliberate, slow, and conscious. System 2 thinking is what we typically refer to when we use the word "thinking." You rely on System 2 thinking when you brief a case, when you try to distinguish two cases from one another, when you decide which reading assignment to start next, when you try to memorize the elements of an implied easement, and when you answer multiple choice questions on a final exam.

Interestingly, even though you rely on System 2 thinking to perform these tasks, your brain is simultaneously utilizing System 1 thinking at each stage along the way. As we do our law school work, or think about what to say in the text message to the friend who hurt our feelings, or decide whether we want to go that party, we generally believe we are exclusively using System 2 thinking. But in reality, our System 2 thinking is often heavily influenced or shaped by System 1 thinking. For example, with respect to the nine-dot problem, you believed you were engaged exclusively in System 2 thinking, but your System 1 thinking (the unconscious assumption your brain reached that it must stay within the apparent box) undermined your System 2 thinking and prevented you from solving the problem.

THE TWO DIFFERENT TYPES OF THINKING 51

The average human brain generates 50,000 to 60,000 thoughts per day. What percentage of these thoughts do you think are unconscious System 1 thoughts as opposed to conscious System 2 thoughts? According to conclusive neuroscientific research, 95% of our daily thoughts are unconscious System 1 thoughts, and only 5% are conscious System 2 thoughts. That's right, we have 47,500 to 57,000 thoughts each day that we are *not even aware of!**

These 47,500 to 57,000 daily thoughts are the ones that are primarily dictating our mood, our resiliency, our well-being, our communications, our decision making, and our overall success. Yet most of us pay zero attention to them. No wonder our stress, emotions, behavioral impulses, and cognition feel so outside our control. They are being formed, molded, and controlled by 47,500 to 57,000 thoughts that we have no awareness of.

---

* You might be wondering how it can be determined how many of our thoughts are unconscious if the individual having the thoughts is not aware of their existence. Neuroscientists first determine the neurological activity occurring when a person is generating conscious thoughts and then track that neural activity across different periods of time when the individual is unaware of having thoughts.

CHAPTER 8

THE GREAT SMUGGLER OF ANCIENT PERSIA

According to Sufi mythology, there once was an exalted smuggler named Nasrudin. He was known throughout the region, especially by border agents. One day, a Persian border agent was startled to see the infamous Nasrudin himself approaching from neighboring Afghanistan. He was walking a donkey who was draped head-to-toe with blankets, bags, and satchels. The border agent's heart began to race as Nasrudin grew closer. He knew this was his moment to catch the acclaimed Nasrudin in an act of smuggling.

As Nasrudin approached, the agent said, "You are the infamous Nasrudin, the great smuggler, are you not?" Nasrudin humbly responded, "I am indeed." The agent then exclaimed, "I know you are smuggling illegal items into Persia. I shall do a full search of every blanket, bag, and satchel!" He spent the next hour removing every individual item and meticulously searching through every compartment and crevice. After an hour of determined work, the exasperated agent was forced to say, "I didn't locate anything, Nasrudin, but I *know* you are smuggling illegal items into Persia! But I have to let you pass." Nasrudin warmly responded, "Very well, thank you."

Two weeks later, the same agent was eating lunch when who again appeared? Nasrudin, once more approaching Persia with a donkey draped with heaps of blankets, bags, and satchels. The agent cried, "Nasrudin, I know you are smuggling illegal items into Persia again, and this time I will catch you!" The agent then conducted an even more detailed search, this time costing him two hours and even more beads of sweat. Yet he found nothing illegal. He bitterly informed Nasrudin, "You may pass. I am certain you are smuggling illegal items into Persia, but I cannot prove it." Nasrudin pleasantly replied, "Very well, thank you."

This same song-and-dance repeated itself every two weeks for the next six months. At that point, the agent was losing his sanity. His confidence in his professional competence was waning, and he spent many long nights stewing over how Nasrudin was managing to deceive him. The agent decided to quit his job and find less stressful work. But on his last day on the job, he again came face-to-face with Nasrudin, accompanied as usual by a donkey draped nose to tail. The agent sullenly remarked, "Nasrudin, today is my last day in my position, as I am going mad and must find other work. You may pass today without search, but please, for my long-term sanity, tell me what you have been smuggling. I have never been more certain of anything! Please tell me what illegal items you have been smuggling into Persia all of these months. I beg this of you."

Nasrudin looked at the agent with compassion and politely said, "Very well, I have been smuggling illegal donkeys into Persia."

This parable is the perfect metaphor for our own attempts to improve our happiness, resiliency, and academic performance. We all care about these things, and we all try to optimize them, yet our efforts are pointed in the wrong direction. We are looking in the wrong place.

It did not matter that the agent was extremely dedicated to finding Nasrudin's smuggled items, or that he exerted great effort. He was simply looking in the wrong place. And why was that? Because he was focusing 100% of his attention and energy on the items right in front of him, without realizing he was unconsciously blind to the real contraband.

Virtually all law students (and humans) make the same mistake. If we are feeling stressed by an event or person, we seek to reduce our stress. But our attention and energy are misdirected to the facts, thoughts, and considerations that our conscious mind "sees." We are blind to the "donkey" of our unconscious thoughts, interpretations, and assumptions – which are the true cause of our stress. Similarly, we want to excel academically in law school, but our attention and energy are misdirected to the conscious factors contributing to success, while ignoring the unconscious thoughts, interpretations, and assumptions that play such a critical role in our success.

It is like the sinking of the Titanic. The ship's captain noticed and then successfully avoided the visible part of the iceberg that floated above the surface. But what he did not account for is the portion of the iceberg that was below the surface. It was that part of the iceberg that tore into the ship's hull, ripped it open, and sank the glorious ship. Similarly, what often sinks our emotional state and academic performance is the collection of thoughts, interpretations, and assumptions that lie below the surface – the ones we never even notice. Any great ship captain, of course, accounts for the visible pieces of the iceberg, but her real focus are dedicated to that which lurks beneath the surface. By mastering that area, she ensures safety, security, and success for the journey.

If we want to flourish emotionally and academically in law school, we must look beneath the surface to our unconscious thinking. That is where our success resides.

Chapter 9

Is That a Doorknob or an Alligator?!

Many years ago, someone in your life likely showed you the popular image below and excitedly asked, "What do you see when you look at this?!" Confused by the question, you glanced at the image, looked up at the seemingly demented questioner, and said, "What do you mean? I see a young woman with a feather in her hair looking away. Why?" That's what approximately 50% of you saw, while the other 50% of you saw an old woman wrapped in a babushka and cozy sweater.

My Wife and My Mother-In-Law, by the cartoonist W. E. Hill, 1915

If you saw the young woman, notice what your brain did. It instantly decoded the image, identified a young woman looking away, and ended its analysis. You did *not* say, "I see a young woman looking away, but perhaps if I contort my interpretation, an old woman may pop out of the same image." In the same vein, if you saw the old woman, you did not remark, "I see an old woman, but if I try to look at the image from a different perspective, another figure might appear."

Why didn't you do that? Because you have a normal, functioning brain! When subjected to a factual input in life (whether it is a two-dimensional image, a difficult reading assignment, a rude text message, an unexpected traffic jam, or any other life event or challenge), the human brain instantaneously deconstructs the factual input, reaches a split-second conclusion about what it represents, and then, critically, *unconsciously assumes that this conclusion is the only conclusion.**

This flawed interpretive process is necessary to function in life. What if, every time you approached a door, rather than unconsciously assuming that the protruding metal sphere is a doorknob, you wondered to yourself, "Is that a doorknob, or an alligator?" Upon considering this possibility, you would no doubt yank your hand back, to make sure that the possible alligator did not sever your hand from your wrist. But what if you then considered a new possibility, "Perhaps it's not a doorknob or an alligator. Maybe it's a slice of pizza!" You would suddenly become jovial, especially if you were hungry, because you always appreciate a good slice of pizza. So rather than reaching for the alleged doorknob with your hand, you would lunge forward with a gaping mouth and take a taste of the metal sphere. "Yuck, that is not pizza!" you would exclaim to yourself. "I wonder if there are any other things it could be, besides a doorknob."

This would be a hard way to live. You wouldn't get much done. In fact, it would probably take you an hour just to leave a room. So, in order to ensure our functionality in the world, our brain causes us to unconsciously assume that our instantaneous, default interpretation of things is undoubtedly correct and the only possible interpretation.

While this neurological mechanism is helpful for functioning in life, it is incredibly unhelpful for emotionally and cognitively thriving in life. This is because when life difficulties or challenges occur, our brain reaches an instant default interpretation of the situation and assumes that interpretation is the only one. And the problem is not *just* that this interpretation is always one of several possible interpretations, but more importantly, that this default interpretation very often is the interpretation that causes us the most stress, upset, and emotional *disease*. This reaction, in turn, over-activates our

---

* Other than the decision to look at the image and the resulting awareness that we see either the young or old woman (which are System 2 thoughts), the entirety of this process is System 1 thinking.

IS THAT A DOORKNOB OR AN ALLIGATOR?!

amygdala, which leads to impaired cognition – and that, of course, hinders our academic performance and overall success.

Below is a Flow Chart that captures the sequential process that leads to elevated stress and impaired cognition in law school.

Life Event → Unconscious Interpretation → Stress Response → Amygdala Hijack → Impaired Cognition → Impaired Law School Performance

So how do we stop this process? The key is to intervene in the process right after the brain reaches its initial, unconscious default interpretation (which is quintessential System 1 thinking). At that moment, if we can *consciously* identify our *unconscious* interpretation, framing, or assumption, we can then elect whether that previously unconscious cognition is benefiting or harming our emotional (and hence cognitive) state. If it is harming, we can replace it or reframe it – which we will discuss below.

We don't recommend challenging your System 1 assumptions every moment in life, such as when you are reaching for a doorknob, driving a car, sitting onto your seat in class, drinking a beverage, or doing the countless routine activities that life and law school involve. That will only derail your functionality. But we do recommend doing so whenever you feel stressed, upset, angry, or overtaken by an emotion that does not feel desirable. In that moment, if you can delve into your System 1 thinking, you will be able to determine whether your unconscious cognition (i.e., interpretation, framing, assumption, etc.) is damaging your emotional state and hence cognitive state. If it is, you can replace or reframe that cognition, and thereby shift your emotional state and resulting cognitive state. We will now discuss how to do that.

CHAPTER 10

HE CUT YOU OFF ON THE FREEWAY?!

Imagine yourself driving in the far-right lane of the freeway when a car from your left swerves across your lane and frantically exits, causing you to hit the brakes to avoid contact. It was not super dangerous, but it was very sudden, and definitely illegal.

What emotion would pop up in you if this happened? Anger. (That is what would arise for almost every one of us.[*]) How long would it take for that emotion to arise after you notice the car cut you off? About one tenth of a second. A clear example of a System 1 reaction.

The question then becomes: Why did the emotion of anger arise in you? The first step in learning to control and optimize our emotions is to understand precisely how our unwanted emotions arise. The emotion of anger arose because you had an unconscious yet firmly held belief that *"all people who cut me off last second on the freeway are jerks."* (Or, perhaps, a more colorful expression.) This belief long preceded this particular event (i.e., the factual input), and it has been stored in your unconscious mind for years. You might disagree with us, thinking to yourself, "I don't hold that belief!" Well, if you would experience the emotion of anger in that moment, then you do hold that belief (or some very similar belief). It is actually impossible to experience the emotion of anger in this situation if you don't hold such a belief. Why is that? Because emotions do not arise randomly. They are the result of a factual event combining with an unconscious belief (or some other cognition, such as an interpretation, mindset, framing, or assumption).

---

[*] It is possible that some of you would experience fear as your first emotion, but the moment you realized you were safe (a split second after the cut-off), that fear would convert into anger.

We call it the "Algorithm of Emotions."

FACT + BELIEF = EMOTION

Now let's change the fact pattern slightly. Imagine that you instead knew that the person who was about to cut you off was rushing to the hospital ER to see a loved one who was on the brink of dying. The driver was crying and overwhelmed, so they were not paying their usual attention to the lane they were in. As the exit approached, they suddenly realized they were about to miss it. Since their loved one could die at any moment, they checked their rear-view mirror and determined they could cut into the open space (ahead of you) without creating any real danger, although it would be a less-than-ideal driving move. They are generally the type of person who hates cutting people off, but they knew the next exit was several miles away, and they feared this could be the difference between arriving on time and arriving too late. So they cut across, feeling quite guilty, but deciding it was probably the best thing to do, all things considered.

Hypothetically, if you knew with certainty (in advance of them cutting you off) that this was all true, what emotion would you experience when they cut you off? Compassion or empathy, right?* So the same behavior on their part would trigger the opposite emotion in you. In the first instance, their action would trigger anger in you, while in the second instance, their identical action would trigger compassion in you. So it is not their action, itself, that determines your emotion. It is *your belief or interpretation of their action* that determines your emotion.

In the first situation, you had an unconscious belief or interpretation that the driver was a jerk (your unconscious mind filled in the blank of uncertainty), while in the second situation, you had a conscious belief or interpretation that the driver was a kind person worried about their dying loved one. The emotion we experience is never the direct result of the life event, it is

---

* We have run this hypothetical and asked this question to thousands of law students and lawyers, and nearly 100% of them answer with compassion, empathy, or some similar emotion. A very small percentage of people say, "I'd still be angry at them!" If you are one of those people, we invite you to pay special attention to the second Mindset Shift – "Judgment to Compassion" in Section II – beginning at page 105.

HE CUT YOU OFF ON THE FREEWAY?! 63

always the direct result of how our mind processes or interprets the event.

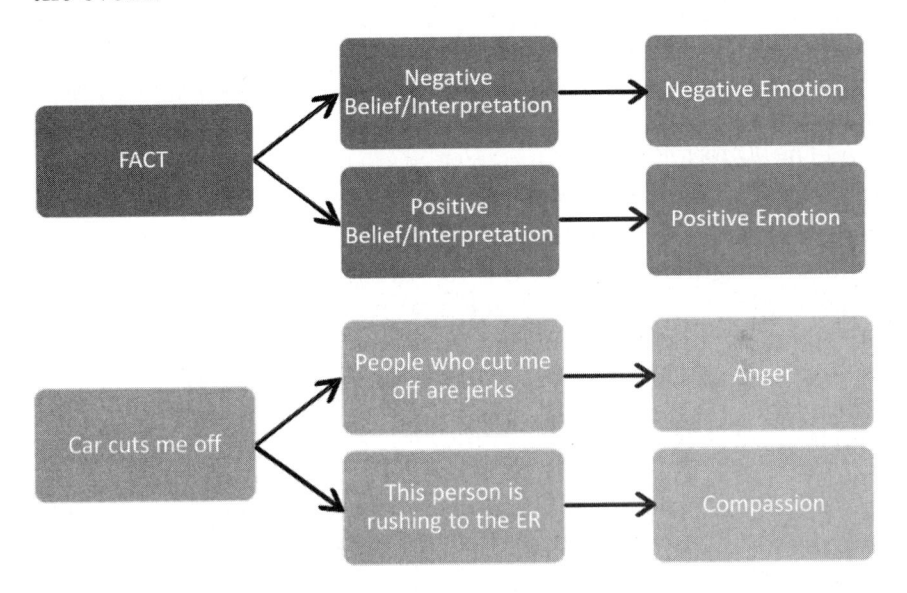

```
FACT → Negative Belief/Interpretation → Negative Emotion
FACT → Positive Belief/Interpretation → Positive Emotion
```

```
Car cuts me off → People who cut me off are jerks → Anger
Car cuts me off → This person is rushing to the ER → Compassion
```

So we invite you to adopt (and begin practicing) a very simple* technique that can transform your resiliency and well-being in law school and life (as well as your cognitive and academic functioning, for reasons we will elaborate on later in this book): any time you are experiencing an uncomfortable or undesirable emotion, use the Algorithm of Emotions to deconstruct your unconscious cognition, and then choose a different cognition that might be true, but that births a more pleasant (happier) emotion.

It's quite simple: If you don't like the emotion you are feeling in response to any event, action, or person in law school or life, shift the underlying cognition that gives rise to that emotion. This technique is often referred to as "Cognitive Reframing" or "Belief Restructuring." Our cognitions are electable, malleable, and changeable. In the Algorithm of Emotions, we often cannot change the *Fact* – because many things occur in life that we simply cannot control, whether it's the length of the reading assignment, the unexpected traffic, the unkind text message we

---

* There is an expression that something can be "simple but not easy." This technique is a perfect example of the axiom. It is simple in form, but that doesn't mean it is easy to remember to do or to effectively perform when our emotions are whirling.

receive, and many other factual inputs. Moreover, we typically cannot change the *Emotion* directly – because emotions cannot just be forced away. Have you ever been stressed or angry, and then yelled, "Go away, stress!" "Go away, anger!" It doesn't work. However, the one thing we have control over in the Algorithm of Emotions is the *Belief* – which is the bridge between the *Fact* and the *Emotion*.

So if you get cut off by someone on the freeway and notice you immediately default to the emotion of anger, shift the underlying cognition (belief) from "all people who cut me off last second are jerks" to "this person is rushing to the ER to see a loved one who is on the brink of dying."

You may object to this suggestion and wonder: Are we advising you to be delusional?

Yes, we are. But to be clear, if you experience anger in response to being cut off, you are already being delusional. We are just suggesting that if you are going to be delusional, you might as well be *happily delusional* rather than *angrily delusional*. The truth is that even if you have no idea why any person cuts you off, you do know they did not wake up that morning and maliciously plot to time their cut-off to perfectly upset you. They were not motivated by evil or a desire to upset your day. You truly do not know why they cut you off, so your brain fills in the uncertainty with the conclusion that they are a "jerk." In other words, you have reached a conclusion that this person is a selfish jerk – with no factual basis for that conclusion and based entirely on an isolated two-second action on their part. This is the quintessence of "delusional."

Now it may not be that they are rushing to the ER, but they likely have some very reasonable motive that is not malicious. They may have been stressed out that they were late to wherever they were going and got distracted before realizing they were about to miss their exit. Or they may have gotten confused by the GPS (or the GPS may have re-routed them at the last moment), and they belatedly realized the exit was upon them. Or perhaps they were just mind-wandering and simply lost focus for a couple of minutes, only to realize they were about to miss their exit. None of these reasons suggests the person is a jerk; they suggest the person is an imperfect human (like the rest of

HE CUT YOU OFF ON THE FREEWAY?! 65

us), who made a mistake. To unconsciously (or consciously) conclude they are a jerk is the height of delusion.*

Not only is this conclusion delusional, but it is also harmful to our own emotional well-being. It launches us into a toxic emotion, anger, and we often hold onto it for minutes (or even longer) after the person exits the freeway. *("I can't believe that person cut me off last second! The nerve!!")* In the next section of the book, we will delve more deeply into the mindset of judgment versus compassion, and we will explore the science that underpins the self-sabotaging effects of anger and judgment.

Let's take a look at a couple of other examples of how our unconscious or programmed thinking, framing, or interpretation of a life event, rather than the event itself, dictates our split-second emotional reaction to the event.†

---

* If you would rather cognitively reframe by selecting one of these options rather than the ER story, or even hinging your interpretation on your inability to know the true reason for the driver's action (rather than on the belief the person is rushing to the ER), that is perfectly fine. That's the beauty of cognitive reframing – you get to decide which is the more empowering belief to adopt.

† Many people also have a biochemical component to their emotions, whether it is depression, anxiety, or some other clinical issue. To be clear, we are not claiming that individual biochemistry plays no role in emotions; it clearly does. What we are claiming is that irrespective of our biochemistry, our beliefs and cognitions often dictate, exacerbate, or otherwise significantly influence the emotions we feel. This is why therapeutic techniques that are based in cognitive reframing, such as cognitive behavior therapy and dialectical behavior therapy, have been empirically shown to be effective in treating the symptoms of clinical depression and anxiety.

Chapter 11

A Symbol of Peace or Genocide?*

If you were walking across campus along a slightly new route and then, upon turning a corner, you were suddenly confronted by a swastika prominently hanging on the outside of a university building, what emotion would you experience?

In that now-familiar one tenth of a second – with no conscious or deliberate thought – you would be flooded with intense emotions like fear, sadness, confusion, or anger. But if an Indian law student attending the Indian Law Institute in Delhi, India, experienced the same event, they would be instantaneously flooded with emotions like joy, peace, and gratitude.

Why is that? Because it is not the symbol, itself, that triggers our emotional reaction, but rather our deeply conditioned beliefs about, or interpretations of the meaning of, the symbol. Importantly, during our lifetime, those beliefs or interpretations are wired into our unconscious mind long before we are exposed to the symbol in any particular instance. For very good reason, the minds of Westerners have been wired to associate the swastika with horror and genocide, but this is a learned neurological association. For equally good reasons, the minds of Indians (and many other Easterners) have been wired to associate the swastika with peace and unity, but this is also a learned neurological association.

The swastika is a 5,000-year-old symbol from ancient India that has long represented well-being, peace, unity, and auspiciousness, so it is no surprise that the average Indian will have a very pleasant System 1 reaction to the mere sight of it. Yet, in the last century, the Third Reich commandeered this sacred symbol of universal unity and began using it in

---

* Trigger warning: In this segment of the book, we are going to reference Hitler and the Holocaust, so if this topic would be at all triggering to you, we encourage you to skip to the next segment of the book, entitled *That is So Disgusting!*

furtherance of its horrific system of bigotry and genocide, causing the average Westerner's mind to have a very unpleasant System 1 reaction to its mere sight. As illustrated in the figure below, the swastika had a very different connotation in the United States until the Third Reich commandeered the symbol.

Photos: Steven Heller

20th Century fad: Fruit packaging, a Coca-Cola pendant, and a pack of cards, all from the US

Until World War II, the swastika was considered a symbol of good luck and prosperity in the United States. It had no connotations of bigotry, genocide, or white supremacy. For example, in 1925, Coca Cola debuted a swastika watch fob across the United States. However, once the United States press began covering the rise of the Third Reich with photos, the connotation of the swastika changed, and its widespread use in the U.S. vanished.

If you show a baby a swastika, regardless of their culture, they will have no emotional reaction to it. Only after receiving the appropriate culture-specific education about its meaning over time will this subjective interpretation become learned by their conscious mind, and eventually, with enough repetition of the interpretation over the years, it will become wired into their unconscious mind. Then, a mere passing glimpse of the symbol will cause a lightning-fast, unintentional, and unconscious cognition that generates the resulting emotion within one tenth of a second. It will feel like an immediate emotional reaction to the sight of the image – *without any cognition* – because the cognition occurs so quickly and so unconsciously. But make no mistake about it, there is a distinct cognition that occurs after the sight of the image and before the emotion arises. It is the essential conduit that converts the image into the emotion.

A SYMBOL OF PEACE OR GENOCIDE? 69

How the human brain gets programmed to generate an automatic emotion in response to a reoccurring image, event, or behavior in life

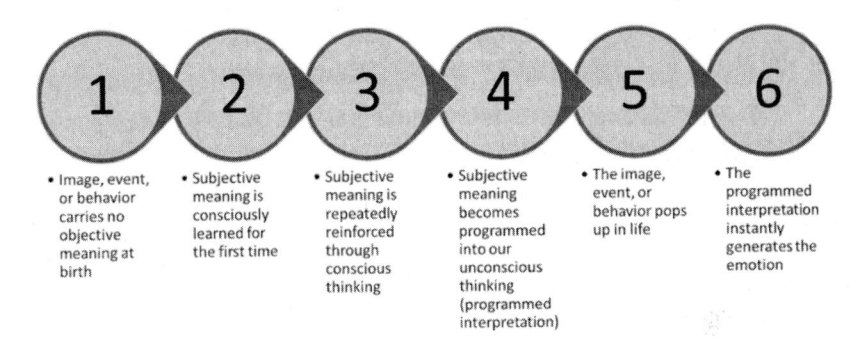

1 • Image, event, or behavior carries no objective meaning at birth

2 • Subjective meaning is consciously learned for the first time

3 • Subjective meaning is repeatedly reinforced through conscious thinking

4 • Subjective meaning becomes programmed into our unconscious thinking (programmed interpretation)

5 • The image, event, or behavior pops up in life

6 • The programmed interpretation instantly generates the emotion

When we begin realizing that all of our emotional reactions in law school and life are the result of learned or conditioned cognitions (i.e., interpretations, beliefs, and meanings), we can begin choosing whether we want our emotional state to be controlled by the programmed cognition that is being triggered by the specific event at issue. If we do not like the emotional reaction we are having, we can identify the programmed cognition and choose a different cognition, and hence, a different emotional response.

This is what the great Holocaust survivor, Viktor Frankl, was referring to with his landmark words: "Between stimulus and response there is a space. In that space is our power to choose our response. In our response lies our growth and our freedom."*

---

* You get to choose if you want to hold onto any particular cognition, even if it leads to difficult emotions. For example, you may choose to hold onto your conditioned interpretation of the swastika because you (very understandably) do not want to desensitize yourself to it. As long as we are making a free choice about whether we want to hold on to our various conditioned interpretations, then we are infusing personal agency into our emotional responses. When you identify conditioned interpretations that are not benefitting or serving you, and that are causing you difficult emotions, we would invite you release or reframe those interpretations.

Chapter 12

That Is *So* Disgusting!

We want to walk you through an experiential exercise as the final illustration of how the human brain generates emotions. We have done this exercise live with over 50,000 lawyers and law students, and we want you to have the experience in writing.

Imagine one of us taking a small dixie cup containing an ounce of purified water and then holding it in our mouth for about four seconds, before spitting it back into the same dixie cup. Then imagine us pausing for a few seconds and then drinking that ounce of liquid in one shot.

What emotion arises in you? Most likely disgust. You were probably grossed out by our mixing water and saliva and then guzzling it down. It's certainly not common for people to do such a thing, so your reaction is very typical. We estimate that 90% of participants who witness us do this live report the emotion of disgust (or some equivalent emotion). As you know, that emotion would arise in you approximately one tenth of a second after we downed the liquid (without any conscious intention, per usual).

Now let us try a different experience. We are confident (*or are we?*) that you will experience the identical emotional reaction. Imagine us taking an adjacent dixie cup containing an ounce of purified water, pouring the water into our mouth, and then holding it in our mouth for about four seconds, before drinking it down.

That is *so* disgusting! Oh wait, is that not your reaction? You likely experienced a very different emotion during the second experience. Rather than experiencing disgust, you likely had no overt emotional reaction. (The second experience consisted of an activity that is generally referred to as *"drinking water."*) If we asked you why you experienced the emotion of disgust after the first experience but not after the second, you would likely struggle to come up with a clear answer, but you would probably point to the fact that the water exited our body during the first experience, but not the second. That is, after all, the only distinction between the two experiences.

As a matter of simple science, this factual distinction does not justify a different emotional reaction. The amount of bacteria in the two cups of water, as a result of mixing them with saliva, is nearly identical. There is a scintilla increase in bacteria levels in the first water cup compared to the second, but the typical meal you eat three times per day is covered with significantly more bacteria cells than were present in the first cup of water.* Yet you do not feel the emotion of disgust every time you eat freshly cooked pasta or a freshly made sandwich. So why did you feel the emotion of disgust in the first experience?†

Because a conditioned belief exists in our society that saliva is disgusting once it leaves the mouth, but completely unremarkable when it remains in the mouth. To state the (now) obvious, this belief makes no logical sense. It is contradicted by basic science and is not tethered to reality. Yet 90% of you felt disgust after the first experience, revealing that you possess (*and are possessed by*) this conditioned belief.

Again, it was not the mixture of water and saliva that caused you to feel the emotion of disgust, it was your own

---

* While eating the typical meal, Americans consume an average of over **450,000** microorganisms, aka microbes, per meal (single cell-bacteria, multicell eukaryote, and other microscopic organisms). Lang, J. M., Eisen, J. A., & Zivkovic, A. M. (2014). The microbes we eat: Abundance and taxonomy of microbes consumed in a day's worth of meals for three diet types. *Peer J, 2*, e659. DOI: 10.7717/peerj.659.

Moreover, you likely are not disgusted by your kitchen sponge, but you should be. The average kitchen sponge has been found to have approximately 50 billion bacteria cells per cubic centimeter, including abundant pathogen cells, and has been shown to be the most bacteria-laden item present in the typical home, apart from the feces in the toilet. See Guglielmi, G. (2017, July 28). Your kitchen sponge harbors zillions of microbes. Cleaning it could make things worse. *Science.* https://www.science.org/content/article/your-kitchen-sponge-harbors-zillions-microbes-cleaning-it-could-make-things-worse; see also Cardinale, M., Kaiser, D., Lueders, T., Schnell, S., & Egert, M. (2017). Microbiome analysis and confocal microscopy of used kitchen sponges reveal massive colonization by *Acinetobacter*, *Moraxella* and *Chryseobacterium* species. *Scientific Reports, 7*, Article 5791. DOI: 10.1038/s41598-017-06055-9.

Ironically, we use *the* filthiest, most bacteria-infested item to *clean* the dishes that we eat off! Yet, because of our conditioned belief that the sponge is a cleaning agent, we do not feel the emotion of disgust that logic and science warrant.

† Incidentally, saliva is a life-supporting substance that is critical to oral hygiene (its microbiomes kill bacteria and fight tooth decay), to digesting food (the enzymes in saliva play a key role in breaking down the food before it enters the intestinal tract, and its viscosity lubricates the food so it can pass through the intestinal track), and to breathing (you would quickly asphyxiate if your salivary glands ceased producing saliva).

THAT IS SO DISGUSTING! 73

conditioned belief about the mixture of water and saliva that caused it. The other 10% of you did not experience the emotion of disgust when subjected to the identical experience. Because you do not possess (and *are not possessed by*) the conditioned belief at issue, you had a very different emotional reaction to the same factual stimulus. When your authors first witnessed this experiment many years ago,* we both experienced the emotion of disgust. But upon self-inspection, we elected to release our delusional conditioned belief and replace it with a factual belief. As a result, we no longer feel the emotion of disgust as a result of this experiment, even though the very same experiment induced disgust in us in the past.

The purpose of this experiment is not to convert you into a bunch of saliva-guzzling law students, but rather, to help you better understand how your brain generates emotions, so that you can more effectively deconstruct your emotional reactions and choose whether you want to continue reacting in the way you always have. When you change your conditioned belief, the same factual event "spits out" a very different emotion. (Pun *desperately* intended.)†

---

* We want to express our appreciation to David Dibble, who exposed us to this wonderful experiment many years ago. Dibble is the author of *The New Agreements in the Workplace: Releasing the Human Spirit*, an insightful book on changing the cultural paradigms present in our workplaces.[7]

† We hope our cheesy puns do not annoy you too much. If they do, we want to warn you that several more are awaiting you in the remainder of the book. Please accept our heartfelt apologies in advance!

Chapter 13

What Is a Mindset?

A mindset is a conditioned belief that influences how we experience various aspects of life. It is a lens through which we interpret the world, including the inevitable challenges and problems that arise in life. The expression, "If you look at the world through rose-colored glasses, everything will look rosy," captures the essence of a mindset. Modern science shows that we never really perceive life events "purely" or "objectively." Rather, we perceive them through the particular pre-existing lens in our mind. This is why two people can have very different interpretations of the same object, such as the beauty of an art piece, the taste of a particular flavor of ice cream, or the smell of a particular perfume. Or why two people can experience different amounts of anger while stuck in the same traffic jam. Or why two law students can have different levels of stress upon realizing that tonight's reading assignment is extraordinarily long.

In the early 1600s, French philosopher Rene Descartes asserted that humans cannot perceive any object or event in the world without that perception being influenced by their own subjective interpretation. Descartes' position was highly controversial and flew in the face of Aristotle's long-accepted assertion that humans perceive reality in a direct and completely objective way. While Aristotle's position was known as "direct realism," Descartes' was known as "indirect realism," in that our perception of reality is "indirect" because there is an intermediary that stands between us and the events we experience: our mind's subjective interpretation.

Four hundred years after Descartes expressed his controversial position, modern neuroscience proves he was right. Neuroscience has shown the brain forms schemas – conceptual frameworks that color our perception of reality. Essentially, schemas are mindsets that are visible in the brain. In technical terms, "Schemas are superordinate knowledge structures that reflect abstracted commonalities across multiple experiences, exerting powerful influences over how events are perceived, interpreted, and remembered."[8] That's a mouthful. But to say the same thing more simply: neurological structures – essentially ingrained mindsets – exist in our brains and influence how we perceive life events. These neurological structures or mindsets – which are unique to each of us – generate our System 1 thoughts and interpretations throughout the day. The good news is that we can challenge these structures and mindsets in the moment, and thus force ourselves to view the life event differently than our pre-existing structure dictates. And when we do this, we not only have a different experience of reality (with different emotional reactions), but we also can modify these structures and mindsets over time.

This is what the Tetris Effect really is: altering our existing cognitive structures and mindsets through deliberate action, so we interpret life events differently. If we are currently wearing rose-colored glasses, we can choose to replace those glasses with aqua-colored glasses with respect to any particular event we are viewing. Or we can choose to keep wearing the rose-colored glasses in that moment. It is our choice. Of course, the more often we choose to switch to aqua-colored glasses, the more those glasses will become our default lens over time.

The fascinating – and promising – reality is this: the science shows that our interpretive lenses and mindsets are highly malleable. And when we alter our mindset about a particular life event, our entire experience around that event can change.

Chapter 14

Housekeepers Who Exercise (That's a Redundancy!)

In a creative study showing the potent effects of our mindset, acclaimed Harvard psychologists Dr. Ellen Langer and Dr. Alia Crum (who has since moved to Stanford) found that when hotel housekeepers learned that their work was the equivalent of exercise, they suddenly began losing weight and becoming significantly healthier — even though their behavior did not change.

In the study, Langer and Crum worked with 84 female hotel housekeeping employees across seven U.S. hotels.[9] The participants had answered polling questions at the outset of the study in which they stated they never exercised, or only did so rarely. Each of the participants was initially measured for their body weight, body fat percentage, body mass index, waist to hip ratio (WHR), and resting blood pressure. Half of the women were placed into the experimental group (whose mindset would be altered), and the other half were placed in the control group (who would continue with their existing mindset).

The experimental group was provided with a set of accurate information, including that the U.S. Surgeon General recommends that individuals accumulate 30 minutes of physical exercise per day to achieve a "healthy lifestyle" and that approximately 200 calories burned per day meets the recommended threshold. They were further told the exercise does not have to be hard or painful, and that it can be moderate as long as they are burning calories and moving their muscles, such as is done during a brisk walk, climbing the stairs, or performing active household work.

Additionally, they were told that the various acts of bending, pushing, lifting, and squatting that they perform throughout their work shift qualify as exercise. They were also provided accurate caloric breakdowns for each of their standard housekeeping tasks (e.g., changing linens for 15 minutes burns

40 calories, vacuuming for 15 minutes burns 50 calories, and cleaning bathrooms for 15 minutes burns 60 calories).

They were further informed that since each of them cleaned an average of 15 rooms per day and worked 32 to 40 hours per week, they were each undoubtedly exceeding the Surgeon General's weekly exercise recommendations for a "healthy lifestyle." (The exercise information was also posted in the employee breakroom.) That's right, these individuals learned – for the first time – that they *were* exercising very regularly and were more than meeting the standard for a healthy lifestyle. They previously had held the belief that they did not exercise (or only did so very rarely), but as a result of this simple intervention, their belief changed. The control group did not receive any of this information, and hence had no reason to change their belief that they do not regularly exercise. All of the participants agreed not to change their diet or the frequency of their outside-of-work exercise over the next four weeks.

At the end of the four weeks, the housekeepers in both groups were re-measured for the same physiological markers. Astonishingly, the members of the experimental group experienced large decreases in body fat percentage, body mass index, waist to hip ratio, and resting blood pressure. They also lost an average of two pounds each. The control group had no changes in any of the categories, which is unsurprising for a four-week stretch.

This study demonstrates the power of our mindset. When the participants unconsciously believed they were not exercising, their bodies did not become healthier. But once they were provided with simple information that altered their mindset about their work, the new mindset induced significant changes to their body and overall health. Their level of physical activity did not change over the course of the four weeks. All that occurred was that their unconscious mindset, that they were not exercising, transformed into a conscious mindset that they were exercising. This change in mindset led to vast physiological improvements.

This is what the research refers to as a "mindset intervention." Participants in a study are provided information or guidance (the "intervention") that is designed to trigger a

HOUSEKEEPERS WHO EXERCISE (THAT'S A REDUNDANCY!)

different mindset – or way of thinking – about some life event, and then the researchers evaluate whether the new mindset leads to improvements in the person's experience or life. The research consistently shows that a change in mindset can have massive effects on participants' mental health, emotional well-being, and cognitive performance.

Chapter 15

Feeling Out of Place Is *Normal*

Research has shown that minority and diverse students entering college often feel more out of place than their white peers. This is even more the case at Ivy League universities. This feeling can have significant effects on minority and diverse students' self-esteem, emotional well-being, and academic performance. Aware of this major problem, Professor Greg Walton from Stanford designed a mindset intervention study intended to partially address the issue.[10] He collaborated with the administration at an Ivy League university to work with African American freshman students. His goal was to provide a mindset intervention to these students that made them believe their sense of non-belonging was not unique to them. He gave them a packet of testimonials from junior and senior students at the university who universally shared that they felt they didn't fit in or belong during much of their freshman year, but that over time, this sense changed, and they eventually experienced very different feelings.

For example, one testimonial that was provided to the freshmen stated:

> When I first got here, I worried that I was different from other students. I wasn't sure I fit in. Sometime after my first year, I came to realize that many people come here uncertain whether they fit in or not. Now it seems ironic. Everybody feels they are different freshman year from everybody else, when really in at least some ways we are all the same.*

After the freshmen read the packet of testimonials, Walton asked them to write an essay reflecting on how their own experiences were similar to those of the juniors and seniors. Finally, when the students completed the written essay, they

---

* We want to thank Kelly McGonigal for the incisive summary of Walton's study she provides in her book, *The Upside of Stress*, on pp. 21–25.

were asked to provide a short video testimonial about their experience so it could be shown to the next year's freshmen to help them, too, discover that a sense of not fitting in is a typical experience for freshmen students. That was the entirety of the mindset intervention. It was intended to modify how these students viewed their sense of not fitting in – from a problem unique to them, to a more universal part of the college experience.

Over the next four years, the African American students who received this brief mindset intervention at the beginning of their freshmen year had higher markers in well-being, happiness, and physical health than did the African American students who did not receive the intervention (the control group). Moreover, at the time of graduation, the students in the mindset intervention group had much higher GPAs than the students in the control group. "Worries about belonging are a reasonable response to our history," Walton said.[11] "By anticipating questions students of marginalized backgrounds ask about their belonging, colleges and universities can create experiences and send messages that help all students recognize that many challenges are normal and inherent in the transition to college, and how they can address them to succeed. That helps students, and institutions, do better." Thus, even a brief mindset intervention that primes underrepresented students to interpret their feelings of non-belonging in a different way can lead to years of emotional, physical, and academic benefits.*

---

* This study, of course, does not suggest that white students face the same obstacles to belonging or feelings of non-belonging as African American and other diverse students. It merely suggests that whether African American and other diverse students interpret their feelings of non-belonging as exclusive to them versus as experienced by most students to some degree can have massive consequences for their long-term health, well-being, and success.

CHAPTER 16

WHEN SHOULD I SHIFT MY MINDSET?

The science is clear that when we change our mindset, vast effects can follow. We can experience the same event or factual circumstances in a very different way – with different mental health, emotional well-being, physical wellness, and cognitive performance. We will be providing various examples below of mindset shifts (supported by rigorous scientific studies) that you can use to optimize your happiness and performance in law school, but before we do, let's address the threshold question: When should you attempt to shift your mindset?

The simple answer is this: whenever you are feeling heavily stressed, angry, sad, or under the grip of any other unpleasant emotion. That intense emotion is a sign that your *current mindset* is contributing to your emotional state. In that moment, if you actively attempt to identify your current mindset and then adopt a different mindset about the challenging event you are facing, you are positioning yourself to change your emotional state. You likely will not be able to change the factual situation, but you can always change your mindset or perspective toward the situation.

CHAPTER 17

SHIFTING IS NOT SUPPRESSING

An important distinction exists between shifting your mindset in response to an unpleasant emotion, on the one hand, and suppressing the emotion, on the other. When you shift your mindset, you are honestly acknowledging the unpleasant emotion and then taking a purposeful action to transform your emotional state. When you suppress your unpleasant emotion, you are refusing to acknowledge that you are even experiencing the emotion. You are bottling it up inside of you and pretending it is not there. "I'm fine, I'm not upset!" we might exclaim to ourselves or others when we are actually feeling quite upset. "Toxic positivity" is a particular form of emotional suppression where we project a blanket sense of positivity despite feeling differently within.* Although the distinction between shifting and suppressing may sound like mere semantics, the difference is actually very real.

In 1863, Russian author Fyodor Dostoevsky provocatively wrote: "Try to pose for yourself this task: not to think of a polar bear, and you will see that the cursed thing will come to mind every minute."[12] Well over a century later, in 1987, Harvard psychologist Daniel Wegner came across this passage and decided to check if the science would confirm Dostoevsky's assurance.

Wegner constructed a study in which he provided participants with a small bell and asked them to monitor their thoughts for five straight minutes.[13] At the outset of the five-minute period, Wegner described a white bear and asked the participants to ring the bell each time they thought of a white bear. However, Wegner instructed half of the participants to try

---

  * Toxic positivity can also manifest interpersonally – when we respond to someone else's unpleasant emotions with positive proclamations that unwittingly minimize their pain or imply they should be reacting differently to the difficulty at issue. For example, if a friend expresses intense stress about the bad grade she got on an important midterm and you reply with, "At least you didn't fail, I'm sure you'll do better on the final!" Or if you respond to a friend's grief about their pet who recently passed by remarking, "He had a long and full life and that's something to be happy about!"

to actively think of the white bear during the five-minute period, while he instructed the other half to try *not* to think of the white bear during the period. Which group of participants do you think rang the bell far more often? Correct, the group that was told *not* to think of the white bear!

Based on this original study, a new psychological doctrine emerged – ironic process theory (also referred to as ironic rebound theory or the white bear effect). According to this theory, which has been confirmed by a myriad of studies over the last few decades, when we attempt to suppress a particular thought or emotion, that thought or emotion usually grows in potency. If you ever had your feelings hurt by someone and then attempted not to think about the pain or the person, yet they kept popping back into your head, you have experienced the white bear effect.

Wegner labeled this process "ironic" because the more we attempt to suppress a thought or emotion, the more active it becomes in our mind. Wegner and his successors in the field concluded that this phenomenon occurs because when our conscious thinking decides not to think about something, our unconscious thinking begins tracking whether we are succeeding in the venture – thereby causing the thing to continually pop back into our mind.

When we feel stressed, angry, or hurt, it can be tempting to "bottle up" or ignore the unpleasant emotion and instead hyper-focus on our law school assignments, distract ourselves with Netflix or some other entertainment, reach for an alcoholic beverage or a smoke, or eat something delicious – *rather than deal with the unpleasant emotion*. We may believe that by paying the unwanted emotion no attention, it will go away – or at least diminish. "If I don't acknowledge it, it won't control me!" Or, "If I pretend it's not there, I'll feel better." Or, "If I think about it, I will just make it worse." Unfortunately, the science shows the opposite is generally true.

A large collection of studies has found that suppressing our unpleasant emotions can cause a variety of detrimental consequences, including intensification of the emotion, heightened cardiovascular activation, slower emotional recovery, worsening of our current mood, increased secondary anxiety, delayed aggression and over-reactivity (aka the "rebound effect" or "boomerang effect"), depletion in will power, impaired memory, reduced relationship closeness and satisfaction, and lower life satisfaction.[14] Simply put, suppressing our emotions is not good for us.*

This is the beauty of shifting our mindset – it is not about suppressing or denying our stress, anger, or sadness; it is about acknowledging it honestly and then taking deliberate action to transmute it. Importantly, the first step is to authentically recognize the unpleasant emotion that has overtaken us. Only then can we adapt our mindset in the most tailored and effective way so as to transmute the unpleasant emotion.†

---

* Emotional suppression has also been shown to be associated with higher mortality rates. A study by a team of doctors from the Harvard School of Public Health, Columbia Department of Health Policy, and the University of Rochester Medical Center tracked individuals over a 12-year period and found that people who bottled up their emotions were 30% more likely to die, including from cardiovascular disease, over that 12-year period than people who did not, and were 70% more likely to die from cancer over the period than the non-suppressors.[15]

Even suppressing physical pain has been consistently shown to backfire. In one prominent study, participants had their hand dunked into a bucket of ice water for two straight minutes (an experimental method for inducing pain known as "cold pressor pain induction"). One group of participants were instructed to suppress their pain by either ignoring it or diverting their attention to a distraction. Another group of participants were instructed to acknowledge the pain by placing their attention on it during the two minutes of dunking. Two minutes after their hand was removed from the bucket, the suppressors experienced heightened symptoms of pain compared to the acknowledgers, even though the suppressors had slightly lower pain symptoms during the two minutes of actual dunking. Moreover, nearly an hour after their hand was removed from the bucket, the suppressors were far more likely to interpret the innocuous vibrations from a disguised neck massager as being painful than the group that did not previously suppress their pain. Cioffi, D., & Holloway, J. (1993). Delayed costs of suppressed pain. *Journal of Personality and Social Psychology, 64*(2), 274–282. DOI: 10.1037/0022-3514.64.2.274. Suppressing our physical pain, as with suppressing our emotional pain, may provide some very short-term "numbing" but does not make it go away and, in fact, leads to exacerbated problems over time.

† In many cases, we can begin transmuting the emotion shortly after it arises. But in other cases, it is important to allow ourselves time to feel the unpleasant emotion, rather than attempt to shift out of the emotion too quickly. If a loved one passes away, for example, attempting to immediately shift our mindset and transmute our sadness is likely the wrong move. Instead, giving ourselves permission and however much time we need (whether it's months or years) to just experience the sadness, grief, and heartbreak before gently beginning the process of shifting is the healthier and better approach. Similarly, albeit to a lesser extent, if a close friend commits an act of betrayal, it may be prudent to experience the hurt, sadness, and anger without prematurely attempting to transmute these emotions. Or, if we receive a bad grade on an important paper or exam, it may be best to allow ourselves to experience the disappointment and stress for a few days before attempting to shift into a more pleasant emotional state – at which point we are more likely to be emotionally ready to shift emotional states and more likely to succeed. The tools of verbalization (Tool #13 at page 305) and emotional granularity (Tool

In the next section, we will provide you with a framework for identifying the mindsets that induce your unpleasant emotions. This will allow you not only to honestly acknowledge your unpleasant emotions, but also to understand why they arose in the first place. And what's more, the framework will equip you to shift into a set of countervailing mindsets that beget the pleasant and empowered emotions that you want to have more of.

#14 at page 313) can support the process of experiencing these difficult emotions in a way that makes them more manageable and less overwhelming in the interim period until we are ready to attempt to transmute them. That being said, for the vast majority of challenges and problems we experience in law school and life, we can briefly experience and acknowledge the unpleasant emotions (so as not to suppress them) and then move to the process of shifting them.

Chapter 18

The 5 Mindset Shifts

Based on our obsessive research on stress and the human mind over many years, we have arrived at five mindsets that lead to virtually all of our stress, anger, sadness and other challenging emotions in life (and law school): **(1) Threat, (2) Judgment, (3) Pessimism, (4) Fixed, and (5) External Control**. We call these the Stress Mindsets. When we are feeling upset or overwhelmed in some way, it is a sign that we are stuck in one of these five **Stress Mindsets**. (Sometimes we are stuck in several of them at the same time, but it is usually one Stress Mindset that is dominating our thoughts and interpretations.) Importantly, each one of these mindsets is associated with heightened symptoms of stress, anxiety, and depression, as well as activation of the amygdala and lower-level survival thinking. Simply put, when we are in one of these mindsets, our emotional state is impaired, and our cognitive functioning is worse.

Each Stress Mindset has a corresponding **Resilience Mindset**. The Resilience Mindset is the "flip side" or inversion of the Stress Mindset on the same issue. Here are the five Resilience Mindsets: **(1) Opportunity, (2) Compassion, (3) Optimism, (4) Growth, and (5) Internal Control**. Each of these mindsets is associated with reduced symptoms of stress, anxiety, and depression, as well as increased activation of the prefrontal cortex and higher-level executive thinking. In short, when we are in any one of the Resilience Mindsets, our emotional state and cognitive functioning are optimized.

Mindset Shifts

Stress & Underperformance
- Threat
- Judgment
- Pessimism
- Fixed
- External Control

Amygdala

Amygdala activation
Prefrontal cortex deactivation

Resilience & Greatness
- Opportunity
- Compassion
- Optimism
- Growth
- Internal Control

Prefrontal cortex

Amygdala deactivation
Prefrontal cortex activation

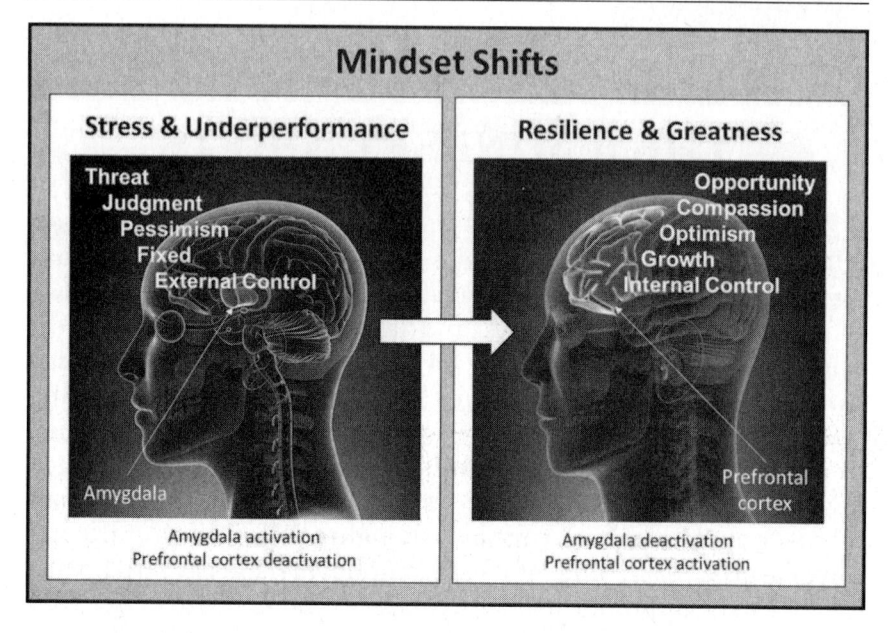

When we are facing a challenge in law school or life, we can view the challenge through the mindset of a "threat" or an "opportunity." When someone in our life does something unfair or unkind, we can interpret their behavior through the mindset of "judgment" or "compassion." When we are facing a problem in life, we can adopt a mindset of "pessimism" or "optimism" as we evaluate the situation. When we make a mistake or fail at something, we can perceive our mistake or failure through a "fixed" mindset or a "growth" mindset. And finally, when life brings us unexpected obstacles, we can interpret the obstacle through the mindset of "external control" or "internal control."

Which mindset we apply is critical to our mental health, emotional well-being, resiliency, happiness, cognitive performance, and academic success. But here's the rub: Our brain is currently wired to automatically interpret most life events and challenges through the Stress Mindsets. They are our default mindsets, which is why we experience so much stress, overwhelm, and upset in life. It takes no effort to apply the Stress Mindsets, since they function automatically at a System 1 level. No problem, though – all we have to do is notice when we have defaulted to one of these mindsets. Once we identify

THE 5 MINDSET SHIFTS 91

which Stress Mindset we currently are in, then we know which Resilience Mindset we need to shift to.

When attempting to shift into a Resilience Mindset, you do not need to actively eliminate the corresponding Stress Mindset. Instead, all you need to do is attempt to cultivate the targeted Resilience Mindset. For instance, if you realize you are feeling stressed because you are stuck in a "threat" mindset, you don't need to diminish your "threat" mindset directly; you only need to cultivate an "opportunity" mindset towards the difficulty at issue. When you implement an "opportunity" mindset, the "threat" mindset that previously gripped you will naturally dissolve. By analogy, if you want to make a room light, you only need to add light, you do not need to actively remove the dark. If you want to fill a cup, you only need to add liquid, you do not need to actively remove the emptiness. And if you want a room to have sound, you only need to add sound, you do not need to actively remove the silence. Similarly, if you want to experience an "opportunity" mindset, you only need to add that mindset to your framing of the situation, you do not need to actively remove the "threat" mindset. This is true for each of the five mindset shifts we outline below. The presence of each Resilience Mindset will organically displace the corresponding Stress Mindset.

We will now provide you with the blueprint for identifying when you are stuck in each Stress Mindset and for shifting into each corresponding Resilience Mindset. The more you notice and override your default Stress Mindsets as you face hardships in life and school, the easier it will become. In fact, as you do this more and more, your brain will start defaulting into the Resilience Mindsets more frequently. In other words, you can slowly rewire your brain to make the Resilience Mindsets easier to access and activate. Each time you shift from a Stress Mindset to a Resilience Mindset when facing a specific difficulty, you will be tapping into improved emotional well-being and cognitive functioning as you navigate that difficulty.

Even better, you will also be taking one small step toward gradually rewiring your brain in the long run. Each time, for example, that you shift from a judgment mindset to a compassion mindset, you will experience the emotional and cognitive benefits of this mindset shift in that moment. But you will also make your brain *slightly* more compassionate for the future. That is, the next time you face unfair or unkind behavior from someone else, it will be ever-so-slightly easier to tap into a mindset of compassion. You may not notice the progress right away, but subtle changes are in fact occurring at the neurological level. And the more you practice this mindset shift, the more noticeable this progress will become. This is how we slowly rewire our brain over time.

Be patient with yourself as you gradually apply these mindset shifts. Maybe for the first three months after reading the guidance below, you only remember to interpret one out of every 10 challenges as an opportunity rather than a threat. But then, in the three months after that, you are able to apply the opportunity mindset to two out of every 10 challenges. Then, in the three months after that, you are able to apply the opportunity mindset to three out of every 10 challenges, and finally, you are able to apply it to four out of every 10 challenges in the subsequent three months. That would mean that one year from today, you will be applying an opportunity mindset in *40% of the challenges* you face in law school and life! That can materially improve your happiness in life and your academic performance in law school. And during each individual challenge to which you apply the opportunity mindset over that one-year period, you will receive an emotional and cognitive boon.

Let's dive into each of the five mindset shifts now.

1. THREAT TO OPPORTUNITY

"Victory comes from finding opportunities in problems."

— Sun Tzu

Think of a time in your life when some contest or challenge was approaching, and you were excited about it. Maybe it was an athletic competition in high school, or a musical recital in your youth, or an exam that you were overprepared for in college, or a performance of some sort in the past. You were fired up about it. Counting the hours until it began. Far from dreading

THE 5 MINDSET SHIFTS

it, you were salivating over it. Naturally, you had some nerves about it because you cared deeply about succeeding, but on the whole, you felt energized, passionate, and positively stimulated by the opportunity. You were eagerly anticipating it – and couldn't wait for it to arrive.

Why were you feeling that way? Was it because you were guaranteed to succeed? No. It's because your brain was unconsciously framing the upcoming contest, performance, or challenge as an opportunity for greatness. As a chance to showcase your talent and to perform to your highest potential. To rise to excellence and achieve your goal. To accomplish what you had set your mind to, and to manifest the results of all of your hard work.

Yet other people in that same situation – whether it was one of your teammates, classmates, co-musicians, or peers – were feeling extremely stressed out by the upcoming event. They felt overwhelmed and paralyzed by the gravity of it, and by the implications of underperforming. They were dreading it.

What explains the completely different emotional states of two people experiencing the same event? It's certainly not the event, itself, that is directly causing each person's emotional state; otherwise, both individuals would be experiencing the same emotions. It is each person's mindset – or *cognitive interpretation* – of the event that determines each person's emotional reaction to the event. As we know from the "driving cutoff" example we discussed earlier, it is *never* the factual event that causes our emotions. It is our cognitive interpretation or framing of the event that does.

The science shows the human mind can frame any challenge in life (including law school) as either a threat of failure or an opportunity for greatness or gain. When we frame the challenge as a threat of failure, we unconsciously think about the ways we can fail and the various ramifications of such a failure. This framing, with the associated thoughts, induces the emotion of stress and reduces our cognitive functioning (by shifting our brain into lower prefrontal cortex activation and higher amygdala activation). However, when the same challenge is framed as an opportunity for greatness or gain, the emotions of excitement, passion, and enthusiasm are induced, and we experience heightened cognitive functioning (with greater activation of the prefrontal cortex and lower activation of the amygdala). So the same challenge can be viewed as either a threat of failure (i.e., a "threat mindset"), or an opportunity for greatness or gain (i.e., an "opportunity" mindset, aka a "challenge" mindset). Just like the "Old Woman/Young Woman" illusion – it can be seen in two completely different ways.

One study provided university-level participants with stressful, cognitive tests involving a series of five images with one missing image. The participants were required to identify the missing image in less than 45 seconds.[16] The researchers intentionally induced the participants into stress in two ways – first, by informing them the test was an "excellent predictor" of academic ability and career success, and second, by informing them that their performance time was being tracked because it was also predictive of long-term success.

Two minutes before providing these instructions, the researchers assessed the participants' baseline emotional state (i.e., level of joy, upset, well-being, etc.), as well as their baseline stress levels as measured through a cardiovascular index. The index was a combined score capturing three key cardiovascular functions: heart rate, blood pressure, and stroke volume (the volume of blood pumped from the left ventricle per heartbeat). And before assessing the participants' baseline emotional state and stress levels, the researchers used a well-established assessment for measuring the degree of each participant's "opportunity mindset" versus "threat mindset" in response to challenges. The various assessments were also performed during the cognitive test to measure how the participants were internally reacting to the challenge in real time.

The results showed that the participants who possessed an opportunity mindset experienced far greater emotional well-being and significantly lower physiological stress while taking the test in comparison to the participants who possessed a threat mindset. So even though their mindsets were assessed before they began the test and before they even knew what sort of test they were going to take, their prevailing mindset powerfully influenced their emotional well-being and stress levels while taking on an unforeseen cognitive challenge.

Another study sought to determine whether priming university students into either an opportunity or threat mindset with a simple two-sentence instruction could affect their cognitive performance and emotional state during an ensuing exam.[17] First, 97 university students were broken up into two groups before taking a working memory exam, which established their baseline working memory levels. The students were also assessed for their current emotional state. The study explained the importance of working memory to academic success as follows: "Working memory (WM) is the capacity to store, retrieve and maintain activation of information in the execution of cognitive tasks, and it is involved in higher-order cognitive processes such as problem solving and reasoning. With central attention and complex cognitive processes (e.g., rehearsal, maintenance, updating and controlled search) as the key components, WM can facilitate students to perform better in various motivated performance tasks such as academic examinations, complex cognitive tasks, and social evaluation tasks. Hence, it is critical to explore how to optimize university students' WM performance in motivated performance contexts."

After completing the working memory exam, the students were told it had just been a "practice test" designed to familiarized them with the style of exam, and that they would now take the "real test." At that point, the researchers provided the first group of students with a two-sentence instruction designed to cause them to frame the test as an opportunity for gain. They told the group that one additional research course credit would be awarded to top performers in addition to the three course credits already at stake. The researchers provided the second group of students with a two-sentence instruction designed to make them frame the test as a threat of failure. They told the group that poor performers would be subjected to an additional interview conducted by their teaching assistant in order to assess whether those students should earn the three credits at issue. The students then took the second working memory test, followed by an assessment of their emotional state.

The results revealed that this two-sentence mindset intervention dramatically affected the students' performance on the second working memory test. Indeed, on average, each student's performance differed by 15% on the second test as compared to the first test, based on whether they were primed into an opportunity or threat mindset. The opportunity mindset students outperformed their former selves, while the threat mindset students underperformed compared to their former selves. The opportunity group also experienced positive emotional changes in comparison to the threat group. As noted by the study, "Risk-focused task instructions debilitated WM performance through intensified threat appraisal and decreased positive affect, whereas opportunity-focused task framing can improve WM performance."

To state the obvious, a 15%-per-person difference in performance is no small feat when no circumstances have changed other than a two-sentence instruction. Indeed, a 15% difference on a "real life" exam could be the difference between a solid "C" (i.e., 75–76%) and an "A-" (i.e., 90–91%). This study also shows how easy it is to alter one's mindset about an imminent challenge – a mere two sentences can substantially alter how we view the challenge, and hence, how we cognitively perform and emotionally feel along the way. A simple shift in perspective about the exam where we consciously think about the gains from possible success, rather than the losses from possible failure, significantly improves our cognitive performance and our emotional state.

Another study reached similar results when university students were primed to frame the challenge as an opportunity for gain versus a threat of loss.[18] 155 students were broken into two groups and were required to make complicated predictions concerning the value of 120 companies' stocks based on a set of manipulated cues. Before beginning, the first group of students were primed to think of the test as an opportunity for gain with the following instruction: "Please write down your name and phone number so that you can be located if necessary. We would like to interview the five best performers. Only 15% of the students who previously participated in the study succeeded on the task." The second group of students were primed to think of the test as a threat of loss with the following instruction: "Please write down your name and phone number so that you can be located if necessary. We would like to interview the five worst

THE 5 MINDSET SHIFTS

performers. 85% of the students who participated in the study previously failed on the task."

Unsurprisingly, the students primed to think of the test as an opportunity substantially outperformed the students primed to think of it as a threat. The "opportunity" students also adapted more effectively to an unexpected change inserted midway through the test. The results, as outlined in the study, "demonstrated that the same level of goal difficulty may lead to high or low performance and adaption to change depending on the appraisal of the situation as challenging [i.e., opportunity for gain] or threatening [i.e., threat of loss]."

A particularly creative study designed to test the power of threat versus opportunity mindsets was conducted with Asian American women students as subjects by Professor Margaret Shih and other researchers at Harvard.[19] The students were provided math tests on two separate occasions. On the first occasion, they were primed to focus on their identity as women, which was intended to induce a threat mindset due to the stereotype that women are worse at math. On the second occasion, the same students were primed to concentrate on their identity as Asian American, which was intended to induce an opportunity mindset due to the stereotype that Asian Americans are better at math.

The result? The students performed far better on the second occasion. This was true even though both tests were the same level of difficulty and no other differences in test instruction or format were provided. A separate group of Asian American women (the control group) were not primed either way, and they performed equivalently on both occasions, as expected. But when the first group was primed into unconsciously focusing on the threat of failure due to being women, rather than the opportunity for success presented by being Asian American, their cognitive performance differed significantly.*

---

* This is an example of "stereotype threat," a specific type of "threat mindset" that involves fear or stress that one's actions or performance will confirm a negative stereotype of a group to which one belongs. This mindset has been consistently shown to lead to cognitive underperformance – even if the individual consciously believes the stereotype is baseless. For an incisive exploration of "stereotype threat" and the decades of fascinating scientific research that supports it, we refer you to the book *Whistling Vivaldi: How Stereotypes Affect Us and What We Can Do*, by Dr. Claude Steele, a

So when you are triggered into intense stress by a particular law school challenge, it is likely a sign that your brain is unconsciously framing the challenge as a threat of failure. In that moment of intense stress, if you can pause and notice how your brain is unconsciously focusing on the various negative consequences that will result from failure, you are halfway there. At that moment, you will have converted your unconscious System 1 thinking to conscious System 2 thinking. Your brain is likely saying things such as, "If I screw this up, I am going to get terrible grades, and I'm not going to get a good job out of law school," or "I am going to embarrass myself and disappoint my family," or "I am going to reveal that I don't belong here and that I am destined to fail." Stress does not arise in a vacuum. This sort of thinking – albeit lightning quick and usually unconscious – is necessary to birth stress.

Once you have identified the underlying thinking that is igniting your intense stress, then change your thinking into an opportunity mindset. "If I hit a home run on this, my grades are going to soar and I'm much more likely to get an awesome job out of law school," or "I am not going to focus on my grade on this stressful writing assignment I am currently working on, and will instead focus on how this assignment is giving me an opportunity to slowly build and refine my legal writing skills so I can excel as a lawyer later," or "Through this challenge, I am going to demonstrate to myself how gritty I can be in the face of stressful challenges by not giving up or backing down," or "The possibility of getting cold-called on in this class, although scary now, is going to help wire my brain in the long run to think fast on my feet in court," or "This overwhelming final exam preparation is the ideal preparation for learning how to master large amounts of information in a short period – which will be critical to becoming a top lawyer."

If you can think of 1–2 *tangible opportunities* presented by the stressful event, and then force yourself to keep thinking of it/them whenever the stress accelerates, you are putting your brain into a position to modulate the stress and enhance your

---

renowned Stanford psychology professor and one of the great thought leaders and researchers on the interplay between stereotypes, mindsets, and cognitive performance.[20]

THE 5 MINDSET SHIFTS

resulting cognition. But what generally occurs in response to a high-stakes challenge is that our brain defaults to a threat mindset – and we unconsciously rehearse the various "terrible" outcomes that will result from poor performance. So we unconsciously catastrophize the situation, causing our stress levels to spike. We believe we are "just stressed out" by the challenge, without recognizing that we are actively – albeit unconsciously – thinking about the challenge in an overtly threat-based manner, which is the real reason for the stress we are feeling.

The brain is wired to frame challenges in this threat-based way, so we should not feel bad that our brain is doing this. Of course, we also should not allow our brain to continue spiraling into threat-based thinking in an unfettered manner. So in those moments of intense stress, we need to interrupt this default neurological process by proactively identifying 1–2 tangible opportunities for greatness or gain presented by this challenge. This subtle paradigm shift can have major effects on our ensuing emotional state and cognitive performance.

A technique for facilitating this mindset shift is to reinterpret your stress as excitement rather than nervousness. In her book *Upside of Stress*, Stanford psychology professor Dr. Kelly McGonigal outlines cutting-edge research on reframing our challenges and stressors in life.[21] "You've probably told yourself or others in moments of stress that if you don't calm down, you'll blow it," writes McGonigal. "This is what most people believe. But is it true?" McGonigal then asks the pivotal question: "What is the best thing to do in this moment: try to calm down, or try to feel excited?" She then goes onto cite various studies suggesting the latter is the superior strategy.

For example, one study run by Harvard Business School professor Dr. Alison Wood Brooks tested whether study participants would perform differently in delivering a speech with little preparation time if they were primed into trying to feel calm versus excited.[22] Half of the participants were told shortly before their speech to try to calm their nerves by saying "I am calm" to themselves. The other half of the participants were told to embrace their nervousness by telling themselves, "I am excited." Each participant then delivered a five-minute speech to a room full of strangers who were instructed not to provide validating head nods or other forms of support.

The group that was told to interpret their nervousness as excitement had higher resilience and confidence scores than the other group. What is more, the objective audience members, who did not know which group each participant belonged to, rated the members of the excitement group as more persuasive, more confident, and more competent than the calmness group.

Rather than trying to force ourselves to feel calm in high-pressure moments, which often does not work, the technique of embracing the natural nerves and reinterpreting those nerves as excitement can help us to healthily process the stress and excel under pressure. It is a tangible way of shifting our brain away from the threat mindset and into the opportunity mindset. Indeed, one would only need to "calm down" *if a threat is presented*, but if a desirable opportunity is being presented, "excitement" is the natural emotion.

Another top researcher in this field is Dr. Jeremy Jamieson from the University of Rochester. As a former college athlete, Jamieson found it noteworthy that top college and professional athletes tend *not* to cope with stress by trying to force themselves to "calm down" before the big game. Instead, they harness their nerves and tell themselves they are "fired up" or "amped up" – and they often excel under the stressful conditions as a result. Jamieson found it interesting how, in contrast, most students and employees try to force themselves to "calm down" before a big test, speech, or other challenge, so Jamieson conducted extensive studies to ascertain whether applying an athlete's mindset to cognitive tests would improve outcomes. The studies uniformly concluded that priming participants to view their nervousness as excitement and as a booster of performance in fact leads to higher stress resiliency and cognitive scores on ensuing exams.[23]

So if you are feeling stressed out when you are about to be called on in class, or before your moot court argument, or in advance of your final exams, perhaps embrace those nerves and tell yourself they are proof that you are excited and fired up about the challenge. This is an opportunity for greatness and gain, and you are understandably amped up about it. Tell

THE 5 MINDSET SHIFTS 101

yourself that these feelings are a performance booster – an energy generator that will help you perform even better. Research suggests that framing the challenge through this "exciting opportunity" lens will boost your resiliency and your performance.*

A business person trying to calm himself down before a big presentation.

Superstar quarterback Patrick Mahomes getting fired up before a big game.

Bricklayers and Higher Purpose

Another way of putting yourself into an opportunity mindset is to recall the specific reason you chose to go to law school and then deliberately think about the details of that reason while you are facing a specific stressor in law school. Have you noticed how the period of time between selecting your law school and the start of law school was filled with excitement and enthusiasm, but the excitement and enthusiasm began to wane once law school began, and continued to wane the more law school

---

* In a compelling example of this sort of reframing, Tyler Adams, the captain of the United States Men's National Soccer Team during the 2022 FIFA World Cup, used the following mantra throughout the tournament to prime his brain for resilience and greatness amidst all of the stress he faced: "Pressure is a privilege."

progressed? The excitement and enthusiasm steadily converted into stress and overwhelm.

Why did this happen? Well, the widespread opportunities presented by law school did not change, but your thinking began to change once the threat of failure became more palpable. Over time, your brain reduced the frequency with which it focused on the manifest opportunities arising from law school, and it began to hone in on the day-to-day assignments, tasks, and stressors. In other words, the focus of your attention shifted from *high-level purpose* before you started law school to *low-level stressors* once you started law school.

A way to override this process is to force yourself to reconnect to that higher purpose. In the related space of employee well-being and performance, a large body of science shows that when employees feel connected to some higher purpose or meaning in their work, their stress levels drop, their well-being and happiness increase, their motivation and job satisfaction grow, and their professional performance improves.[24]

As we have discussed, framing a challenge through the litany of possible losses and bad outcomes induces stress, which is why connecting to a higher purpose or deeper meaning is so effective. When we do this – in the midst of a law school (or work) challenge – we force our brains to transcend or circumvent the possible losses and bad outcomes that we selfishly fear, and instead focus on the possible impact on others or on something greater than ourselves. We shift from our small, self-centered interests to some larger interest beyond ourselves.

A classic parable captures this shift. Two men are working on a construction site, laying bricks. A passerby notices that they are doing the same thing, but the first man looks fatigued, disengaged, and perturbed by his work, while the second man looks energized, engaged, and impassioned by his work. So the passerby approaches the first man and asks, "I'm sorry to interrupt you, sir, but may I ask what you are doing?" The man despondently replies, "I'm laying bricks." The passerby then walks 20 feet away to the second man and asks him, "I'm sorry to interrupt you, sir, but may I ask what you are doing" The man enthusiastically responds, "I'm building a cathedral!"

THE 5 MINDSET SHIFTS

Both men were doing the identical work, but how their brains framed that work was completely different. The first man conceptualized the challenging task in a vacuum based on his own narrow interests, i.e., in isolation from the higher purpose of the task. The second man conceptualized it through the lens of that higher purpose. That conceptualization shift caused a vast difference in their mental and emotional states.

There is a famous story about President John F. Kennedy's first visit to NASA's headquarters back in 1961. During his tour of the facility, he noticed a janitor carrying a broom. He interrupted the tour, walked over to the man, and said: "Hi, I'm Jack Kennedy. What do you do here at NASA?" "Well, Mr. President," the janitor responded, "I'm helping to put a man on the moon." Make no mistake about it, this janitor was not exaggerating. Neil Armstrong never could have landed on the moon in 1969 had this janitor and the rest of the janitorial staff not effectively done their job in cleaning and sterilizing the NASA headquarters for those many years. Without daily janitorial services, the NASA headquarters would have deteriorated to the point where it could no longer function. So the janitors were an essential "but for" cause in our crowning achievement of putting a man on the moon. Rather than viewing his sweeping, mopping, and cleaning in isolation from the higher purpose to which they were attached, this janitor cognitively tethered those tasks to their higher purpose.

You can do the same. Perhaps you want to be a public defender because you want to defend the Constitution or protect the indigent. Or maybe you want to be a prosecutor because you want to uphold the rule of law and create a safer society. Or maybe you want to do international law in order to advance legal initiatives that have global ramifications. Or maybe you want to do legal policy work so you can catalyze social change in our nation. Or maybe you want to work at a large law firm so you can contribute to high-profile matters that affect our financial markets. Or maybe you to want to do civil rights work so you can advocate for equality and create a more equitable society. Or maybe you want to get a high-paid job so you can financially support your parents or some family member in need. Or maybe you don't know what kind of work you want to do, but you are pursuing your law degree because it will allow you to protect your friends and family from exploitation or injustice.

Regardless of the higher purpose behind your legal education, you are likely to become temporarily disconnected from it while grinding out stressful deadlines on a day-to-day basis. At 11:00 p.m. when you are struggling to comprehend your Contracts reading, or when you walk into your Torts class and feel the butterflies in your stomach from the cold call that could ensue, or when you are stressed while studying for your Civil Procedure exam, *that* is the moment to consciously think of your higher purpose. That is the moment to think of the faces of the people you want to help, or the particular aspect of society you want to reform, or the critical cause you want to fight for. That is the moment to connect the struggle or discomfort you are experiencing to the reason you are choosing to experience it.

Studies show that even a momentary connection to a purpose beyond ourselves changes the way our brain responds to cognitive tasks. One study found that when radiologists were shown a photo of the patient whose x-ray they were about to scan, they wrote longer reports and had significantly higher diagnostic accuracy. Yet when the radiologists were shown the same x-rays (unbeknownst to them) three months later without the photo, their reports shortened and their diagnostic accuracy dropped.[25] Even a brief connection to the higher purpose behind the cognitive task causes our brain's performance to elevate.

In his book, *Start With Why*, corporate culture and leadership expert Simon Sinek refers to this higher purpose as the "why."[26] Most people, explains Sinek, get stuck focusing their attention exclusively on the "what" (i.e., "What do I need to complete today?" or "What are the necessary steps to success?" or "What would be a respectable GPA?") and the "how" (i.e., "How am I going to get all of this done?" or "How should I approach this assignment?" or "How will others perceive me if I fail?"). But we forget the most important thing: the "why." That is, the reason we are doing the "what" and the "how" in the first place.

When we clarify and consciously connect to the "why" as we are taking on an academic challenge, we ignite a sense of passion and resiliency that sets us up for success. But when we are unclear about our "why," or if we do not consciously connect to it in the midst of our academic task, the very same task feels deeply burdensome and stressful. In the words of Sinek, "Working hard for something we do not care about is called stress, working hard for something we love is called passion." So a key aspect of mental optimization in law school is converting the constant difficult, mundane academic tasks into something more meaningful and passion-stoking. The way to do that is by consciously connecting those tasks to some higher purpose or cause beyond ourselves. When we do this in a moment of stress, we powerfully shift our brain from a threat mindset into an elevated opportunity mindset. Friedrich Nietzsche put it well nearly 140 years ago: "He who has a strong enough 'why' can bear almost any 'how.'"

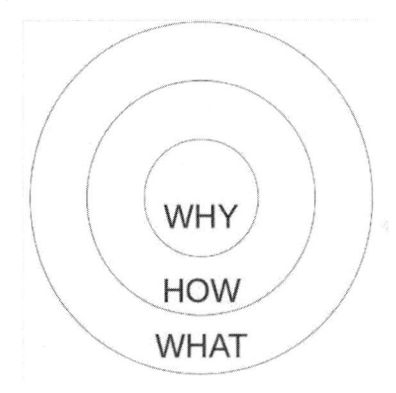

The "golden circle" from Simon Sinek.

Focusing on the "why" allows us to animate and more effectively execute the "what" and the "how."

2. JUDGMENT TO COMPASSION

"If you want others to be happy, practice compassion. If you want to be happy, practice compassion."

— the Dalai Lama

Let's face it, the law school experience presents ample opportunities for judgment and resentment, whether it is the gunner in your Property class, the humongous reading assignments, the students who hold opposing political opinions to yours, certain professors who seem insensitive or tone deaf, school administrators whose leadership decisions you question, student organizations you do not support, the torturous Socratic method, your law school friend who occasionally lets you down, cases you read that feel fundamentally unjust, the problematic curve grading system, your roommate or neighbor who occasionally annoys you, your school's sometimes antiquated institutional norms, the brutal examination schedules, your friend from college or family member who thinks you should be more available to chat because they don't understand how intense law school really is, and a host of other realities that trigger irritation in you. In other words, notwithstanding that law school is a great privilege bestowed on a lucky few like yourself, there is plenty to be judgmental and frustrated about.

Although having judgments and frustrations at times during your law school experience is completely natural and predictable, how you respond internally to those judgments and frustrations plays an important role in your overall happiness, well-being, and academic performance. If you allow yourself to ruminate over and mentally fuel those fleeting triggers, then those triggers grow within you and begin to undercut your well-being and success. The more you dignify them with your thoughts and attention, the more powerful and destructive they become.

An ancient Cherokee tale involved a wise elder teaching his young grandson about life. The grandfather explained, "We all have a battle between the two wolves that live within each of us. One wolf is judgment, anger, resentment, envy, hate, pride, superiority, greed, arrogance, and ego. The other wolf is compassion, kindness, empathy, love, forgiveness, generosity, humility, understanding, benevolence, and peace." The grandson thought about it for a minute and then asked his grandfather, "Which wolf wins?" The grandfather replied, "The one you feed." When law school and life regularly trigger the judgmental wolf, you get to choose how much you want to feed it versus starve it. If you choose to starve the judgmental wolf and instead feed the compassionate wolf – even in the face of unfair

THE 5 MINDSET SHIFTS 107

or ugly behaviors from others – the science says you will be a happier person and better student.

But before we get into the science, let's first establish what compassion means. Law students and lawyers tend to resist automatically when they are invited to practice compassion towards people who act unfairly in their lives. But what we have realized is that most people have this ingrained aversion because they do not actually understand what compassion entails.

Compassion is <u>not</u> condonation, agreement, or acquiescence. It is not letting people off the hook or absolving them of responsibility. Compassion is an understanding of the unique facts and life events that led the person to act in the unfair or unacceptable manner in this moment, or, where understanding is not possible, an openness to and curiosity about such facts and life events. A genuine desire to arrive at such explanations. It is trying our very best to put ourselves in the other person's shoes and determine what underlying challenges, difficulties, fears, or pain points spurred their distasteful behavior. It is staying open to what we cannot easily see, i.e., the possible motives and struggles that shaped their behavior, rather than assuming malicious or selfish intent simply because we do not like their behavior.*

In psychology, the "fundamental attribution error" is the cognitive bias whereby our brains are wired to unconsciously attribute other peoples' unfair or undesirable actions to their character or integrity, as opposed to circumstances or situational factors. For example, if you see a student bump into another student while rushing down a crowded law school hall, you are more likely to automatically attribute that action to the student being careless or inconsiderate, rather than stressed out from being late to a destination. Yet, we tend to do the exact opposite

---

* From a technical perspective, empathy is generally described as the ability to feel, understand, or connect with another person's emotions, experience, or situation, i.e., to put oneself in the shoes of another, while compassion is generally described as empathy plus a desire to help or support the person. We have nevertheless elected to use the word "compassion" for this mindset, rather than "empathy," because it is more commonly referenced in mainstream terminology and a more familiar term in our industry. However, if the word "empathy" resonates more with you, or it feels like a more technically accurate descriptor of this mindset, we invite you to use that term for yourself instead.

when it comes to our own actions. This is the actor-observer bias, the cognitive bias wired into our brains that causes us to be more likely to attribute our own poor actions to circumstances or situational factors instead of our character or integrity. So when we are the one who bumps into another student while we are rushing down the hallway, we are more likely to automatically attribute that behavior to our stress over being last to class, as opposed to a confirmation that we are a careless or inconsiderate person.

Why do we do this? Psychologists believe our tendency to interpret the other person's poor behavior as a reflection of their poor character, and our own poor behavior as a reflection of our unfortunate circumstances in that moment, is the result of the asymmetry of available information. At the moment of the other person's poor behavior, we generally do not have full access to the detailed factual circumstances, internal struggles, and emotional drivers that gave rise to their behavior. So our brain's desire for certainty causes us to prematurely conclude it is a reflection of character. It may not be an accurate conclusion, but at least it's a conclusion! And that feels good to our brain and creates clear parameters for our responsive action, in contrast to the discomfort and paralysis that comes from floating in vast, indefinite uncertainty. However, when it comes to our own poor behavior, we have real-time access to the complex set of circumstances, struggles, and drivers that triggered the behavior. So we are far more likely to assign the behavior to those factors, rather than to our character defects.

THE 5 MINDSET SHIFTS

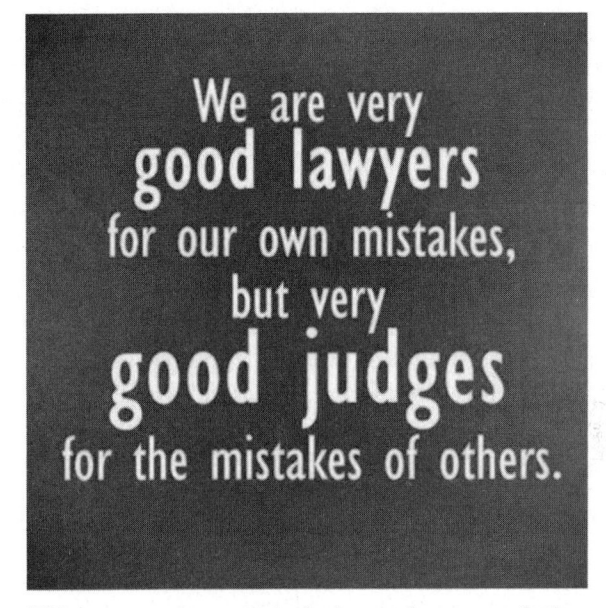

> We are very **good lawyers** for our own mistakes, but very **good judges** for the mistakes of others.

This meme seems particularly worth contemplating for the average law student.

In his classic 1989 book, *The 7 Habits of Highly Effective People*, Stephen R. Covey shares a personal example from his own life of how our brain tends to leap to character judgments of others:

> I remember a mini-paradigm shift I experienced one Sunday morning on a subway in New York. People were sitting quietly – some reading newspapers, some lost in thought, some resting with their eyes closed. It was a calm, peaceful scene.
>
> Then suddenly, a man and his children entered the subway car. The children were so loud and rambunctious that instantly the whole climate changed.
>
> The man sat down next to me and closed his eyes, apparently oblivious to the situation. The children were yelling back and forth, throwing things, even grabbing people's papers. It was very disturbing. And yet, the man sitting next to me did nothing.
>
> It was difficult not to feel irritated. I could not believe that he could be so insensitive as to let his children run

wild like that and do nothing about it, taking no responsibility at all. It was easy to see that everyone else on the subway felt irritated, too. So finally, with what I felt like was unusual patience and restraint, I turned to him and said, "Sir, your children are really disturbing a lot of people. I wonder if you couldn't control them a little more?"

The man lifted his gaze as if to come to a consciousness of the situation for the first time and said softly, "Oh, you're right. I guess I should do something about it. We just came from the hospital where their mother died about an hour ago. I don't know what to think, and I guess they don't know how to handle it either."

Can you imagine what I felt at that moment? My paradigm shifted. Suddenly I saw things differently, and because I saw differently, I thought differently, I felt differently, I behaved differently. My irritation vanished. I didn't have to worry about controlling my attitude or my behavior; my heart was filled with the man's pain. Feelings of sympathy and compassion flowed freely. "Your wife just died? Oh I'm so sorry! Can you tell me about it? What can I do to help?" Everything changed in an instant.

Covey's experience sheds light on how our brain takes a small amount of available information and rapidly converts it into a broad and wholistic conclusion about the other person's character. Have you ever sent a very thoughtful text to a friend only to receive radio silence for several days? What did your brain do at that point? If your brain is like most, it probably reached some sort of judgment that your friend is being selfish, rude, or disrespectful in their delay. And have you ever received a belated reply in that situation that gushes with gratitude for your caring text and offers a heart-felt apology and explanation of the unique life events the person was dealing with that caused the delay? While stewing over the non-reply for several days, you had never even considered the possibility that your friend was going through a struggle. Instead of staying open to the possibility of an unknown struggle or life event, your brain leaped to the concrete – and completely misguided – conclusion that your friend was being "bad" in some way.

We all have had countless experiences of this neurological phenomenon in our lives, yet we do not seem to temper our judgment when the next opportunity to be offended arises. Although the truth of the situation gets revealed in some instances, such as this friendship example, we often make a sweeping judgment based on incomplete information *and then never receive the full story*. So we move to the next life event, completely unaware that our judgmental conclusion – and the corresponding large energy expenditure – may have been unjustified.

You may be wondering what is wrong with relying on this default "judgment tendency." You may be thinking, "There are lots of bad behaviors committed by selfish people in life. So who cares if I arrive at a few erroneous judgments? In the vast majority of situations, my judgments are justified."

Your judgments may be justified, but that does not mean they are beneficial. In the words of Nelson Mandela, paraphrasing St. Augustine, "Resentment is like drinking the poison and hoping the other guy dies." Indeed, the science makes clear that far from being beneficial, our judgments and resentments decrease our well-being, happiness, and stress resiliency. It can feel cathartic and deceptively satisfying *in the moment* to ruminate judgmentally about a person or situation, but the research shows that this small, seeming benefit has enormous mental, emotional, and cognitive costs. We cut off our nose to spite our face. When we are judging a person or a situation, and wallowing in that hostility, we are actively framing the person or situation as a "threat" to us, which causes our stress response to ignite.

In other words, viewing a person or situation through a judgmental lens activates our amygdala, elevates our stress levels, and reduces our happiness. From a strictly self-serving perspective, it is not a prudent thing to do. For these reasons, judgment can be conceived of as *self-generated stress*. All we are doing is poisoning ourselves. The antidote is compassion. The more we cultivate compassion, and the more we limit our tendency to judge, the happier, more resilient, and more successful we become.

One study tested the effects of thinking of a past offense in a judgmental versus compassionate way.[27] Participants in the judgment group were instructed to think of an offensive event in a judgment-focused way for two minutes by contemplating the unfairness of the behavior and the ramifications of that unfairness. Participants in the compassion group were instructed to think of an offensive event in a compassion-focused way for two minutes by contemplating the behavior as "a bad act by a human being" and simultaneously aiming to find compassion or mercy for why they committed the act. At the end of the two minutes, the participants' emotional states and physiological stress levels were assessed. The participants in the compassion group were in a state of far higher emotional well-being and far lower physiological stress. They had more positive emotions and higher feelings of resiliency and control, while experiencing lower heart rates and less eye muscle tension – two physiological markers of stress. Both of these markers spiked, as did negative emotions and a sense of being helpless or out of control, in the judgment group. Just two minutes of thinking of an offensive event in a judgmental versus compassionate manner substantially affected stress levels and emotional well-being.

There is an extensive body of research reaching similar conclusions, namely, that deliberately attempting to interpret an upsetting event through the lens of compassion, rather than ruminating judgmentally, improves our well-being, happiness, and stress resiliency. As one study concluded, "[R]umination intensifies and prolongs negative emotion" and induces "greater sympathetic nervous system activation."[28] So judgmental rumination not only triggers our fight-or-flight response (sympathetic nervous system), but it also causes us to stay in that negative, stressed-out emotional state for much longer. For this reason, the study concluded that when a life event upsets us, how we choose to think about the emotional event is critical to our subsequent emotional state: "[T]hese findings provide compelling new evidence that how one thinks about an emotional event can shape the emotional response one has."

Thinking about the event through the lens of compassion shapes our emotional response in a positive and empowered way.

Abundant studies have reached similar findings about the vast benefits of compassion. One study found that compassionate reframing of an upsetting event, in contrast to a judgmental framing of it, stimulated an increase in positive emotions such as joy and confidence, a reduction in negative emotions such as anger and sorrow, and a calming of the cardiovascular and sympathetic nervous systems.[29] Another study found that compassionate framing, as compared to judgmental framing, decreases our blood pressure and speeds up the process of recovering physiologically from the upsetting event.[30] An additional study assessed the effects of a compassion mindset (referred to as "cognitive empathy" by these researchers) on depression, anxiety, and stress.[31] The study found a direct link, concluding "[C]ognitive empathy was negatively related to levels of depression, anxiety, and stress." In other words, the more the participants attempted to reframe an offense through compassion, the lower their levels of depression, anxiety, and stress. Relatedly, a study of 155 college students found that the more judgmental and hostile a student's attitude, the less resilient they were to the academic and life challenges they faced in college, prompting the researchers to recommend "specific teaching programs" to reduce judgments and hostility in order to enhance resiliency.[32]

In the final study we will discuss on this topic, participants were induced into a judgmental mindset for two minutes through the following instruction: "For the next two minutes, think of the person you blame for hurting, offending, or wronging you. Think of the ways the offense harmed you when it happened, and how it continued to negatively affect you. During your imagery, actively focus on the negative thoughts, feelings, and physical responses you have as you think about the negative ways the offender and offense harmed you."[33] Then, after a short period of emotional assessments, the participants received the following instruction to induce them into a compassionate mindset regarding the same offender: "For the next two minutes, try to think of the offender as a human being whose behavior shows that person's need to experience a positive transformation or healing. Try to give a gift of mercy and genuinely wish that person well. During your imagery, actively focus on the thoughts, feelings, and physical responses you have as you cultivate compassion, kindness, and mercy for this person."

Unsurprisingly, the two minutes in the judgmental mindset plunged participants into impaired emotional and cardiovascular states. It caused them to experience intense negative emotions, contractions of the eyebrow muscles and under-eye muscles (associated with the stress response), "significant cardiac acceleration" (spiked heart rate), and "impaired parasympathetic nervous system functioning" (reduced relaxation response in the nervous system). Moreover, spending two minutes in the judgmental mindset left the participants with "low levels of positive emotions, including happiness, joy, empathy, forgiveness, and gratitude."

But after shifting into the compassion mindset for just two minutes, the participants experienced a substantial increase in each of these positive emotions, including "significantly up-regulated control, happiness, and joy," as well as marked decreases in the negative emotions they were previously experiencing. Additionally, their heart rates slowed, their eyebrow and under-eye muscles relaxed, and their parasympathetic nervous system activated. In short, they became happier, less stressed, and more empowered.

At a certain level, this is all intuitive, right? We bet you were not surprised by the outcomes of the studies. Most of us theoretically know that thinking judgmentally does not make us happy or induce an optimal mental and emotional state. Yet we continually choose – *albeit unconsciously* – to spend our time ruminating judgmentally and resenting the various outrages we witness in law school and life. When we witness something irritating or unfair, it is so tempting and so easy to default into righteous judgment, yet in doing so, we launch ourselves into a state of mental and emotional darkness. We undercut our own happiness, our own resilience, our own feelings of control, and our own physiological equilibrium (and by logical extension, our own cognitive and academic performance).

Yes, it does take much more discipline to resist the temptation to judge and instead force ourselves to think of the

THE 5 MINDSET SHIFTS

triggering event from a compassionate perspective. And it may not feel very satisfying, in the moment at least, not to fuel our righteous outrage. But resisting that negative urge makes us much happier, healthier, and emotionally stronger.

So if we want to induce compassion in response to unfair or ugly behaviors, the research suggests that we attempt to think of the actors as normal humans who are flawed, like the rest of us, and purposefully try to think of unique factors or challenges that they may be going through that gave rise to the conduct. The research further suggests that we consciously contemplate how they are in need of growth or healing, that we attempt to wish them well in our own heads, and that we do our best to try to forgive them and give them mercy. This, again, is not to condone or acquiesce to their conduct, it is only to forgive them (whether mentally or verbally) while continuing to hold them accountable for that conduct.

We can also deliberately acknowledge to ourselves that even if (as may often be the case) we cannot figure out a valid explanation for why they committed the unfair behavior, we are nevertheless refusing to leap to the conclusion that they are necessarily a maliciously motivated or bad person who deserves our judgment. We are choosing instead to stay open-minded and to separate the person's character from their behavior – especially knowing that if we do not, we will be the ones who suffer.

This approach is often referred to as "assuming positive intent." Rather than allowing our brain to automatically conflate "undesirable behavior" with "evil intent," we actively rebut this tendency and instead assume their intent is positive, even if – *and especially when* – we don't have full information about their intent (which, incidentally, is *almost always* the case). Indra Nooyi, regularly ranked among the most successful and influential women in the history of business, was the CEO and Chairperson of PepsiCo from 2006 through 2019, when she led the company through historic growth and profitability. When asked by a journalist from *Fortune Magazine* to identify the advice that had most contributed to her massive success, she pointed to the technique of assuming positive intent:

My father was an absolutely wonderful human being. From him I learned to always assume positive intent. Whatever anybody says or does, assume positive intent. You will be amazed at how your whole approach to a person or problem becomes very different. When you assume negative intent, you're angry. If you take away that anger and assume positive intent, you will be amazed. Your emotional quotient goes up because you are no longer almost random in your response. You don't get defensive. You don't scream. You are trying to understand and listen because at your basic core you are saying, 'Maybe they are saying something to me that I'm not hearing.' So 'assume positive intent' has been a huge piece of advice for me.[34]

As revealed by Nooyi, building the habit of assuming positive intent allows you to significantly reduce your anger, emotional turmoil, and conflict in life, not to mention significantly increase your professional success. Sometimes this just involves consciously acknowledging that although we dislike the person's behavior, we are refusing to assume a malicious motive. We do our best to stay open and curious, and perhaps to even ask some open-minded questions about the person's intentions or goals, but we do not allow our brain to hijack us into presumed malice. Assuming positive intent is an implementable technique that can help us tap into a compassionate mindset in the face of behavior we resent.*

---

* A cute parable for how the brain works in so many situations is this: A kindergarten teacher wants to teach a young boy, Jimmy, how to count to higher numbers. So he starts with something simple that Jimmy will undoubtedly already know. The teacher hands Jimmy one apple and then another apple, and asks, "How many apples do you have now, Jimmy?" The boy answers, "Three apples." A bit dismayed, the teacher snatches the two apples back and says, "Let's try this again. I am handing you one apple at this time, and now I am handing you another apple. How many apples do you have now, Jimmy?" Again, the boy responds, "Three apples." The teacher's blood begins to boil. "Jimmy, this should be very simple! How is it possible if I hand you one apple and then another apple that you say you have three apples?!" Jimmy then reaches into his pocket and pulls out another apple and states, "My mother gave me an apple to take to school today." This parable is a microcosm of countless of our interactions in life. Like the teacher, we are constantly *certain* that other people are acting irrationally or poorly, but we often possess only a limited amount of information that provides the context for their actions. Despite that limited information, we assume we have full context and leap to judgments about the other person without realizing that our judgments are misguided.

Another technique for doing so is offered by Don Miguel Ruiz, author of *The Four Agreements* and many other bestselling books. Ruiz suggests viewing peoples' unfair or ugly actions as the emotional equivalent of physical crutches. When we see a person limping towards a door with a cast on their leg and crutches under their shoulders, explains Ruiz, we instinctively rush to the door to open it for them. This is because we, as humans, have an innate yearning to help people who are injured or suffering. Upon seeing the crutches and cast, our compassion automatically swells. Yet Ruiz points out that people who are emotionally injured or suffering do not wear a cast or crutches.

So how can we know they are injured and suffering? They commit unfair or unreasonable behaviors, says Ruiz. Indeed, if you think back to the last few times you snapped at someone or acted unfairly, you were probably in an unhappy emotional state just before you committed that behavior. Your messy behavior was largely a manifestation of your underlying emotional state. Yet when others display these clear signals of emotional suffering, i.e., behaving poorly, we tend to meet them with judgment, rather than compassion. Usually, it is only when they display clear signals of physical suffering, such as crutches and a cast, that we meet them with compassion, not judgment. So Ruiz invites us to cultivate a compassionate mindset in response to undesirable behaviors by honing in on the truth that the person (despite possibly appearing inconsiderate, selfish, or even arrogant) is nevertheless suffering inside.

In addition, deliberately recalling some of our own ugly actions or unfair behaviors can sometimes help us find greater compassion for the person who is currently acting unfairly (even though this person likely had no relation to those prior experiences). We have a tendency to sweep our past transgressions under our mental rug when we are righteously condemning the other person. Gently reminding ourselves of our own human frailties can help soften the grip of resentment.

We can also use the technique discussed in the above highway cutoff example (see page 61) of making up a possible explanation that might better explain the unfair behavior. If we get cut off unexpectedly, for instance, we can replace the default assumption that the other driver is a terrible jerk with the possibility that they are rushing to the ER to see a loved one who may be on the brink of death. Or perhaps they are running late to an important meeting or interview, and their stress caused them to miss the approaching exit. They may be stressed or overwhelmed, but they are not necessarily bad people. We are not creating an *excuse* for their behavior, just a possible *explanation*. The possible explanation can sometimes help us soften our judgment and move into a place of greater compassion. Unlike an "excuse," which releases someone from responsibility for their undesirable behavior, an "explanation" simply provides context for why they committed the undesirable behavior, and hence can help us cultivate compassion for them while still holding them responsible for their behavior.

As another example, perhaps a person's upbringing or social conditioning led them to hold positions we deem unfair or unreasonable. But if we consider their unique life path and developmental experiences (some or many of which they may not have had control over), their arrival at those positions may make a bit more sense to us. Again, it is not about excusing or condoning their position, it is about refusing to become toxified by it. This allows us to be emotionally liberated as we stand against the position or attempt to hold them accountable for it.

We can even apply this approach to grave injustices. Indeed, many of the great change agents in history have done precisely this. Whether it is Nelson Mandela, Martin Luther King, Jr., Mother Teresa, the Dalai Lama, or Mahatma Gandhi, many of the most impactful humans our planet has seen found the ability to meet racism, bigotry, and other extreme injustices with compassion rather than judgment. Each of these transformational leaders somehow separated the perpetrators from their despicable conduct and thus avoided holding judgment and hate in their heart for the perpetrators. They still fought ferociously and ceaselessly for change and justice, yet they did not sabotage themselves – *or their sacred cause* – with personal animosity. Martin Luther King, Jr.'s immortal words speak to this reality: "Darkness cannot drive out darkness; only

THE 5 MINDSET SHIFTS 119

light can do that. Hate cannot drive out hate; only love can do that."*

When we witness an action that offends us, whether it is a small slight or a fundamental injustice, we have a tendency to ruminate in condemnation. We get stuck in a judgment mindset, and it temporarily feels so good to righteously judge the offender. When your authors invite people to try to find compassion for the perpetrator in that moment, the most common response we get is an irritated utterance, "They don't *deserve* my compassion!" We generally respond by asking, "Do *you* deserve to extend them your compassion?" Regardless of whether the perpetrator deserves our compassion, we can nevertheless choose to extend it to them if we want to receive the windfall of emotional, physiological, and cognitive benefits that will follow.

Consider, too, the application here of our earlier discussion about rewiring your brain: The more we practice shifting from a judgment mindset to a compassion mindset in these moments, the more we wire our brain to do so, and the easier it gets. And the more we raise our baseline levels of emotional thriving in life.

Years after the Dalai Lama escaped China and fled to Tibet, he was asked by a journalist whether he experienced fear when he was falsely imprisoned and tortured by his captors in China. He responded directly: "Oh yes, I felt fear. I feared I would lose my compassion for my captors."

---

* Interestingly, modern science has revealed the strategic benefits of shifting from judgment to compassion in attempting to persuade others. Resentment has been shown to make us less effective at persuasion, a skill that is obviously a critical aspect of succeeding as a lawyer (and as a person in any relationship). In a recent meta-analysis study of the relationship between anger and persuasion, it was found that even moderate levels of anger reduce persuasive abilities, even when argument strength is high.[35] Researchers at Harvard Business School have found that being overly assertive and aggressive also reduces our persuasive abilities, and that we should instead soften our intensity and hedge our language in order to increase our odds of flipping the other side.[36]

Simply put, being an outraged and overly assertive advocate makes us less, not more, persuasive. Advocating from a place of passion *and compassion* makes us most persuasive.

3. PESSIMISM TO OPTIMISM

"We can complain because rose bushes have thorns, or rejoice because thorn bushes have roses."

— Abraham Lincoln

A deer is walking along a path in the forest. She suddenly hears a faint rustling of leaves 30 feet to her left, and her head snaps in that direction to notice a tiger lurking in the bushes. The barely audible sound was that of a single step taken by the tiger as its foot pushed down on a bed of leaves while it stealthily approached the deer. A millisecond after noticing the tiger, the deer bolts into a full sprint in the opposite direction, in a desperate attempt to survive the imminent attack.

At the moment the tiger took that step, there was a symphony of different sounds in the forest. There was wind blowing through the branches of the trees, water trickling down a stream, birds chirping, cicadas buzzing, a swinging monkey rattling the branches in the trees, a moose bellowing in the distance, and even a woodpecker drumming at a nearby tree. Yet the deer's head swiveled instantly to the tiger's single step on compressed leaves. Why did it do that? How did the deer tune out all of the other sounds and instead laser in on the single step of the tiger?

The negativity bias. This is a cognitive bias that is hardwired into the brain of all mammals and reptiles. It is a critical component of our survival instinct, and it causes us to disproportionately notice and focus on problems and threats (i.e., negative information), and disproportionately filter out neutral and positive information. Said differently, our brain unconsciously weighs negative information more heavily than it does similar neutral and positive information.

If the deer in the above vignette did not have the negativity bias, its brain would have given equal attention to each of the many sounds that were simultaneously hitting its ears, as well as the many other factual stimuli available to its brain, such as the shortest path to its destination, the pleasant feeling in its

THE 5 MINDSET SHIFTS

hoof, or the fact that it was not currently thirsty. A democratic allocation of attention would have diluted the relative significance of the rustling leaves, and the deer likely would not have noticed the threatening sound, or it would not have noticed it nearly as quickly. This, of course, would have led to the death of the deer (or increased the likelihood of death). So the deer's brain is wired to filter out all of the sounds, sights, and impressions that are neutral or positive (such as those beautiful nature sounds, the successful steps the deer keeps taking towards its destination, the impression that it is not currently hungry, and immeasurable other factual inputs), and to fixate on any sound or input that presents a possible risk of death.

Without the negativity bias, the average deer's lifespan would plummet. As would the lifespan of the average human. Have you ever crossed a street while checking your phone only to whip your head up in sudden awareness of a fast-approaching car? Have you ever been on a hike with a friend when a precarious cliff emerged, causing you to instinctively hyper-focus on each step you took along the edge as you tuned out your friend's story about their annoying roommate? Have you ever been in your apartment and suddenly panicked upon seeing a spider in your periphery, while the rest of the items in the room vanished into the background? Have you ever been driving your car when you abruptly found yourself slamming on the brakes upon spotting a car that might hit you, all while filtering other visible stimuli out of your attention? That is your negativity bias keeping you alive.

The negativity bias is wonderful for survival, but terrible for happiness. Although we need this bias to maximize survival even in this modern society, it causes us great emotional strife in countless situations we face that are unrelated to survival. The reality is that we humans rarely face the threat of death or serious injury in this day and age, but our brain's negativity bias apparently didn't get the memo. So it is firing on all cylinders throughout the day in countless situations having no implications for our survival or physical safety. Have you ever gone to sleep fixating on the one unimpressive thing you said in class while filtering out the many impressive things you said? Have you ever taken for granted the large collection of wonderful traits possessed by your friend or significant other while obsessing over the one trait you most dislike? Have you ever felt frustrated at the end of the day because 2 things didn't go your way without acknowledging the 15 things that went well? Have you ever complained about the many problems with the law school experience without equally appreciating its many gifts? Have you ever fallen into self-judgment over one of your personal weaknesses or imperfections without proportionately valuing your vast collection of strengths?

This is also the negativity bias in action. Our brains are wired to hyper-focus on the problem or threat presented in every situation, while filtering out positive and neutral information about the situation. When the situation involves an actual risk of death, the negativity bias is a life saver. But when the situation involves no such risk of death, the negativity bias is a well-being killer. The overwhelming majority of situations we face in life do not involve a threat of death, which means that our negativity bias is frequently being unnecessarily triggered. Our brain is wired to prioritize survival at all costs and is therefore ineffective at discerning the difference between survival and non-survival situations, leading to the constant invocation of the negativity bias in inappropriate situations. From a survival perspective, it is better for the brain to over-assume risk than under-assume risk – so the brain does exactly this. In short, our brain is reacting as if we might be physically attacked at the restaurant we are dining in, but all that is happening is that the waiter forgot to bring us the side order of french fries.

You can think of this phenomenon as evolutionary pessimism. What's worse, law school instills another layer of pessimism in us beyond our hardwired negativity bias. We call it "professional pessimism." People regularly say law school teaches us "how to think like a lawyer." One aspect of this lawyerly thinking is the ability to read a case and rapidly "issue spot" every nuanced fact that could potentially implicate a particular conclusion or application of the legal rule. When we issue spot, our brain is unconsciously filtering out any information that is not potentially dispositive to the ultimate legal analysis and filtering in every piece of minutia that may.

THE 5 MINDSET SHIFTS

For example, here is some information expressly included in a landmark U.S. Supreme Court case you have read or will read in your Constitutional Law class:

- Counsel for appellants included Robert L. Carter, Spottswood W. Robinson, III, Louis L. Redding, Jack Greenberg, George E. C. Hayes, William R. Ming, Jr., Constance Baker Motley, James M. Nabrit, Jr., Charles S. Scott, Frank D. Reeves, Harold R. Boulware and Oliver W. Hill.
- The case arose from a set of related cases from the States of Kansas, South Carolina, Virginia and Delaware which "are premised on different facts and different local conditions."
- In all but one of the underlying cases, the district court consisted of a three-judge panel.
- The Supreme Court case involved original oral arguments and then re-arguments on two separate dates across two separate Supreme Court terms.
- One of the State laws being reviewed, as referenced in the *20th sentence* of footnote 1 (*that's a hefty footnote!*), is the Revised Delaware Code, section 2631.
- The citation of the primary Supreme Court precedent on the issue is 163 U.S. 537.
- The Supreme Court clarified that the "the Attorney General is again invited to participate" in the subsequent oral arguments on the appropriate relief implicated by the holding in the case.

When you originally read this case, your brain unconsciously filtered out all of this information – and countless other pieces of information in the case – because they were irrelevant to the legal issue. So what case is this? *Brown v. Board of Education*. And in case you are wondering, the citation of 163 U.S. 537 attaches to the notorious *Plessy v. Ferguson* case that *Brown* overruled. Even though the facts and holding of *Plessy v. Ferguson* are critical to analyzing *Brown*, the citation to *Plessy* could not be more irrelevant.

The pieces of information above are obvious examples of irrelevant information that are easily filtered out. As you proceed through law school, your brain gets better and better at making hair-splitting distinctions in less clear instances about what information is relevant to the analysis and outcome, and what information is not. The ability to make these distinctions – which particularly requires you to hone in on risks, errors, problems, and soft-spots – becomes critical to succeeding as a lawyer.

For example, let's say you become a litigator and are cross-examining the opposing side's star witness. The witness provides her lengthy explanation on the dispositive issue, which testimony – if accepted as true – would destroy your entire case. You pause for a moment, look down, scratch your head, look up at the judge, and then proclaim, "That sounds fair, Your Honor, I have no further questions!" You would *not* be a very good litigator if you did that. Here's what would happen instead: Your brain will have scanned through her entire explanation as she was speaking, filtering out all of the information that is neutral or positive for your case, and then lasering in on each piece of information that presents a problem or threat to your case. You would then attempt to undermine her testimony on each of these pieces of information, methodically moving through each grain of threatening information with probing questions designed to undermine the veracity or basis of her position on each grain. Make no mistake about it, her original two-minute explanation was littered with non-threatening details (including many basic facts that both parties agree upon), which your brain rapidly filtered out in order to seize on the problematic details.

As with the deer, if your brain weighed all of the information testified to equally, the relative visibility of the problematic details would become diluted. The legal risks would become murkier, and your success as a lawyer would suffer. So as a law student and lawyer, you calibrate your brain to detect the most amount of risk in the shortest amount of time. The more your brain engages in this cognitive process in analyzing legal issues, the more your brain *unconsciously* replicates this problem-focused thinking in other areas of your life. That is, the more pessimistic your brain becomes in all aspects of life. Remember the Tetris Effect, and how our brain builds neural pathways and thought structures based on prior thinking habits?

The same thing will likely occur if you become a transactional lawyer who focuses on contracts or negotiations (or any other type of lawyer, frankly). Say opposing counsel emails you his 70-page first draft of the agreement on the core transaction at issue, and you reply to his email with, "Looks great, we're ready to sign!" Again, this wouldn't be considered exquisite lawyering. Interpreting the *content* of opposing counsel's draft agreement through an optimistic lens will undermine your client's best interests. What you will do instead is open up the document and then shred every sentence, word, and comma that creates legal risk or issues for your client. You will then respond with alternative language for each and every concerning detail. To be clear, the vast majority of the 70 pages will consist of material that is unobjectionable to you, so your brain will unconsciously filter all of that out and zero in on each and every minutia that creates a problem or threat. Again, the more your brain goes through this exercise in the practice of law, the more it will become wired to unconsciously parrot this process in other areas of your life.

The professional pessimism instilled in law school and perpetuated by lawyering is an important professional competency. Without it, you will not succeed as a lawyer. So we are not suggesting that you reject this training; we are suggesting that in embracing this training, you actively resist the impulse to indiscriminately apply these same thought patterns to other areas of your life. Consider this: If a CIA terrorist interrogator chooses to subject her spouse to sophisticated interrogation techniques when he overcooks her lasagna, it probably will not bode well for their marriage. Simply because these interrogation techniques are useful to her success as a terrorist interrogator does not mean she should robotically implement this behavior in other areas of her life. Similarly, simply because professional pessimism is useful to your success as a lawyer (and law student) does not mean you should robotically apply this thinking in other areas of your life.

A 2009 study, "Stemming the Tide of Law Student Depression: What Law Schools Need to Learn from the Science of Positive Psychology," published in the *Yale Journal of Health Policy, Law, and Ethics*, touches on this very point:

> Law schools teach students to look for flaws in arguments, and they train them to be critical rather than accepting. This ability is a crucial skill for lawyers in practice, but, if applied to one's personal life, may have significant negative consequences. Training in critical analysis may lead students to apply the same critical approach to their own life and the problems that they encounter in personal relationships. That may lead students to overestimate the significance and permanence of the problems they encounter, which is precisely the kind of pessimistic explanatory style that leads to stress and depression.[37]

The combination of the negativity bias that is wired into our brain by evolution and the professional pessimism that is wired into our brain by the legal industry can be a dangerous combination for our happiness, stress resilience, and emotional well-being. Together, they calibrate our brain to disproportionately focus on threats and problems in our life, while filtering out all of the things in our life that are wonderful. This makes us more pessimist, and less optimistic, as people.

From a scientific perspective, pessimism does not refer to the stereotypical "Debbie Downer" or "Darren Downer" concept. It means the propensity, relative to optimism, to filter out – *and hence not give appropriate attention to* – a high percentage of real information and life events that are positive or beneficial. In a similar vein, optimism does not refer to the widely stigmatized notion of being naïvely happy or gullible; it means a propensity, relative to pessimism, to filter in – *and hence give appropriate attention to* – a higher percentage of real information and life events that are positive or beneficial. Both optimists and pessimists are hinging their viewpoints and emotions on actual facts. But since the brain is filtering out approximately 95% of the factual stimuli it is subjected to over the course of the day, one's optimistic versus pessimistic lens dictates which 5% of facts "get through" to our conscious awareness. That 5% plays a key role in our happiness, resilience to stress, and overall emotional well-being.

The scientific research shows that optimists are happier and healthier in a variety of ways. Optimists experience less stress, anxiety, and depression than pessimists.[38] They are more resilient to life challenges and problems.[39] They lead happier and more joyful lives.[40] They have better interpersonal relationships, are more effective at accomplishing goals, and recover more aptly from life difficulties.[41] "Optimism is also beneficial for physical health," explains a major study on the interplay between lifespan and mindset.[42] "All else being equal, optimists live longer and are healthier. The effects can be quite substantial, with one survey of 97,000 individuals reporting that optimists are 14% less likely to die between the ages of 50 and 65, and 30% less likely to die from cardiac arrest. Optimism has also been related to extended survival time of cancer and AIDS patients."

In the academic context, optimism is associated with better academic performance and GPAs.[43] Moreover, a 2007 study assessed 61 first-year law students as having optimistic or pessimistic mindsets and then checked in with them 10 years later, finding that the optimists were making an average of $32,667 more per year than their pessimistic colleagues.[44]

An Optimistic Mindset Can Be Cultivated

The good news is that regardless of where you currently fall on the optimism versus pessimism spectrum, you can cultivate a more optimistic mindset through simple practice. Like all other mindsets, our pessimism-optimism mindset is highly malleable. A 2016 meta-analysis study, for instance, assessed 29 previous peer-reviewed studies on building an optimistic mindset and found that "the meta-analytic results indicate that optimism interventions are successful in increasing optimism."[45] As explained by Dr. Aparna Iyer, an expert on optimism and a psychiatrist at the University of Texas Southwestern Medical Center, "[O]ptimism can definitely be a learned trait. Just because you have been a pessimist for most of your life does not mean that you are destined to always be a pessimist. In fact, there are many effective ways to adopt an optimistic mindset."[46]

A very simple way to begin rewiring your brain to be more optimistic is to establish a regular gratitude practice. A consistent gratitude practice allows us to override our brain's negativity bias (and professional pessimism) and to begin noticing more of the positive aspects of our life that we are currently unconsciously filtering out. For this reason, purposeful gratitude is widely considered the ultimate antidote to our brain's propensity for negativity. We like to think of gratitude as "optimism in action." Indeed, it is impossible to hold a pessimistic mindset at the same moment you are engaging in gratitude. Gratitude is an instant "pessimism override." A large collection of studies has shown that a simple gratitude practice can enhance optimism, reduce pessimism, increase our stress resilience, and improve our overall happiness in life.

For example, one study found that spending just four minutes thinking about one's mother with appreciation induced a reduction in heart rate and neurological stress response, while spending four minutes thinking of an unlikeable person produced the opposite effects.[47] Another study found that spending just one day per week for five minutes writing down gratitude-inducing experiences from the week improved life satisfaction for that day *and the next week*, yet writing down problems from the week once per week for five minutes reduced life satisfaction ratings for that day and the subsequent week.[48] In another study, participants took 20 minutes each day, for three straight days, to write down three positive experiences from their life. The control group wrote about neutral experiences for the same 20 minutes per day for three days.[49] Unlike the control group, the positive writing group experienced spikes in happiness during the 3-day period and also had fewer symptoms of illness three months later.

Another study provided 1–2 short gratitude reminders via text message to 55 undergraduate students at the outset of the semester after assessing their emotional well-being and cognitive focus markers.[50] The other 55 students, also assessed but in the control group, did not receive the gratitude reminders. At the end of the semester, all 110 students were reassessed for the same emotional and cognitive markers from the beginning of the semester. The students who received the text messages and did a brief gratitude practice three or more times per week, unlike the control group, experienced elevated emotional and

THE 5 MINDSET SHIFTS

cognitive markers compared to their own scores at the beginning of the semester. The simple gratitude practice led to lower stress levels, higher overall well-being, and improved focus throughout the semester in all aspects of academic performance, whether in class, while studying, or while taking exams. The control group, of course, experienced no such improvements.

In yet another study, participants who wrote a 20-minute letter of gratitude to a different person in their life once per week for three straight weeks (even if they didn't send the letters to the recipients) experienced major improvements in their mental health that continued for *three months* after the gratitude practice ended: "[T]hose in the gratitude writing condition ... reported significantly better mental health than those in the expressive writing and therapy-as-usual control conditions about 4 weeks and 12 weeks after the conclusion of the writing interventions."[51] That's right, a total of 60 minutes of gratitude spread across three weeks led to "significantly better mental health" for *three months* afterwards.

Another study tested the effects of a 21-day gratitude practice on emotional well-being.* Half of the participants were put in the gratitude group, which involved a once-per-day practice, for 21 straight days, of identifying a few things from the day the person was grateful for or appreciated. In accordance with the usual practice, the other half of the participants were put into the control group. Both groups were regularly assessed throughout the 21-day period on various measures of emotional well-being. Unsurprisingly, the control group did not experience changes in their emotional well-being over the 21-day period, but the gratitude group did.

Specifically, the "participants in the gratitude condition reported considerably more satisfaction with their lives as a whole, felt more optimism about the upcoming week, and felt more connected with others than did participants in the control condition." The study concluded that "participation in the gratitude condition led to substantial and consistent improvements in people's assessments of their global well-being." Another 21-day gratitude study found that individuals

---

* This was a separate sub-study within the same overall study previously referenced.[52]

who wrote down a few things to be grateful for each day for 21 days, unlike those in the control group, experienced improved emotional well-being for the 21-day period and were still experiencing these improvements at a two-month follow-up.[53] A simple 21-day gratitude practice can have major positive effects.

Even a one-week gratitude practice has been shown to have substantial effects. In one such study, participants in the gratitude group were asked to write down each night, for one week, "three good things" that occurred that day.[54] The "good things" could be something big (e.g., having a safe place to sleep at night or a loving family member) or small (e.g., that delicious slice of pizza from lunch) – all that mattered is that they were specific. The control group was asked to write down three early life memories each night for one week. Although the control group's mental and emotional states remained unchanged during the one-week period and beyond, the gratitude group experienced "increased happiness and decreased depressive symptoms for six months."

That's correct, a *one-week* gratitude practice led to *six months* of elevated happiness and reduced depressive symptoms! By forcing the brain to *consciously* think of three positive things each day for one week, participants calibrated their brains to *unconsciously* think of positive things for many months, which elevated their happiness and mental health long after the brief calibration exercise ended. It's a beautiful example of converting System 2 thinking into System 1 thinking.

This is how you rewire your brain. This is how you begin converting your naturally pessimistic mindset into a more optimistic mindset. Positive thinking and gratitude do *not* come naturally to us humans, especially to us humans who choose to go into the law. So if we continue to go through law school and life without actively working to reshape our pessimistic mindset, we are going to experience less happiness and lower well-being along the way (and hence, impaired cognitive performance and overall success). But if we choose to challenge our default pessimistic mindset by forcing ourselves to consistently yet briefly see the positive things in our life, we can rewire our brains. The result is that we begin to see – and experience – our life in a different way.

Dr. Wayne Dyer, the late psychologist and a prolific author on mindsets, has said, "If you change the way you look at things, the things you look at change." Dr. Dyer's words capture the essence of the neurological feedback loop resulting from deliberate optimism: When we force ourselves to look for positive things, our brain becomes more positive, and soon we effortlessly begin seeing the world more positively. And that causes our happiness and well-being to elevate.

We invite you to begin a 21-day gratitude practice. Each day for 21 straight days, simply write down three things from your day that you are grateful for or happy about. (Each evening, you can think of three things from that day you are grateful for, or, if you do this practice in the mornings, you can think of three things from the prior day you are grateful for. You can choose which point in the day is best for you, but we recommend aiming to do it at a relatively consistent time each day in order to make it easier to remember to do it.*) We are providing a 21-day gratitude sheet below as a sample, and you can go to www.LawSchoolThriving.com to print a one-page PDF of this sheet.

The first few days you do this, you may notice it is sometimes hard to identify three things you are grateful for; your mind may feel like it's slogging through mud. Don't worry, this is totally normal – your negativity bias is still in full control. But after about 7–10 days, you will likely notice positive things pop into your head more quickly and easily, as the grip of your negativity bias loosens. And by day 21, it will probably be difficult to limit it to just three positive things. Just in that 21-day window, you will directly experience how your brain and your thinking can be reshaped. The research shows these benefits will likely last several months after you complete this 21-day exercise because your re-calibrated brain will unconsciously interpret things differently going forward.

---

* This is a habit-building technique explained in more detail in Tool #10, "Goals & Habits" in the subsection, "Tie the Goal to a Pre-Existing Cue," found at page 265.

Gratitude Practice

Every day for the next 21 days, write down three things you are grateful for. They can be anything (big or small). Make them specific and try not to repeat them. Then watch your brain rewire!

1. _____ _____ _____
2. _____ _____ _____
3. _____ _____ _____
4. _____ _____ _____
5. _____ _____ _____
6. _____ _____ _____
7. _____ _____ _____
8. _____ _____ _____
9. _____ _____ _____
10. _____ _____ _____
11. _____ _____ _____
12. _____ _____ _____
13. _____ _____ _____
14. _____ _____ _____
15. _____ _____ _____
16. _____ _____ _____
17. _____ _____ _____
18. _____ _____ _____
19. _____ _____ _____
20. _____ _____ _____
21. _____ _____ _____

After the 21-day written exercise ends, we recommend that you convert the practice into an ongoing mental exercise. Once per day, quickly think of three things from the day you are grateful for or happy about. This will not only ensure

THE 5 MINDSET SHIFTS

maintenance of the benefits of the 21-day written practice, but will also allow your brain to continue to rewire even further in the direction of optimism.

At some point down the road, you can also experiment with building a *self-gratitude* practice. In other words, you will shift to making your three positive or grateful thoughts per day specifically about *you*, rather than your life. Think of the "mini-victories" you achieved that day or specific examples of how your character strengths manifested that day. Remember, your day is full of these mini-victories and character moments, but your brain has a tendency to filter them out and focus only on your errors, failures, shortcomings, and imperfections. For example, you can briefly think of how you succeeded in completing that painfully long and complex Civil Procedure reading and generally understood the issues, or how you selflessly listened to and supported your stressed-out friend who is going through that hardship, or how you figured out that confusing Torts doctrine after meeting with your professor during office hours, or how you complimented that student you don't know very well because you thought it would make him feel better, or how you held the door open for that stranger who was entering the building behind you, or how you made a little progress in your outlining even if you didn't get through as much as you were hoping to, or how you thought about your grandma and wished her happiness even though you didn't find time to call her.

The more you do this for yourself, the more your brain will get reformatted to begin seeing yourself in a manner that accurately accounts for your successes, strengths, and character – rather than improperly (and unfairly) discounting these realities and only harping on the flaws. Your sense of self and your overall well-being will improve.*

In addition to these gratitude practices, you can cultivate more optimism and free yourself from the negativity bias on a

---

* A self-gratitude practice is probably the most powerful way of weakening imposter syndrome, which grips countless law students and humans, because the unfounded feelings of being inadequate or a fraud that comprise imposter syndrome so often result from the negativity bias being directed towards oneself in an unchecked manner over time. You can alternate between self-gratitude and life-gratitude, perhaps one week doing one, the next week doing the other, and alternating going forward. Or you can blend the two forms of gratitude into the same practice. Experiment to determine what works best for you.

moment-by-moment basis by using another simple technique. Unlike gratitude practices, which tend to be *retroactive* in nature (in that we reflect back upon the day or week to identify positive developments that our brain may have downplayed or filtered out), this technique is about *present-moment optimism*. Here it is: when a problem, difficulty or frustration arises during our day, pause and ask yourself three simple questions. *First*, what negative or burdensome information is my brain noticing in this moment? *Second*, what positive or beneficial information about this situation is my brain filtering out or downplaying in this moment? *Third*, what is the relative weight or magnitude of the positive information compared to the negative information?

This is a simple and instantaneous way of interrupting and derailing the negativity bias before it takes hold of us. The second question forces us to uncover the truth that the negativity bias is suppressing, while the third question forces us to fairly assess the negative information in the context of the positive information – rather than in a vacuum. This simple re-calibration practice often causes our perspective to shift, and makes us feel less upset about, less victimized by, and more resilient to the problem that arose.

Here is an example from our own experience. We applied this re-calibration process to a "problem" that arose in our work a few days ago (as of the time we were originally drafting this portion of the book). We were recently retained by one of the largest law firms in the world to speak at their Partners' Global Retreat at a fancy coastal resort. We would be presenting a "break-out session" (i.e., ours would be one choice from among several concurrent sessions for which attendees could opt) on the overlap between well-being and leadership in law firms. But three days before the retreat, we both tested positive for Covid and were forced to withdraw from the retreat. Immediately, the negativity bias took over: We had lost a valuable opportunity to influence how top partners treat their associates and staff members – which could have positively affected peoples' lives; we had lost a hefty professional fee; we had lost our first gig ever with this particular law firm – which likely would have yielded more work in the future; we had maybe lost our only chance ever to work with that firm, etc., etc., etc. *The negativity bias was in*

THE 5 MINDSET SHIFTS   135

full swing! We were feeling stressed, frustrated, and upset with the situation. "Why did this happen to us?!," we internally moaned. We were stuck in this emotional state for about an hour or so.

But then we interrupted this dark state by asking ourselves the re-calibration questions. The second question yielded nectar – and revealed that we were, in fact, filtering out vast pieces of positive information due to the negativity bias: We will get to recommend another wonderful well-being colleague to replace us who will do a fantastic job and generate positive impact for the people in need; we will be supporting that colleague by giving him/her an instant and valuable gig and new client that he/she didn't have to pitch for; we will be supporting this law firm in an innovative way by selflessly offering them someone of really high quality whom it otherwise would not be able to locate on such short notice; we will likely build greater trust with this firm that will probably yield additional business, including over the next few months; we very possibly will be invited to speak at next year's Global Partners' Retreat and this time we will attempt to secure a plenary session (where we speak to the entire partnership, which will lead to greater impact than if we presented this year); our professional fee will likely be substantially larger next year (for various reasons); and we are freeing up a couple of valuable days of work that will allow us to focus on an imminent, high-profile writing deadline that was going to be difficult to meet if we traveled to the retreat.

When we asked ourselves the third question, we immediately realized the positive information weighed *about the same as* the negative information. Our stress and upset plummeted. They didn't disappear entirely, but the overall feeling dropped from about a level 8 to about a level 2. In a matter of moments. It was now very manageable – just a small irritant, rather than a major stressor. If we hadn't proactively intervened on the negativity bias, it would have had a field day with our emotional well-being and left us feeling demoralized.

Life brings continual unexpected problems and challenges to all of us, so the negativity bias has constant opportunities to exert its will. Your authors don't always remember to intervene in this way, but when we do, it makes a huge difference. And the more we do it, the easier it is to remember to do it, and the more proficient we become. The negativity bias's power over us is weakening month-by-month, as a result. If *you* start proactively attacking the negativity bias when the inevitable problems of law school and life emerge, you, too, can re-calibrate your perspective on the problem and substantially dampen the stress. And the more you do this, the better your brain will get at it. But it is an active practice, which requires continual effort to override your neurological predisposition. The practice, however, is worth its weight in gold.

Michael Josephson, a former law professor and now thought leader in legal ethics, reminds us that even with all of the hardships in life, there is plenty of fodder for gratitude in every moment: "The world has enough beautiful mountains and meadows, spectacular skies and serene lakes. It has enough lush forests, flowered fields, and sandy beaches. It has plenty of stars and the promise of a new sunrise and sunset every day. What the world needs more of is people to appreciate and enjoy it."[55] Once you make gratitude a consistent daily practice, by spending even 30–60 seconds per day doing it, and once you begin challenging the negativity bias when problems arise by using the 3-question re-calibration process, you will start to notice there is a *lot* to be grateful for – *at this very moment* (and each moment thereafter). And you will be rewiring your brain for greater happiness, resilience, well-being, and cognition now and for the future.

4. FIXED TO GROWTH

"The only real mistake is the one from which we learn nothing."

— John Powell

You are going to mess up. You are going to fail. And you are going to underperform on some goals. How do we know this? Because you are a *human being*! We are all imperfect, we all make mistakes, and we all have performance flaws.

THE 5 MINDSET SHIFTS

The question is: When these errors or shortcomings arise, how do you interpret them? The science says your *interpretation style* plays an important role in your happiness, well-being, and academic success. In 2006, Dr. Carol Dweck, a psychology professor at Stanford, published a book that introduced a groundbreaking concept into the mainstream: the difference between a "fixed mindset" and a "growth mindset." Her book, *Mindset: The New Psychology of Success (How We Can Learn to Fulfill our Potential)*, is widely considered one of the most important works on emotional well-being, academic success, and professional success ever published.

Based on a mountain of scientific studies, Dweck explained that people with a fixed mindset hold the unconscious belief that their intelligence, talent, and abilities are fixed or static, while people with a growth mindset hold the belief (usually conscious) that their intelligence, talent, and abilities can be grown and improved at any time. According to the research, people with a fixed mindset experience higher levels of stress, shame, sadness, depression, and anxiety, as well as lower levels of academic achievement and career success, than people with a growth mindset.

Having a fixed mindset is a difficult way to live because it causes us to think that every assignment, every test we take, and every mistake is a litmus test of our very intelligence or value as a human. If we don't understand a case we just read, we feel unintelligent and unqualified to be in law school, and that we are never going to succeed. If we get a bad grade, we feel inept and incompetent as a person. And if we make a mistake that hurts someone in our life, we feel horrified and ashamed by the blunder.

In contrast, having a growth mindset allows us to interpret each such event as an opportunity to learn, grow, and expand. So if we don't understand a case we just read, it is an opportunity to get better at comprehending cases in our ongoing journey to become an expert in case law interpretation. If we don't get a good grade on the test, it is a chance to identify new ways of studying or performing that will help us improve next time and achieve ultimate success in the long run. And if we make a mistake that hurts someone in our life, it is a chance to take full accountability and to better understand ourselves so we can slowly grow as a person and hopefully treat the person better in the future.

People with a growth mindset have been continually shown to be happier, more healthy mentally, more resilient to stress, and more successful academically and professionally. In light of that, let's cut to the chase: your goal should be to develop (or to maximize) a growth mindset. The problem, however, is that most people, especially those in highly competitive fields like law, possess a fixed mindset. Most likely, therefore, you, too, possess a fixed mindset – through no fault of your own. If you happen to possess a growth mindset, you likely only "lean subtly" towards growth, while still maintaining many fixed tendencies. So regardless of which you possess, deliberately attempting to build or strengthen a growth mindset has the potential to materially improve your life, your happiness, and your success.

I [*your co-author Rebecca*] can say that *nothing* has more positively affected my emotional state, well-being, or success than building a growth mindset. I possessed a fixed mindset my whole life, and I didn't even know it. When I read *Mindset*, my life completely changed. I realized that I could deliberately cultivate a growth mindset that would allow me to navigate the constant stressors, challenges, and mistakes in a very different way. The more I practiced implementing a growth mindset, the more I benefited. Over time, I became a much happier and healthier person who also achieved more success. I have had the great fortune of teaching this mindset shift to many students and lawyers over the years, and I have witnessed many of them transform as a result. My sincere hope is that after reading this segment of the book, you will choose to cultivate a growth mindset going forward.

Let's start by establishing where you currently reside on the fixed-growth spectrum. Dweck has created a simple assessment for quickly determining this. Check out this link: https://blog.mindsetworks.com/what-s-my-mindset. You answer 8 quick, multiple-choice questions and then the system will auto-generate a summary of your fixed-growth mindset. Knowing

THE 5 MINDSET SHIFTS

where you currently stand, as we have repeatedly mentioned, is the first step in transformation.

Lightbulbs and Babies

Thomas Edison began obsessively trying to invent the lightbulb in 1878. He worked on it every day for 10–20 hours per day for over 14 months, experiencing failure after failure. After having over 10,000 failed lightbulbs, he finally broke through and created a functioning lightbulb. We're pretty sure his mother was nagging him along the way, "Tommy, dear, are you still working on that silly lightbulb idea? You should really get a job. They are hiring at the local tavern – you'd be perfect for that job! They have delicious sandwiches!" (To be clear, the part about his mother nagging him is fictional, it just feels like it happened.)

After Edison succeeded in inventing the lightbulb, a journalist famously asked him, "Mr. Edison, how did you have the wherewithal to continue trying to invent the lightbulb after 10,000 failed lightbulbs?" Edison apparently looked confused by the question before responding, "I didn't have 10,000 failed lightbulbs. I had 10,000 attempted lightbulbs that I learned from, which is what allowed me to invent the lightbulb." Edison did not view the 10,000 non-functioning lightbulbs as *failures*. He viewed each one as an essential step in his journey towards success. Edison had a growth mindset.

If you were in Edison's clogs (that's what they called shoes in the 1800s), would you have continued after even 5,000 "failed" lightbulbs? Actually, a more realistic question (perhaps): would you have continued after 500 straight failures? How many times do you generally "fail" at something before you determine you are bad at it, or destined not to succeed? For most of us, the number is probably around two or three times. Maybe 10 times. But 10,000 times? That's a different mindset altogether. Edison is an inspiring example of an extreme growth mindset – he did not lose his confidence or conviction simply because he was facing failure after failure. His failures and errors did not define him, they illuminated him (we simply couldn't resist that pun). Rather than feeling ashamed by his failures, or believing they were a signal that he was destined to fail in the long run, he extracted a tangible learning lesson from every failed lightbulb, and then incorporated that information going forward. He made 10,000 micro-refinements, which ultimately led to radical success.

Do you want to know someone else who is a shining example of a growth mindset? Your *former* self. That's right, when you were a toddler, you had a strong growth mindset. All toddlers do. Have you ever watched a toddler learn how to walk? They fall hundreds of times before they succeed. The first time they try to stand unsupported, they wobble before buckling over to one side and crashing down to the ground. They immediately get back up, this time shifting their weight disproportionately to the other side to compensate for the prior fall, and of course, go crashing down that way. Then they pop back up, this time fastidiously trying not to fall either left or right – which inevitably leads to a faceplant. This exercise goes on for weeks, as they slowly get better and better at standing, walking, and balancing – through the process of falling, over and over again.

Research shows that toddlers fall an average of 17 times per hour when they are learning to walk. Yet they don't feel embarrassed, they don't get stressed, they don't turn on themselves, and they don't quit. They never conclude, "I am terrible at walking, and will never succeed. So I am going to just crawl for the rest of my life!" By the way, how many times do you currently have to fall in public while trying something new before you promise to never try that thing again? We're guessing fewer than 17 falls per hour.

As we grow up, we slowly lose this growth mindset. We begin to associate our falls with failure rather than growth. We see our mistakes as reflecting our incompetence, not our journey to mastery. We begin to stress over the prospect of failing, instead of embracing the failures as the path to long-term expertise. So at this point in your life, you likely have a fixed mindset, or at least many fixed aspects of thinking. That's the bad news.

The good news is that the science shows it is not too hard to begin forming a growth mindset. Several studies have provided participants with a growth mindset intervention, and those participants have responded with immediate improvements in their well-being, resiliency, and cognitive performance.

THE 5 MINDSET SHIFTS

For example, a study by Professor Jeremy Jamieson from the University of Rochester (remember him from the "Threat to Opportunity" mindset?), as well as colleagues David Yeager and Hae Yeon Lee from the University Texas at Austin, found that a 25-minute reading and writing assignment on growth mindset can yield these results.[56] The participants in the study were high school students who were broken into two groups and told they would be performing stressful tasks. All students were measured for their baseline stress levels, including heart rate and blood pressure, and then given a background reading and writing assignment that took about 25 minutes total. Half of the students received a growth mindset reading and writing assignment that scientifically (and accurately) explained that people can change and grow (without referencing growth mindset in the academic context), while the other half of students – the control group – received an assignment based on the general science of learning (which contained no mindset intervention). The students then were given three minutes to prepare a speech based on their assignment, which they then delivered. At this point, they were given a math test. The students' stress levels were then re-evaluated.

The students who were taught about growth mindset had lower physiological stress and better cognitive performance compared to the control group. In the words of the researchers, the growth mindset students "exhibited improved cognitive, physiological (neuroendocrine and cardiovascular), and behavioral (task performance) responses to acute social stress compared with control participants." In other words, the mindset intervention students were less stressed than the control group, they delivered better speeches than the control group, and they had higher math scores than the control group. Importantly, the growth mindset students not only had lower stress markers than the control group, but their post-intervention stress levels were markedly lower than their pre-intervention levels. So the growth mindset students were not just less stressed than the control group, they were less stressed *versions of themselves*. It only took a simple 25-minute assignment about growth mindset to induce these major improvements.

A 2021 study tested whether upper division college students enrolled in a one-semester Biochemistry class would perform differently in the class based on whether or not they received a growth mindset intervention consisting of a brief discussion of growth mindset at the outset of the semester and periodically during the semester.[57] The study encompassed students from four separate semesters of the course to increase the testing population. The results? The benefits of the mindset intervention were vast. According to the study, "[S]tudents receiving growth mindset interventions significantly outperformed students who did not receive interventions on the final cumulative exam[.]" The study concluded that a growth mindset intervention "can be an effective tool to improve student academic performance in a biochemistry course."

Similarly, another study found that a less than one-hour written growth mindset intervention provided to high school students at the beginning of the school year led those students to experience a substantial increase in growth mindset and reduction in fixed mindset that remained by the end of the school year. Moreover, those students saw an average 0.11 improvement in GPA at the end of the year, compared to their prior GPA.[58] In contrast, the control group experienced no improvement in their GPA and no change in their mindset.

Another study found that inducing a growth mindset in students improved their academic achievement during challenging school changes and increased their resiliency and completion rates across difficult math classes.[59] A further study of university students found that a mere 25-minute growth mindset intervention led to a substantial increase in growth mindset at the conclusion of the intervention, and that this change in the participants' mindset remained five days later when the researchers performed a follow-up assessment.[60] An additional study found that "a growth mindset is positively associated with resilience, school engagement, and psychological well-being."[61] Finally, a study found that underrepresented minority students in a college Chemistry I course experienced improved performance as a result of a growth mindset intervention provided at the beginning of the course.[62]

THE 5 MINDSET SHIFTS

While this is just a sampling of the extensive growth mindset research, we hope it is abundantly clear that you would benefit from proactively adopting a growth mindset. If you embrace the science-based truth that your intelligence, talents, and abilities are not fixed, but can continually grow and become enhanced through your efforts, you are setting yourself up to maximize your law school success. If you *choose to believe* that each week in law school, and each alleged "mistake" or "failure" along the way, is an opportunity to slowly get better, the science says this belief will improve your academic performance and overall success in law school.

What if You Fall into the Lake?
No Problem, You Can Swim!

Adopting a growth mindset will also do wonders for your day-to-day stress levels. This is because of a concept referred to as *anticipatory anxiety*. Anticipatory anxiety is a special form of anxiety we experience about a future event or possible occurrence. Say we get called on in class and feel anxiety as we try to think of the answer. This would be "garden variety" anxiety. However, if it is the morning of class, and we are feeling anxious about the mere possibility of being called on in class later today even though we are currently sitting comfortably on our living room couch, that is anticipatory anxiety.

If we have a fixed mindset, we are perpetually in a state of low-grade anticipatory anxiety. This is because we know, at a certain level, that every possible mistake or failure we make will derail us emotionally. Remember, when we have a fixed mindset, we interpret every mistake or failure as an indictment of our value and competence, so when we suffer one of these blows, we tend to spiral down into shame, overwhelm, sadness and major distress. These consequences necessarily raise the stakes of each and every possible future mistake or failure. In this way, a fixed mindset causes us to have very low *mistake tolerance* or *failure tolerance*. Because we cannot stomach mistakes or failures, we are in a chronic state of anticipatory anxiety over the mere *possibility* of making a mistake or failing. Every homework assignment, every case briefing, every answer we give in class, every practice test we take, and every other tangible action we take that *could go wrong* triggers our anticipatory anxiety (even if it's at a subtle, unconscious level) – because, in the back of our mind, we know that if we mess up, we are going to plummet.

However, if instead, we know that even if we mess up or fail, we can stomach it and move forward, our present-moment experience transforms. That is, once we know we can tolerate mistakes, we experience a greater sense of calm in each moment along the way because we do not dread the possibility of failing. And what is the easiest and most powerful way to embrace the possibility of a future failure or mistake, rather than to dread it? A growth mindset. Because if we view every failure or mistake as an opportunity to learn and grow, it ceases to be so scary. When there is nothing redeeming about our failures or mistakes, on the other hand, they become dread-worthy.

We liken a fixed mindset to walking around the edge of a deep lake by yourself. If you know you cannot swim, then every step becomes stressful and precarious – because one mistake can cost you your life. So as you walk along the perimeter of the lake, you are in a constant state of low-grade anticipatory anxiety. You are unable to enjoy the beauty and tranquility of the water, trees, and vast nature. However, if you know how to swim, then the same stroll becomes serene and calming. You don't experience anticipatory anxiety because you know that if you make the mistake of falling into the lake, you will just swim to shore without incident. You will be wet, but no real harm will occur. Your awareness that you can *tolerate* a mistake – if you happen to make one – transforms your present-moment experience.

Similarly, having a fixed mindset puts us into a state of perpetual anticipatory anxiety about making a mistake or failing. But if we develop a growth mindset, like learning how to swim, we free ourselves of the anticipatory anxiety and can instead experience each moment with far greater calm. We are no longer dreading the future error so much, which allows the present to be far more peaceful.

One of our all-time favorite examples of someone actively attempting to become more tolerant of failure and rejection is Jia Jiang. He was a corporate employee who always dreamed of starting his own business, but he struggled his whole life with

THE 5 MINDSET SHIFTS   145

fear of failure and rejection. He finally overcame his fear and decided to start his business, but the business epically failed – causing him to spiral into a dark state of self-doubt for years. He didn't think he could ever try to start his own business again. Anytime he would experience failure or rejection, no matter how small, he would collapse into shame, embarrassment, and self-judgment. As a result, he was never calm and relaxed, because he so deeply dreaded failure and rejection – which in his view were constantly lurking around every corner. He was stuck in a highly fixed mindset, and it was controlling his life.

But one day, Jiang decided to take radical action to overcome his fear of failure. He came up with an extremely creative way of building greater tolerance for failures and rejections. What did he do? Rather than attempting to avoid failure and rejection, as he had his whole life, he decided to actively pursue failure and rejection. He promised himself he would experience failure or rejection at least one time every single day for 100 straight days. That's right, he created a 100 Day Challenge where he would do one thing each day that was *guaranteed* to lead to failure or rejection. He believed he could eventually build a tolerance for failure and rejection through this extreme challenge. He documented it by video and later turned his experience into a viral TED Talk titled, "What I learned from 100 days of rejection,"[63] as well as a book, *Rejection Proof: how I beat fear and became invincible through 100 days of rejection.*[64]

Some of our favorite things Jiang did that, *unsurprisingly*, led to rejection or failure included:

- ask a stranger to borrow $100
- request a "burger refill" at a fast-food restaurant
- play soccer in a stranger's backyard
- convince FedEx to send his package to Santa Clause
- become a live mannequin at Abercrombie & Fitch
- get a free room from a hotel
- drop off a tire for drycleaning

- get a haircut from a groomer at PetSmart
- order a quarter of a shrimp at a restaurant
- become a Girl Scout Cookie salesman
- set up his own beverage stand inside Starbucks
- interview then-President Obama

Through this innovative challenge, Jiang was able to transform his relationship to failure and rejection. As he explains in his TED Talk and book, he realized through his 100-day journey that his success and value are not defined by his failures; in fact, each daily challenge allowed him to have fascinating conversations with new people, learn about himself, and weaken his fear of failure. So even though he was failing, he was growing and improving through each failure. Through this process, his anticipatory anxiety faded away, as he no longer dreaded the possibility of failure and rejection. He built a deep-seated courage and self-confidence that have guided the rest of his life and launched him into becoming a very successful entrepreneur. This is a compelling example of changing one's relationship to failure and rejection, and one we hope inspires you in some way.

The Key Question to Ask Yourself Whenever You Fail or Fall

Short of doing your own 100 Day Challenge, what can you do to transform your relationship to failure? What can you do to build (or deepen) a growth mindset?

One thing you can do is to *choose to believe* the science showing that our intelligence, talent, and abilities are dynamic and capable of growing over time through effort. This is the scientific reality, but whether you choose to believe it is a different story. Perhaps you can read (or listen to) Dweck's *Mindset* book, or poke around *YouTube* for short video summaries of it, or do some casual Googling of this topic so you can arrive at this position on your own. Remember, several studies show that less than 30 minutes of learning about growth mindset can lead to a shift in belief and performance. (What you have already learned in this portion of the book should, itself,

THE 5 MINDSET SHIFTS

deliver some results, but we invite you to continue the exploration.) By deliberately attempting to cultivate this belief, you will be doing yourself a major solid.

The second thing you can do is to ask yourself one quintessential question every time you fail, make a mistake, commit an error, or underperform on anything: *What is one thing I can learn from this failure, mistake, or struggle that will make me a better law student or person?* This question has the potential to change your life. At the moment of failure, error, or struggle, this question can instantaneously redirect your mind to the growth opportunity. It reframes the event from one of disappointment and shame to one of growth and improvement. You can think of it as the "**Thomas Edison Question.**" Every single time Edison produced a failed lightbulb, he extracted one learning lesson or one piece of value from the failure. As a result, he converted each failure into a critical step towards success – and simultaneously stripped the disappointment and shame from each failure.

So if you struggle to comprehend your Contracts reading, or if you believe your question in class came out incoherent, or if you feel shaky and anxious whenever you get called on in class, or if you get a low grade on your Research & Writing paper, or if you succumb to procrastination on your evening reading a few nights in a row, or if you can't seem to figure out how to make your research terms broad enough to cover all of the potentially relevant results but narrow enough to capture the most important cases, or if you feel like you are getting behind on outlining, or if you take a practice test that doesn't go well, or if you keep coming up with excuses not to take any practice tests even though you think you should take some, or if you feel like the quantity of information is simply too massive to eventually memorize for the final, do not just "power through" your stress and move on. And do not believe the illusion that this is an insurmountable issue or an indicator that you are going to fail in law school or in the profession. Reject, too, the myth that any given issue or struggle is destined to be a weakness of yours, rather than something you can convert into a defining strength over time.

Instead, pause and ask yourself the Thomas Edison Question with each such issue. *("What is one thing I can learn from this failure, mistake, or struggle that will make me a better law student or person?")* If you purposefully view each struggle or failure not in isolation, but in the context of a *larger process* of you methodically and consistently becoming an amazing law student over time and an incredible lawyer in the long run, then the struggle or failure will feel very different. We can't tell you how many of the best trial lawyers and oral advocates we meet tell us they were terrible at answering Socratic method questions in law school, but they slowly learned how to advocate "on their feet" over the course of several years and eventually became great at it. Or how many first-year law students struggle mightily with outlining in the first semester but slowly overcome the issue and become excellent outliners in their second semester or second year of law school.

Or, to share a personal one, students who dramatically improve their legal writing. I [*your co-author Jarrett*] did poorly on all of my writing assignments in my 1L Research & Writing class because I was having a really hard time adjusting my prior writing style. I had been a philosophy major, which involves a writing style diametrically opposed to the legal writing style. I felt demoralized and highly stressed by my low grades on my 1L writing assignments and by the bloodbath of red edits and comments left by the professor on each assignment. Yet by the time I was a first-year lawyer, I was continually told by supervising attorneys how exceptional my legal writing was. My continual stress and fear in the first semester of my 1L year came from my fixed mindset (despite not having heard of the concept at that point), which told me that my writing struggles were an indicator that I was not ever going to be a great legal writer. If I had known about growth mindset and viewed these struggles as a temporary stage leading to my long-term success, I would have been a much happier and more resilient 1L.

The Thomas Edison Question can also apply to your personal relationships. If you snap at a friend or family member during a phone call and then feel guilty afterwards, rather than just going into a shame spiral, ask yourself: What is one thing I can learn about myself from this reactive moment? In other

THE 5 MINDSET SHIFTS

words, how can you use this imperfect moment to gradually become kinder or less reactive in similar situations in the future? Perhaps you notice your tendency to be extra reactive when friends or family imply you have done something wrong, so you identify an opportunity for the future to respond to their judgmental statement with, "I am feeling a little judged, do you feel that I did something unfair here?", rather than lashing out with your usual counterattack. Or maybe you notice you tend to be reactive when you are under seemingly unrelated law school stress, so you determine you can start certain conversations off with a pre-disclosure, "I'm so excited to catch up with you, but just so you know, I'm under some intense law school stress right now, so if my tone feels a bit intense or rushed at times, that's why." Sometimes this sort of pre-disclosure can make the other person more gentle and less judgmental throughout the conversation, or it can help us become less reactive during the conversation because we have aired the truth in advance. Or perhaps you notice that you should have given yourself some alone time to process your stress, rather than hopping on the call to placate that friend or family member who really wanted to speak with you. This reactive moment might be a signal that you have a tendency to ignore your own self-care needs and to make yourself available to others even when you would rather not. So instead of just feeling bad about your reaction, you can use this reaction to catalyze different and more empowered behaviors in similar situations in the future. As such, this experience can become part of your gradual, long-term growth as a human.

Remember, you are going to make a lot of mistakes and fumbles in both law school and life. It is part of the human experience. But if you can begin viewing each such fall or failure as an opportunity for self-awareness and gradual growth, your law school experience – and your future – will transform. You get to choose: Will each failure or mistake take you down into a state of darkness? Or will you deliberately use each such instance to gradually grow and expand into a better version of yourself? Thomas Edison used a growth mindset to illuminate the world through the lightbulb. You can use a growth mindset to illuminate your happiness, resilience, and long-term greatness.

5. EXTERNAL CONTROL TO INTERNAL CONTROL

"If you don't like something change it; if you can't change it, change the way you think about it."

— Mary Engelbreit

In 2016, neuroscientists and psychologists at University College London (UCL), one of the most prestigious research institutions in Europe, ran a fascinating study in which they hooked the participants up to a machine that would administer a series of painful electric shocks to their hands, while assessing their real-time stress responses based on the probability of being shocked in each instance.[65] (Hats off to UCL's lawyers for drafting an air-tight liability waiver that allowed their scientists to electrically shock kind-hearted Londoners!) To assess the participants' stress levels in anticipation of each electrical shock, the scientists used instruments to measure the participants' pupil dilation, skin conductance (which is the variation of electrical activity in the skin in advance of sweating), and cortisol levels. These are three well-established physiological symptoms of the stress response.

Interestingly, when participants knew they had a 100% chance of getting shocked, their stress levels elevated in the moments before the shock occurred. But when they knew they had only a 50% chance of getting shocked, their stress levels *skyrocketed* in the moments before the possible shock. That's right, participants had significantly higher stress levels in the moments before a 50% probability of being shocked than in the moments before a 100% guarantee of being shocked.

Why would participants have more stress from a possible good result (i.e., a 50% chance of avoiding pain) than from a guaranteed bad result (i.e., a 100% chance of receiving pain)? This makes no *logical* sense, but it does make *neuro*logical sense. This is because the human brain fears and despises uncertainty more than anything else – including certain pain and certain bad outcomes. Nothing triggers us into stress, anxiety, anger, and despair more quickly than uncertainty, unpredictability, and

THE 5 MINDSET SHIFTS

unforeseen events. The UCL study is one of many studies that show that uncertainty, unpredictability, and unforeseen events are the greatest cause of stress and anxiety – even more so than terrible events.

Unfortunately, life is unavoidably riddled with uncertainty, unpredictability, and unforeseen events. So the very things our brain hates the most are perpetually prevalent in life – and law school. And why does the brain hate these things so much? Because they strip us of feeling *in control* of our lives. They eliminate our pre-conceived narrative of how the situation or event is "supposed" to unfold, which leaves us feeling powerless and overwhelmed. The science is clear that all humans have an innate psychological need to feel in control, so when our sense of control is undercut, we plummet into stress and anxiety and upset.

One way we cope with these feelings is to take a decisive action or exert a decisive position that makes us feel more in control than we really are. A few years ago, Amy Robach, a 40-year-old news journalist at ABC, appeared on *Good Morning America* with a new haircut to discuss her breast cancer diagnosis, which at that time had led to a double mastectomy and two of eight total planned rounds of chemotherapy. As she explained in a video recorded right before she cut her long hair, she decided to take clear action in the face of the uncertainty over how much of her hair would fall out or become thin. "I am taking control of something that I have very little control," she remarked.[66] "I am going to cut my hair very short, I've never done this before. I want to say I had something to do with how I look, not the cancer." This is a completely normal coping mechanism in response to a horrific life event that makes one feel powerless. When a life situation makes us feel an absence of control, whether big or small, it is very common to take some tangible action to feel more in control than we truly are.

When you are overwhelmed with law school stress, do you ever notice yourself suddenly cleaning your apartment, or doing your laundry, or playing a video game you excel at, or maybe even doing a small assignment that is not time-sensitive or important but that makes you feel like you "accomplished" something? I [*your co-author Rebecca*] can say that my go-to activity when I am stressed by life or career is to organize the house by putting things back in their rightful place, opening Amazon boxes, and of course filing mail in my unnecessarily elaborate filing system. Boy, do I feel *"in control"* when I do that!

One of the earliest researchers on how humans cope with a perceived loss of control was the late Stephen Sales, a psychology professor at Carnegie-Mellon University. In the early 1970s, Sales conducted studies that found that during times of great societal stress that are outside anyone's control, people tend to take individual actions that create greater perceived control in their own life. For example, Seller compared the membership records of various churches during times of widespread strife, such as the Great Depression. He found a spike in new memberships to churches whose doctrines instilled a sense of individual control in their parishioners by providing them with clear behavioral guidelines for qualifying for heaven.[67] Yet new memberships to churches that did not as overtly affirm parishioners' sense of control, such as Presbyterian and Episcopalian churches, floundered. Interestingly, once more prosperous times returned and people otherwise felt more in control of their lives, these membership trends inverted.

Sellers also analyzed registration records maintained by the American Kennel Club over the course of the 20th century and found that during times of war, Americans acquire dogs that are perceived to be more protective, like Doberman Pincers, German Shepherds, and similar breeds, at an approximately 40% higher rate than during peaceful times.[68] Relatedly, Pomeranians, Boston Terriers, Chihuahuas, and other breeds perceived to be less protective drop in popularity during times of war but increase in popularity during times of peace. So, either a Doberman Pincer named Smokey is capable of defeating a foreign military invasion, or we tend to take tangible actions that make us feel more in control during times of uncertainty and fear.*

---

* Researchers have documented just how essential a sense of control is for both mental and physical health. For instance, people who feel more in control of their lives report better health, lower physical pain, and faster recovery from illnesses than other people do. They also live longer.[69]

THE 5 MINDSET SHIFTS

When we feel a lack of control, we also have a tendency to manufacture baseless theories and mental conclusions about the outside world that restore a perception of control in our own minds. As explained by former Wall Street Journal writer Joseph T. Hallinan in his book, *Kidding Ourselves: The Hidden Power of Self-Deception*, "Having a sense of control is so important that if we don't have it, we make it up." Among many other scientific studies he references,* Hallinan documents a groundbreaking study in 2008 conducted by Jennifer Whitson from the UCLA Anderson School of Business and Adam Galinsky from the Columbia Business School that demonstrated that "when people are made to feel as if they have no control they will literally see things that don't exist, such as patterns where there are no patterns." Indeed, the more the participants were subjected to information and stimuli they could not control (based on the careful manipulations of Whitson and Galinsky), the more likely they were to "perceive a variety of illusory patterns, including seeing images in noise, forming illusory correlations in stock market information, perceiving conspiracies, and developing superstitions."[70] Yet, the more Whitson and Galinsky increased the amount of control the participants had over the information and stimuli, the less likely they were to perceive illusory patterns within it. Experiencing a loss of personal control can induce us to attempt to make sense of the outside world by imposing illusory patterns and theories on reality. That is how much the human brain craves control.

All of which brings us to the biggest problem with law school. It is rife with circumstances, situations, and policies that are *de facto* beyond our control. These things may change in the future, but the reality is that most of them are not going to change any time soon. This can wreak havoc on our mental health and emotional well-being. It could be your Torts professor's teaching style, or your Crim Law professor's cold-calling Socratic method, or the sheer quantity of nightly reading in your Property class, or the absurd guidelines governing your Research & Writing paper, or your school's unique grading system or strict bell curve, or your Contracts professor's final

---

* We would like to acknowledge Joseph T. Hallinan for his incisive analysis and research on the power of perceived control, which we have relied upon heavily in the above citations.

exam format ("What, all essays?!" or "What, no essays!?"), or your school's policy on externships, or an article published by a prominent professor at your school that deeply upsets you, or your Civ Pro class's disproportionate focus on jurisdiction issues compared to the class taught by the other Civ Pro professor, or your school's winter break dates, or your Con Law professor's inability to ever answer a question in a helpful way, or your school's outdated technological platforms, or the seeming randomness as to which doctrines will appear in your final exams, or the recent policy decision issued by your school's board of directors, or any one of the additional aspects of your law school experience that make your blood boil or make you feel you would be happier or more successful if this aspect were different.

Notwithstanding that you undoubtedly face several of these obstacles (all law students do), the scientific research reveals that you can interpret these obstacles through either an *external locus of control* mindset or an *internal locus of control* mindset. If you have an external locus of control, you feel that your life and your success are largely influenced by factors and events outside your control. So you look at these inevitable obstacles and believe your success hinges on your ability to remove or change them. As a result, you dedicate a large amount of your valuable time, energy, and thought to resisting the obstacles, trying to modify them, or complaining about them. You become consumed by the obstacle at issue and view it as central to your ability to succeed. When you fail or are not happy, you tend to point to the obstacle as the reason for that outcome.

If you possess an internal locus of control, on the other hand, you believe that your life and your successes are primarily determined by your own choices, efforts, and actions. You do not deny the existence or magnitude of the obstacles, but you believe you can succeed despite the obstacles. As a result, you dedicate the vast majority of your valuable time, energy, and thought to transcending or overcoming the obstacles, rather than trying to remove or change them. When you fail or are not happy, you tend to take personal responsibility for that outcome and ask yourself how you can behave differently to obtain a different outcome in the future.

THE 5 MINDSET SHIFTS

The good news is that we can cultivate an internal locus of control (or strengthen it if we currently lean in that direction). And why would we want to do this? Because the science is clear that an internal locus of control leads to a host of mental, emotional, and academic benefits. For example, a 2021 study assessing the relationship between locus of control and well-being reviewed a collection of prior studies before concluding, "[I]n all of these studies, the internal locus of control was positively related to positive mental health indicators while the external [locus] showed the opposite pattern."[71] Moreover, people with an internal locus of control score higher across various dimensions of happiness than people with an external locus of control.[72] Another study found that individuals with an internal locus of control had lower stress levels and symptoms of depression in response to negative life events.[73]

Additionally, individuals with an internal locus of control manage health problems better than individuals with an external locus of control. A study involving patients facing a high risk of cardiovascular disease found that the patients with an internal locus of control took better care of their health and had lower health burdens after their original diagnosis.[74] A study involving patients with Type II diabetes determined that the patients who were trained to cultivate an internal locus of control improved their self-care and management of their diabetes, while the patients who were trained to cultivate an external locus of control experienced the opposite outcomes.[75]

Other studies reveal that an internal locus of control enhances functioning in the employment and academic arenas. A major meta-analysis study reviewing 213 published studies across 20 years of locus of control research in the employment context found that, on average, having an internal locus of control increased job satisfaction by 33%, increased mental well-being by 36%, and increased life satisfaction by 35%.[76] Another study from the employment arena found that when employees experience burnout, an internal locus of control and sense of personal agency are crucial to the process of recovering from the burnout.[77]

A study involving college students found that "learning performances of the students with internal locus of control are high, and they are more proactive and effective during the learning process," while "the ones with external locus of control are more passive and reactive during this period."[78] An additional study of college students found that those with an internal locus of control had higher levels of academic achievement compared to the ones with an external locus of control.[79] Another study assessed the locus of control of 3,000 first-year university students before the start of the school year and found that, when controlling for ACT scores, the students possessing an internal locus of control obtained significantly higher GPAs in their first year than the students with an external locus of control.[80] Several other studies have found that students with an internal locus of control outperform students with an external locus of control.[81]

The benefits of an internal locus of control, as outlined above, are manifold. The more we accept that there are things in law school and life that we simply cannot control, and the more we become laser-focused on the things we can control (such as our attitude, decisions, and effort), the happier and more successful we will be. In her best-selling book, *Loving What Is*, which has been translated into 35 different languages and has helped countless people across the globe improve their mental health and emotional well-being, author Byron Katie, a woman named after her father, provides a powerful analogy for developing an internal locus of control (using slightly different terms). She says it is the single most important thing we can do to improve our resilience and happiness in response to life stressors.[82] Katie would know, as she struggled with clinical anxiety and major depression for a 10-year stretch from age 33 to 43 that often left her bedridden and unable to leave her home. At that point, she began to build an internal locus of control and her entire life changed, as she explains in her book.

The deliberately simplistic analogy Katie uses for what causes virtually all of our stress and upset in life is our unconscious belief that "**A dog *should* meow, not bark**." That is Katie's representation of a common life occurrence: Something happens in our life that is a fixed reality, we cannot control it, but we want the reality to be different, so we push against that reality and get upset that it won't change. In this way, we cause

THE 5 MINDSET SHIFTS   157

our own stress and upset, says Katie, because we are refusing to accept the reality of the moment. We might as well get upset because a dog barks when we want him to meow, she explains. It does not matter how much we want the dog to meow; he is *not* going to meow. We cannot control this external reality.

If we can accept the reality that the dog is not going to meow (even if we like the sound of a "meow" more than a "bark" or believe our life would be better if the dog meowed), we free ourselves to focus on our own internal reaction and behavioral response to the bark. But if we instead stay stuck obsessing over the undesirability of the bark, and we try to convert the dog from a barker into a meower, we are going to cause ourselves unnecessary stress, sadness, anger, and feelings of powerlessness – and we are also going to divert our attention away from successfully overcoming the challenges presented by the barking. "I am a lover of what is, not because I'm a spiritual person, but because it hurts when I argue with reality," writes Katie. "When we argue with it, we experience tension and frustration. We don't feel natural or balanced. When we stop opposing reality, action becomes simple, fluid, kind, and fearless."

So perhaps ask yourself: what aspects of your law school experience are akin to a dog barking when you want him to meow? What things do you wish you could change by waiving a magic wand? Is your attachment to changing these things, however unfair or wrong they may be, causing your own suffering? Would you be better served to redirect your focus and energy to transcending or navigating these obstacles, rather than changing them?*

Perhaps for some of them, it makes sense to keep focusing on trying to change them (while also ensuring your focus on your own response). But for others, it may be better for you to accept

---

* Martin Seligman, the father of Positive Psychology, coined the term "learned helplessness" to refer to a person's chronic perception that they lack control in life. Learned helplessness, which cannot arise where a person has an internal locus of control, has been shown by Seligman and others to be a major contributor to depression, anxiety, and other mental illnesses. For a detailed exploration of learned helplessness and tools for combatting it, we refer you to Seligman's book, *Learned Optimism: How to Change Your Mind and Your Life*.[83]

that you cannot change those things, and to pivot your attention to what you can control.*

Beware of Self-Handicapping

Before we share a simple, three-part structure for gradually cultivating an internal locus of control, we want to discuss a specific form of external locus of control that can be particularly rampant and insidious in law students. It is called self-handicapping. Self-handicapping is generally defined as an "anticipatory self-protective strategy in which individuals create or claim obstacles to success prior to an important performance to excuse potential failure." Those obstacles could be illusory. But more commonly, they are objectively real obstacles – but they are not necessarily the reason, or the entirety of the reasons, for a future failure. In other words, success could still occur in the face of these obstacles, but we use these obstacles to preemptively brace for and "cushion the blow" from a possible failure. Self-handicapping is recognized as a method of preserving one's self-esteem, as well as managing the impressions of others, in the event of failure.

---

* We would like to offer an important clarification about internal locus of control. An internal locus of control is *not* about passively accepting injustice or inequity, or refusing to take action to make one's school or society better or more equitable. There are, indeed, many external circumstances in law school and life that are worth standing up to and many causes worth fighting for. Spending your time, energy, and talent to ignite positive change is a noble act that should be encouraged, and it certainly is not emblematic of having an external locus of control. Instead, the locus of control analysis relates to the various problems and issues that routinely arise in life that do not go to the heart of equity or justice; they are irritating or imperfect circumstances that we would prefer to be different, but that either are not going to change or that are not worth our effort. Our valuable energy and time would be better directed to overcoming the circumstances. Internal locus of control is about identifying, in every situation, what we have control or influence over, and then injecting our energy and passion into those things. It is also about taking responsibility for our own well-being and exerting our effort and internal resources towards maximizing our well-being, rather than allowing law school's various flaws to derail our well-being. Moreover, internal locus of control is not about denying reality. It is not pretending that external circumstances do not *influence* success, or that external circumstances *equally* influence success across different groups. Indeed, the objective evidence reveals that various external factors – including unconscious bias and other biases against women, BIPOC individuals, and members of various other underrepresented groups – influence success, performance, and feelings of belonging. Internal locus of control is about taking overt action to attempt to change these deeply ingrained biases if we are moved to do so, while simultaneously ensuring that our commitment to external change does not derail our own well-being, thriving, and success. We capitalize on everything we have control and influence over, while letting go of the battles that will only sink our thriving or success.

Consequently, when we have stress about the possibility of not succeeding on an upcoming performance (e.g., final exams or a major writing assignment), we identify obstacles to success (such as the ones identified above on page 153), and use them to mentally justify possible failure. For instance, as we are starting to study for our Property final, we focus on the Property professor's poor teaching style throughout the semester, the irrational format of the Property final, and the mandatory curve governing the final. These considerations not only make us feel "behind the 8-ball" throughout the study period, but they also provide us with preemptive protection of our self-esteem if we receive a poor grade. If we, in fact, end up receiving a poor grade on the final, it was not our effort, talent, study strategy, decision not to take enough practice exams, daily study routine, or preparation that caused the poor grade. It was these external obstacles.

Although self-handicapping can have a verbal component (where the preemptive excuse is articulated to someone in advance of the performance), it is primarily an internal thinking pattern that protects our self-esteem in the event of failure or underperformance. We anticipatorily blame external factors for our possible failure or underperformance in order to avoid personal responsibility and preserve our self-identity. Law students can be quite good at identifying various "outrages" about their law school experience *(we speak from experience, as former law students!)* – and, ironically, doing this could hamper their own success. It often serves to self-handicap them. This way, if they don't perform as well as they would like, they have a compelling excuse to point to, which allows them to keep their identity as a star student or super bright person intact.

One of the most common forms of self-handicapping I [*your co-author Rebecca*] witnessed as a full-time law professor was the withholding of full effort. I coached and supported a myriad of students who were intensely stressed that they would not excel in law school. So counterintuitively, they withheld full effort – so that if they ultimately did not excel, they had a built-in excuse that preserved their sense of self. "I didn't do too well on finals, but I really didn't study that hard." (Their underlying motive for withholding effort was often not consciously known to them at the time they were withholding that effort; it would only emerge in some later coaching session.)

Although self-handicapping is extremely common in law school, it plainly hampers well-being and success. Indeed, self-handicapping, like other forms of external locus of control, has been shown to impair mental health, stress resilience, and cognitive performance on the challenge at issue. For example, a study of 366 university students found "self-handicapping [to be] a proximal determinant of depression, anxiety and stress."[84] So even though self-handicapping is done to protect one's sense of self, it actually causes far more damage to one's self-identity than benefit. Another study found that self-handicapping causes students to be less motivated in their preparation for the test, prepare less intelligently for the test, and perform less effectively on the test.[85] An additional study found that self-handicapping led to lower academic success in the student population at issue, and then noted, "[T]his finding supports previous findings that relate the self-handicapping behaviors of students to low levels of academic success."[86] By giving ourselves a preemptive excuse for not succeeding, we tend to underperform as a result of self-handicapping.

For similar reasons, it has been found that self-handicapping increases our propensity for procrastination in advance of an exam.[87] In a creative experiment on the cognitive effects of self-handicapping, researchers at University of Florida divided 193 undergraduate students into two groups. Each group took a cognitive test while crowd noise was played on a stereo system in the test room.[88] The first group was told in advance that background noise interferes with concentration and creativity, while the second group was told the noise should have no effect. So the first group was primed to self-handicap, while the second group was primed to reject self-handicapping. As expected, the students who were given the preemptive excuse for not performing well, in fact, performed far worse than the students who were not given the excuse.

This is the fundamental problem with self-handicapping: We are preemptively relying on an excuse for possible future failure so we feel better about ourselves if we do fail, yet this unconscious thinking, itself, impairs our performance along the

THE 5 MINDSET SHIFTS

way and, hence, makes us far more likely to fail. Dr. Jennifer Crocker, a professor at Ohio State University and expert on the psychology of self-esteem, summarized self-handicapping in this way: "[T]he short-term emotional benefits of pursuing self-esteem are often outweighed by long-term costs."[89] Dr. Susan David, a psychologist at Harvard Medical School and author of *Emotional Agility*, a book about the importance of emotional adaptability to succeeding in life, similarly notes that when we self-handicap, we are unwittingly choosing short-term protection of our self-esteem over our long-term well-being, thriving, and success. "We humans are funny," remarks David. "Often we create beliefs or engage in behaviors that seem to help us in the short term, only to discover they get in the way of the lives we really want to live, or the people we want to become." The reason self-handicapping is so dangerous, says David, is because it is generally unconscious (System 1) and *difficult for us to detect* when we are doing it: "This kind of behavior is often so subtle and habitual that we don't notice we're doing it."[90]

When you are facing a stressful challenge that includes an external obstacle that seems capable of interfering with your success, if you mentally "buy-in" to the notion that this obstacle can, in fact, interfere with your success, then it likely will end up doing just that. If you give the obstacle that power in your own mind, you will likely perform worse as a result, according to the science. But if you acknowledge the obstacle and even note that you wish it were not here, *while simultaneously refusing to believe that the obstacle will interfere with your success*, then you are priming your brain to overcome the obstacle. The science says that this mindset will actually improve your performance and increase your chances of success.

So whenever an obstacle arises (which will frequently happen) as you are taking on an academic challenge, we'd like to propose the following questions for you to self-reflect on – in order to increase your self-awareness, minimize self-handicapping, maximize an internal locus of control, and optimize your chances of success as you navigate that challenge:

- What obstacles to success exist that I lack control over and am realistically not going to change during this challenge? *[specify as much as possible]*

- What about this challenge do I nevertheless have control over? *[specify as much as possible]*
- Do I feel a temptation to self-handicap in my own mind (by mentally attaching to any obstacles from the first bullet-point), so I will feel better about myself if I do not succeed on this challenge? *[try to identify any subtle or unconscious impulses, anxieties, or thoughts that may relate]*
- If I were to engage in self-handicapping or implement an external locus of control during this challenge, what would that look like? *[how might I evade personal responsibility for my ultimate success in this sort of situation?]*
- Should I allow my frustration or upset about the obstacles identified in the first bullet-point to derail my success on this challenge?
- Can I still succeed on this challenge, despite the obstacles identified in the first bullet-point?
- How can I exploit what I *can* control to maximize my odds of succeeding on this challenge? How can I implement an internal locus of control?
- How will I feel if I ultimately succeed on this challenge, notwithstanding the obstacles identified in the first bullet-point?

By pausing to ask yourself these sorts of questions, you may arrive at some self-awareness, as well as tangible strategies for resisting self-handicapping and applying an internal locus of control. And as is the case with all of the mindset shifts, the more you practice shifting into an internal locus of control, the more you will wire your brain to begin thinking this way on its own.

One of the most profound examples in history of a person applying an internal locus of control is holocaust survivor Viktor Frankl. In his book, *Man's Search for Meaning*, Frankl documents his three years in Nazi concentration camps, including Auschwitz. He explains how he was completely stripped of his control over any of his external circumstances in life. He could not control his schedule, what he wore, where he slept, when he could use the restroom, what work he did throughout the day, how much food he could eat and when, whom he interacted with, and, of course, whether he would die at any moment. Due to his total loss of external control, however, Frankl decided to change his thinking and absorb himself in his sense of internal control, which could not be touched by the Nazis. Unlike during his pre-Holocaust life, when his emotional well-being and attitude constantly fluctuated based on external events and unpredictable stressors (e.g., the ups-and-downs of his income, business success, community reputation, relationship with his wife, children's success in school, etc.), Frankl somehow developed a perpetual internal locus of control and thereby emotionally freed himself from his horrific circumstances. He was regularly seen socializing and laughing in the concentration camps, and he built a rich sense of life purpose and meaning during the Holocaust. He had no external control, but he had the *ultimate* internal control. His life actually became more fulfilling and meaningful than it ever was before the Holocaust. In Frankl's words: "Everything can be taken from a man but one thing: the last of the human freedoms – to choose one's attitude in any given set of circumstances, to choose one's own way."

If Viktor Frankl could build an internal locus of control in Auschwitz, we can build an internal locus of control in law school.

Section III

Tangible Tools for Law School Success & Thriving

Section II of this book was designed to provide you with guidance on how to master your thinking and mindsets in order to improve your happiness and cognitive performance. This section, on the other hand, is intended to provide you with a wide collection of tangible behavioral tools to achieve the same results. In other words, Section II involved high-level cognitive mastery and mindset reframing, while this section involves ground-level behavioral change techniques, i.e., concrete micro-actions you can take to enhance your happiness and cognitive performance.

Sections II and III provide independent yet complementary approaches. If you apply only the cognitive techniques of Section II, you should experience vast benefits. Similarly, if you apply solely the behavioral techniques of Section III, you should also experience vast benefits. That being said, the greatest benefits will come from applying both the cognitive techniques of Section II and the behavioral techniques of Section III.

Regarding the behavioral techniques in Section III, each technique is entirely self-contained, so applying the prior or subsequent technique is irrelevant to your ability to effectively use – *and receive full benefits from* – any particular technique. Of course, the more techniques you use, the greater the total benefit.

You can think of this section of the book as a "brain buffet" – a lengthy assortment of behavioral techniques that will hack your brain into heightened resilience and peak performance. When you go to a real buffet, you stroll along the line and inspect each option individually. If the item looks tasty, you shovel some of it onto your plate. If it does not look yummy, you skip to the next option. That is what we invite you to do with each of these brain hacks. Read each one to determine if it looks "cognitively tasty" to you, and if it does, begin incorporating it into your law school experience. If it does not look tasty to you, skip it and move to the next one.

Even if you end up adopting just five of these techniques (although it would be hard to select just five because they are *so succulent*), those five techniques have the ability to meaningfully improve your well-being, resilience, cognitive functioning, and academic performance in law school.

Enjoy the brain buffet!

Tool 1

Face: Chopsticks Will De-Stress You

"Sometimes your joy is the source of your smile, but sometimes, your smile can be the source of your joy."

— Thich Nhat Hanh

Imagine yourself working later today on your most stressful law school task. Visualize yourself "locked in" on your textbook or laptop, or whatever is in front of you. Now place a single chopstick in your lips, held tightly by your lips without using your teeth. Yes, we said chopstick! If you do not have a chopstick handy, no problem, go ahead and place a pen or pencil between your lips in the same fashion. It should extend out from the front of your mouth – as if you are pursing your lips onto a cigarette. Go ahead and hold that pose as you imagine yourself working on your high-stress task.

Good, now let's change the positioning of the chopstick or writing instrument. Place it *horizontally* across your back molars, so that the chopstick or instrument is lying across your mouth atop your tongue while being held by your left and right molars. With the item in this position, visualize yourself working on that high-stress task.

Now the million-dollar question: Is it possible that the difference between holding the chopstick the first way versus the second way could have a material effect on your stress levels and overall mood while working on that highly challenging task? The answer is "yes." In fact, a 2012 study from psychologists and neuroscientists at the University of Kansas determined that this simple difference in chopstick placement yields a significant difference in stress levels and emotional recovery.

Before we get into the details of that study, we want to provide you with some background. We all know that when we are happy, we smile. And when we are stressed, we scowl.

But modern neuroscience and psychology have proven that the opposite is also true. When we smile, no matter how stressed we were at the moment we begin smiling, the act of smiling reduces our stress and improves our mood. And when we scowl, no matter how stressed we were at the moment we begin scowling, the act of scowling increases our stress and hampers our mood. Why is this? Because the brain (whom we call "the loyal messenger") is constantly observing our facial expressions and then regulating our sympathetic nervous system and endocrine system based on the cues it detects. There is a body-brain feedback loop whereby our facial expressions communicate signals to the brain, which, in turn, either actives or deactivates our endocrine and sympathetic nervous systems. The scientific literature refers to this feedback loop as "facial feedback."

When we are scowling, the brain determines we are under some sort of physical threat (since clenching of the face is an evolutionary reflex to a physical attack). So the brain, in order to help us survive this assumed physical attack, ignites the stress response, floods our system with stress hormones and catalyzes each of the physiological reactions we discussed in Section 1 – including reducing our high-level executive thinking and activating our low-level survival thinking. We are now in a far better position to successfully flee or fight off the physical attack. The only problem is, of course, there is no physical attack. We are sitting quietly at our desk trying to comprehend a mind-numbingly confusing case.

So we are *miscommunicating* to our brain. That is, we are sending incorrect messages to the brain. In response, it increases our stress levels – and hence, reduces our cognition. So regardless of what level of stress we were experiencing until we started scowling, the moment we began to scowl, our stress elevated and our thinking worsened. In this way, our facial response to our existing stress materially increases our stress and impairs our thinking.

Back to the chopsticks study.[91] If researchers want to study participants' emotional reactions to different facial expressions without the participants knowing what facial expression they are holding, it can be rather challenging. If the participants are asked to smile or scowl, their awareness of their facial expression could influence the results of the study. So, is it possible to get participants in a scientific study to smile or scowl *without them even knowing they are smiling or scowling*? Yes, via chopsticks! As you may now realize, holding the chopstick pursed between one's lips as if it were a cigarette creates an automatic "stress scowl," while holding it horizontally along the back molars creates an automatic smile. The participants in the study were asked to hold the chopstick in one of the positions, without being told they were making a smile or scowl, while performing a deliberately stressful task. The results revealed that holding the chopsticks in a way that created an unwitting smile produced lower stress and faster stress recovery during the stressful task than when the participants held the chopsticks in an unwitting scowl, which increased stress and slowed stress recovery.

A collection of other studies have also shown that our facial expression powerfully affects our stress levels and overall mood in response to factual stimuli. For example, one study assessed participants' hormone levels at baseline and then again when the participants were asked to hold a pen in their mouth in a way that generated a de facto smile; the study found that the unwitting smile stimulated the release of happy hormones.[92] Another study fastened a chain of adhesive bandages to the cheeks of participants that contorted their face into a de facto smile or non-smile by lifting or lowering their cheek muscles to replicate those expressions. While their facial expressions were manipulated by the bandages, the participants assessed a series of images.[93] The participants rated the images more favorably and positively when their cheeks were raised into a de facto smile, causing the researchers to conclude that their facial expressions influenced their brains' interpretation of outside events. The researchers further noted that "these results confirmed the hypothesis that participants may feel happier when the cheeks are raised than lowered."

A similar study that involved adhesive bandages on the forehead and eyebrow region that induced participants into either a scowl or a neutral expression found that participants interpreted images more negatively and pessimistically when induced into a scowl.[94] Participants in another study rated a series of cartoon clips as funnier when their face was unwittingly positioned into a smile as a result of holding a pen in their mouth in a particular way instructed by the researchers, and rated other cartoons as less funny when their face was unwittingly positioned into a more serious expression as a result of repositioning the pen in response to the researchers' instructions.[95]

In a fascinating line of studies involving Botox, the cosmetic injection designed to smooth out wrinkles, doctors stumbled upon the possibility that Botox can reduce symptoms of depression. For years, patients across the U.S. anecdotally reported more positive and less depressed moods in the weeks following Botox injections, but most doctors presumed it was because these individuals intensely valued a "wrinkle free" face, and hence, their happiness increased when the wrinkles temporarily disappeared. It seemed that a smoother face *does* bring happiness after all! But eventually, it was realized that Botox injections primarily target the lower forehead and eye muscles, which are disproportionately involved in frowning and scowling, rather than smiling. So it was theorized that Botox might have been causing improved happiness for some patients because it was freezing their ability to frown and scowl, which in turn was altering their brain's functioning and resulting mood. A classic case of facial feedback. It was time to scientifically test this theory.

So what did the resulting science reveal? Strong evidence that Botox (clinically known as the botulinum toxin) reduces symptoms of depression through facial feedback. In one study involving participants suffering from treatment-resistant depression (where several different types of medications and therapeutic interventions over time had caused no material reduction of the patients' depression symptoms), it was found that injecting Botox into the participants' frown muscles reduced depression symptoms by an average of 47.1% over the course over the 16-week period that Botox is most effective.[96] The control group, which received saline placebo injections into those same muscles, experienced a 9.2% reduction in depression symptoms over the same period (consistent with the placebo effect).

For context, people with treatment-resistant depression are individuals who have not received any meaningful relief from FDA-approved medications or evidence-based psychotherapy; they are estimated to constitute 10% to 30% of people with depression. A 47.1% decrease in depression symptoms among any group of people, particularly across treatment-resistant depressants, is nothing short of spectacular. "In summary, our study provides new evidence that [Botox] to the glabellar region [the area between the eyebrows necessary for frowning] may be an effective, safe, and sustainable intervention in the treatment of depression," concluded the study. "It provides clinical support for the concept that the facial musculature not only expresses, but also regulates, mood states." In other words, how we hold our facial expression is not just an expression of our mood, but a determinant of it. The study found that "[a]t this juncture, [Botox] may be considered for depressed patients with the objective of inducing mood-lifting side effects."

Another Botox study found that 52% of the participants suffering from major depression who received a single Botox treatment in their frown muscles experienced an over 50% reduction in their depression symptoms that persisted six weeks after the treatment, as compared to 15% of the placebo group.[97] The study concluded, "[A] single treatment [of Botox] appears to induce a significant and sustained antidepressant effect in patients with major depression." And another Botox study that assessed over 40,000 FDA records from Botox recipients found that Botox patients with depression "had a significantly lower number of depression reports when compared to patients undergoing different treatments for the same conditions."[98] The study remarked that "[t]hese findings suggest that the antidepressant effect of [Botox] is significant." This collection of studies provides strong support for the notion that our facial expressions play an important role in our emotional state.

Studies have also shown that our facial expressions influence our perception of pain. For example, one study found that "making a standardized pain face" in response to a painful stimulus increases the perceived magnitude of the pain in comparison to receiving the same painful stimulus without making such a face.[99] The study noted that "facial expressions of pain are an important part of the pain response, signaling distress to others, and eliciting social support." However, the study concluded that such facial expressions of pain, although serving valid self-protection purposes, cause the stimulus to feel more painful. Another study determined that "pain [facial] expressions resulted in higher pain ratings compared to all other facial expressions" when participants were subjected to a succession of deliberately painful stimuli.[100] The study confirmed the validity of facial feedback, noting "[t]hese findings demonstrate that the modulation of pain and emotion is bidirectional with pain faces being mostly prone to having mutual influences." An additional study subjected participants to a painful vaccine-like needle injection and found that smiling participants experienced 40% less pain than their neutral-faced counterparts.[101]

There is widespread evidence that our facial expressions communicate important signals to the brain that influence our perception of the experience and our resulting emotions. So the next time you are working on something that is stressing you out, pause for a moment to notice your facial expression. We can virtually guarantee you that you will be holding a stress scowl – with pursed lips, a clenched jaw, and contracted jowl muscles. That means you are communicating to your brain that you are anticipating an imminent attack, so you are causing your brain to ignite the stress response, which we know also impairs cognition. In that moment, if you can override your default stress scowl with a smile or confident expression, you will be signaling to your brain that it is safe to reduce stress and elevate cognition.

Thus, a simple technique to combat stress and enhance cognition is to notice whenever you are stuck in a stress scowl while doing your law school work, and to convert that facial expression into a smile or expression of confidence. The loyal messenger (your brain) will pick up this signal and shift you into a more resilient and heighted cognitive state. And the more you do this over time, the more you will begin to rewire your brain

FACE: CHOPSTICKS WILL DE-STRESS YOU 173

not to default to a stress scowl when you are facing an academic challenge, and you will slowly elevate your baseline resiliency.

The difference between these two facial expressions can have a large impact on this law student's stress levels and cognitive performance.

TOOL 2

BODY: THE "90-DEGREE RULE"

"The mind and body are not separate units, but one integrated system."

— Dr. Bernie S. Siegel

Imagine you are camping in the Amazon (the rainforest, not the website). You are sitting comfortably in a chair, roasting marshmallows, wondering how long it has been since you've showered. Suddenly, a huge jaguar comes bolting out of the woods in a lightning-fast sprint directly at you. In a matter of milliseconds, the jaguar is airborne, leaping towards you with its fangs and claws fully exposed, leaving you no time to run or intelligently fight back. What will you reflexively do in that instant? (Other than drop your perfectly roasted marshmallow.)

You will tuck your head downward and hunch your posture in order to brace yourself for the imminent impact. This will require zero conscious or deliberate thought (it is the ultimate example of "System 1" thinking), and it will occur, yes, in about one-tenth of a second. This is a mammalian defense reflex wired deeply into our neuropsychology: When we are about to be subjected to an unavoidable act of blunt force, we instantly recoil into a constricted, hunched posture. This bracing reflex also occurs when you are walking through a haunted house on Halloween and a horrifying demon pops out unexpectedly. Or when you are riding as a passenger in a car and the driver does not see that another car is about to crash into you. Or when you are on a rollercoaster approaching the enormous drop that you mortally fear.

Now we want you to try something: Hunch over in this moment into a tight bracing position, as if a jaguar were lunging at you. Now raise both of your arms up so they are parallel to the ground, while keeping the rest of your posture the same. In other words, put your arms into a "mummy" position, where your arms are extended forward (while keeping the rest of your body in the bracing position). Finally, start wiggling your fingers continuously.

What do you look like in this moment? You look like *you* while frantically working on your laptop trying to meet your typical law school deadline! That's right, you are hunched over with your back, shoulder, and neck muscles constricted, and your head tucked downward, as you stare feverishly at the laptop or text book. If you ever walk through the law library during the final exam period, you will notice virtually all of your colleagues intensely hunched over their work product in this same way. If you ever meander through the halls of a law firm or other legal organization, you will immediately be able to determine who is working on a high-stress deadline: the people who are hunched over their work product in this intense, bracing posture. We call this the "stress posture."

Just as the stress scowl increases our existing stress levels, the stress posture does the same. Regardless of the amount of stress you are experiencing when you fall into the stress posture, the stress posture is signaling to the loyal messenger (your brain) that you are about to be attacked by that leaping jaguar. So your loyal messenger boosts your cortisol and stress levels so you have a better chance of somehow surviving this vicious predator after bracing the unexpected leap. But as we know, you are not actually facing a lunging jaguar, you are facing an evasive legal doctrine. So your stress jolt is only making you less happy and less cognitively effective.

To optimize our emotional and cognitive state in stressful moments during law school, we must notice when our body unconsciously defaults into a "stress posture" (i.e., a hunched, slumped position), and then override this reflex by shifting into an upright or erect posture where our head is up and our shoulders are back. If your spine is straight and upright, rather than folded over, you are signaling to your brain that you are physically safe and not under threat, which in turn causes your brain to reduce the existing cortisol and stress levels. Similar to facial feedback, this particular mind-body loop is referred to as postural feedback. The posture we hold in any given moment sends signals to the brain, which modifies our hormones and emotions accordingly.

A voluminous body of research has shown that holding an upright or erect posture, as opposed to a hunched or slumped posture, positively impacts our overall mood, emotional well-being, resiliency, self-confidence, and cognition. Indeed, a minimum of 46 studies in peer-reviewed journals have found this positive impact.[102] For example, one study found that when individuals unknowingly held an upright posture (with the assistance of a physiotherapy tape) while undergoing the stressful task of preparing for and engaging in a mock interview for their dream job, they experienced lower physiological stress, subjective fear, and self-doubt than individuals who unwittingly held a hunched posture (again, with the assistance of a physiotherapy tape).[103] The content of their interview answers also differed: linguistic analyses revealed that the hunched interviewees were much more negative in their responses than the non-hunched interviewees. The researchers concluded, "[S]itting upright may be a simple behavioral strategy to help build resilience to stress." They elaborated that "[a]dopting an upright seated position in the face of stress can maintain self-esteem, reduce negative mood, and increase positive mood compared to a slumped posture." Furthermore, the researchers concluded that "sitting upright increases rate of speech and reduces self-focus."

A large body of research has identified similar mental, emotional, and cognitive benefits from holding upright versus hunched postures in a wide variety of contexts. For example, one study found that being in an upright seated posture led to improved overall mood (based on factors of well-being, energy, and stress) and faster processing speeds on an objective attention test as compared to being in a hunched posture;[104] another study found that individuals induced into a negative mood were far less successful in shifting out of the negative mood when they held a hunched seating posture rather than an upright seating posture;[105] another study found individuals were far better at positively reframing stressful thoughts when they were in an upright versus hunched seated posture;[106] another study involving Japanese students found that those who were trained to sit with an upright posture were more productive than their colleagues on writing assignments;[107] another study found that individuals in an upright or "power" posture experienced greater stress resilience, self-confidence, and risk-taking abilities than individuals in a hunched posture;* another study found that individuals in a hunched seated posture recalled negative memories far more easily than positive memories, yet in upright postures recalled positive memories far more easily;[110] another study found that individuals learning a foreign language experienced less anxiety based on both the General Anxiety Scale and the Foreign Language Anxiety Scale when they practiced the new language while in an upright versus hunched posture;[111] another study found that individuals learning a foreign language had greater self-confidence and a more positive outlook on their learning abilities when holding an upright versus hunched posture;[112] another study found that individuals struggling with mild depression experienced improved moods and reduced anxiety and fatigue when they kept their posture upright rather than slumped;[113] and finally (phew!), another study found depressed individuals in a hunched posture were far more susceptible to "recall bias" about themselves (a cognitive bias where individuals unconsciously filter out strengths and positive personality traits about themselves and disproportionately notice and focus on weaknesses and negative personality traits) than when they were seated in an upright posture.[114]

---

* This particular study,[108] which formed the basis of Dr. Amy Cuddy's viral 2012 TED Talk, "Your body language may shape who you are," has received considerable attention and criticism from certain individuals in the field, primarily due to the absence of subsequent replications of certain of the study's findings and also due to some data collection weaknesses and statistical analysis errors relied upon by the study. Importantly, however, the key finding of the study (what Dr. Cuddy calls "the power posing effect") has been replicated by at least nine published studies and at least four unpublished studies. Most importantly, there have been at least 46 studies published in peer-reviewed journals supporting the postural feedback doctrine and showing that how we hold our posture has significant effects on various components of our mental, emotional, cognitive, and behavioral functioning, such as our mood, emotional state, resiliency, self-confidence, reputation, decision making and actions.[109]

A less technical illustration of these issues can be found here: Singal, J., & Dahl, M. (2016, September 30). Here Is Amy Cuddy's response to critiques of her power-posing research. https://www.thecut.com/2016/09/read-amy-cuddys-response-to-power-posing-critiques.html.

Dr. Cuddy's TED Talk can be found here: https://www.ted.com/talks/amy_cuddy_your_body_language_may_shape_who_you_are.

BODY: THE "90-DEGREE RULE" 179

Here's a simple rule of thumb we call the "90-Degree Rule": if the angle between your spine and pelvis is less than 90 degrees (i.e., hunched or slumped), you are signaling to your brain that you are in danger; if the angle is 90 degrees or greater, you are signaling to your brain that you are safe.

Stress Pose: hunched and contracted

Empowered Pose: upright and dignified

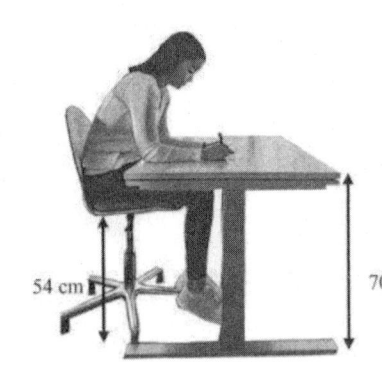

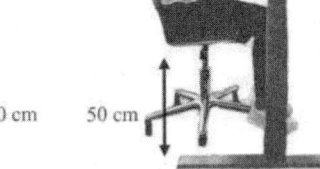

54 cm   70 cm   50 cm   85.5 cm

This image appeared in the following study: Awad, S., Debatin, T., & Ziegler, A. (2021). Embodiment: I sat, I felt, I performed – Posture effects on mood and cognitive performance. *Acta Psychologica*. *218*. Article 103353. DOI: 10.1016/j.actpsy.2021.103353.

If you are feeling stressed out while doing your law school reading, it is extremely likely that you are unconsciously hunched and constricted into a "stress pose" in that moment. So when you feel stressed out, pause for a split second and ask yourself whether your posture is hunched and constricted. When you (likely) notice that it is, simply shift into a more open and confident posture that produces at least a 90-degree angle between your spine and pelvis. Feel a sense of power and dignity running through your body, rather than a sense of bracing and constriction. And then get back to your reading – with the upgraded emotions and cognition that await you.

You will notice that your facial expression and bodily posture are often synchronized. So when you are stressed, both your face and your body simultaneously go into a tight, constricted position – which exponentially increases your stress levels. So in moments of stress, notice the constriction of *both* your face and your body – and then simultaneously convert them both into empowered, confident poses. You'll have executed two techniques for the price of one!

Tool 3

Movement: Micro-Exercise Every 3–4 Hours*

"Me thinks that the minute my legs begin to move my thoughts begin to flow, as if I had given vent to the stream at the lower end and consequently new fountains flowed into it at the upper."

— Henry David Thoreau

Have you ever watched a wildlife documentary on the Discovery Channel or National Geographic where a tiger is hunting a deer? The deer is desperately fleeing the tiger, and the tiger is narrowing the gap with every step. Somehow, the deer miraculously escapes the tiger and lives to see another day. What is the one thing every deer in that situation will do the moment it gets to safety?

Shake. Yes, shake. It will do a full-body shake to release the stress from the traumatic experience. Then it will likely rest, but it will not be able to rest until it removes the stress that flooded its system.

If any of you own a dog, think of the last time you were taking your dog for a walk when an aggressive dog in the neighborhood lunged at her, spurring one of those intense barking stand-offs where both dogs are simultaneously lunging at each other and being pulled back by their respective leashes. After the other dog finally relents, your dog takes a few steps, notices she is in the clear, and then does a full-body shake. She then looks completely calm, as if the incident never occurred, before joyfully trotting along to her next experience in life.

---

* This tool involves bodily movement. If you have a physical limitation or condition that restricts bodily movement, please feel free to modify the recommendations in this section according to your own needs.

Why do both your dog and the deer immediately shake after a stressful event? Because they know instinctively – *without even reading the scientific studies** – that stress is held at the cellular level and is released through bodily shaking.

In fact, virtually every mammal in the animal kingdom uses bodily shaking or movement to release stress. Except we humans. Why don't we? Because using this instinctual stress-negator probably would not be good for our reputation in society.†

Say you get cold-called in Contracts class with the following question: "What is the central issue addressed by the court in *Adams v Lindsell*?" You suddenly feel your stomach drop, and a rush of stress floods into your system. But instead of immediately attempting to answer the question, you stand up, push your chair a few feet away, and then launch into a ferocious, full-body shake – flailing your limbs in every possible direction while erratically whipping your head left-to-right and up-to-down at warp speed. You do this for a full 10 seconds, then you stop, pull your chair back to its original position, calmly sit down, and confidently state, "The central issue presented by *Adams* is whether an expiring written offer is deemed legally accepted at the time the written acceptance is placed in the mailbox by the offeree, or at the time it is received by the offeror."

Although this frenzied shaking would be a prudent thing to do before answering the question in order to reduce your stress and improve the quality of your thinking while you are on call, it is likely something you would never do. The reality is that we, as a species, have chosen to prioritize the appearance of calmness over the actual experience of calmness. If you wildly shook and flailed around before answering the question, you

---

* We did not mean to imply that your dog is not well read or is somehow unscientific. We just meant to acknowledge her innate wisdom in knowing how to rapidly release stress.

† The rest of the mammalian kingdom not only releases stress differently than humans, but also gets triggered into stress only when facing an attack or physically threatening act. So they tend to suffer from stress-related health conditions at infinitesimal rates, far lower than do humans. For a deeper understanding of the biology and physiology of the stress response and of the differences between humans and other species' relationship to stress, we recommend *Why Zebras Don't Get Ulcers*, by Stanford neurobiologist Robert Sapolsky, originally published in 2004 and widely considered the landmark book on the science of stress.

would undoubtedly feel calmer inside for the entire time you were on call, but you would be perceived by the professor and your colleagues as a maniac. So we elect to sacrifice our own well-being and clarity of thought in order to protect our reputation and convey the appearance of calmness and sanity. It is a simple exchange we make constantly throughout our day and life.*

Our society has nevertheless sanctioned one particular form of visceral movement as "acceptable" and "normal": exercise. Apparently running in place for 20 straight minutes on a moving ramp that literally prevents you from traveling anywhere is considered totally "sane" (although members of most indigenous tribes might have a different impression upon seeing you exerting all of that effort on a treadmill only to remain completely stationary). We all know that, in addition to improving physical health, exercise improves mental, emotional, and cognitive health. The science conclusively proves that exercise decreases stress, reduces symptoms of anxiety and depression, increases energy and vitality, reduces fatigue and lethargy, improves mood and happiness, and enhances focus and overall cognitive functioning.[116]

Yet most law students tend to be highly sedentary. They struggle to find time to exercise regularly, and if they do exercise regularly, they tend to spend the rest of the day sitting at a desk – both during class and while studying. The vast majority of law students we meet across the country tell us how fatigued they feel throughout the day. They also tell us how sedentary they are in a typical day. This is no coincidence.

In terms of the brain-body feedback loop, what message do you think we are sending to our brain when we are highly sedentary throughout the day? Answer: We are passively sitting in our cave and hence do not require energy! Again, the brain is the "loyal messenger" who is observing our use of our body in real time to determine how to deploy its various neurochemical assets most beneficially. If we are highly sedentary, we are

---

* The practice of deliberate shaking has recently become formalized into a therapeutic technique, titled "Tension and Trauma Releasing Exercises" (aka "TRE") by David Berceli, Ph.D. Although in its infancy, the emerging scientific research suggests that TRE can help reduce stress, increase resilience, improve mood, and elevate quality of life.[115]

signaling to the brain that we do not require high levels of energy; if we are physically active, we are signaling to the brain that we are in need of energy to execute our various actions.

So we can use this simple hack to trick the brain into spiking our energy levels throughout the day: Every three hours (or four hours max), do 30 to 60 seconds of "micro-exercise" that leads to some shortness of breath and elevation of heart rate. For example, 60 jumping jacks, 20 pushups, walking up three flights of stairs rather than taking the elevator, 45 seconds of planking, two rounds of vinyasa flow (such as Surya Namaskar) if you do yoga, 10 deep lunges, 30 seconds of visceral shaking, or any other micro-exercise you prefer.

The key is that it needs to speed up your breathing and heart rate. If this happens, then you are guaranteed to experience three physiological benefits from this simple act: (1) reduced cortisol (nothing burns cortisol faster than exercise, and the stockpiling of cortisol elevates both your baseline stress levels and your baseline fatigue levels); (2) increased oxygenation of the blood (you are getting a spike of oxygen into your entire blood stream, which elevates your energy levels and makes you feel more vibrant); and (3) flooding of oxygenated blood into the brain (which boosts alertness, attention, and mental clarity).

Several meta-analysis studies, which each rely upon dozens of underlying studies over the course of many years, have found that even a single, short burst of exercise improves energy, mood, and cognitive functioning.[117] Moreover, cutting-edge studies have shown that even ultra-short sessions of movement lead to many of these beneficial effects. For example, one study found that one minute of stair climbing (which can be done in the typical law school or apartment building, *as long as you bypass the elevator!*) improved the participants' cognitive performance on a task-switching exercise, as compared to their scores before the stair climbing. "In addition," found the study, "following the stair climbing participants reported feeling more energetic, less tense, and less tired." The control group did not experience a change in their mood, energy levels, or cognitive performance over that same stretch of time.

MOVEMENT: MICRO-EXERCISE EVERY 3-4 HOURS

Another study found that a short session on the stationary bike, unlike the control condition, led to enhanced alertness and energy, as well as improved working memory, among the participants.[118] Even a 10-minute, brisk walk outside has been shown to improve mood and energy activation.[119] In fact, a mere 2-minute session of walking or stationary biking has been shown to increase learning abilities and working memory in the period that follows.[120] In short, even an isolated and extremely short session of movement can cause marked energetic, emotional, and cognitive benefits.

We know that when you are exhausted and grinding your way through your reading, the *last* thing you want to do is get up to do something physical. Just thinking about it might sound painful to you. But the ROI is so very high that we believe you will quickly see it is worth the 30–60 seconds of discomfort every 3–4 hours. By adding this simple practice throughout your day, you will be consistently injecting energy into your neurobiological system, hacking your brain into reducing lethargy, and spiking your cognition.

Tool 4

Study Breaks: Make Sure They Are *Non-Intellectual*

"The paradox of relaxation is the renewal of the mind, rekindling of spirit, and revitalizing of strength."

— Lailah Gifty Akita

Say you have been doing your Civ Pro reading for two straight hours and come to a natural pause when you finish that assignment. You decide to take a break. It's 6:35 pm, so you determine you will take a 25-minute break until 7:00 pm – and then start your Torts reading for the night. You have been working hard since class ended, and you are excited for your precious 25-minute break.

What activity do you do during your short break? Most likely one of the following five – which we have found are five of the most common activities law students (and, really, all humans) engage in during their short breaks from studying or working: (1) web-browsing a favorite website; (2) scrolling through social media; (3) texting friends or family; (4) emailing friends or family; and (5) in-person socializing (chatting with colleagues in the law library, friends, or housemates.)

And why do you engage in these activities? Because they are all emotionally satisfying. But there is one problem with them – they are all *cognitively depleting*. Unattuned to this reality, you decide to spend your 25-minute break perusing your favorite political website. You click on an enticing article covering a decision or policy position taken by a politician you dislike, and you begin reading.

Tell us, what does this activity remind you of? Oh yes, law school reading! You know, that thing you do *all* the time, and that you are (supposedly) trying to take a break from in this moment. But you surge ahead, engaging your reading comprehension faculties and firing up your high-level cognition. As you read, your brain is unconsciously making both objective assessments (this assertion is "true" or "false") and normative assessments (this position is "unjust" or "just" or has "terrible" or "wonderful" public policy implications). Your memory formation faculties are firing on all cylinders as you soak up every detail and store it in your short-term memory and then convert it into your long-term memory.

Upon reading a disingenuous quotation from the politician you despise, you are triggered into outrage and stress. Your brain then taps into its memory retrieval system, observing that this very politician expressed an inconsistent position three months ago on a different issue when it suited him/her. Your brain then does another shift and launches you into a hypothetical future conversation with your crazy uncle, who somehow adores this toxic politician. Your brain rattles off the three points you would make to expose your uncle's misguided political positions. And even more – your marvelous (it really is!) brain then activates its highest-level executive thinking, pondering whether there is anything you can do to curtail the unjust policy that is being advanced and stewing over other unjust policies that are being advanced in the world.*

What a relaxing and rejuvenating study break! You must feel extremely calm, restored, and ready to focus your mind on Learned Hand's three-part formula for determining whether there is a duty to protect third parties from harm. No? That's right: The activity you engaged in during your study break actually further depleted your cognition and your willpower, even though its theoretical purpose was to enhance these things.

One of the biggest mistakes law students make is that they spend the vast majority of their short study breaks doing highly intellectual activities. Each of the five activities identified above qualifies as that. This happens because we unconsciously conflate two very different types of activities: (1) emotionally satisfying activities; and (2) cognitively rejuvenating activities.

---

* The vast majority of these cognitive processes are occurring unconsciously and rapidly but are nevertheless cognitively exhausting.

STUDY BREAKS: MAKE SURE THEY ARE NON-INTELLECTUAL

Just because an activity is entertaining does not mean it is rejuvenating to the brain.

Engaging in the political website "study break" we have described above would be the equivalent of Lebron James (or whoever your favorite athlete is) coming out of the game to take a recharge break, but instead of sitting on the bench, walking through the tunnel and into an open space to play some casual tennis with his best friend. The 10 minutes of tennis would be highly emotionally satisfying for Lebron. He would be having fun with his best friend, there would be no score kept, and he would no longer be in the view of the 50 million people who pick apart every mistake he makes.

So Lebron's "break" would be emotionally satisfying. But if he went back into the game after those 10 minutes of tennis, would he be physically rejuvenated? Of course not. Because Lebron's primary instrument of performance is his body. Your primary instrument of performance is your brain. You are a "cognitive athlete." So if you use your break to further push your brain and your cognition, you are obviously not going to feel neurologically recharged and optimized at the end of it.

Let's say you have taken a high-cognition break. When you come back to your Torts reading, you notice yourself feeling fatigued, unmotivated, and distracted. Paying attention to the reading feels like pulling teeth. So you say to yourself, "Maybe I'll just read one more article and *then* I will do my Torts reading," or "Maybe I'll just check social media one last time, and *then* I'll do my Torts reading." You wonder why you feel so exhausted and unfocused when you just took a 25-minute break. If you are like your authors when they were in law school (long before they understood this simple science), you may even question if there is something wrong with your brain. "I just took a 25-minute break, I should be alert, motivated and focused. What's wrong with me?!"

We have just described a devastating problem for almost all law students. Yet there is an easy fix. We all must recognize the difference between "emotionally satisfying" and "cognitively rejuvenating" – and then we must dedicate a *portion* of each study break to cognitive rejuvenation. This does *not* mean you should entirely deprive yourself of emotional satisfaction during your study breaks and thus become an isolated law school hermit who exclusively prioritizes cognitive rejuvenation. It just means that you should make an intentional choice about how you want to spend each study break, based on a conscious awareness of the impacts of your choice, and that you ideally dedicate some portion of each break to rejuvenation – even though it will likely be less emotionally satisfying. But you will find yourself more rejuvenated, energized, focused, and productive – which itself creates far more emotional well-being than reading a seventh political article in the afternoon.

So if you take a 25-minute break, perhaps you spend the first 20 minutes doing an emotionally enjoyable but cognitively depleting activity – but then you spend the last five minutes doing a cognitively rejuvenating but emotionally less satisfying activity. Even that five minutes of cognitive rejuvenation will make a material difference in your focus and productivity in the subsequent period. But more importantly, consistently carving out that five minutes will start to compound over time, and your baseline levels of exhaustion and distractibility will start to lower. And, if you instead divide your 25-minute break into 15 minutes of cognitive depletion and 10 minutes of cognitive rejuvenation, you will notice an even larger benefit.

EXAMPLES OF COGNITIVELY REJUVENATING ACTIVITIES

The obvious question becomes: what activities induce cognitive rejuvenation? Well the short answer is any activity during which your analytical and intellectual thinking is not being used. A short-hand tip is to try to avoid activities involving the two "Ls" – "language" and "logic." If the activity centers on the use of language (e.g., reading, speaking, texting, crossword puzzles, playing Wordle or other language-based games, or doing anything else that turns on the use of language), it will not be cognitively rejuvenating. Similarly, if the activity involves the application of logic (e.g., strategizing, planning, problem solving, scheduling, comparing, etc.), it will not be cognitively rejuvenating.

If, however, the activity does not center upon either language or logic, it will probably be cognitively rejuvenating.

Some examples of cognitively rejuvenating activities that can be done in short spurts include meditation, stretching, breathing exercises, a short walk outside, playing a musical instrument, listening to music (unless you are simultaneously analyzing the details of the lyrics), drawing, doodling, adult coloring books, watching YouTube videos that don't involve language or logic (e.g., adorable animal videos), petting or cuddling your cat or dog, looking at a plant or tree through the window or up close, deliberately daydreaming (where you give yourself permission to just let your mind wander wherever it wants to go for a few minutes), imagining a beautiful sunset or terrain, playing Tetris or other spatial manipulation games (that don't involve language), recalling a wonderful memory or life experience, or any other activity that is not *analytical* in nature. Several of these activities are elaborated upon elsewhere in this book.

Keep in mind, though: When engaging in these activities during short breaks, do not get caught up in whether you are "good" at them (or even whether you are "enjoying" them). Instead, remind yourself you are doing them to rejuvenate and optimize your analytical thinking when you get back to work. So if your drawing is not going to end up in the Louvre, or if your musicality is not going to win you a Grammy, don't let that deter you from doing it!

By spending a few minutes of each study break (or most study breaks) deliberately engaging in non-analytical tasks, you will notice an enhancement in your energy and analytical thinking when you resume your studies. You should feel less lethargic and more focused. And the more you sprinkle in these short non-analytical periods during the day, the more rejuvenated and powerful your analytical thinking will consistently be during your law school work.

Finally, there is a particular, non-analytical activity we highly recommend you do each day that is probably one of your most dreaded experiences: boredom.

BOREDOM IS ELECTRIFYING!

In 1990, a 25-year-old British secretary and researcher for Amnesty International frustratedly endured a four-hour delay on a train ride from Manchester to London, where she lived. As a lover of books, she was rarely seen by friends and family without a novel or some reading material. Yet she somehow did not have a book in her hand on this day, when she needed one most. How would she pass the four hours without anything to read? What an epic wasted opportunity, she thought to herself. Boredom quickly set in. Smart phones had not yet been invented, so there was nothing for her to do but sit there, stewing in the agony of doing nothing and getting nothing accomplished. This was the most intense boredom she had ever experienced.

At some point, though, an interesting image popped into her head. She saw a scrawny boy with brown hair and big round glasses. She then imagined him fighting off evil wizards. She became energized by these ideas, and as the train delay prolonged, she allowed her creative imagery to expand. More details of this boy and his adventures unfolded. By the time her train finally arrived at her stop, she had experienced several waves of unprecedented creativity, and she had formed the essence of what she believed could be an actual book. She exited the train, rushed to her apartment, and typed up several pages. Harry Potter was born.

It is likely that J.K. Rowling would never have created Harry Potter had she not been stuck in the longest and most painful stretch of boredom of her life. Was this coincidental? Absolutely not. Well-established science shows that when the brain is placed into a state of boredom, a *cognitive craving* is ignited for creativity, engagement, and productivity. Neuroscientists refer to the state of boredom as "relaxed dissatisfaction" because the brain simultaneously experiences relaxation and rejuvenation, on the one hand, and dissatisfaction and hankering for stimulation, on the other hand. This rare neurological state primes us for elevated cognition when the boredom ends. Boredom is the soil out of which heightened cognition blossoms. So even though boredom is not fun (by definition), it electrifies the brain.

In one study, 80 participants were broken into two groups of 40. One group was asked to copy phone numbers from a phone directory for 15 minutes (yawn!) to stimulate boredom, while the other group (the control group) was allowed to keep themselves

STUDY BREAKS: MAKE SURE THEY ARE NON-INTELLECTUAL

entertained during the same 15-minute period.[121] At the end of the 15 minutes, both groups took a well-established scientific test of creativity that involves trying to think of as many possible alternative uses of two items, for example, two cups. The 40 participants who were primed into boredom thought of a significantly larger number of alternative uses, and their alternative uses were also vastly more creative.

In a second study, the same researchers wanted to see if making the boring task of copying numbers *even more boring* would further enhance creative thinking.[122] So they broke the participants into three groups – a control group that was entertained for 15 minutes, a second group that was primed into boredom through the same copying exercise as in the prior study, and a third group that was primed into even greater boredom by just reading the phone numbers for 15 minutes – without even copying the numbers on a separate page. Just staring at an endless list of phone numbers for 15 straight minutes without at least being able to copy the information elsewhere is the height of boredom. The three groups then performed the creative thinking test. As hypothesized by the researchers, the "regular" boredom group significantly outperformed the entertainment group, and the "super" boredom group substantially outperformed the "regular" boredom group. So the state of boredom induced far greater creative thinking than the state of entertainment. And the more intense the boredom, the greater the creativity.

Another study found that boredom increases problem-solving abilities.[123] Researchers primed half of the participants into a state of boredom by having them sort beans by color for 30 minutes. There was a large bowl of red and green beans plus two empty bowls, and participants were asked to use one hand to put the red beans in one bowl and the green beans in the other bowl. *Snooze fest!* The other half of participants were given 30 minutes to engage in a fun art project involving paper, beans, and glue. After the 30 minutes, all participants were given a problem to solve: they were two hours late to an important work meeting and had to come up with feasible and justifiable explanations that accounted for their tardiness without offending their work colleagues or making themselves look bad. The boredom group significantly outperformed the art group based on assessments of the explanations by "blind" graders (who did not know which group each participant belonged to). Boredom caused the participants' brains to more effectively problem-solve a real-world problem, compared to the participants who were entertained by the enjoyable art project.

Neuroscientist and professor of cognitive science at Rensselaer Polytechnic Institute, Dr. Alicia Walf, explains that when we are bored, the brain's default mode network is activated. This is a set of interacting brain regions that are active during passive rest and mind-wandering. At the same time, the brain's dorsal attention network, which is a set of interacting brain regions that are active during high-focus and analytical cognitive task performance (such as reading cases, briefing, outlining, memorizing, etc.), is deactivated.[124] In other words, when we put our brain into even a short window of boredom, we are overriding the intensely analytical thinking that typically dominates our day, and we are providing our brain a much-needed break from that sort of cognitive performance. The default mode network takes over while the dorsal attention network restores and rejuvenates. By the time we complete the short period of boredom, the brain regions responsible for our high-level analytical thinking (and necessary for law school success) have been replenished and primed for enhanced performance. So from a neuroscientific perspective, one of the best things we can do to amplify our "law school thinking" is to give ourselves short periods of boredom.

Very few law students ever experience even brief moments of uninterrupted boredom. Whenever we feel a jolt of boredom, we immediately reach for our smart phone, which provides an unlimited well of boredom-killing apps and activities. None of us enjoys feeling bored (*does anyone list "boredom" as one of their favorite hobbies in their online dating profile?*), so the moment we feel even a hint of boredom in life, we frantically fill the space with a nugget of stimulation or entertainment. Unfortunately, this causes us to be deprived of the rich cognitive and academic benefits of boredom.

So we invite you to begin introducing boredom into your life with a simple daily "Boredom Exercise." You can create a

STUDY BREAKS: MAKE SURE
THEY ARE NON-INTELLECTUAL   195

calendar entry in your phone (that's putting your phone to good cognitive use) called "Boredom" that pops up once per day. When your boredom reminder chimes, finish whatever you are doing, and then put your phone down, turn away from your laptop or textbook, and then stare at a blank wall for three minutes. What?! Yes, we said stare at a blank wall for three minutes.

Go ahead and try this *now* – and see how it goes. Set your alarm for three minutes, and then stare at a blank wall until the alarm goes off. We will be here when you are done. Have fun! We mean, have boredom!

How was that experience? Boring? We're thrilled to hear that! That means your brain experienced "relaxed dissatisfaction" (and a deactivation of its dorsal attention network). If you were to turn to your challenging law school reading right now (though we would prefer it if you stick with us a bit longer!), your brain is going to function with greater engagement, creativity, and productivity than it would have three minutes ago. If you do this simple practice once per day (annoying as it may be), you will be giving your brain critical rejuvenation and motivation to enhance its performance.

Tool 5

Phone: Is Your Smart Phone Making You Dumb?

"It is okay to own a technology, what is not okay is to be owned by technology."

— Abhijit Naskar

Let's face it: we are all *addicted* to our smart phones. If you doubt this statement, we invite you to leave your smart phone at home all day tomorrow when you go to campus. Did you feel that sudden panic in your gut?? That's your addiction talking!

Smart phones are obviously extremely useful in life, in law school, and in the legal profession these days. They allow us to handle a variety of law school tasks from afar, to instantly look up information that previously required an entire law library, and to communicate with friends, family, and law professors on the fly. Once you are a lawyer, your smart phone will allow you to be more responsive to clients and handle urgent work matters while "out and about," rather than chained to a desk like so many lawyers of the past. In short, smart phones can be a major law school and communication optimizer – increasing our efficiency, freedom, and autonomy.

However, as with any good thing, excess can actually undermine the very benefits the good thing is designed to achieve. The average person in the U.S. checks his or her smart phone between 150 and 262 times per day (depending on the study). So that means we are checking our phones every four to six minutes throughout the entire day. (Before starting the next paragraph, you may want to quickly check your phone!)

Have you ever stood in line at the grocery store and noticed you have repeatedly checked your email every minute or two without even thinking about it? Have you ever been working on a lengthy writing assignment on your laptop and realized you keep pausing your writing in order to reach for your phone? How about during a phone call with a friend, or during a law school class: Do you ever find your attention pulled away from the discussion at issue, so you can covertly check your phone? If you are a typical human being, the answer to each of the above questions is almost certainly: "Yes!" (By the way, extra points if you, like your authors, are ever guilty of checking your phone on the walk from your home computer to the bathroom. Really?! We can't even walk *15 steps* without neurotically checking our phone?)

The problem for the vast majority of law students (and humans) is that they do not control their phone; *their phone controls them.* Rather than *strategically* using their phone to accomplish more in law school and life, they *mindlessly* and *impulsively* use their phone throughout the day. This leads to major impairments in productivity, efficiency, and overall law school success. And why is that? For two primary reasons: (1) our smart phones lead to excessive task switching while we are doing our law school work; and (2) the mere sound and visibility of our smart phone impairs our cognition during law school work.

TASK-SWITCHING HINDERS OUR COGNITIVE PERFORMANCE

Let's first address reason number one. Many law students like to believe they are good at "multitasking." While working their way through their law school reading on a typical evening, they are bouncing back and forth between their reading assignment and the various irresistible temptations perpetually offered by their phone, such as text messages, emailing, web-browsing, and a variety of social media apps, from Tik-Tokogram to FacialBook.*

The problem with "multitasking" is that it is not a real thing. (Which is why we put that word in quotation marks.) Although we can walk, chew gum, and think about that criminal law doctrine simultaneously, modern neuroscience has proven

---

* Please forgive us if we are not remembering the correct names of these apps. If you have any complaints about our background research, please log into your Twitter account and send a "chirp" to the publisher of this book.

that the human brain cannot *simultaneously* perform two tasks that involve executive or high-level thinking. So when we believe we are "multitasking," what we are really doing is rapidly switching back and forth between tasks. We are not "multitasking"; we are "task-switching."

If you doubt us and still believe you are a multitasker, we hereby extend the following challenge to you. Right now, please think of the three most important emails you need to send out later today *and simultaneously* try to recall the elements of the most recent criminal law case you read. Whoops! Can't do it, can you? That's ok, it's just how the human brain works. Of course, your brain can think of the three most important emails you need to send out later today, *or* it can think of the elements of the most recent criminal law case you read. But it cannot do both cognitive tasks simultaneously. If it tries to do both at the same time, it will be rapidly oscillating between the two tasks, in a way that may feel as if you are somewhat multitasking. But the truth is, you are rapidly task-switching.

As explained by Dr. Anthony Wagner, the Chair of Stanford University's Psychology Department, and one of the world's foremost experts on the neuropsychology of learning, memory, and cognitive performance, "[M]ultitasking is almost always a misnomer, as the human mind and brain lack the architecture to perform two or more tasks simultaneously. By architecture, we mean the cognitive and neural building blocks and systems that give rise to mental functioning. . . . To this end, when we attempt to multitask, we are usually switching between one task and another. The human brain has evolved to single task."[125]

The problem with task-switching is that it is a productivity, time, energy, and performance *killer*. You know this at an instinctual level. Say we were to offer you one million dollars if you scored 90% or higher on a 30-minute test, but we gave you two options to take the test: (a) 30 uninterrupted minutes; or (b) 45 total minutes in which you work on the test in five-minute increments (for six total increments), with each increment separated by a three-minute forced break of texting and emailing. Both options would involve 30 total minutes of testing time, but with the latter option, you would be alternating between five minutes of testing and three minutes of phone time for the entire 45-minute window. Which option would you select if a million dollars were on the line?

Option (a)! Sorry to put words in your mouth, but we were extremely confident you were going to say that! The reason you went with this option (assuming you did) is because you have an innate understanding that you will perform faster and better in an uninterrupted work block than in a work block of equal total duration that is broken up by secondary cognitive tasks. Yet most law students, in practice, go with the equivalent of option (b) throughout the entire day: they break up every hour into a large collection of separate cognitive tasks, which requires continual task-switching every hour of the day.

The science shows that every time we switch from the primary task to a secondary task and then back to the primary task, the brain incurs "task switch costs." According to Dr. Wagner, "[a] switch cost is a reduction in performance accuracy or speed that results from shifting between tasks. A rich body of research in psychological science has documented that the behavioral costs of task switching are typically unavoidable: individuals almost always take longer to complete a task and do so with more errors when switching between tasks than when they stay with one task." Dr. Wagner explains that brain scan studies validate that task-switching unduly taxes the brain, leading to neurological inefficiencies, attention depletion, and resource allocation problems.

The two primary "task switch costs" that occur every time we task switch are resumption inefficiencies and attention residue. A resumption inefficiency is the loss of neurological resources and performance time resulting from our brain's attempt to recalibrate back to the primary task. Attention residue is the reduction in focus and attention on the primary task that prolongs after the task-switch due to our brain's inability to fully detach from the demands or implications of the secondary task.

Say you are drafting a lengthy brief for your Legal Research & Writing class. You are continually feeling the "itch" to check your phone, so every few minutes, you pull away from the brief, quickly check texts and emails, and then return to the brief. Each time you return to the brief, you incur resumption

PHONE: IS YOUR SMART PHONE MAKING YOU DUMB?

inefficiencies, as your brain burns valuable cognitive resources attempting to reorient back to the brief's nuances. Your brain rapidly (and unconsciously) processes a laundry list of key factors the moment you return to the brief: What point was I writing about when I left to check my phone? What are the primary goals of this section of the brief? How do the goals of this section relate to or advance the overall goals of the brief? What cases was I about to cite? When should I cite those cases? And in what order? What guidance did the professor provide during class that may be applicable to this section of the brief? What mistakes did I make in my last writing assignment that I want to avoid in this section of the brief?

Make no mistake about it, just because you are not consciously processing these inquiries does not mean they are not occurring at your "System 1" level. They are. And they are burning valuable cognitive resources that you desperately need to execute this complex writing assignment efficiently and proficiently. The more you task-switch during this stretch of writing, the more you bleed out your brain's limited resources, and the more inefficient and impaired your cognitive performance becomes.

In addition to the resumption inefficiencies that occur every time you task switch, you are also incurring attention residue after each task switch. Each time you jump back from your phone to your brief, a part of your brain is still focused on and attached to whatever you just experienced on your phone. So you are now working on your brief again, yet part of your attention and cognition is being misdirected (albeit unconsciously) to what you just read or processed on your phone.

Your unconscious mind may be spiraling around such topics as: Why did it take that person so long to reply to my text? Why do I always seem to reply more quickly to them than they reply to me? Oh boy, I really need to call my grandma! Should I have added another attachment to that email I just sent? Was that the best attachment to have sent in the first place? Should I have edited it first? I wonder what their response will be. That reminds of that related email I need to send. Why haven't I gotten to that yet?! Oh right, in order to send that email, I first have to confirm certain information, which is going to be so boring and annoying. Do I really need to do that before responding to the email? Why is a simple email so complicated and overwhelming?!

This is how the mind works.

And modern research shows that these sorts of internal dialogues – which are triggered with each task-switch we conduct – materially impair our cognitive performance on the primary task we are working on. So even though you are back working on the brief, part of your attention and neural processing is being misdirected back to your texting and emailing, all of which reduces the efficiency and proficiency of your brief writing.

Moreover, the more we task-switch throughout the day, the more we wire our brain to be distracted and inefficient *even when we are not task-switching*. A study published by Dr. Wagner and other Stanford scientists in 2009 found that heavy task-switchers are far more easily distracted and far less productive while taking a cognitive test than individuals who generally task-switch less frequently (even though none of the participants task-switched during the particular test).[126] In other words, excessive task-switching not only has negative ramifications each time we task-switch, but also long-term ramifications that harm our overall cognition.

Because task-switching reduces the quality and speed of our cognitive performance on the primary task, it is important to create a tangible system that will reduce the amount of task-switching we perform throughout the typical law school day. Before we discuss how to establish such a system, let us explore the secondary reason our smart phones impair our cognition and law school performance.

THE SOUND AND SIGHT ARE *IRRESISTIBLE!*

In the Greek epic, *The Odyssey*, a set of dangerous creatures, the Sirens, were infamous for using their irresistibly enchanting singing and beauty to lure passing sailors to their island, only to shipwreck and kill the sailors when they drew near. Well aware in advance of the dangers of the Sirens' deadly charm, the protagonist Odysseus instructs his crew to tie him to his ship's mast and orders them not to release him, however ferocious his demands to be released become. As a result of this plan, Odysseus is able to experience the intoxicating sounds and vision of the Sirens without succumbing to his own death. He knew he could not resist these magnetic temptations without physical restraint.

In our modern society, the sounds and sights of our smart phone can be nearly as alluring. And nearly as destructive to our cognitive viability. In fact, the research reveals that unlike the Sirens, our smart phones can capsize us through their mere sounds and sights, without any subsequent attack.

In one study, participants filled out registration forms that asked them to provide their cell phone number, among other information.[127] Each participant was then assigned to one of three groups, provided their own testing room, and given a cognitive test that required focused attention. The researchers' interns in the back room then surreptitiously sent text messages or made phone calls to certain participants at pre-designated times (using the cell phone number the participant provided in the registration form). One group of participants received text messages, the second group received phone calls, and the third group received neither. The researchers monitored whether the participants touched or interacted with their smart phones with each "buzz," "chime," or "ring." The majority of the participants did not touch or actively engage their phone in response to the notifications. But when they did, each such notification was specifically noted and later assessed by the researchers.

The study found that in the period that followed each notification, the participants' cognitive performance plummeted, even when they did not touch or look at their phones. "We found that cellular phone notifications alone significantly disrupted performance on an attention-demanding task, even when participants did not directly interact with a mobile device during the task," explained the study. "Although these notifications are generally short in duration, they can prompt task-irrelevant thoughts, or mind-wandering, which has been shown to damage task performance." So even if we resist the urge to check our smart phones, the mere sound of the device can impair our cognitive performance.

Interestingly, the study found that the impairment in test performance from merely hearing the notifications was equivalent to the impairment from actively checking one's phone upon hearing the notifications. "The magnitude of observed distraction effects was comparable in magnitude to those seen when users actively used a mobile phone, either for voice calls or text messaging." That's right, the mere "ding," "chime," or "ring" of the phone caused cognitive performance to drop to levels comparable to when the participants began using their phones after the notification.

In another study, researchers planted an alleged "participant" in a mock classroom whose smart phone periodically rang while the larger group of real participants took rapid memory tests as they learned new information.[128] The researchers found vast differences in the participants' cognitive performance in the periods after the ring versus during longer windows of silence, concluding, "[T]he presence of a ringing cell phone in the classroom led to significant disruption in students' memory for information presented while the cell phone was ringing." Even though it was not their own phone that was ringing, the results "clearly demonstrated that cell phone rings disrupted cognitive performance." If our learning and memory are impaired from the sound of a stranger's smart phone, one can only imagine the extent of the impairment from the sound of our own smart phone.

Although the mere sound of our smart phone can hamper our cognition, is it possible that the mere sight of our smart phone can also impair it? It would seem inconceivable that just having the phone next to us while working, without hearing it or using it in any way, could hamper our cognition. Well, actually, this is precisely what the science proves.

In a creative study designed to assess this very issue, researchers from McCombs School of Business at the University of Texas at Austin provided participants with a series of cognitive tasks to perform, and each participant performed half of the test with her/his smart phone on her/his desk and the other half of the test with the smart phone stowed out of sight.[129]

PHONE: IS YOUR SMART PHONE MAKING YOU DUMB?

In order to induce this condition and protect the integrity of the study, the researchers informed the subjects they should keep their smart phone on the desk and face-down for half of the test in case using the phone might be helpful to answering some of the questions in that portion of test. Of course, none of the questions implicated their smart phone in any way, so the participants never once picked up or used their phone during this portion of the test. The phone merely sat next to them, visible in their peripheral vision. During the other portion of the test, the participants were told they would not need their smart phone, and they were asked to stow their phone out of sight.

So how did the participants perform on the two different portions of the test? They performed more productively and more accurately when the phone was stowed, compared to when the phone was in their peripheral vision. A lead researcher on the study, Dr. Adrian Ward, explained that "as the smartphone becomes more noticeable, participants' available cognitive capacity decreases."[130] Ward elaborates, "[Y]our conscious mind isn't thinking about your smartphone, but that process – the process of requiring yourself to not think about something – uses up some of your limited cognitive resources. It's a brain drain."

Another study reached similar results. Half of the participants were asked to silence their smart phone and place it face down on the left side of their desk as they took learning and memory tests. They were also asked not to touch their phone during the test. The other half of the participants were asked to hand the researchers their phone at the outset of the tests, and their phones were placed out of sight behind a thin panel on the researcher's desk. Which group performed better on the tests? You know the answer! That's right, the group that could not see their phones had better learning and memory scores than the group who could merely see their phones, even though they never used them.

So even if you resist the impulse to check your phone while you're doing your law school reading, writing, outlining, or studying, the mere sight – or sound – of your phone can impair your cognitive and academic performance (and emotional well-being).* Asking humans to do important cognitive tasks with their cell phone visible or audible is like asking a monkey to do important cognitive tasks with a delicious banana resting next to him. It's just not fair to the monkey's brain; the mere presence of the banana destroys his focus and cognitive performance, no matter how much he wants to excel on the cognitive tasks.

In light of these scientific findings, there is a clear and obvious solution to protect yourself against the alluring sounds and sights of our modern-day Sirens: *"Silence-Stow-Set."*

DANGER ZONE: If your phone is visible while you do your law school work, prepare for excessive task-switching and reduced productivity!

THE SOLUTION: SILENCE-STOW-SET

To combat the "task switch costs" of our smart phone, and to prevent its mere sight and sound from further impairing our cognition, we need a tangible system of defense. Luckily, there is a simple – and very effective – method for combatting these cognitive hinderances. We call it: "Silence-Stow-Set."

---

* A litany of studies show that frequent smart phone and email checks increase our levels of stress and anxiety.[131]

PHONE: IS YOUR SMART PHONE MAKING YOU DUMB?

Whenever you are doing law school work of any kind, we recommend you:

(1) **Silence** your phone: Either flip the volume to "Silent" or activate the "Do Not Disturb" feature.*

(2) **Stow** it out of sight: Place your phone in a drawer, backpack, or purse, or any other location where you cannot see it while working.

(3) **Set** a time boundary specifying the frequency of your phone checks.

Whether it's every 45 minutes, every 30 minutes, or every 15 minutes, establish a concrete timeframe that dictates when you will be checking your device. If even 15 minutes feels stressful at this point, start with 7 minutes, and then slowly increase that number over the subsequent days and weeks. Once you have established the specific timeframe with which you would like to begin, set your phone alarm for that number of minutes (yes, you can use your phone's alarm to enforce your limit on using your phone!), and simply do not pull your phone out of its cave until you hear the alarm. Then check your phone as you see fit, and when you are done, re-set the alarm and place the phone back into its cave.

Without a pre-established boundary, the Siren-like temptations of the phone are simply too intoxicating to resist. When we ask law students and lawyers across the globe what determines the frequency of their phone checks, nearly 100% say something to the effect of, "I just feel the urge and feel it's time, so I reach for it." There is no system for managing or overriding the incessant impulse to check the phone. So we begin checking the phone every time we feel the urge, which only deepens the brain's addiction to the phone. (See the section below on "Acting Opposite" to better understand the importance of violating the impulse to check our phone.)

---

* If there is an important call or message you are awaiting from a specific person or group of people, you do not need to have your volume on to notice it. Instead, keep your phone on the "Do Not Disturb" mode, and then pre-set into your phone these specific individuals, so that their calls or messages will still "buzz" or "ring" through, while all other incoming communications will remain silenced. Here are simple instructions on how to set these Contacts into your phone: https://www.nytimes.com/2019/01/24/smarter-living/how-to-use-do-not-disturb-iphone.html.

By establishing – and regularly honoring – a time boundary for our phone checks, we protect ourselves against the vast cognitive and academic impairments that unavoidably flow from the unregulated use of our phone. We begin to reduce task-switching and increase uninterrupted work blocks, yielding an enhanced quality and efficiency of cognition. Moreover, we methodically rewire our brain to become less addicted to checking our phone. As a result, we are more mentally, cognitively, and emotionally present in all that we are doing, whether it is listening to a class lecture, reading our homework assignment, studying for finals, or engaging in a deep conversation with our best friend. The constant "itch" of the phone slowly begins to weaken.

So starting today, we urge you to begin the "Silence-Stow-Set" technique. Your focus, attention, productivity and performance will begin to improve. And you will start to build a more empowered, less addictive relationship with your phone.

Although you will immediately begin to realize cognitive and performance benefits from the "Silence-Stow-Set" technique, remember that changing your brain's addiction to the phone is a process, not an instantaneous effect. Importantly, by applying "Silence-Stow-Set," you will be bringing self-awareness, purposefulness, and accountability to your smart phone use. This will likely feel frustrating and difficult at first, since your smart phone is accustomed to ruling you with boundless authority and no limitations. By creating a clear boundary for the first time, you are re-establishing your authority over your phone. You are declaring to yourself (and to your phone!) that you will use your phone only for your benefit, and not for your detriment. You are choosing to prioritize your cognitive functioning and academic performance above your impulses and distractions. This change occurs methodically over time, but the rewards will be bountiful.

Tool 6

Tech Buffer: Build a "Perimeter of Protection" Around the Beginning and End of Your Day

"Great is the art of beginning, but greater is the art of ending."

— Henry Wadsworth Longfellow

One of the best things you can do for your mental health, emotional well-being, and academic momentum throughout the day is to start and end your day without a flood of technology. That is, erect a tech boundary – particularly with your smart phone – protecting the very beginning of the morning and the very end of the evening. Unlike the prior technique, which is about changing your relationship to your phone throughout the day, this technique is specific to the very beginning and very end of your day. (We can already feel your anger bubbling up, but please read on.)

The vast majority of law students (and humans) check their phones first thing in the morning and right before falling asleep. This leads to a litany of adverse consequences. Let's look at the morning and evening windows one at a time.

RISE AND SHINE WITH YOUR SMART PHONE?

Upon peeling open your eyelids in the morning, how many minutes (*or seconds?!*) does it take before you check your phone? For the vast majority of you reading this book, we estimate "immediately" or less than a minute. Countless law students and lawyers we speak with say they use their phone as their alarm, and upon turning off their alarm, they automatically check their phone. Does this *ring* true for you? (We apologize for that awful pun.)

According to a study run by IDC, a global market research firm, about 65% of Americans between the ages of 18 and 44 check their phone as the first thing they do upon waking up.[132] This figure is probably even higher for law students, who fall in the lower segment of this age range. Our anecdotal experience suggests that over 90% of law students check their phone first thing in the morning.

But don't worry, you are not alone. A study by the Braun Research Center and Bank of America found the first thing American adults think of upon waking up is their phone. Immediately thinking of one's phone is more than twice as common as immediately thinking of coffee, and more than 3.5 times as common as thinking of one's spouse or significant other. (Who is our *real* true love in life?)

When we check our phone immediately after waking up, we are choosing to start our day by inundating our brain with an avalanche of information, stressors, obligations, and emotional triggers. This immediately induces our brain's beta brainwaves, which are the fastest and most arousing brainwaves. But the brain is actually designed to gently transition from the delta brainwaves of sleep to theta brainwaves – which is a transitory state between sleep and wakefulness. Theta brainwaves are induced when we are daydreaming, meditating, tapping into intuition, or engaged in peaceful self-perception. We feel relaxed, tranquil, non-analytical, and sometimes a bit groggy. This is how we are meant to begin our day: in a gentle and peaceful mental state that is detached from analytical thinking and strategic processing.

When we check our phone upon waking up, we rob our brain of its natural desire and propensity to start the day with gentle theta processing. Instead, we harshly launch it into beta processing, which is the least gentle, most volatile, and most aroused neurological state. It is as if your brain wakes up in a state of serenity only to have a glass of ice water thrown onto it! The phone forcibly thrusts your brain into a hectic and overactive state that it is not yet ready for. This is a harsh and unkind thing to do to your brain and to your nervous system.

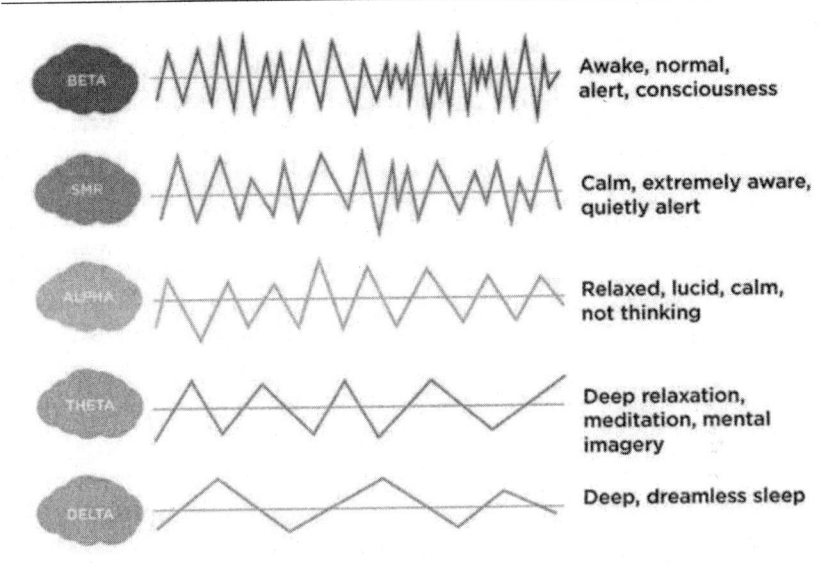

TECH BUFFER: PROTECT THE BEGINNING AND END OF YOUR DAY

BETA	(waveform)	Awake, normal, alert, consciousness
SMR	(waveform)	Calm, extremely aware, quietly alert
ALPHA	(waveform)	Relaxed, lucid, calm, not thinking
THETA	(waveform)	Deep relaxation, meditation, mental imagery
DELTA	(waveform)	Deep, dreamless sleep

Neurofeedback Alliance. https://neurofeedback alliance.org/understanding-brain-waves/.

According to Julie Morgenstern, author of the book, *Never Check Email In The Morning*, when you check your phone first thing in the morning, "[Y]ou'll never recover. Those requests and those interruptions and those unexpected surprises and those reminders and problems are endless."[133] In other words, by checking your phone first thing in the morning, you start your day off with a palpable sense of stress and overwhelm – *before your brain is ready to process it all*. Talk about a self-inflicted wound to your emotional well-being!

Tristian Harris, Google's former Design Ethicist, agrees. "When we wake up in the morning and turn our phone over to see a list of notifications, it frames the experience of 'waking up in the morning' around a menu of 'all the things I've missed since yesterday.'"[134] Harris further explains that this allows the phone to hijack our morning routine – and the detrimental effects ripple throughout our day. That is, in addition to the obvious damage to your morning, starting your day this way can set a negative tone for the entire day – where the foundational anxiety from the morning can permeate the remainder of the day. Just as starting your day with exercise or meditation can set the tone for an emotionally healthier and happier day, starting your day by shocking your nervous system into premature activation can set the tone for a day of emotional disarray.

So rather than beginning your day in this self-sabotaging way, we invite you to begin each day with a window of 10–30 minutes without using your phone or other devices. We recommend 30 minutes, but if that feels too challenging, start with 10 minutes (and slowly build up to 30 minutes, if you'd like). It is extraordinarily unlikely that checking your texts and emails at 7:10am (or 7:30am), rather than 7:00am, will have any adverse effect on your personal relationships or academic success. But protecting that small window will have a vast, positive impact on your nervous system and emotional state. Then, when you eventually check your phone, you will be doing so in a mindful and non-reactive way, and your brain will have been in a theta state for long enough that the same emails, texts, and other triggers will feel less stressful and less overwhelming.

SMART PHONE LULLABY?

Several years ago, an associate attorney at one of the most prestigious and high-stress law firms in the world, Skadden Arps, came to me [*your co-author Jarrett*] for coaching to help him with a very specific and urgent problem. He was suffering from major sleep problems: He had been getting only two to three hours of sleep per night for the last couple of months. Every single night he struggled to fall asleep. But once he fell asleep, he would wake up in the middle of the night thinking about work, often lying in bed for hours before falling asleep again for another short window. He said the sleep deprivation was taking a major toll on his mental health and professional performance. He was delirious throughout the workday, and his resiliency and joy were nose-diving. His brain was not functioning effectively in his work, as most aspects of his cognition were noticeably impaired from the sleep deprivation. He signed up for an 8-session package of telephonic coaching.

During our first session, I learned that he, like many lawyers, was stuck in a cycle of thinking obsessively about his work, including the constant deadlines, the firm's perfectionist standards, and whether he would fail or succeed at the firm. When he tried to sleep, these worries were particularly intrusive

TECH BUFFER: PROTECT THE BEGINNING AND END OF YOUR DAY

and derailed his ability to fall asleep and stay asleep. I sensed that if he was to overcome his major sleep problems, this coaching relationship would require a deep dive into various aspects of his emotional processing and behavioral patterning in life, which would likely span beyond the 8 sessions.

One of the first questions I asked him during our first session was how many minutes before he put his head down to the pillow, on the typical night, did he last check his phone. His answer was "It's the last thing I do before putting my head down. I do one final check of work emails and such, and then I put my phone down and close my eyes." I immediately knew this was an issue. I also asked him how many minutes after waking up in the morning did he first check his phone. Unsurprisingly, he said he turns off the alarm on his phone and then immediately checks his work email. "So a matter of seconds," he said.

During this first session, we explored his relationship to his litany of work stressors and his deep-seated fear of disappointing his boss and of damaging his reputation at the firm. At the end of the session, he agreed to a tangible "self-commitment" for the next week until our second session: He would put his phone onto airplane mode *one hour* before going to bed each night and wait *30 minutes* after waking up to first check his phone each morning. He also agreed not to check his email on his laptop during these protected windows. He originally resisted these suggestions, but ultimately said, "I'm desperate, so I'm willing to try anything for a week." I anticipated that this seemingly small restructuring of his relationship to his phone would take some of the edge off his stress and provide him with some mental "breathing room" to dig deeper into the sleeping issues he was experiencing.

One week later, I began our second session by asking, "How has the last week gone?" To my astonishment, he said: "I'm doing amazing. That first night after our session, I got a decent night's sleep for the first time in forever. Fell asleep pretty quickly, and then got a good chunk of sleep before waking up in the middle of the night, but I actually fell back asleep. I probably got a good 5 hours of total sleep that night. It was a miracle. And I have been sleeping better and better each night since. In fact, last night I think I slept seven hours! I don't think I have slept this well since I joined the firm." He said that not checking his phone or email for the last hour of the night and the first 30 minutes of the morning had completely changed his sleep quality and that he now felt a **"perimeter of protection"** where he could truly disconnect from work and ease into sleep. He thanked me profusely and said he was now "good to go." He did not feel the need for additional coaching, since the sole issue for which he sought coaching was resolved. So I happily returned his payment for the remaining seven sessions.

Let's be clear, this was not a typical situation. It is rare that a single session combined with a single behavioral change eradicates a major problem a client has been dealing with for months. But individuals we coach, as well as law students and lawyers who attend our presentations, regularly inform us that this simple technique of creating a "perimeter of protection" made a material difference in their sleep quality and stress levels. Even recently, the managing partner of one of the top law firms in the U.S. shared that this simple technique made a significant difference in her mental ease at night and her stress levels during the day.

A large body of research explains why. In a 2020 study published in the journal of *Nature and Science of Sleep*, researchers assessed the evening smart phone usage and consequent sleep patterns of 1,925 university students aged 17 to 23.[135] The study found that nearly 90% of the students regularly used their smart phones in bed after turning off the lights, with only four percent of the students enabling their phone's blue light filter while doing so. According to the researchers, the "supreme finding of this study was that using a mobile [phone] for at least 30 minutes after the lights have been turned off (without a blue light filter in mobile) correlates with poor sleep quality, daytime sleepiness, sleep disturbances and increased sleep latency." In other words, university students who spend at least 30 minutes on their phone after turning off the bedroom lights experience an increase in *every* category of sleep problem. It takes them longer to fall asleep (sleep latency), they wake up more often in the middle of the night (sleep disturbances), the depth of their sleep is lower when they are

TECH BUFFER: PROTECT THE BEGINNING AND END OF YOUR DAY

actually sleeping (sleep quality), and they feel sleepier during the day (daytime sleepiness).*

Similar results were found in a study of adults ages 18 to 94 in Belgium.[137] Although only 60% of these individuals kept their smart phones bedside as they slept (clearly the participants in their 80s and 90s skewed this figure), the study found that "using a mobile phone after lights out was associated with negative sleep outcomes," including "poorer sleep quality and more insomnia and fatigue symptoms." For individuals who spent any time on their smart phone after lights out, they were more than twice as likely as individuals who did not use their phone after lights out to struggle to fall asleep and more than three times as likely to wake up in the middle of the night.

Another study of Belgian smart phone users, this time ages 18 to 25, found that bedtime phone use "was related to a considerable decrease in sleep quality."[138] Specifically, the study found that individuals who spent less than 30 minutes on their smart phone after lights out were 3.3 times more likely to experience sleep problems compared to individuals who spent no such time on their phone; individuals who spent 30 to 60 minutes on their phone after lights out were 6.0 times more likely to experience sleep problems; and individuals who spent over an hour on their phone after lights out were 8.9 times more likely to experience sleep problems.

A study of Japanese adolescents reached similar conclusions that bedtime use of smart phones is associated with all forms of sleep problems, from sleep latency, to sleep disturbances, to sleep quality: "Our finding that mobile phone use after lights out was associated with all forms of sleep disturbance, each different in nature, suggests that the use of mobile phones after lights out has various effects on sleep."[139]

Evidence supports various theories for the clear conclusion that bedtime phone use impairs sleep, whether it is the late-night exposure to the blue light emanating from our phones (blue light suppresses melatonin, a hormone released at night that is essential for good sleep because it regulates the sleep-

---

* A study of 532 university students ages 18 to 39 in Norway found that 95% percent of the students used their smart phone in bed after lights out, and further found that the incidence of such smart phone use was associated with impaired sleep.[136]

wake cycle), increased mental processing and cognitive arousal from the information presented by the phone, or enhanced stress and anxiety triggered by the content delivered by the phone. Regardless of the *reason* for the sleep impairment, it cannot be doubted that late night phone use impairs our sleep.

In light of this research, we encourage you to put your phone onto airplane mode at least 30 minutes, and ideally 60 minutes, before you close your eyes for the evening.* This will allow you to spend the final segment of your evening "winding down" mentally and emotionally, so that when you put your head onto the pillow, your brain will be in a state where it can truly let go. And if you use your laptop to watch Netflix or other entertainment at the very end of the night, we recommend only using the laptop for streaming (not to web browse or check social media). We further suggest fully closing your email or opening a separate window for the streaming, to avoid inadvertently noticing your email inbox when you navigate the tabs. Finally, we also recommend using a blue light filter on your laptop.†

By building this "perimeter of protection," you will be ensuring that you end each night and start each morning in a place of mental tranquility and emotional groundedness.

---

* Less than 20% of people who keep their phone bedside while they sleep ever turn their phone to airplane mode.[140]

† You may also reflect on whether you ever experience "Bedtime Revenge Procrastination," a term coined in 2020 by Chinese journalist, Daphne K. Lee. It refers to the phenomenon in which people delay going to sleep to engage in activities and entertainment they don't have time for during the day. It's essentially an act of unconscious rebellion against the lack of personal time or self-care opportunities during the day. "If I'm too stressed or overwhelmed during the day to enjoy some peace and quiet, I'm going to do so at the end of the night!" The problem with this approach is, depending on the person, it can possibly lead to a vicious cycle, where we go to sleep too late as a result of our late-night entertainment, then feel sleep deprived and fatigued the next day, causing us to be less efficient throughout that day, leading us to resort to more bedtime revenge procrastination that evening, which of course leads to a continuation of the cycle. Other people, however, experience rejuvenation the next day even if they get a little less sleep, because that personal time at the end of the night uplifts and replenishes them for the next day, so it is a worthwhile exchange for them. For this reason, bedtime revenge procrastination can harm some people but benefit others. So if you ever do this, perhaps ask yourself if this exchange benefits or harms you. Let that answer guide your future behavior.

TECH BUFFER: PROTECT THE BEGINNING
AND END OF YOUR DAY   217

Moreover, you may be surprised at how much this affects your stress and mood during the many hours you are awake.*

---

* If you find this practice to be difficult or aggravating as you start implementing it, know that these are natural, short-term symptom of rewiring your brain's relationship to your smart phone and other technology. As outlined in detail in Tool #8, "Impulsivity" (see page 237), this sort of behavioral change will slowly cause restructuring of the brain and different emotional responses. But in the beginning, it is uncomfortable, due to your current neurological wiring. It may also be helpful to use the set of behavior change techniques outlined in Tool #10, "Goals & Habits," (see page 255), including "small victory" theory and the other techniques specified.

TOOL 7

MICRO-DECISIONS: ELIMINATE AND SHORTEN SOME

"Energy saved is energy generated."

— Anonymous

In 1998, a psychologist named Roy Baumeister conducted a landmark study on human cognition that made him a giant in the world of psychology.[141] College students who had volunteered for a food taste test in exchange for an extra unit of class credit walked into a room containing ovens that had just baked piping hot chocolate chip cookies, so the aroma of the fresh-baked cookies filled the entire room. The students had been told to refrain from eating any food for at least three hours before the tasting session, so they were nice and hungry upon entering the cookie wonderland. Let the salivation begin! Baumeister then broke the students into three groups. Group 1 was given a plate of chocolate chip cookies that they were told not to eat, as well as a plate of cold radishes that they were told to eat with no limitation. Group 2 was given the same two plates but were told they could eat from whichever plate they preferred. Group 3 was given no food at all. (This was the late 1990s, so *everyone* wanted cookies! Nowadays, many people avoid cookies for health reasons and would be grateful to receive a nutritious radish. But in 1998, being required to eat radishes while others around you are eating fresh-baked cookies was a cruel form of torture.)

Baumeister then stepped out of the room and gave the students five minutes to rate and assess the food they had been assigned to, if any. After the five minutes elapsed, Baumeister returned to the room and provided the students with a cognitive puzzle that was deliberately impossible to solve – unbeknownst to the students. He then recorded how long it took for each group of volunteers to quit on the puzzle. Since it was impossible to solve, everyone would eventually quit – it was just a question of when.

So what did the experiment reveal? On average, the participants from Groups 2 and 3 persisted with the puzzle for over *twice* as long before quitting, as compared to participants from Group 1. And why was this? Because the participants in Group 1 had burned valuable willpower and cognitive energy in attempting to resist the deliciously tempting cookies that sat inches from their nose, depleting the very resources they needed to solve the unrelated complex cognitive puzzle that followed.

Baumeister's new theory was born: Humans have a limited amount of willpower each day, and when we needlessly burn some of that precious fuel on one task, we have reduced attention and willpower for subsequent, unrelated tasks. This phenomenon is now widely referred to as "decision fatigue" or "willpower depletion" (although Baumeister originally called it "ego depletion"). The participants who were provided cookies but prohibited from eating them expended cognitive fuel that the others did not, according to Baumeister, leaving them depleted and more likely to quit the puzzle sooner.

Later studies on willpower depletion reached the same results even when controlling for the possibility that the original results were influenced by the sugar rush, glucose spike, or voluntary emotional withdrawal that may have been induced by the cookie snub. If we needlessly burn our limited willpower and cognitive fuel on small tasks throughout the day, our cognition begins to erode, and we have depleted the willpower and self-control needed to execute more important tasks later in the day.

There have been hundreds of studies published in peer-reviewed journals supporting the existence of willpower depletion. What the studies generally reveal is that with certain limited exceptions,* each and every micro-decision, micro-action, and micro-cognition we commit throughout the day causes a palpable reduction in our willpower and energy, which in turn,

---

* A collection of activities, several of which are outlined in this book, that require an outlay of willpower nevertheless lead to a *net increase* in willpower at the completion of the activity. Examples include certain forms of exercise, meditation, music, art, and various other tools found in this book. But with rare exceptions, each of the activities we perform throughout the day causes a net reduction in our available willpower.

MICRO-DECISIONS: ELIMINATE AND SHORTEN SOME

impairs our cognitive performance on more challenging tasks later in the day.

For example, in a classic study commonly referred to as the "jam study," psychologists from Columbia and Stanford set up an experiment at an upscale grocery store that is known for its extensive selection of niche goods, including roughly 250 varieties of mustard, 75 varieties of olive oil, and over 300 varieties of jam.[142] A tasting booth of jams was set up on consecutive Saturdays that did not fall on a holiday weekend and that were predicted to have a similar flow of costumers. On one Saturday, the researchers offered 24 varieties of jam at the tasting booth, and on the other Saturday they offered only six varieties. On the day of the more extensive offerings, 242 customers interacted with the tasting booth, while 260 customers interacted with the booth on the other day. The researchers hypothesized that a lower percentage of customers would purchase jam when 24 varieties were displayed because reviewing that many options would burn their willpower, which would, in turn, reduce the willpower necessary to make a final purchasing decision.

The hypothesis was confirmed. Only 3% of the customers purchased jam when 24 varieties were displayed, yet a whopping (nearly) 30% of the customers purchased jam when only six varieties were displayed. Importantly, the customers in the two groups interacted with the booth for approximately the same amount of time, so the length of time was not a contributing factor to the contrasting purchasing decisions. This study shows that even when a decision is preceded by a couple of minutes of slightly more stringent cognitive analysis, as opposed to a couple of minutes of slightly less stringent cognitive analysis, our subsequent decision can be significantly affected.

Another study in the consumer purchasing realm found that shoppers leaving IKEA (who were presumably decisionally fatigued from making a large collection of micro-decisions during their perusing) scored much lower on tests measuring their ability to plan for future life events than shoppers arriving at IKEA.[143] That's right, a stroll through IKEA fatigues our brain and makes us far less likely to intelligently plan for the future – an activity that requires attention and energy.

Based on these and other decision fatigue studies, many retail companies now deliberately choose to limit the number of options they offer their customers. They want to avoid fatiguing their customers' brains during the evaluation process in a way that reduces the available energy needed to make the most important decision in the end: whether to purchase the item. Walking away from an item burns far less energy and willpower than internally justifying its purchase.

In another study, university participants in one part of the study were asked to rate how often they had previously used items in a list of products (e.g., certain colored pens, scented candles, popular magazines, colored t-shirts, etc.), while the second group of students was asked to actually make decisions on which of these products to select.[144] Another part of the study involved a different set of students, who either reflected on hypothetical course options for the next semester (the control group) or actually selected which courses they would take among the hypothetical options (the experimental group). The time provided to each group to either reflect or decide was the same.

Across both parts of the study, the students who made actual decisions subsequently performed worse on various tests of willpower and self-control. These tests included taking a cognitive test without succumbing to the distraction of video games and entertaining magazines that the researchers provided the students simultaneously with the test; drinking a beverage that was healthy and nutritious but deliberately bad tasting (a classic test of choosing what is best for us over what feels good!); keeping one's hand in an uncomfortably cold bucket of water in order to earn a prize (another classic test of willpower that measures our willingness to endure discomfort in order to achieve a goal); and giving up on an unsolvable cognitive puzzle (or a solvable but complex puzzle). While most of the "reflect or decide" periods were just 10 or 12 minutes in length, one component of the study found material losses in willpower and self-control from a mere four minutes of decision making.*

---

* You know that dread you feel when you go to a new doctor and the receptionist hands you a clipboard with pages of questions for you to complete about your medical history? That dread results from your awareness that you are about to burn a lot of willpower in a short period of time – even though they are basic questions that you know

MICRO-DECISIONS: ELIMINATE AND SHORTEN SOME

In another study, college students attended a 20-minute networking session with other students where they were broken into clusters of six students and were told at the end whether any of their colleagues wanted to collaborate with them going forward.[145] However, this was a farce, as the collaboration decisions were randomly made by the researchers on a 50/50 basis across the entire population of students: half of the students were told they received no collaboration requests and the other half that they received collaboration requests.

Each student was then given a bowl of 35 mini cookies and told to rate them based on flavor, texture, mouth feel, and several other enumerated criteria. But what the researchers were covertly assessing was whether the students who felt rejected would eat more cookies (due to a reduction in willpower) than the students who felt socially accepted. Consistent with the researchers' expectation, the socially rejected students ate more than double the number of cookies than the socially accepted students. This is one of many studies showing that feeling rejected causes willpower depletion that impairs our ability to exercise self-control over subsequent temptations.

Being mindful of your feelings of rejection and acceptance (both socially and professionally) is important, so you can track whether your self-control reduces after feeling rejected in some way. For example, do you become more distracted by social media, streaming videos, or other entertainment when you are feeling rejected by a friend's text message, a social media post that makes you feel excluded, or a law school or professional opportunity that you desire but do not get? If the answer is "yes" (which it is for the vast majority of us), then you can begin to become consciously aware (i.e., a System 2 awareness) of the heightened risk of succumbing to study distractions when you are feeling rejected or less confident on particular days. With that clear awareness, you can begin to consciously override the temptation, rather than unconsciously succumbing. "We cannot change what we cannot see," as we like to remind you.

In another study, students were instructed to memorize novel pieces of information regarding the anatomy of the human

---

off the top of your head. Indeed, it is not the complexity of the cognition, but its mere occurrence that matters.

eye for 5 minutes.[146] Half of the students had been provided simple willpower-depleting tasks immediately before the five minutes of memorization, while the other half had not.

All of the students were then provided a one-minute distraction task, which consisted of simple arithmetic problems, before being asked to recall as many pieces of information as possible about the human eye. "The ego-depleted participants," explained the study, "performed significantly worse in the knowledge retrieval [i.e., memorization] task than non-depleted participants." Notably, the two groups of students did not perform differently on the simple arithmetic problems, so those problems did not appear to influence the difference in memorization. Thus, a brief expenditure of attention before performing a memorization task can impair our memorization abilities.

Another study found that individuals who engaged in a brief cognitive analysis suffered from greater confirmation bias in a subsequent, unrelated cognitive task. Specifically, they were far more likely to confirm their pre-existing political position after receiving new information that would suggest the need to change, in comparison to individuals who did not engage in the brief, unrelated cognitive analysis before performing the politically related cognitive task.[147]

Finally, we want to mention a study that conducted a review of many prior studies on willpower depletion in the educational context. The researchers in each prior study first subjected one group of students to a short task that depleted cognitive resources (the "depletion condition") and the other group of students to a similarly short task that did not deplete cognitive resources (the "non-depletion condition"). They then subjected both groups of students to a cognitive task that required self-control and willpower to complete.[148] According to the reviewing study, "[i]t has been reliably found [across the collection of prior studies] that in the depletion condition performance in the secondary self-control task is significantly worse than in the non-depletion condition."*

---

* Emerging research is suggesting that will power depletion could be the consequence of an overaccumulation of the excitatory neurotransmitter glutamate in the prefrontal cortex resulting from the initial decision making and cognitive

MICRO-DECISIONS: ELIMINATE AND SHORTEN SOME

So as law students, if we deplete our willpower during the many, brief *non-law school tasks* we perform throughout the day, we are setting ourselves up for impaired self-control and effectiveness in completing the law school tasks that follow. Those seemingly small considerations, ruminations, and decisions you make throughout the day, having nothing to do with law school, can actually affect your willpower and cognitive performance on your law school tasks later in the day. Optimizing your mental health and academic success in law school therefore requires you to mindfully navigate your micro-decisions on matters *unrelated to law school*.*

JUDGES AND DOCTORS PLAGUED BY WILLPOWER DEPLETION

Research has shown that willpower depletion can directly affect how judges dispense justice and how doctors dispense medicine. In a study published in the *National Academy of Sciences* by a team of Israeli and Columbia University psychologists, the question was whether willpower depletion, rather than just the merits of a case, impacts judicial rulings.[150]

The researchers analyzed 1,112 parole rulings over the course of 10 months made by eight judges in the Israeli criminal justice system. What was the number one factor that contributed to whether parole was granted to a convicted criminal, you wonder? Here is a list of factors that were *not* the primary factor in determining whether an inmate was granted parole:

- The gravity of the crime committed
- The unique facts involved in the commission of the crime
- The amount of time served thus far by the inmate
- The inmate's number of prior convictions

---

performance.[149] More research will be needed to better understand the biochemical components of will power depletion, but progress is being made.

* Why do law students dream about car mufflers so often? Because they often wake up *exhausted* due to decision fatigue! (That joke was so horrible that we believe our book contract should have been cancelled by the publisher the moment they read it. Miraculously, the joke made it into this book!)

- The amount of personal responsibility taken by the inmate at the parole hearing
- The inmate's proposed rehabilitation plan
- The race, ethnicity, sex, or religion of the inmate

The number one factor – *by far* – that determined whether parole was granted in any particular case was the ***time of day*** of each parole decision. That's right, it was not the law, or the facts, or recidivism risk, or societal safety, that played the critical role in determining whether an inmate was released on parole. It was the random time of day when each inmate's parole hearing happened to be scheduled.

Each day, the judges conducted three separate parole sessions: (1) the start of the day until the morning break (with the break lasting an average of 38 minutes); (2) after the morning break until the lunch break (with this break lasting an average of 57 minutes); and (3) after the lunch break until the end of the day.

Over the course of the 10 months, parole was granted at a rather consistent rate of about 65% at the beginning of the morning session, with the grant rate then steadily dropping over the course of the morning session until hitting an average of almost 0% just before the morning break. It then rose again to approximately 65% at the outset of the post-break session, before steadily declining over the course of that session to nearly 0% just before the lunch break. After the lunch break, it again spiked to about 65%, and again plummeted to nearly 0% at the very end of the day.

Here is a chart that depicts the grant decisions and time of day (i.e., "ordinal position") for these 1,112 judicial rulings:

MICRO-DECISIONS: ELIMINATE AND SHORTEN SOME

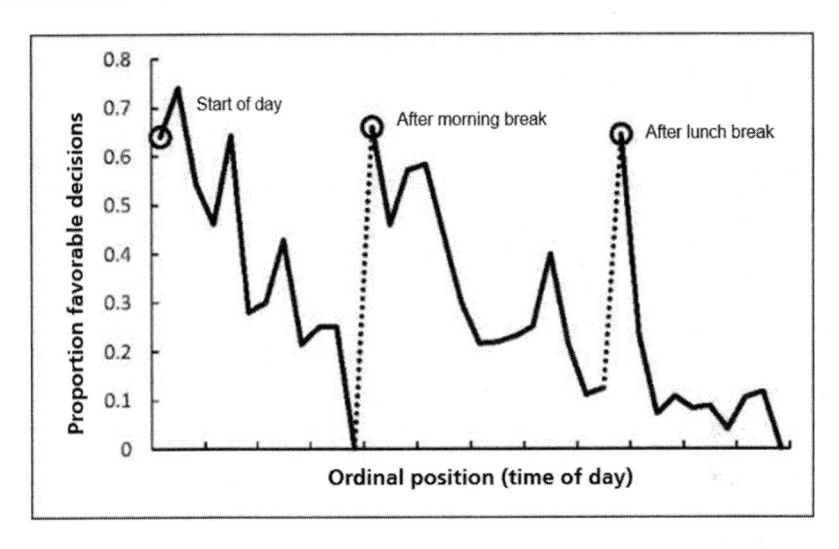

[Figure: Proportion favorable decisions vs. Ordinal position (time of day), with markers at Start of day, After morning break, and After lunch break]

Danziger, S. Levav, J. & Avnaim-Pesso, L. (2011). Extraneous factors in judicial decisions. *Proceedings of the National Academy of Sciences (PNAS) of the United States, 108*(17), 6889–6892. DOI: 10.1073/pnas.1018033108

Because the decision to grant parole requires far more effort, thought, and legal justification than denying parole, the willpower depletion that occurred over the course of the parole sessions led to a diminished reserve of willpower in the judges, which in turn led to impaired decision making and diminished parole grants. The more decision fatigue the judges experienced, the more likely they were to take cognitive "short cuts" by denying parole, rather than exerting the willpower required to make the best decision on the merits.

One of the lead researchers on the study, Jonathon Levav, now a professor at the Stanford Graduate School of Business, explained that the study "shows the consequences of mental fatigue on really important decisions even among excellent decision-makers."[151] These judges were not aware that their own mental fatigue was playing a critical role in their decision-making process. They believed they were making decisions on the merits, but their own internal fatigue was really what was dictating whether they released an inmate into society. "It is really troubling and quite jarring – it looks like the law isn't exactly the law," noted Levav.

Do you believe doctors' medical decisions might also be influenced by their current level of decision fatigue, rather than the medical needs of each patient? If you answered, "Yes," you win a free chest x-ray! In a study published by the American Medical Association in *JAMA Internal Medicine*, researchers assessed whether doctors' antibiotic prescription decisions regarding possible respiratory illness were impacted by the time of day of each appointment.[152] The study analyzed 21,867 prescription decisions by primary care physicians across 23 different medical practices treating patients presenting with symptoms of acute respiratory infections.

At the outset of the study, the researchers explained their hypothesis on the connection between decision fatigue and prescription decisions: "In primary care, prescribing unnecessary antibiotics for acute respiratory infections (ARIs) is a common, inappropriate service. Clinicians may prescribe unnecessary antibiotics – again, the easy, safe option – due to perceived or explicit patient demand, a desire to do something meaningful for patients, a desire to conclude visits quickly, or an unrealistic fear of complications. We hypothesized that decision fatigue, if present, would increase clinicians' likelihood of prescribing antibiotics for patients presenting with ARIs as clinic sessions wore on."

This is precisely what occurred across the 21,867 prescription decisions. The predominant factor in determining whether a prescription was ordered, concluded the study, was how late in the day each patient happened to arrive, as opposed to the respiratory symptoms the patient was experiencing. "We found that primary care clinicians' likelihood of prescribing antibiotics for ARIs increased during clinic sessions, consistent with the hypothesis that decision fatigue progressively impairs clinicians' ability to resist ordering inappropriate treatments." In other words, the later in the day it becomes, and the more prescription decisions the physicians make over the course of the day, the more likely they are to prescribe unnecessary and inappropriate antibiotics to each remaining patient. As elucidated by the study, the decision to deny a prescription requires more willpower and medical analysis than a decision to approve a prescription, leading to an inflated rate of approval over the course of a lengthy shift.

You might be thinking, "Sure, decisions on antibiotics are somewhat important, but certainly decisions on a critically important medical issue such as whether to order surgery could not possibly be impacted by decision fatigue, could they?" If you answered your own question in the affirmative, congratulations, you win a free surgery!

In a study of 848 patient appointments in which eight orthopedic surgeons assessed the need for surgery over the course of 133 separate work shifts spread across three months, researchers hypothesized that as the day progressed, the surgeons' decision fatigue would lead to a reduced frequency of ordering surgery.[153] "Theoretically, decision fatigue should therefore make orthopedic surgeons more likely to postpone their decisions or mak[e] conservative recommendations without thoroughly considering the pros and cons of an operation," said the researchers. "We therefore hypothesized that there would be fewer patients scheduled for operation by doctors who had already seen many patients during their work shift."

This hypothesis was validated by the study. "We found a strong link between the surgeons' decisions to operate and the sequence of patient appointments they face throughout the day: much fewer patients are scheduled for operation by surgeons who are nearing the end of their work shift. We attribute this effect to decision fatigue; that surgeons become more inclined to rely on heuristics and go with the status quo option when tired." Importantly, the objective health symptoms of the individual patients (i.e., the case characteristics and the patient characteristics) were not particularly influential in whether surgery was ordered; it was the timing of their appointment that was pivotal. "Our interpretation of the data is supported by the fact that the sequence of patient appointments was associated with the decision to operate, in the expected direction, but not with case characteristics or individual patient characteristics."

Thus, even when it comes to high-stakes decisions about operating on a person's body, or paroling a person from prison, decision fatigue impairs the cognitive process and the quality of decision making. And as we explored earlier in this segment of the book, the routine decisions we make throughout the day also have these effects. If we are not mindful about our own decision fatigue in law school, and if we do not take deliberate steps to defeat or transcend it, we are likely to suffer from impaired decision making and cognition that will impact our happiness and success in law school.

WHY DO THEY WEAR THE SAME OUTFIT EVERY DAY?!

Considering you are inundated with information, decisions, and obligations every day in law school, what can you do to curb decision fatigue? Let us examine a technique that can be instructive to your process.

Aware of the science of decision fatigue, many of society's greatest thinkers wear virtually the same clothes every day. They are conscious that the cognitive resources spent on deciding on the right outfit in the morning will quite literally reduce the cognitive firepower available for far more important decisions later in the day. Think of Steve Jobs and the black turtleneck, blue jeans, and white New Balance sneakers he wore virtually every day. Or Mark Zuckerberg and the same grey t-shirt and grey zip-up hoodie he wears every day. Or President Obama and the small collection of gray suits and blue suits, with the universally matching undershirts and ties, that he wore virtually every day for his eight years in the White House. Or business mogul Richard Branson wearing the same blue jeans and white shirts every day. Or Elizabeth Holmes, who wore a black turtleneck every day in building Theranos into a company valued at $10 billion. Or Matilda Kahl, the Head of Creative at Sony Music, wearing the same white silk blouses and black pants every day.

While he was the President in 2012, Obama explained "[Y]ou'll see I wear only gray or blue suits. I'm trying to pare down decisions. I don't want to make decisions about what I'm eating or wearing. Because I have too many other decisions to make."[154] Obama elaborated on the importance of proactively fending off decision fatigue. "You need to focus your decision-making energy. You need to routinize yourself. You can't be going through the day distracted by trivia."

MICRO-DECISIONS: ELIMINATE AND SHORTEN SOME

In citing the decision fatigue doctrine in referring to his own repetitive wardrobe, Zuckerberg has elaborated, "I really want to clear my life so that I have to make as few decisions as possible, other than how to best serve this community."[155] He sees a direct connection between renouncing small decisions in his life and his ability to succeed in his career, explaining, "I feel like I'm not doing my job if I spend any of my energy on things that are silly or frivolous about my life."

When asked in 2015 about wearing a black turtleneck every day, then CEO Elizabeth Holmes responded, "[I]t's my uniform. It makes it easy, because every day you put on the same thing and don't have to think about it – one less thing in your life. All my focus is on the work. I take it so seriously."[156] (In January 2022, Holmes was convicted of three counts of fraud and one count of conspiring to commit fraud. We would advise you to emulate Holmes' commitment to defeating decision fatigue, but probably not her commitment to fraud.)

Matilda Kahl is undoubtedly passionate about creative expression, as evidenced by her position as Head of Creative at Sony Music. But she knows that the creative expression in her work is advanced by reducing the creative expression in her wardrobe.[157] Having worn the same essential outfit for years, Kahl is often asked why such a creative professional would be so bland in her wardrobe. "When I get those questions, I can't help but retort, 'Have you ever set up a bill for online autopay? Did it feel good to have one less thing to deal with every month?' " By wearing the same thing each day, Kahl has optimized her well-being, her time, and her sense of personal power: "The simple choice of wearing a work uniform has saved me countless wasted hours thinking, 'What the hell am I going to wear today?' And in fact, these black trousers and white blouses have become an important daily reminder that frankly, I'm in control. Today, I not only feel great about what I wear, I don't *think* about what I wear." (Emphasis in original.)

So how does this apply to you? The takeaway here is not that you should wear the same grey t-shirt every day in law school. Some of you may get energized and inspired by picking your outfit each day, while others of you may get drained and stressed from it.* The takeaway here is to use your creativity to establish some daily routines that will allow you to mechanize some of the micro-decisions you consistently make in your life. Perhaps you won't create a daily routine for your wardrobe selection because that does not feel beneficial to you. But you may find many other aspects of your life that you can routinize, whether it is the food you eat,† the time you arrive on campus each morning, the number of hours you spend in the library after class on the typical day, your schedule for taking practice tests over the course of the semester, the length of your dinner break each evening, the days and times you exercise each week, the days and times you make calls to family and friends to catch up, or the times you check social media throughout the day.

These are just some examples to get your creative juices flowing. We suggest that you take some time to identify *three* new daily routines you can implement. Just as Matilda Kahl said her wardrobe routine creates an ease similar to putting her bills on autopay, if you establish three new routines, you will quickly notice the newfound ease that results. In these three areas of your life, you will no longer have to spend valuable cognitive resources toiling over decisions. They will now be automated, freeing up sacred willpower and cognitive fuel that you can use to listen more carefully in class, do your homework more efficiently, and resist the litany of study distractions more effectively.

---

* We are also mindful of the gender implications of a repetitive wardrobe. The ability of Zuckerberg, Obama, Jobs, and other men to streamline their wardrobe as a way to reduce decision fatigue may not be equally available to women in similar roles – as several studies have confirmed that women's clothing choices are much more scrutinized, rendering a "voluntary uniform" potentially imprudent and risky for the average woman in law or business. *See* Emma Rees, (Apr. 5, 2018). *Clothes do not make the woman: What female academics wear is subject to constant scrutiny*, THE (TIMES HIGHER EDUCATION) MAGAZINE. https://www.timeshighereducation.com/features/clothes-do-not-make-woman-what-female-academics-wear-subject-constant-scrutiny. In addressing wardrobe decision fatigue, Arianna Huffington has commented on the gender inequity women face in this space: "Men have a competitive advantage. They don't have to waste the kind of energy we waste."[158]

For both gender equity and decision fatigue reasons, Huffington deliberately wears the same outfits in different contexts, as she explained in a 2019 tweet: "While decision fatigue is real, there's another reason why I'm a big proponent of style #repeats: Like men, women should be free from the expectation to reinvent the wheel every time they leave the house."[159]

† Cornell University researchers have found that people make an average of 221 micro-decisions every day about the food they eat.[160]

MICRO-DECISIONS: ELIMINATE AND SHORTEN SOME

In addition to establishing three new daily routines, we invite you to begin approaching *ad hoc* micro-decisions throughout the day through the lens of decision fatigue. Can you begin to view every action, decision, and thought process expressly from the perspective of balancing outcome *and energy*, rather than just maximizing the outcome? As we navigate the day, we typically default into making the "best" decision or taking the "ideal" action in every micro-situation that is presented throughout the day – *without accounting for the costs of that outcome* (and without considering that this outcome will have no material impact on the quality of our life). In other words, we unconsciously view every micro-decision and micro-action in isolation, aiming to achieve the optimal outcome in each and every micro-situation, without consciously considering how this energy burn will impact our energy levels and cognitive performance on far more important issues later in the day.

Instead, let's try a new approach. As the plethora of ordinary micro-decisions percolate throughout the day, we can begin to consistently ask ourselves: *How much energy and willpower should I dedicate to this particular decision or action? Would I be better served by preserving some of that energy for other decisions and actions in the day that will advance my law school performance (even if it means making a slightly "worse" micro-decision in this moment)?*

For instance, do we really need to engage in a 12-minute debate with our law school friend over whether to go to Chipotle or Baja Fresh for lunch, simply to obtain a *slightly* better burrito? When we engage in the classic "restaurant debate" (one of most common debates of all time), we are usually not thinking about how the energy loss from this conversation will reduce our ability to resist social media temptations later that afternoon while doing our Civil Procedure reading. We are myopically focused on getting the exact burrito we want, regardless of the latent consequences on our energy and cognition.

Similarly, if we find ourselves in a political debate with a classmate or family member, or a social media argument with a stranger, we tend to be oblivious to the energetic and cognitive ramifications of this power outlay. We want to be "right" and prove them "wrong," without considering how this conversation will affect our ability to focus and complete our homework later that day. Nor do we typically consider the fact that, regardless of how much time, energy, and passion we bleed out, the other person is highly unlikely to alter a position they have held for years based on this single conversation (despite our *obvious genius*). So it truly is an ill-advised resource expenditure.

Because law school attracts principled individuals who tend to enjoy zealous debate (and law school further trains us to excel in such debate), and because social media provides limitless opportunities for principled debates, we are surrounded by constant temptations to deplete our precious energy and willpower in ways that will impede our focus and productivity later in the day.

Drafting emails is also a repeated source of *ad hoc* willpower depletion. Every person who is reading this paragraph is likely guilty of having spent *twice* as much time as necessary on a particular email earlier today, when the extra effort realistically had no discernible effect on the situation.

Think of an email you spent 10 minutes on earlier today that could have been done in five minutes. Sure, it would not have been quite as artistic, nuanced, or eloquent, but did that extra genius improve your life or law school experience in any real way? If you can identify even just four emails per day that you can compose in five minutes rather than 10, you will have saved yourself 20 minutes of time that can be more beneficially used, *but far more importantly*, you will have preserved valuable energy and willpower that will translate into greater productivity and performance later in the day when you are trying to "lock in" on your homework. The extra 20 minutes is nice; the enhanced productivity and cognitive performance is exquisite.

The same reasoning applies to your text messages. Certain text conversations, like emails, require your full energy and quality, but plenty of them do not. With regard to the latter, can you recognize those conversations as they are occurring and mindfully cut your time and energy expenditure in half? If you are able to do so on even a handful of text conversations per day, you should experience a bump in willpower and cognition as a result.

MICRO-DECISIONS: ELIMINATE AND SHORTEN SOME

In closing, a tangible goal you may consider is identifying *five ad hoc* micro-decisions each day that you will eliminate (e.g., skip the Facebook debate or let your friend pick the lunch restaurant) and *five ad hoc* micro-decisions each day that you will spend half as much time on. When you implement this strategy, you will begin building up new reserves of energy and willpower, and you will prepare yourself to experience greater energy, resilience, focus, and cognitive firepower later in the day on your important law school work.

TOOL 8

IMPULSIVITY: ACT OPPOSITE TO THE STRESSOR*

"Emotional self-control – delaying gratification and stifling impulsiveness – underlies accomplishment of every sort."

— Daniel Goleman

Back in the 1950s, intimate partner violence in the United States was occurring at staggering rates. The overwhelming majority of intimate partner abusers were men, and when certain of these men sought help from a psychologist or other mental health professional (whether voluntarily or via court order), a common piece of professional advice they would receive was to hit an inanimate object when they were angry, instead of their wife. The notion was that if these men took their anger out on a pillow, they would have an outlet for their anger and violent expression, and their wife would be spared any abuse. By giving the men permission to hit an inanimate object, the professionals reasoned, the anger would be released and nobody would be hurt. Makes logical sense.

Unfortunately, something very tragic occurred: This professional advice led to an increase in physical abuse in many households. Why would men hitting an inanimate object, rather than their wife, also lead to an increase in hitting their wife?

Because of neural pathways, which were not understood by psychologists at the time. Each time an abusive man hit the pillow in response to his anger, the neural link in his brain between the emotion of anger and the behavior of physical violence was validated and deepened. The more the man reacted to his anger by unabashedly hitting the pillow (knowing that it

---

* Trigger warning: This section of the book contains a discussion of intimate partner violence. If this subject matter would be at all triggering to you, we encourage you to skip to the next section of the book, Tool #9, at page 243.

was not hurting anyone), the more his brain became conditioned to release the emotion of anger through the behavior of hitting. Hitting the pillow created a short-term release of the anger, but in the long-term it also wired his brain to require physical violence in order to release the anger. Moreover, by repeatedly and systematically allowing the emotion of anger to be fully released through violence (rather than curtailed through self-restraint), his brain's capacity for restraint weakened and its propensity for unregulated anger increased. From a neurological perspective, the emotion of anger was being continually validated and rewarded, causing his brain's patterning for anger to solidify and deepen.

Eventually this neural rewiring resulted in increased physical violence towards his wife. Consequently, the professional advice the man received actually boosted his angry impulses and made him more violent.

Modern psychology now recommends the opposite approach. If a man (or anyone) has an anger management problem that is associated with physical violence, and he wants to break or weaken this loop, the man must *violate* the urge to commit violence in reaction to anger. So when a jolt of anger pops up within him, instead of following the impulse to hit, he should "act opposite" to the impulse. This technique is commonly called "acting opposite" (also known as "opposite action"): We deliberately engage in a behavior that is contrary to the behavioral impulse generated by the emotion.

So when the emotion of anger arises, the man is advised to commit any action – *other than an act of physical violence*. Whether it is doing five slow breaths, taking a walk around the block, thinking of something for which he is grateful, cuddling with the dog for 30 seconds, or watching a silly video on YouTube, the key is to violate the impulse to hit. Each time he "acts opposite" to the impulse to hit, he interrupts his neural connection between anger and violence. The more he interrupts this neural connection, the weaker this neural connection becomes, and the easier it is to resist violence – and over time, the weaker the impulse for anger becomes. That is how he rewires his brain to become less violent and less prone to anger.

IMPULSIVITY: ACT OPPOSITE TO THE STRESSOR

How does this apply to stress, you may be wondering? Well, just as the emotion of anger generates an impulse to commit the behavior of violence, the emotion of stress ignites an impulse to commit a specific behavior. That behavior is "powering through" or "white knuckling" our school work. Or taking some sudden and hasty act in reaction to the stressor.

Say you are studying and you abruptly think of a doctrine that you know nothing about that could potentially be on the test. In that moment, a jolt of stress wells up within you, and creates an impulse to immediately look up the doctrine so you can be relieved of this intense emotion. Or, if you receive an email about an upcoming assignment from a professor that makes no sense and triggers you into stress, you will likely feel an impulse to reply immediately to gain clarification and alleviate your uncertainty. Or, if a friend or family member sends you a text message that judges you for being "MIA" since you started law school, you might be triggered into stress and upset and feel an impulse to reply ASAP so you can defend yourself and clarify the record. Or, if you are in an argument with your significant other and they say something unfair or unkind, your intense stress and hurt may create an impulse to blurt out an immediate counterpoint without any delay.

In each of these situations, the emotion of stress ignites an irresistible urge to take immediate, hasty action (which is usually not our finest action, and often one that we later wish we could take back). Nevertheless, at the moment we take the impulsive action, we feel temporary relief from the stress (just as the man who hits his wife feels temporary relief from his anger). But we are also validating and strengthening this neural connection in our brain. Over time, we wire our brain to only feel *de-stressed* if we take such an action. We condition our brain not to be able to feel peaceful and centered unless every email is sent, every text is replied to, every assignment is completed, every task is accomplished, and every unfair accusation is corrected. In each instance, we feel momentary stress relief as a result of our impulsive action – *until* the next life event arises soon thereafter to trigger us into the next round of stress. What's more, by continually and loyally acting at the behest of our stress, we neurologically validate and reward this emotion, causing its control over us to expand. This cycle continues perpetually and we become more stressed and less resilient people over time.

We recommend breaking this cycle. When you feel a jolt of stress from any of the above triggers, resist the impulse to take immediate action, and instead "act opposite" to that impulse. Each time you violate that impulse, you will weaken the neural connection, and over time, you will notice a heightened sense of resiliency whereby the same emails, texts, assignments, and tasks fail to trigger you into the same level of stress.

In his book *Destressifying*, Davidji, a former Wallstreet finance wiz and now mindfulness teacher, provides a powerful acronym to support us in resisting the urges of our emotional reactions. (Don't all law students love acronyms?!) When something occurs in your life that suddenly triggers you into stress or anger, Davidji recommends reaching for a "SODA." You may be wondering how reaching for a sugary, caffeinated drink could help you navigate this unexpected stressor. Here's how:

Stop: pause what you are doing; take no action.

Observe: look inward and objectively observe your emotional state; identify what emotion you are feeling at this moment (e.g., stress, hurt, anger, sadness, etc.).

Detach: do some act of physical detachment from the stressor to signal to your brain that you are interrupting the fight-or-flight response (e.g., put the phone down after reading the triggering text, turn 90 degrees from your laptop after reading the upsetting email, tell your significant other you'd like to take a minute for silent self-reflection, etc.).

Ascend: take some action that is opposite or contrary to the impulse created by the emotion; do something proactive and empowering, rather than reactive and disempowering (many of the recommended techniques in this book qualify).

IMPULSIVITY: ACT OPPOSITE TO THE STRESSOR

After 30–90 seconds of "acting opposite,"* return to the difficulty you are facing. Although the difficulty will not have gone away, your relationship to it will be different. By engaging in that brief *"pattern interrupt,"* you are far more likely to proactively respond, rather than hastily react. And more importantly, each time you "act opposite," you are taking a small but tangible step in rewiring your brain so these sorts of difficulties in the future do not rattle and stress you to the same degree. Instead of "death by a thousand cuts," you are engaging in "happiness by a thousand cuts."

This is how you become a less reactive, more peaceful, and more resilient person amidst the unpredictable chaos of life. There is no magic pill for ultimate peace; it requires a lot of small actions over time. But repeated instances of "acting opposite" will accelerate your progress towards this hallowed destination.

---

* Dr. Jill Bolte Taylor, a renowned Harvard neuroscientist, has proven that the biochemical component of an emotional reaction lasts a mere 90 seconds. She accordingly coined the term, the "90-Second Rule," to capture the special importance of acting opposite to the impulse created by the emotional trigger *for the first 90 seconds following the trigger*. The longer into this period we can resist the impulse, the more the biochemical reaction will dissipate and the more likely we are to take an action unshackled (or less shackled) by the emotion.

"Peace is not the absence of chaos or conflict, but rather finding yourself in the midst of that chaos and remaining calm in your heart," said political diplomat John Mroz. You will regularly find yourself in the midst of chaos and conflict as a law student, as a lawyer, and as a human living in this world. But that does not mean you cannot experience inner peace in the face of it all. By slowly transforming your relationship to stress – and other difficult emotions – by violating the behavioral impulses generated by these emotions, you will begin to emancipate yourself from the bondage of your emotions and impulsive thoughts. You will begin to experience calm in your heart – even when the outside world is completely uncalm. That is precisely the type of freedom the legendary Bob Marley was referring to in 1980 when he wrote: "Emancipate yourself from mental slavery. None but ourselves can free our minds."

Tool 9

Procrastination: Apply the 10-Minute Rule

"I'm going to stop procrastinating! Starting tomorrow."

— Sam Levenson

Battling with procrastination was a very personal issue for me [*your co-author Jarrett*]. Well, it was not *that* long a battle, it was more like a short window of my life. Sort of a blip on the screen. Barely detectable.

Okay, 36 years. That's right, I struggled with procrastination for *36 straight years*! I'm pretty sure that qualifies as more than a "blip." After perpetually battling this major issue throughout my life, I thought to myself, "How long do I need to desperately struggle with this issue before I am willing to take action?" Apparently, the answer was *nearly four decades.*

At that time, I became obsessed with studying and mastering the science of procrastination with the goal of eventually freeing myself from its anguishing grip. I delved deeply into the vast research on the underlying motives for and causes of procrastination, the variables that strengthen and weaken its grip, the neurological and personality influences, the behavioral correlations, the cognitive performance ramifications, and various other aspects of the half century of scientific studies on the topic.

Based on these countless hours of inquiry, I eventually arrived at a clear understanding of what occurs inside ourselves when we procrastinate, and I found a tangible technique that allows us to break free of the bondages of procrastination. I was then able to fundamentally transform my relationship with procrastination and overcome this demoralizing issue that had plagued me my whole life. These days, it occasionally pops up as a minor issue, but it is largely a non-factor in my life. As a result of this science-based technique, my overall productivity, efficiency, resilience, self-confidence, and emotional well-being have been materially elevated. (In fact, my sections of this book would never have been written if it were not for this technique.)

If you struggle with procrastination (occasionally or continually), I now want to provide you with a synthesis of my findings and the simple technique that can help you defeat this ruthless beast.

Let's start by acknowledging that procrastination is extremely prevalent. The research suggests that an estimated 80% to 95% of college students engage in procrastination, and approximately 75% of college students consider themselves procrastinators.[161] College students report that procrastination occupies over one third of their daily activities,[162] often effectuated through activities like streaming videos, watching TV, scrolling through social media, engaging with various smart phone apps, web-browsing, calling a friend or family member, cleaning one's apartment, doing laundry, and napping. So if you struggle with procrastination, you are not alone. Rare is the law student who is not affected by procrastination. In fact, procrastination is the most common performance struggle we personally see among law students and lawyers alike – across the globe.

So what is procrastination? Well, we all know what it looks and feels like, but let's establish a clear definition. Procrastination is generally defined as the voluntary delay of an intended activity even though that delay will have negative consequences. It consists of our desire to do take some action in the moment, yet not being able to motivate ourselves to take that action. "You know what you ought to do and you're not able to bring yourself to do it," explains Dr. Timothy Pychyl, a psychology professor at Carleton University in Ottawa, Canada, and one of the world's leading researchers on procrastination. "It is the gap between intention and action," says Dr. Pychyl. So despite intending to take an action, we delay that action while having simultaneous awareness that such delay will have

PROCRASTINATION: APPLY THE 10-MINUTE RULE   245

negative ramifications in our life, whether mental, emotional, financial, academic, professional, or relational.

Most of us think that procrastination is a problem of time management or discipline. Or that it is a result of motivation problems or character flaws. The science shows it is none of these things. To the contrary, the research reveals that procrastination is a problem with our ability to *regulate our emotions*. As explained by Dr. Pychyl, "Procrastination isn't a unique character flaw or a mysterious curse on your ability to manage time, but a way of coping with challenging emotions and negative moods induced by certain tasks – boredom, anxiety, insecurity, frustration, resentment, self-doubt and beyond."[163] When we are unable to effectively regulate the challenging emotions brought about by the school work and deadline at issue, those emotions get the better of us and induce us to procrastinate. For this reason, it is widely accepted in the scientific community that "procrastination is an emotion regulation problem, not a time management problem," says Dr. Pychyl.

This emotion regulation problem obviously manifests as time management and self-discipline issues. But those are just the symptoms, not the underlying problem. Nobody would say that an injured athlete who is limping has a "limp problem." They would say that she has torn cartilage in her knee, and that injury is causing her to limp. The root problem is her torn cartilage, which leads to several symptoms, such as pain in the joint, swelling of the knee, locking of the joint, difficulty bearing weight, inability to fully straighten the knee, restricted joint mobility, and – of course – a limp. Similarly, procrastination's root problem is emotional regulation, which gives rise to a host of symptoms, including struggles with time management and self-discipline.

In a 2013 study, Dr. Pychyl and his colleague, Dr. Sirois, confirmed the well-established finding that procrastination is an emotion regulation issue while offering a more technical articulation of the phenomenon: procrastination results from "the primacy of short-term mood repair over longer-term pursuit of intended actions."[164] In other words, when we are facing a deadline or obligation that triggers unpleasant emotions (and hence a bad mood), we prioritize repairing or eliminating those unpleasant emotions over completing the intended action that is triggering those emotions. It is not that we are lazy, undisciplined, unfocused, or imprudent when we procrastinate; it is that we are experiencing uncomfortable emotions we are struggling to process. So we procrastinate to temporarily nullify those emotions.

And what are those emotions, you might ask? According to the research, the most central emotions are fear of failure, perfectionism, self-doubt, task aversiveness (a term of art defined below), and impulsiveness.[165] Each of these emotions – *when unregulated* – deters us from beginning the task at issue. These emotions are interrelated and mutually reinforcing: They work together to overwhelm us into inaction. A fear of failure causes a sort of *paralysis by analysis*, where we hesitate to begin a task that we dread failing on. Feelings of perfectionism cause us to erect such a toweringly high standard of performance that we cower from even beginning it. Self-doubt (also referred to as low self-efficacy in the research) causes us to question our own capacity to excel on the task, leaving us deterred from even starting. Task aversiveness, which is a feeling of unpleasantness arising from the contemplation of an intended task, causes us to recoil from or avoid the intended task.* Impulsiveness, which is a tendency to act on momentary urges without accounting for the consequences, causes us to reach for an activity that is more pleasant, comfortable, or enjoyable than the intended task.

When we boil these various factors down to their essence, and let go of some of the nuanced technicalities, we can say that procrastination is most commonly the result of the interplay between **perfectionism** and **monsterism**. ("Monsterism" is a term we coined for the phenomenon we describe below.) Perfectionism tells us that we must perform this particular task with complete and total genius if we want to achieve success, avoid failure, and uphold our reputation. If we cannot achieve impeccable mastery on this particular task at this moment, then it's not worth starting at all. These brutally high standards

---

* Frustration with the task, resentment about the task, and boredom with the task are the most common triggers of task aversiveness.[166]

PROCRASTINATION: APPLY THE 10-MINUTE RULE

cause us to feel stressed and intimidated by the task, leading us to cower from it.

Monsterism is our mind's tendency to artificially inflate the relative complexity of intended tasks. It is a form of cognitive distortion where the intended task feels harder and bigger than it actually is. Our mind tells us that we do not – at the moment we are attempting to start the task – possess the energy, willpower, and cognitive resources to take on this grueling task. Just as we are wanting to start the task, our mind turns the task into a giant "monster" – where it appears far too complex and unwieldly to take on *at this particular moment*. We doubt our ability to muster up the energy and resources needed to slay this monster.

When we procrastinators eventually do commence the task (typically in a desperate charge, at the very last second), we usually realize something very unsettling: the task was not *nearly* as complex as our mind made it out to be! We realize our brain distorted the magnitude and complexity of the task, leading us to ask ourselves, "Why didn't I start this sooner? It really isn't so bad. I didn't have to procrastinate and put myself through all of that torment." Yet, at the moment we were trying to begin the task, it appeared so vast and complicated, and the notion of mustering up the necessary resources to masterfully perform it felt overwhelming. And, by the way, the more stressed and fatigued we are, the more likely our brain is to overinflate the relative magnitude and complexity of the task.

The interplay of perfectionism and monsterism makes the task seem extremely unpleasant. When we try to convince ourselves to start it, we feel a collection of negative emotions, from stress, to resentment of the task, to doubt about our ability to excel at this moment, to self-judgment about our current motivation or discipline, to general overwhelm. This is not a fun emotional experience to have.

Guess what action temporarily masks or numbs these swirling emotions? That's right, procrastination. In the face of this grossly unpleasant task, and all of the unpleasant emotions that are bubbling up inside us, procrastination acts as an immediate and short-term numbing agent. Although procrastination certainly does not resolve or healthily process those emotions (and they tend to rebound even more powerfully later), it does instantaneously numb them. Which is why every act of procrastination of a law school task *also* involves some other overt activity.

Remember the list from above? When you are procrastinating about that law school task, you turn to some discernible activity, such as streaming videos, watching TV, scrolling through social media, engaging with smart phone apps, web-browsing, calling a friend or family member, cleaning your apartment, doing laundry, or napping. (Napping can be described as becoming *literally unconscious* to the unpleasant emotions). Even doing a less challenging law school assignment can be a diversion from the intended task. None of us just sits in calm silence while procrastinating. That would deprive us of the essential benefit of avoiding the unpleasant emotions. We would be avoiding the challenging law school task, but we would be staring directly at the unpleasant emotions – which is precisely what procrastination is performed to prevent.

So procrastination invariably involves *both* (i) retreating from the intended task, and (ii) lunging towards a distracting task. We project our attention away from the firestorm of unpleasant emotions within us, and towards a more pleasant activity. In so doing, we obtain short-term relief from the intensity of the unpleasant emotions. Those emotions do not disappear, but they feel less pungent and disturbing. That is why procrastination is an emotion regulation problem, and not a time management problem.*

---

* When the distracting task we lunge towards is not just entertainment or household projects but another school or work project, we are committing precrastination. ***Pre***crastination, the act of initiating less urgent and less important tasks in a manner that generates time management problems for more urgent and more important tasks that are being simultaneously avoided, works hand-in-hand with procrastination. Precrastination and procrastination are a destructive duo that work in tandem to wreak havoc: Jumping on less urgent and less important tasks when the urgent "big one" needs to be performed allows us to feel as if we are doing *something* productive and, hence, makes it easier and more justifiable to avoid the necessary task. Precrastination is essentially an *enabler* or *facilitator* of procrastination. If procrastination is the bank robber, precrastination is the friend who drives the robber to the bank and serves as the "lookout" person during the robbery. So as you are procrastinating an important task, notice if you reach towards less urgent and less important law school tasks to complete instead, such as emails, easier homework assignments, paperwork, tallying legal research, etc. This is often your brain tricking you into doing tasks that will make you feel decently productive and therefore less guilty,

SHOULD I WORK ON THAT PAPER...? NAH!

Let's look at a classic "procrastination vignette" that many of us have faced. It's 8:45 p.m. and you are finishing up your study break and late dinner while watching Netflix. Your Legal Research & Writing paper, which you have been meaning to start, is now due in three days. You finished your reading assignments before your dinner break with the intention of spending two hours on writing the paper from 9 to 11 p.m. These two hours of writing will allow you to finally start this paper and will spark some momentum for you to make good progress on it tomorrow.

You finish your meal and watch the last few minutes of your Netflix show until the clock hits 9 p.m., signaling that it is time to begin writing. You close Netflix and open up a new Microsoft Word document. There it is – the blank white page. Your brain suddenly feels just as blank. Blood is rushing from your brain to your stomach to aid in digestion, and it is dark outside. You are starting to feel groggy, reflecting on the long and stressful day you have had. You feel some brain fog setting in. You think about all of the willpower and cognitive resources you will need to marshal in order to write for the next two hours, and you start to feel emotionally discontent. Several of the emotions we mentioned above are percolating within you. You fantasize about closing the document and watching Netflix for the rest of the evening, but you tell yourself you can't do that.

As you struggle to muster up the discipline you need, you find yourself clicking on your favorite websites for a few minutes, and you read a few enticing articles. You then briefly consider starting to write but find yourself scrolling through your favorite social media app. You "like" and comment upon a few posts, but you mostly scroll through the never-ending feed. You again think you should start to write, but now you realize there are a couple of school-related emails you need to send. So you hop into your account and send those two emails. After sending those emails, you decide to pop into YouTube to watch a couple of funny clips.

---

which further masks the unpleasant emotions about the primary task that led you to procrastinate in the first place.

You now glance at the clock and see it's 9:37 p.m. You have gotten zero writing done in the 37 minutes so far, and you suddenly notice how much more exhausted you are. You feel twice as groggy as you felt at 9:00 p.m., and the idea of starting this writing project now feels even more crushing than before. You putz around your array of online distractions for another 15 minutes and then realize it is nearly 10 p.m. You are feeling drained and demoralized, and you decide there is no way you are going to get any writing done tonight. "I will definitely jump on this first thing in the morning," you tell yourself. You close Microsoft Word and open Netflix.

Your stress, shame, and frustration are palpable, and then you begin zoning out on your favorite show. You are not able to enjoy the show as much as you ordinarily would, but the show is still entertaining and helps to numb some of your emotional intensity. At a perhaps unconscious level, there is a part of you that is relieved that you don't have to write your paper tonight or muster up the massive willpower needed to do so. You don't consciously process any of the inner workings that factored into your procrastination decision: the fear of failure that was present as you attempted to write, your perfectionist standards, your palpable aversion to the paper, or the possibility that you may be inflating the actual complexity of the paper. You instead sink your attention into your Netflix show, while allowing the set of unpleasant emotions and considerations to slowly fade into the distance.*

Procrastinating allowed you to temporarily avoid and numb these unpleasant emotions and considerations. *No wonder you procrastinated!* Every time you thought about starting the paper, your unconscious mind (via "System 1" thinking) loudly proclaimed, "I am so fatigued and depleted, I am simply not capable of doing two hours of genius writing right now!" Your belief that you were not capable of doing two hours of genius writing at that time prevented you from beginning to write. The notion that you needed to do two hours of genius writing was too unrealistic and too emotionally jarring, so you had no choice but

---

* To be clear, we are not implying that every reader has experienced this particular chronology of internal events. It is an archetypical account designed to be used as a teaching opportunity.

PROCRASTINATION: APPLY THE 10-MINUTE RULE 251

to turn to procrastination to escape the unfair predicament and the unpleasant emotions triggered by the predicament.

But there was another option: change the predicament and change the emotional unpleasantness of beginning to write. This can be done by implementing the "**10-Minute Rule**,"* a science-based tool for overcoming procrastination. It is also the tool that allowed your co-author to conquer his life-long struggle with procrastination. This potent technique is very simple: Rather than unconsciously saying to yourself, "I am not capable of doing two hours of genius writing right now," the 10-Minute Rule invites you to consciously say to yourself, "I *am* capable of doing *ten minutes* of <u>average</u> writing right now!"

You then set your alarm for 10 minutes and write from 9:00 p.m. to 9:10 p.m. with an intentionally *average* quality, knowing you will improve the quality in the morning. When your alarm goes off, you stop writing and take a 10-minute break. After the 10-minute break, you return to 10 minutes of average writing. After that, you take another 10-minute break before returning for another 10-minute writing block. You do this back-and-forth process for the entire two-hour window between 9:00 p.m. and 11:00 p.m., and when you arrive at 11:00 p.m., you will have completed one hour of total writing. Importantly, you will have finally broken through the impenetrable starting point and dedicated a full hour to writing. The procrastination did not defeat you. You will go to sleep (and wake up) in a very different emotional state, and you will have put yourself in a position to be far more productive in your writing the next day.

But here is the best thing about the 10-Minute Rule: in either the first or second (or possibly third) 10-minute increment of writing, you will likely plow through the scheduled 10-minute break. When the alarm sounds, indicating it is time for a 10-minute break, you will realize how locked in you are to the writing, and you will somewhat effortlessly choose to continue writing, rather than taking that break. Before you know it, 11:00 p.m. will arrive, and you will have written for nearly the entire two-hour block.

---

* The tool has several other names and permutations, but we use the "10-Minute Rule."

The brilliance of the 10-Minute Rule is that it allows you to trick your brain into starting the writing (or whatever task you are intending to start) by giving yourself permission to write (i) for only 10 minutes, and (ii) with average quality. These two variables completely alter your emotional reaction to the prospect of writing. They extinguish the perfectionism and monsterism that make that prospect so distasteful and so emotionally overwhelming. Once you give yourself overt permission to do average writing for just 10 minutes, it becomes a very doable, bite-size task.* And once you start writing – and quickly build momentum – the prospect of continuing to write beyond the 10 minutes becomes perfectly palatable. Continuation is *much easier* than initiation. As we know, procrastination is about the devastating barrier to initiating the task. The 10-Minute Rule allows us to surreptitiously circumvent this barrier, at which point the procrastination is stripped of its power.†

---

* The 10-Minute Rule is rooted in some overlapping science as "Small Victory Theory" (aka "Behavioral Shaping"), which is outlined on page 260 of Tool #10 ("Goals & Habits: Achieve What You Seek").

† If for some reason you are not inspired to continue writing through the breaks, do not fret over this. Take each of your 10-minute breaks without shame, and then keep returning to your 10-minute blocks of writing. At the end of the two hours, you will still

PROCRASTINATION: APPLY THE 10-MINUTE RULE

You will likely notice something else that is interesting. Despite giving yourself express permission to perform "average" writing, the quality of your writing will be far better than that. The reasons for this are two-fold: (1) the permission to lower your standards will reduce the tension and stress that obstruct the writing process, so paradoxically, this permission will induce greater ease and flow; and (2) once you are writing, you will discover that the assignment is not nearly as complex as your brain envisioned it to be, and hence you actually have plenty of energy and resources to perform it with quality.

If you are concerned that you will not be able to trick your brain with this technique after the first time you implement it (since your brain will "know" what you are doing), you need not be. The more you apply this technique, the more you will rewire your brain to consistently pierce the veil of procrastination and, paradoxically, the easier it becomes to trick your brain in each successive instance and the more you will methodically turn this tool into a habit. Also, if you struggle with this tool in the beginning, do not become discouraged. Remember that your brain is deeply wired for procrastination at this point in your life, so each time you practice this technique, you will be slowly rewiring your brain to embrace it and effectuate it.

So whenever you are feeling the urge to procrastinate an intended task, overtly reject the oppressive notion that you need to perform genius-level work for several hours, and instead remind yourself of an undeniable truth: You *are* capable of doing *10 minutes* of *average work* right *now*.*

---

have completed an hour of writing (as opposed to the usual absence of writing), and you will have positioned yourself for success on this paper.

    * The 10-Minute Rule is a modern outgrowth of the ground-breaking Pomodoro Technique, developed by Francesco Cirillo in the late 1980s, which involves setting your alarm for 25 minutes of uninterrupted work (which he called a "pomodoro"), before taking a five-minute break, then returning for another 25 minutes of uninterrupted work followed by another five-minute break. After every three pomodoros, you take a longer break of 20–30 minutes. Then you repeat the same cycle. Although this method is very effective, we believe the 10-Minute Rule captures all of its strengths while mitigating its primary weakness: it has become scientifically clear over the last 30 years that uninterrupted working blocks of 25 minutes are simply too long to induce most of us to start a dreaded project, particularly in light of the incessant distractions and temptations created by smart phones and the internet (neither of which existed in the late 1980s). The Pomodoro Technique is a wonderful tool for enhancing one's general time management skills, but with respect to the specific challenge of overcoming procrastination, we recommend the 10-Minute Rule.

Tool 10

Goals & Habits: Achieve What You Seek

"Motivation is what gets you started. Habit is what keeps you going."

— Jim Rohn

Law school involves an ever-growing array of personal goals we set for ourselves (*as you well know!*), yet very few law students have ever been taught science-based tools for achieving goals and building habits that support goal achievement. As a result, we may set goals for ourselves or desire new behavioral habits, but that is very different than actually achieving those outcomes. For this reason, most law students (and humans) remain "stuck" in old habits and falter in achieving the goals and targets they seek. This impairs their emotional well-being and their academic success.

We would therefore like to share a collection of science-based techniques that can help you accomplish your goals and build better habits in law school and in life. While we could write an entire book on this one topic (indeed, several wonderful books have been written on it), we believe it would be valuable to provide you with some "golden nuggets" on this topic in a streamlined manner.

Importantly, you will be able to enjoy the full benefits of several of the other tools shared in this book if you are able to turn those tools into regular habits. So this segment of the book should help you implement several of the other tools found in this book. For example, you can use the habit formation techniques below to bolster your ability to build a daily meditation practice (Tool #11), "Silence-Stow-Set" (Tool #5), erect a Tech Buffer (Tool #6), practice visualization (Tool #12), use vulnerable verbalization (Tool #13), and engage in mid-day movement (Tool #3), among other tools outlined in this book. You can even use some of the techniques below to expedite the process of turning the 10-Minute Rule (discussed in the last section) into a habit. You can also use these habit formation techniques to more effectively turn the Mindset Shifts (from Section II) into habits in your life.

As you set your sights on behavioral changes, we invite you to shift how you conceive of the targeted changes. Instead of asking yourself, "How can I accomplish this goal?", we invite you to ask, "How can I build a habit that will naturally lead to this goal being achieved?" This is a subtle, yet important, paradigm shift. Instead of focusing on the external result, you focus on building the internal habit that will organically yield that result. In the section below, when we use the term "goal," we are referring to behavioral change goals (i.e., targeted habits), rather than result-centric goals.

When it comes to any behavioral goal or new habit you are trying to achieve, whether or not it is a tool found in this book, the techniques below can serve as a blueprint to convert what you *intend to achieve* into what you *have achieved*. In that vein, here are seven science-based tips that will help you actually achieve your targets.

1. PICK JUST ONE MAJOR BEHAVIORAL GOAL AT A TIME

The habit research shows that building a new habit is most effective when we place laser-like focus on one new behavior at a time. The willpower required to build a new habit or break an old habit is immense, and if we dilute our willpower across several different habits or goals at the same time, we are likely to achieve none. If, for example, you try to build a new meditation practice during the same week you attempt to build a new exercise routine, while simultaneously attempting to reduce your television and social media consumption, you have created the perfect recipe for becoming a non-meditating couch potato who watches television and scrolls through social media all day!

A mistake that many law students (and humans) make is they arrive at an inflection point in their academic career or life where they feel motivated to make key changes, and then they set too many separate goals at the same time. The likely result is they fail to achieve any of them. Ironically, this outcome can mean their levels of well-being, resiliency, and self-confidence drop even lower than they were when they set the well-being goals in the first place. Sometimes setting goals and failing to accomplish them can be more demoralizing than never setting them in the first place. So the intention to improve one's well-being, if mismanaged in this way, can actually lead to a net reduction in well-being. To avoid this outcome, position yourself for success by not setting too many different goals at the same time.

Of course, in any typical week you will have multiple micro-goals that you set for yourself, e.g., paying your rent, going to the grocery store, printing out that set of Westlaw cases, emailing the Registrar's Office, etc. We are not naïvely suggesting that you should only focus on one of these micro-goals at a time and disregard the rest of them. What we are referring to is not the mound of micro-goals that you have in any given week, but rather the major *behavioral goals* you identify that will help you become a happier, healthier, or more productive human. That is, not the one-off goals that pop up throughout the week, but the deeply ingrained habits and behavioral patterns that you want to change. For example: changing your reading or outlining schedule, building a new study habit, establishing a new workout routine, adopting some of the tools in this book, changing your eating habits, breaking an unhealthy or unfair relationship habit, implementing a system for paying bills timelier, or any other "behavioral goal" of this nature.*

---

* Several of the examples and studies we reference in this Goals & Habits Tool relate to physical exercise or weight loss. This is not because we have a singular focus on physical well-being. Instead, it's because these areas provide rich soil for valid and reliable scientific studies and findings since they involve rather objective, measurable, and easily comparable results. It's easier to measure and prove changes in minutes exercised per week, or pounds lost per month, than hours per week spent on digital distractions or the intensity of one's emotional reactions towards family members per month. However, the studies and findings apply with equal force to behaviors and habits with less objective and measurable success metrics; they are simply harder to effectively quantify across a large collection of study participants over the course of an entire experiment period.

Select one *behavioral goal* you would like to accomplish and then harness your available willpower into turning that behavior into a habit. You can use the habit-formation techniques that follow. Once that habit is firmly entrenched in your life (and your psyche), then you can begin working on the next goal.

2. BREAK THE GOAL INTO BABY STEPS

Once you have identified the single goal you would like to focus on at this time, it is time to break it into smaller pieces. Approximately 95% of New Year's resolutions fail, despite the strong desire for change and regardless of the character of the person involved. Why? The research shows that the primary reason resolutions fail (with over half failing before the end of January) is because we set a goal that is simply too idealistic as a starting point.

Habit researchers classify goals into two separate types: "ultimate goals" and "interim goals." Most people make the mistake of setting their ultimate goal as the first goal in the New Year. So despite not having exercised for two years, their resolution is to go to the gym three days per week for 45 minutes per session. They buy that gym membership (including the hefty non-refundable "initiation fee") and within weeks, their gym card is on a shelf serving as a coaster for their car keys.*

This occurs because the gap between our available willpower and the willpower required to go to the gym three days per week is simply too vast. By aiming for too lofty a goal from the outset, we have set ourselves up for failure. So researchers suggest identifying your ultimate goal (i.e., "go to the gym three days per week for 45 minutes per session"), and then breaking the ultimate goal into at least 5–10 interim goals. The interim goal should meet what we call the *"extremely doable"* standard, which means it should sound realistic at first glance and should not require a crushing expenditure of willpower. If the next

---

* A woman joined a gym in January and was frustrated that the parking lot was always full, typically requiring a 10-minute delay before she could find a spot. So she approached the gym's owner to express her discontent. The owner smiled and said, "All of those cars are from the 'New Year's resolution exercisers.' Just wait until February 1st – the parking lot will be empty by then."

GOALS & HABITS: ACHIEVE WHAT YOU SEEK

interim goal does not feel "extremely doable" to you, it is a sign that it is too lofty.

For example, what follows is a set of progressive interim goals that can lead to the ultimate goal of going to the gym three days per week. Very important: Do not move on from any interim goal until it has become a consistently performed habit.

- Walk around the block once every Tuesday and Thursday.
- Walk around the block twice every Tuesday and Thursday.
- Jog around the block once every Tuesday and Thursday.
- Jog around the block once every Tuesday and Thursday, and after each jog, do 10 pushups and 10 sit-ups.
- Jog around the block twice each Tuesday and Thursday, and after each jog, do 15 pushups and 15 sit-ups.
- Jog around the block twice each Monday, Wednesday, and Friday, and after each jog, do 15 pushups and 15 sit-ups.
- Jog around the block three times each Monday, Wednesday, and Friday, and after each jog, do 15 pushups, 15 sit-ups, and 15 jumping jacks.
- Go the gym every Monday and run on the treadmill for the equivalent of three blocks, followed by 15 pushups, 15 sit-ups, and 15 jumping jacks. Every Wednesday and Friday, stick to the same routine as before.
- Go the gym every Monday and Friday to do the above routine, while continuing to do the home workout every Wednesday.
- Go to the gym every Monday, Wednesday, and Friday, following the above routine.

- Slowly increase your time in the gym by 5 minutes, adding a new exercise technique, once each level becomes a habit.

Before you know it, you will be going to the gym three days per week for 45 minutes each session, and you will have formed a deeply ingrained exercise routine that is built to last and that does not overwhelm your willpower reserves. It will take longer to build this habit than suddenly proclaiming that you are going to go from no workouts to three gym days per week, but unlike the sudden proclamation, this process will actually lead to long-term success.

In behavioral psychology, this technique is called "behavioral shaping"; in executive coaching it is often called "small victory" theory. The key is to make the first interim goal extremely easy to achieve (i.e., the "extremely doable" standard), and once that becomes a habit, make the next successive goal equally easy to achieve (from that new starting point). You will know when each interim phase has become a habit because you will notice yourself doing it rather reflexively – without engaging in a big internal debate about doing it or not doing it, and without having to exert a large amount of willpower to execute it. At that point, you can move to the next interim phase.

If the first interim goal does not feel extremely doable, lower the goal. And if you don't feel like creating an entire list of interim goals (i.e., the overall blueprint), no problem – you can skip that. Just start by picking a first-level goal that is extremely doable, and once that goal becomes a habit, increase it slightly to the next extremely achievable level.

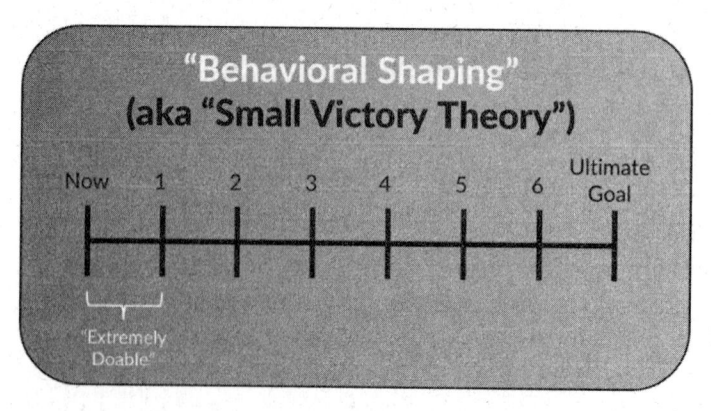

"Behavioral Shaping"
(aka "Small Victory Theory")

Now   1   2   3   4   5   6   Ultimate Goal

"Extremely Doable"

We have helped thousands of lawyers, legal professionals, law students, and corporate employees build a daily meditation practice using this technique. We often meet law students and others who say, "I've tried to meditate, and I just can't do it! I've decided it's not for me." The first question we usually ask is how many minutes did they attempt to meditate for each session? Invariably, they respond with, "15 minutes" or "20 minutes." *Who do they think they are, the Dalai Lama?!* Trying to build a meditation habit by starting with 15–20 minutes of meditation per session is like trying to learn how to swim by being dumped into the middle of the Pacific Ocean from a helicopter during your first swimming lesson.

In our anecdotal experience, the single most common reason that people fail to establish a daily meditation routine is that they set a gaudy and unrealistic target as their initial goal. Doing so converted the experience of meditating into a conceptual "monster" that felt intimidating and overwhelming. They simply did not have the willpower to continue at that rate, so they stopped meditating, leading them to feel like failures and to spiral further downward than where they were before trying to meditate.

So if you are wanting to build a daily meditation practice, using "small victory" theory is the way to do it. Begin meditating each morning for one minute maximum! If that feels uncertain, set 30 seconds of meditation as your daily goal. Once meditating for 30 seconds each day becomes a habit, you can increase it to one minute. Before you know it, you will be organically meditating 10 minutes every day, and it won't be that hard.

If you have been wanting to start outlining for your classes but have not been able to motivate to do it, you probably don't want to suddenly proclaim, "Next Monday I am going to begin outlining for all of my classes! Every week I am going to outline for all of the lectures that week going forward!" It's an inspiring thought, but it is likely too great a leap from where you are to where you want to be. (Countless law students, including your co-author Jarrett when he was in law school, have succumbed to this overambitious proclamation.)

Instead, break that ultimate goal into a set of interim goals. Perhaps, starting on Monday, you outline one case from each class that week. And if that feels like too much, maybe you just do a high-level outline of one case per class that includes just the case name and the statement of the rule. This seemingly small step has the potential to be the inflection point that eventually leads you to conquer the beast of outlining. That is just an example, but we invite you to determine for yourself what would meet the "extremely doable" standard for the first week or two of outlining. That approach will allow you to obtain a "small victory" (albeit a very important one) by breaking your non-outline streak, and you can then leverage that momentum into the next phase of outlining.

Many students who have not begun outlining despite a desire to do so simply don't know this technique (Jarrett certainly wishes he knew it while in law school!). So instead, they leap to an "all or nothing" approach to outlining. No surprise: it backfires for the vast majority of students. If you are already consistently outlining, then this particular example does not apply to you. But if you have been struggling to outline, a "baby steps" approach is more likely to succeed than the aspirational notion that you will suddenly transform on a random Monday from a non-outliner to a full-outliner. It's just not the way human beings experience transformation.

Or perhaps you have a tendency to focus so intensively on your school work that you regularly get behind on your bills and other "real world" obligations. To change this aspect of your life, you might tell yourself, "On Monday I am going to knock out all of these bills and ministerial matters that have piled up." But come Monday morning, this "ultimate goal" will likely feel overwhelming when you realize how brutal your law school responsibilities are looking for the week, and the notion of somehow completing all of the ministerial tasks in one day may feel soul-crushing. So you likely will complete none. But if you instead tell yourself that you are going to complete one real-world obligation each day (or every other day) starting on Monday, that is likely a more realistic and more prudent approach. Going forward, can you establish a monthly structure built upon a "small victory" approach to such obligations? If not, you are likely to suffer from Einstein's definition of insanity – "doing the same thing over and over and expecting different results." Small victory theory allows us to break this defective cycle and re-establish our sanity.

So whatever goal you choose to set, be sure to attack it by using "small victory" theory. As the ancient Chinese philosopher Lao Tzu said long ago, "The journey of a thousand miles begins with one step."

3. MAKE THE GOAL SPECIFIC, TANGIBLE, AND MEASURABLE

New goals often fail because they are vague or amorphous. Behavioral modification research reveals that goals such as "start meditating daily," "begin exercising regularly," "reduce the time I spend each day on social media," or "eat healthier" are significantly less likely to lead to modified behavior than goals such as "meditate each morning for one minute right after I wake up," "jog outside for 10 minutes on Mondays and Thursdays as a break after completing two hours of school work," "spend a maximum of 90 minutes per day on social media" (if the typical average has been 2 hours), or "eat only the following 6 types of foods for dinner this week."

Vagueness is the enemy of habit formation. That is a foundational principle of habit reformation, and one that is highlighted in James Clear's best-selling book on habits, *Atomic Habits*. Countless studies show the more specific, tangible, and measurable we can make each interim goal, the more likely we are to achieve it. In other words, how we phrase or frame the goal *in our own mind* plays a critical role in our probability of achieving it. If we can articulate it with great detail and concreteness, we are positioning ourselves for success.*

Scientists call this an "implementation intention," which is a specific plan that describes the how, when, and other circumstances under which you will engage in the targeted

---

* In the early 1980s, the "S.M.A.R.T." approach to goal achievement became popular. "S.M.A.R.T." is a mnemonic device for the following criteria: Specific, Measurable, Achievable, Relevant, and Time-Bound. The first two criteria, Specific and Measurable, are the basis of this particular tip. Various of the underpinnings of the "S.M.A.R.T." approach are contained in the goal achievement and habit formation tips we are sharing. But our tips have the benefit of an additional 40 years of behavioral change research that was not available at the time the "S.M.A.R.T." approach was established.

behavior. An easy structure to create an effective implementation intention is the following:

> **I will [BEHAVIOR] at [TIME] on [DAYS OF WEEK] in [LOCATION] for [DURATION].** *

Although it is rather easy to concoct this sort of statement, the research reveals that doing so significantly elevates the success rate of our goal. In one study, researchers worked with 248 people interested in starting a workout routine.[167]

The participants were broken into three groups. The first group was the control group. The second group was the "motivation" group, so they listened to a presentation from the researchers on how exercise could reduce the risk of heart disease and improve cardiovascular health, and they also read some materials on the various benefits of exercise. The third group was the "implementation intention" group. They listened to the same presentation as the "motivation" group, but they also were asked to complete the following sentence in writing: "During the next week, I will partake in at least 20 minutes of vigorous exercise on [DAY] at [TIME] in [PLACE]." The researchers then tracked whether the participants exercised over the next two weeks.

The results showed that 35% of the control group exercised at least once per week, while 38% of the "motivation" group did so. Yet 91% of the "implementation intention" group exercised at least once per week. By simply writing down the specifics of *when* and *where* they would exercise, the participants' success rates soared. It was not the participants' motivation to exercise that led to success, it was their conversion of that motivation into a specific plan of action. In a meta-analysis study that aggregated the findings of 94 different studies on the effects of an implementation intention, it was concluded that a short implementation intention "substantially increases the likelihood of attaining one's goals."[168]

---

* Once you have read the next technique ("Tie the Goal to a Pre-Existing Cue") about effectively using "cues," we recommend replacing **[TIME]** with **[CUE]** in this skeletal structure. But since you have not yet arrived at that technique, we are temporarily using **[TIME]**, a less effective alternative, as a placeholder.

Without this detailed articulation of our intention, our inertia and lethargy almost always win out. If we simply tell ourselves, "I am going to meditate for one minute tomorrow," we inevitably come up with an excuse for not doing it when we wake up, whether it's "I have to check email" or "I have to brush my teeth," or "I have to make breakfast for the kids." Then a couple of hours later when meditation crosses our mind, we quickly utter to ourselves, "I need to finish this urgent task, I'll meditate later." Then in the afternoon, we say, "I am feeling pressed for time and still have one more class I need to prepare for, so I'll meditate later." This continues throughout the day, until we arrive at the end of the night, when we say, "I'm exhausted, the last thing I want to do is meditate, so I will meditate tomorrow!" This cycle continues for days, or weeks, until we conclude that we are apparently incapable of meditating, and we are left feeling dejected and disempowered.

A highly tangible "implementation intention" (preferably written at first) is a tool we can use to induce self-accountability and defeat the inertia and distractions that are waiting in the wings to undermine our goal. Your "implementation intention" should be succinct (e.g., one sentence), so you can easily commit it to memory and draw on it throughout the day. By articulating your goal in this highly specific, tangible, and measurable way, you are boosting your chances of success.

4. TIE THE GOAL TO A PRE-EXISTING CUE

In the early 1990s, neuroscientists at the Massachusetts Institute of Technology discovered a breakthrough in habit research: all habits involve a three-part neurological reaction. First, there is the cue, a trigger that tells your brain to go into automatic mode and initiate the particular habit. Second, there is the routine, which is the behavior or action at issue. Third, there is the reward, which is the neurological validation (e.g., lighting up of reward centers of the brain, a release of endorphins, etc.) that immediately follows and validates the habitual behavior.

In *The Power of Habit*, a landmark book on habit formation, author Charles Duhigg labeled this three-part process (Cue-

Routine-Reward), which is present in all habits, the "habit loop." The MIT neuroscientists found that each time we commit the relevant behavior and the habit loop is triggered, the behavior becomes slightly more habitual, and our brain requires fewer resources to convince us to commit the behavior. With each triangulation of the habit loop, the behavior becomes more and more habitual. Over time, the behavior becomes automatic, i.e., it becomes a habit.

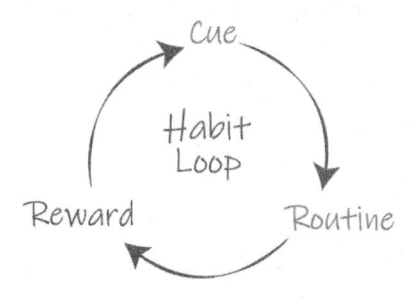

Cue → Routine → Reward → (Habit Loop)

In his groundbreaking book, Duhigg thoroughly elucidates the habit loop and offers various techniques for exploiting the brain's wiring in order to build new habits. One of the most effective things we can do, according to Duhigg, is to identify a "cue" that we predictably experience in our life, and immediately follow that "cue" with the desired behavior. If we use the same "cue" every time we commit the behavior, the behavior will get ingrained into the brain as a habit far more quickly. (Some neuroscientists call this "habit stacking," as we are stacking the desired habit upon a pre-existing habit, in order to neurologically link the two.)

Let us give you an example of the role of a "cue" in building a habit. Think of your least favorite drink, but one that does not have alcohol, caffeine, or some other addictive ingredient. Have you thought of a beverage that truly grosses you out? Good! Keep that disgusting beverage in mind as we walk through this exercise. Let's hypothetically say you chose grapefruit juice. If we asked you to stock your refrigerator with grapefruit juice, and we then asked you to drink three sips of grapefruit juice every day for 25 straight days – at randomly occurring times throughout the day – how do you think you would feel about grapefruit juice at the 30-day mark? You would still find it disgusting.

Now let's change the "fact pattern" a bit. (See what we did there?) Say we asked you to stock your refrigerator with grapefruit juice but this time we asked you to drink one sip of grapefruit juice immediately each time you enter your home for the next 25 straight days. In other words, every time you return home from anywhere, you open up your front door, immediately walk straight to the fridge, and take one sip of disgusting grapefruit juice before going about your business.

So every time you return from class, you immediately have one sip of grapefruit juice. You go outside to take the garbage out and immediately return. It's grapefruit juice time! You go to your car to retrieve a textbook you accidentally left in the trunk. Can someone say, "Grapefruit juice?" You do this for 25 straight days.

How do you think you would feel about grapefruit juice at the 25-day mark? You would *still* hate the taste of it! In fact, you might find it even more disgusting than you did at the outset of the experiment. But something fascinating will likely have occurred over the 25-day period: Your brain will have developed a craving for grapefruit juice. At some point during this experiment, whether it is 15, 20, or 25 days into it, you will notice something very perplexing: Every time you turn the handle of your front door and take that first step into your home, your brain will suddenly think of grapefruit juice! Not only will it think of grapefruit juice, a craving for it will also arise. To be clear, this is a neurological craving; your taste buds will still detest grapefruit juice. But your brain will have a "System 1" yearning for it, at which point your conscious "System 2" thinking will utter something to the effect of, "Why am I craving grapefruit juice?! It's so repulsive."

This example illustrates how we can wire our brain to crave something (whether a beverage or a behavior) even if we dislike it. The key is to consistently pair the targeted behavior with the same cue. Said differently, to engage in the targeted behavior every time a particular cue is triggered. By replicating the "Cue-Routine" component of the habit loop, we can trick the brain into thinking that the behavior is more of a habit than it actually is.

So if you want to start meditating one minute per day, rather picking an arbitrary time of day (such as "11:00 a.m. each day"), select an event that occurs at the same approximate time each day and make that the trigger for your new behavior. For example, meditate for one minute right after waking up, right when you are about to start eating lunch (or if that feels torturous, right after your last bite of lunch), right after you park your car upon arriving home from school, right after eating dinner, or right after your evening shower. Pick one of these cues (or any other one you prefer), and meditate each day immediately after that cue. (You can now edit the above "implementation intention" by replacing "TIME" with "CUE".) Each time you meditate immediately after the same cue, you will be exploiting your brain's habit loop and accelerating the habituation of this behavior.

This same reasoning applies to any law school behavior you want to turn into a habit. If you want to do some outlining every day, rather than doing it at random or arbitrary moments of each day, you can pick a single cue and then continually pair outlining with that cue. If you are exhausted and want to skip outlining for that day, we would invite you to nevertheless open the outline on your computer when the cue is triggered and simply read a portion of the outline for a minute. You can then close the outline. You will have succeeded in neurologically entwining the cue with outlining, thereby deepening the habit loop (even without having actually worked on the outline).

5. SET UP THE GOAL

A simple hack that increases the success rate of building a new habit is proactively removing the barriers that prevent us from taking action once we are "cued." Shawn Anchor, the Harvard professor we discussed in Section II, found in his research that our ability to build new habits is often undermined by small, logistical barriers to the desired action.

For example, in a study assessing peoples' ability to build a morning exercise routine, it was found that that the participants who were instructed to leave their exercise shoes and socks by the front door the night before were more than twice as likely to succeed in building the new routine than the participants who were not given this simple instruction. Because they had put their shoes and socks out the night before, these participants required less "activation energy" (i.e., the amount of energy needed to initiate the desired act) at the pivotal moment, and therefore were less deterred from working out.

When the alarm goes off and it is pitch black outside, our rapid cognition recognizes that in order to engage in the targeted behavior, we not only have to exert "execution energy" – the large amount of energy needed to exercise (which is *challenging enough*) – but we also have to exert "activation energy" to find our shoes and socks ("Where the heck did I leave my shoes?") – just so we can have the *privilege* of exercising in the dark. This combination is often too much for our psyche to handle, so we impulsively hit "snooze" on the alarm and tuck ourselves back into bed. The additional layer of effort, having to locate our shoes, can often be the breaking point for our willpower. It's the straw that broke the camel's workout. We otherwise may have just enough willpower to motivate to exercise, but that additional burden of also having to muster up the willpower to "prepare" to work out makes the entire experience a willpower overload, and we break.

In *The Happiness Advantage*, Anchor explains that an effective hack in building a new habit is completing as many as possible of the small logistical items in advance, followed by break. Then, when it's time to do the actual behavior, we can dedicate 100% of our energy and willpower to executing the actual behavior. Even the smallest of logistical hurdles can derail our momentum in taking the desired action, so the idea is to eliminate as many of these micro-hurdles as possible in advance. When we have to exert activation energy and execution energy back-to-back, we often fail to perform the action, yet when we separate the activation process from the execution process, our odds of success spike.

And if we are trying to *break* an undesired habit, we can add artificial activation energy, by making it slightly harder or more annoying to commence the habit. Often this small obstruction deters us from impulsively reaching for that bait in the moment of temptation. So Anchor advises, "Lower the activation energy for habits you want to adopt, and raise it for habits you want to avoid. The more we can lower or even eliminate the activation energy for our desired actions, the more we can enhance our ability to jump-start positive change."[169]

If you are trying to build a daily practice of gratitude journaling, leaving the journal and pen out on the very piece of furniture you intend to use while you journal can be the difference between succeeding and failing. Anchor explains that if we have to scramble for more than 20 seconds to find the logistical items necessary to perform the act, we are exponentially less likely to complete the act. He calls this the "20-Second Rule," because if we are burdened by even 20 seconds of activation energy to start an undesirable but beneficial act, it is often the death knell to that act. If you are sitting in the living room working and decide to do 30–60 seconds of gratitude journaling, but you then realize your journal is on the nightstand in your bedroom, your journaling inspiration will likely suffer an instantaneous demise. The small but mighty burden of walking to the bedroom and back – *on top of the energy expenditure of subsequently journaling* – is simply too much for our unconscious minds.

For this reason, a person trying to build the habit of playing the guitar every day is far more likely to succeed if the guitar is stored in a visible location next to where they intend to play each day, as opposed to being tucked away in the closet. That's right, the *anguish* of having to walk *all the way* to the closet and open that closet door is often the difference between building the habit and not.

If you want to build the habit of starting your outline first thing in the morning, without getting pulled away into time-consuming and energy-zapping distractions, consider expending the activation energy the night before. When you typically sit down at your computer in the morning with the intention of launching into your outline, you actually are *not* in a position to immediately start writing (no matter how much you want to). It is hard enough to motivate to write first thing in the morning, but you have additional (likely unknown) obstacles to writing: you first have to pull up your outline on the screen, locate your class notes, pull out your textbook and open it to the right case, and locate and open any supplemental materials or documents you will reference during the outlining process. So not only do you have to muster up the energy to outline (which is brutal enough), but you also have to engage in this tedious and exhausting process just to earn the right to begin the brutal process of outlining.

But guess what is just one, effortless click away at that very moment? Social media, web browsing, and a litany of other fun allurements. It's not a fair competition. Your "System 1" thinking scans all of this in a matter of milliseconds and before you know it, your strong intention of starting the day with outlining has been derailed. However, if you were to exert all of the activation energy the night before, as your final task of the evening, then you are far more likely to launch into outlining first thing the morning. What if, when you sit down at the computer, your outline is already up and all of the digital and hard-copy materials you will use in the process are already fully set up? Now 100% of your energy and willpower can be directed to typing the first sentence. You have astronomically increased your odds of immediately outlining.

The same occurs in reverse. If we are trying to break an undesirable habit, deliberately creating logistical hurdles advances the process by *increasing* the activation energy required to commit the habit. As Anchor notes, "Our best weapon in the battle against bad habits . . . is simply to make it harder for ourselves to succumb to them."[170] So if we are trying to reduce our television consumption, Anchor recommends taking the batteries out of the remote control and placing them in the kitchen drawer. Then when we are on the couch and have an impulse to watch TV, our unconscious mind scans the situation and realizes we have to go through the agonizing process of walking all the way to the kitchen, opening the drawer, and somehow figuring out how to put the batteries into the remote. "Why on earth do they require the batteries to go in opposite directions, and why do I always put them in the wrong way?!", we indignantly ask ourselves. And then we make a split-second decision to avoid this annoyance, and we continue on without turning on the TV.

If we are trying to reduce the frequency of our email distractions while working on a key document (such as an outline), Anchor suggests turning off email notifications, hiding the email icon in a file that requires several "clicks" to arrive at, and if necessary, deleting the auto-storage of our username and password. "What?!", you are likely thinking. "I'm supposed to type in my username and password every time I check email – *are you insane?*" Please don't shoot the messengers! We are just sharing Anchor's science-based suggestion (which we happen to fully endorse). If you are having discipline problems around email checking (ignore this suggestion if you are not), it is a powerful way to re-establish control. Rest assured, if you have to go through all of these annoying steps just to check email, your self-sabotaging emailing will plummet, and your productivity on the outline or other important task will skyrocket. Same thing with social media or web browsing. If you are struggling to reduce the amount of time you spend each day on those activities, make the process of initiating them less effortless and more irritating. You are going to become much better at resisting them.

So in order to enhance your ability to build your new habit, be sure to set up the habit by preemptively eliminating the micro-barriers to success. And if you are trying to break an old habit, create micro-barriers that make it harder and more aggravating to succumb to the temptation. As you master the art of activation energy, your habit reformation skills will blossom.

6. REWARD YOURSELF FOR THE GOAL

One of the best things we can do to help build a habit is to reward ourselves each time we engage in the targeted behavior (until it becomes a habit). James Clear, the previously mentioned author of the book *Atomic Habits* and one of the world's leading experts on habits, describes self-rewards as "the cardinal rule of behavior change."

As Clear explains, "In the beginning, you need a reason to stay on track. This is why immediate rewards are essential. They keep you excited while the delayed rewards accumulate in the background."[171] Over time, the "delayed rewards" of the habit (for example, the improved productivity and sense of control from a new study habit, or the increased health, vitality, and energy from a consistent exercise regimen) become pronounced, and the artificial self-rewards become unnecessary.

By giving ourselves a reward each time we complete the desired behavior, we are replicating the brain's "reward" component of the 3-part habit loop, and thereby jump-starting the brain's habit formation mechanism. For this reason, Charles Duhigg encourages us to provide a truly enjoyable reward each time we complete the targeted behavior. When it comes to building a new workout routine, for example, the research shows that one of the most effective ways to do so is to eat a small piece of chocolate or other delicious treat right after each workout.[172]

You read that correctly: the research shows that eating a post-workout piece of chocolate (or another yummy treat) is one of the most effective ways to build this new habit. The increase in calories from this unhealthy treat is likely to be less than the calories you burned from the exercise session. But more importantly, you are tricking your brain into thinking that exercise is more of a habit than it already is. Duhigg explains that if we eat an unhealthy treat right after exercising, we are activating the "reward" component of the habit loop, and thereby speeding up the habit formation process. Conversely, if we just eat something healthy right after exercising, like salad, we are deactivating the "reward" component and neurologically slowing down the habit formation process. From a neurological perspective, we are punishing ourselves for completing the desired act. That doesn't sound like an effective way of building a long-term habit, does it? Once the habit loop begins to concretize in the brain, your real neurological rewards will begin to activate after exercising, and you can phase out the artificial reward. It's a prudent tradeoff you are making in furtherance of this new habit: you choose to consume some extra calories during the habit formation process in exchange for increasing the odds and speed of building the habit.

This is why one of your co-authors, who shall remain nameless due to shame, would eat Taco Bell after every yoga class they attended many years ago when they were trying to build a yoga habit. Their guilty pleasure in life was Taco Bell (who doesn't love artificial, highly processed, chemical-infused Mexican food?) at the time they read this research, which also happened to be the time they were failing to build a 3-day-per-week yoga habit. This was the first piece of research on habit formation they read, and they were immediately skeptical of it: "There is *no way* that eating unhealthy food after exercising will help me build an exercise habit," they assured themself. So they figured they would call the bluff on this research by taking the challenge. They allowed themself the forbidden ecstasy of Taco Bell, but only right after a yoga class. As the other yogis would follow class with a green juice or kale salad, your co-author would make a beeline to Taco Bell and engorge themself with quesadillas and gorditas. (They went a little overboard on the "small treat" idea.)*

Something mystical then occurred: your co-author built a 3-day-per-week yoga routine, and after a couple of months into the experiment, the Taco Bell reward became unnecessary and was phased out (as the delayed rewards of enhanced energy, mental health, and fitness bloomed). By "mystical," by the way, we mean "scientific." Consistent with the scientific evidence, that delicious reward supercharged their ability to build a habit they likely would not have built. Your co-author maintained that habit for many years in a row, until the yoga studios closed due to the pandemic, at which point the habit paused.

The reward you select for any given habit formation does not have to be food related. It can be allowing yourself to watch your favorite trashy show on Netflix, or taking a mid-day nap, or getting your nails done, or sunbathing for an hour, or playing an hour of video games, or taking a long hot bath. Think of what brings you short-term pleasure and then hold off on that activity until you commit the targeted act. Each time you follow the targeted act with that specific reward, you will turn the act into more of a habit.

So whatever behavioral goal you set for yourself, be sure to immediately follow each successful act with a small reward. Your brain will thank you.

---

* Because we believe in transparency, we will disclose that Jarrett is the co-author at issue. You can refer to him as Jarrett "Taco Bell" Green going forward.

7. TRACK YOUR PROGRESS

Our final tip for building a new habit is this: Track your progress through a very simple self-monitoring tool. The "Hawthorne Effect" (also known as "Psychological Reactivity") is a long-standing phenomenon of behavioral psychology whereby people's behavior improves when they are being observed by others. Have you noticed that you improve your behavior when your professor is looking at you versus when you are alone in your apartment? Don't feel bad — even electrons behave differently when being observed, as proven by the observer effect in quantum physics.

What is fascinating, though, is that recent research reveals that a person's behavior also improves when the person observing them is *themself*![173] As long as we track our self-observation *in writing* (whether on paper or via our phones), the science shows our behavior improves, as compared to when we behave with no formal tracking mechanism — during which we tend to notice our behaviors only in an unstructured, *ad hoc* way.

This effect was discovered when behavioral change therapists would ask new clients to track in writing, in between sessions, the behavior that brought them into therapy, so that the therapist could establish a baseline of the client's normal functioning (essential to measuring future improvements). What kept occurring is that the clients would return to the therapist's office the next session to share that their monitored behavior in between sessions was not representative of their typical behavior because, oddly, they experienced *marked improvement* in their behavior while they were tracking it. This eventually led to research studies and the conclusion that merely tracking one's own behavior in a concrete manner mysteriously improves the behavior.

Habit researchers have studied this phenomenon and now recommend a simple "self-tracking" process when attempting to build a new habit. In one such example, as featured by Duhigg in *The Power of Habit*, 1,600 obese individuals participated in a nutrition-based weight loss study in 2008 funded by the National Institute of Health.[174] Participants were broken into several groups, with each group subjected to one experimental variable. The purpose of the study was to determine which variable or factor led to the largest weight loss. One group was provided a food journal and asked to write down what they ate one day per week.

Six months into the study, the participants who conducted this once-per-week food journaling had lost twice as much weight as the participants who did not. The simple act of tracking their food once per week transformed their ability to eat healthier and lose more weight. Some researchers theorize that tracking one's own behavior over time creates a different level of self-accountability, while others believe it generates more insights about one's patterns and idiosyncrasies that help improve behavior. Whatever the reason, a large body of research reveals that it works.

So here's what we suggest: Create a simple "Yes-No" chart when you are about to start building the new habit. It can be a single piece of paper, with the dates listed for the next four weeks in a single column on the left side of the page. This can also be done on your smart phone in the "Notes" App. Then at the end of each day, simply mark a "Y" (for "Yes") or "N" (for "No") next to each date, reflecting whether you completed the behavior.

So if you are aiming to build a daily meditation habit, pre-list the next 14–28 dates (you can choose the number of days you want to start tracking and can always extend it later!) on your phone or paper, and at the end of each evening, simply type or write the letter "Y" if you meditated that day and the letter "N" if you did not. If you are trying to reduce the amount of time you watch TV or Netflix (or engage in social media) each day, pre-list the next 28 dates on your phone, and at the end of each evening, enter a quick estimate of how many minutes you spent that day doing the activity. For example, 150 minutes, 130 minutes, 240 minutes, 190 minutes, etc. Don't worry about exactness – if you are 15–20 minutes off, it is no big deal. Just listing the rough estimate will serve the purpose of creating a self-tracking system. You can adjust the structure of the chart to conform to the specific goal you set.

GOALS & HABITS: ACHIEVE WHAT YOU SEEK 277

Meditation Tracking

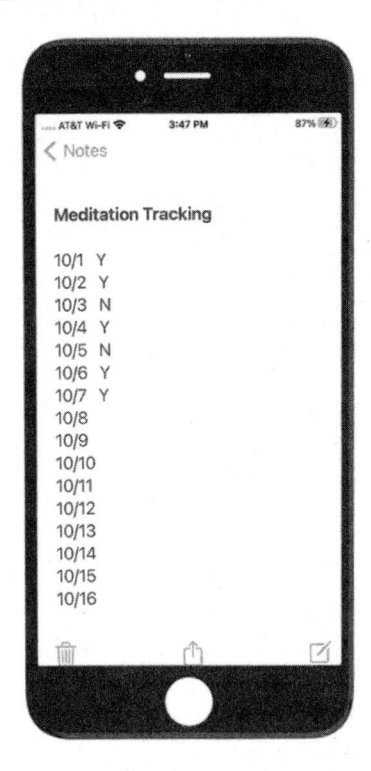

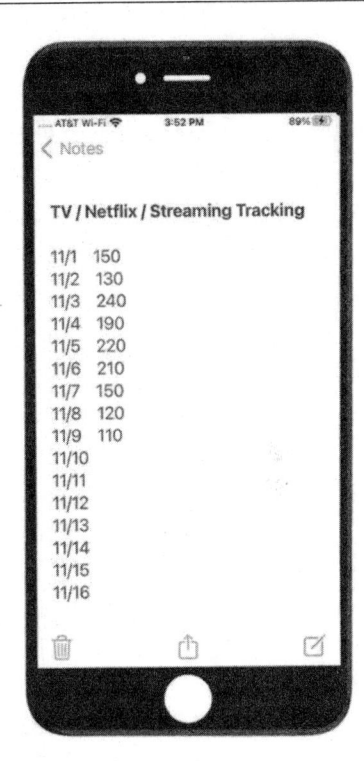

10/1 Y
10/2 Y
10/3 N
10/4 Y
10/5 N
10/6 Y
10/7 Y
10/8
10/9
10/10
10/11
10/12
10/13
10/14
10/15
10/16

TV / Netflix / Streaming Tracking

11/1 150
11/2 130
11/3 240
11/4 190
11/5 220
11/6 210
11/7 150
11/8 120
11/9 110
11/10
11/11
11/12
11/13
11/14
11/15
11/16

Even though this self-tracking takes just a few seconds per day, the research reveals it will materially increase the likelihood of you succeeding in building or breaking the habit at issue.*

SUMMARY

To summarize, here are the seven tips for habit reformation:

- **One goal at a time:** Don't "goal juggle"; attack one major goal at a time.

---

* There is an abundance of "habit tracking" apps available in your app store. If you type the words "habit tracker" into the "search" field of the app store, a list of habit tracking apps will appear, e.g., "Habit Tracker"; "Done: A Habit Tracker;" "Productive – Habit Tracker"; "Strides: Goal Tracker"; "Habitify: Habit Tracker"; "Way of Life – Habit Tracker"; and many others. They have slightly different graphics, features, user experiences, etc., but any one of them will allow you to effectively track your targeted habit. You can poke around the options and pick the one that most resonates with you. Moreover, if you would like additional information on the power of tracking a desired habit, we refer you to this piece from James Clear: https://jamesclear.com/habit-tracker.

- **Baby steps:** Break the ultimate goal into easily achievable interim goals.
- **Tangible and measurable:** The more concrete and detailed the goal, the better.
- **Pre-existing cue:** Perform the behavior immediately after the same cue each time.
- **Set up the goal:** Eliminate the small, logistical barriers to your goal in advance, or create such barriers for a habit you are trying to break.
- **Reward yourself:** Immediately follow the targeted behavior with an enjoyable reward.
- **Track your progress:** Create a simple chart to monitor your progress each day.

In approximately 350 B.C., Aristotle famously said, "We are what we repeatedly do. Excellence, then, is not an act, but a habit." Now that you have these science-based tips in your repertoire, you are well-equipped to methodically achieve excellence. We encourage you to identify one major behavioral goal at this time – and to begin taking it on!

Tool 11

MEDITATION: IT'S *SUPER* ANNOYING! (YET LIFE-CHANGING)

"The goal of meditation isn't to control your thoughts. It's to stop letting them control you."

— Anonymous

You are constantly inundated with pro-meditation exhortations, such as "You have to start meditating!" or "You *really* should meditate, it's sooo good for you!" It's super annoying; we get it. We even considered not including this particular tool in the book because we thought the last thing you need is to be told to meditate *by more people*. But we have found that a big reason law students (and others) do not meditate is because they have received misinformation about what meditation is, and what meditation should feel like. Our society – and many well-intentioned meditation teachers – propagate a collection of "meditation myths" that have the effect of dissuading people from trying to meditate or staying with meditation when they struggle. These myths make us feel like meditation failures, and they cause us to reject a tool that can significantly enrich our lives.

Your co-authors were duped by these myths for many years, and consequently, we both failed to build a consistent meditation practice despite much effort. Eventually, we were fortunate to study under some of the world's wisest meditation teachers, and we learned that much of what we believed for all of those years was false. Once those veils were lifted, we both built a daily meditation practice without much strife, and the benefits have been immense and multi-faceted.

We have since helped thousands of law students, lawyers, legal professionals, and corporate employees build a daily meditation practice by exposing the myths and revealing the truths. We would now like to do that for you.

Here is what we have determined to be the top five meditation myths – and the corresponding meditation truths:

Meditation Myths	Meditation Truths
1. Meditation should feel peaceful and relaxing.	Meditation is boring and turbulent!
2. Meditation is intended to quiet the mind.	You cannot quiet the mind!
3. You should meditate in a distinguished lotus position.	Those meditation photos on Instagram are charades!
4. You are bad at meditating.	There is no such thing as being bad at meditating!
5. I didn't get much from meditation, so I stopped.	You won't receive the rich benefits of meditation until you commit to it for a few weeks.

We are going to expound upon each one of these. But before we do, we want to address the threshold question: What are the benefits of meditation? Overcoming the meditation myths in order to build a meditation practice would only be a worthwhile endeavor if meditation will ultimately benefit your life. The good news is that the scientific evidence decisively shows that it will. And it's not just a small amount of evidence; there have been *hundreds* of studies published in peer-reviewed journals that have found that meditation provides tangible benefits, including mental, emotional, relational, cognitive, and academic benefits.

Let's put it in terms you will relate to: There is more scientific evidence supporting the vast benefits of meditation than there are unread books in your law library. *(Shout-out to the 1983 Federal Supplement, Third Series! "F. Supp. 3d." in the house!)* Here is a very brief summary of some of the well-established benefits of meditation:

- increases working memory, cognitive functioning, verbal fluency, and attentional functioning, and reduces fatigue and anxiety[175]
- decreases mind-wandering and daydreaming[176]

MEDITATION: IT'S SUPER ANNOYING! (YET LIFE-CHANGING)

- increases the efficiency and effectiveness of multi-tasking (i.e., task-switching), and reduces the incidence of distraction[177]
- increases gray matter in the brain, including the left hippocampus, which is responsible for learning, memory, and emotional regulation[178]
- improves reading comprehension skills, working memory, and GRE test scores[179]
- improves decision making and reduces one's propensity for sunk-cost bias[180]
- improves brain signaling and cognitive speed by increasing axonal density (the signaling connections in the brain) and axonal myelin (the protective tissue around the axons)[181]
- increases cortical gyrification (wrinkling of the brain), which is associated with improved cognitive functioning[182]
- increases attention span and ability to control allocation of attention between competing stimuli, and reduces the "attentional blink" deficit (a neurological phenomenon whereby the brain's allocation of attention to one item causes it to fail to notice a rapidly succeeding second item)[183]
- reduces the brain's pain activation response, increases pain tolerance, and improves the ability to remain mentally focused while being subjected to a painful stimulus[184]
- improves several aspects of attention and focus, including attentional control, attentional endurance, and distraction resistance[185]
- improves creative thinking and problem-solving abilities[186]
- improves working memory and sustained attention while performing a task[187]
- decreases cognitive rigidity during problem solving, and increases the ability to achieve novel solutions

to intellectual problems, rather than being "blinded" by one's past experience[188]

- is associated with the thickening of the cerebral cortex (which is associated with increased cognitive abilities and overall intelligence markers)[189]
- reduces mind wandering, including mind wandering to negative topics[190]
- is associated with more rational decision making and heightened activation of related brain networks in response to unfair actions from others[191]
- increases psychomotor vigilance (i.e., the speed at which we convert cognition into motor action)[192]
- rapidly alters gene expression and improves mitochondrial energy production and functioning, which is associated with improved health benefits from reduced psychosocial stress[193]
- increases alpha brain wave modulation and, hence, attention during cognitive task performance, as well as working memory[194]
- improves performance decrements among individuals experiencing "stereotype threat" (where inclusion in a perceived unfavorable group impairs cognitive performance)[195]
- reduces stress, due to decreases in distractive and ruminating thoughts, and improves positive mood states[196]
- reduces stress and increases compassion and forgiveness[197]
- lowers stress, anxiety, and fatigue[198]
- lowers stress and anxiety and improves mood[199]
- reduces stress, including heart rate and physiological biomarkers of stress[200]
- reduces stress, and increases self-compassion and quality of life[201]

MEDITATION: IT'S SUPER ANNOYING! (YET LIFE-CHANGING)

- increases well-being and emotional control in response to stressful images[202]
- decreases emotional intensity and increases internal calmness when under stress[203]
- reduces the negativity bias and increases optimism[204]
- reduces stress and increases feelings of self-efficacy and positive states of mind[205]
- reduces symptoms of anxiety and panic among individuals with general anxiety disorder and panic disorder[206]
- reduces heart rate, blood pressure, and mental stress among individuals with hypertension[207]
- improves cognitive reframing of stressful events and thereby reduces stress from those events[208]
- increases stress resiliency and decreases sleepiness and fatigue[209]
- decreases symptoms of depression and anxiety[210]
- reduces depression, anxiety, and stress[211]
- decreases symptoms of depression and addictive disorders[212]
- decreases unconscious bias on the basis of race[213] and age,[214] bias against traditionally stigmatized groups,[215] sexist attitudes,[216] and age-related stereotyping[217]
- is associated with greater acceptance of one's romantic partner and greater overall satisfaction with one's romantic relationship[218]
- reduces relationship negativity and increases perceptions of support in relationships[219]
- is associated with improved relationship satisfaction[220]

In sum, meditation has been scientifically shown to improve our brain structures, various aspects of our cognitive functioning, our stress resiliency and emotional well-being, our symptoms of mental illness, our energy and sleep, our interpersonal relationships, and our overall mindsets and mood in life. We think it is safe to assume you would benefit from some of these effects.*

Because we have addressed the threshold question of whether a daily meditation practice would benefit you, the question now arises whether you are capable of building a daily meditation practice. We feel strongly that the answer is "yes," especially after we expose the "meditation myths" and the corresponding "meditation truths." Once you have a more accurate understanding of what meditation truly is and how it should feel, we believe building a daily meditation practice will become exponentially easier. So without further ado, here are our explanations of what we believe to be the five "meditation myths" and "meditation truths."

Meditation Myth #1: Meditation should feel peaceful and relaxing.

Meditation Truth #1: Meditation is boring and turbulent!

---

* A small percentage of people have negative effects from meditation, as reflected by a meta-analysis study that found that 3.7% of participants in experimental studies experienced unwanted effects.[221]

This is a rather small percentage, as even therapy leads to negative effects in approximately 10% of the cases (but has a much higher failure rate than meditation, i.e., the incidence of no positive effect, as opposed to a negative effect). Therapy has immense empirical support, but that does not mean there are not some rare negative effects of therapy. The same goes for meditation, although to an even lesser extent. More importantly, the rare negative effects reported from meditation likely are not caused by meditation, but rather *noticed* and more directly felt during meditation. Indeed, a major aspect of meditation is "turning toward" and observing our internal state, which often involves stress, turmoil, and other emotional volatilities. Directly observing these volatilities is not always pleasant, and can make the volatilities feel more pronounced than when we suppress or distract ourselves from them. However, just as a captain of a ship in the middle of the ocean who observes a leak in the hull will experience fear and other difficult emotions but can now take action to address this pre-existing problem, a meditator who observes her underlying emotional turmoil will also experience fear and other difficult emotions (which she could have avoided by not meditating), but she can now take action to address this pre-existing issue.

Importantly, by remaining in ignorance, neither the meditator nor the ship captain is benefitted; in fact, they are harmed. A meditator who is uncomfortable upon learning of the "leaks" in their emotional hull can then begin to process, heal, and transform those emotional issues in ways that will lead to far greater well-being and happiness in the long-run. As we will further explain in "Truth #1," below, meditation can be turbulent and uncomfortable, but the benefits far outweigh these costs.

MEDITATION: IT'S SUPER ANNOYING! (YET LIFE-CHANGING)

About 20 years ago, I [*your co-author Jarrett*] decided I wanted to learn to meditate, so I joined a Sunday meditation group. A few minutes after I arrived at the opening session, it was apparently time to start meditating. The meditation teacher gave no background on what we were about to do, before abruptly saying, "Okay, let's close our eyes and meditate for 20 minutes." I snapped my eyes shut, and within about 10 seconds was begging to open my eyes. The next 20 minutes felt like some sort of slow torture being inflicted on a prisoner of war. My mind was frenetically pinballing from thought to thought, and I felt extremely irritated, turbulent, and impatient inside. I wondered if other people were struggling, so I would occasionally crack my eyes barely open (so it still looked like my eyes were closed if anyone was watching) and scan the room. What I saw was highly disturbing: everyone else looked completely peaceful and blissful. Their relaxed, serene faces suggested they were experiencing none of the internal chaos I was. I became angry at them for being so tranquil while I was in misery, and I became angry at myself for being so "bad" at meditating. Great, now I was not only internally chaotic, but I was also full of rage!

For the rest of the session, I oscillated between rage, impatience, frustration, and mind-numbing boredom. I identified dozens of activities I could be doing that would be infinitely more productive and beneficial than this. When the 20-minute torture session ended, I wondered what was wrong with me. How come everyone was so peaceful and happy meditating, while I was so agitated and bored?

Due to the (false) belief that only I found meditation boring and irritating, and everyone else found it euphoric, I struggled mightily with meditation for years and rarely did it. At that time, I had not received any proper instruction on "how" to meditate, i.e., how to navigate all of the emotions and thoughts, so meditation basically consisted of me closing my eyes and waiting for the agony to end.

Many years later, I learned that meditation is generally not euphoric, but challenging, frustrating, and turbulent. When we close our eyes and go within, we come into direct presence with our "monkey mind," which is the tumultuous and volatile generator of 50,000 to 60,000 thoughts per day. We also come face-to-face with our emotional "stuff," e.g., our fears, anger, judgments, jealousy, sadness, self-doubts, and insecurities. Turning toward this stuff is not comfortable. But make no mistake about it, whether we meditate or not, those chaotic thoughts and intense emotions are inside us. And they are dictating our sense of peace, emotional well-being, and happiness. Meditation is the brave act of observing these uncomfortable aspects of self, rather than willfully ignoring them.

Our mentor and life coach, Victoria Allen, says "[M]editation requires us to choose truth and growth over comfort." When we meditate, we courageously choose to look at the truth of what is within us, which is invariably uncomfortable. And it is only upon seeing these uncomfortable truths that we truly begin to grow in life. As we mentioned earlier in this book, "We cannot change what we cannot see." Meditation helps us see. But what we see is not always comfortable. Because most people seek comfort over truth and growth, they look away from their internal state and they reject meditation.

Many things in life that are highly beneficial are also uncomfortable and unenjoyable. Exercise, eating well, studying for a complicated test, forgiveness, communicating openly and honestly with loved ones – to name a few. People who have built a regular exercise routine praise the vast benefits they receive (and the science confirms these benefits). But that does not mean that exercising is comfortable or enjoyable *while doing it*. The rich benefits flow to them after exercising, not while exercising.

"We don't meditate for the feelings during meditation," our teacher Deepak Chopra says. "We meditate for the feelings after meditation." The reality is that most of us do not feel tranquil or peaceful during meditation, but meditation leads us to feel far more tranquil, peaceful, and resilient for the rest of the day. Both of us can say that we find our daily meditation practice to be challenging and uncomfortable. Every morning, our mind comes up with an excuse to skip it. But the colossal benefits are worth the discomfort and lack of enjoyment. So if you find meditation to be boring, agitating, and uncomfortable, welcome to the club!

MEDITATION: IT'S SUPER ANNOYING! (YET LIFE-CHANGING)

Meditation Myth #2: Meditation is intended to quiet the mind.

Meditation Truth #2: You cannot quiet the mind!

One of the great falsehoods of meditation is that it is intended to quiet the mind. It sounds lovely, but the problem is that the human mind cannot be quieted. So when we meditate with the expectation or intention of quieting the mind, we are setting ourselves up for disaster. It's like going to an NBA basketball game with the expectation or intention of seeing a fabulous Broadway musical. It ain't gonna happen. This misguided expectation is going to lead to epic disappointment and frustration during the basketball game. One of the reasons people struggle so mightily with meditation is because, through no fault of their own, they have been led to believe they will quiet their mind during the meditation. The experience that follows is predictably disappointing and frustrating.

One of our old meditation teachers used to say, "The mind generates thoughts like the mouth generates saliva." We cannot quiet the mind any more than we can halt the salivary glands. Here's a personal challenge for you: For the next five minutes, try to prevent your salivary glands from generating saliva. Go ahead, you can do it! Actually, no matter how much you focus or try, you are not going to stop your salivary glands from generating saliva. And no matter how much you focus or try, you are not going to stop your brain from generating thoughts. That is what the brain does. "If you have stopped your thoughts," our meditation teacher, Davidji, is fond of saying, "then you have flat-lined and are now dead." Indeed, death is the only way of stopping the brain from generating thoughts.

So if you want to be alive, you better get used to an active mind. Here's the truth: Meditation is not about quieting the mind, it is about being present to the volatility of the mind. We like to say that meditation is "the dance between attention and distraction." We briefly experience present-moment attention by placing our attention on a specific focal point (e.g., our breath, a specific body part, an image, an affirmation, etc.), but then the mind inevitably slips into distraction. We go down a succession of associative thoughts, and then eventually notice that our attention has spun out of control. So we gently release those distractions, and then bring our attention back to the focal point.

We are able to hold our attention on that focal point for a couple of seconds, perhaps, and then it flits away again. At some point, we realize that our mind has taken us down a wild path of associative thoughts, and at that moment, we non-judgmentally release those thoughts and lovingly place our attention back on our focal point.

"It doesn't matter how many times you get pulled into distractions," says Chopra. "What matters is how many times you *notice* you've gotten pulled into distractions."

When I [*your co-author Rebecca*] was learning to meditate from my teacher Dr. Jeremy Hunter, an executive leadership expert and professor at the Drucker School of Management, he emphasized that distractions were actually the *key* to meditation. I had come to his office hours to confess that I was failing at meditation, as evidenced by the constant barrage of distractions that ravaged each meditation. He looked at me with warm compassion before saying, "Rebecca, I am so happy to hear you have been experiencing so many distractions." As my brain contorted to comprehend this befuddling comment, he added, "noticing the distractions *is* meditation." The moment I heard this, everything changed for me.

Here is an example of an extremely standard five second period of distraction that occurs in the mind of a meditator during a typical meditation.

> I am paying attention to my breath, awesome. Here is my inbreath, and there is my outbreath. I can feel my back when I breathe, that's weird. My back is kind of sore, is that from sitting all day? Sore. Soar. I never remember which spelling this is. Do birds sore or soar? Spelling. . . . I was never good at spelling, thankfully I never had to do Spelling Bees. I would have been eliminated in the first round. Guaranteed! Is it 'i before e' or 'e before i'? I hope I didn't have any spelling errors in that email I sent out earlier, that wouldn't look good. I had so little time that I didn't proofread it as carefully as normal. Today is so time-crunched, will there be time for lunch? Oooh lunch, I want pizza. A delicious pizza pie! It's funny how they still call it a pie. Has anyone ever put whipped cream on a pizza? I should put

MEDITATION: IT'S SUPER ANNOYING! (YET LIFE-CHANGING)

whipped cream on more things. Is it unhealthy to eat whipped cream for breakfast?

Within five seconds, our mind has taken us from present-moment awareness to realizing we should be eating whipped cream for breakfast. That is what the human mind does. But at some point, we notice what has occurred, and then we gently say to ourself, "Oh right, I'm meditating. I am going to let the thought about whipped cream for breakfast go for now, and bring my attention back to my breath. Here I am breathing in, and now breathing out."

That is what meditation feels like. It is the oscillation or dance (albeit an often *inelegant* dance) between attention and distraction. We simply go back-and-forth between attention and distraction, attention and distraction, attention and distraction, attention and distraction, until the meditation ends. When we release the myth that meditation involves quieting the mind, we can embrace what meditation truly is, and it becomes markedly easier to build a meditation practice. It is true that as we meditate more and more, we can sometimes keep our attention a little longer before the distractions take us over, but ultimately, our attention will get hijacked by distracting thoughts sooner or later. If we don't have any of these distracting thoughts, it's time to call the morgue.

Meditation Myth #3: You should meditate in a distinguished lotus position.

Meditation Truth #3: Those meditation photos on Instagram are charades!

Another meditation myth that obstructs the process of building a consistent meditation practice is the notion that we should "look" a certain way when we meditate. Instagram is littered with photos of highly fit individuals rocking the latest fashion trend while perfectly positioned atop a natural overhang in an elegant lotus posture. It could be the cover photo of "Meditation Magazine" (does that exist?), but is it really meditation? No, not really. While there is nothing wrong with holding an elegant lotus posture, it is not at all necessary. And for many people, holding certain postures – especially while seated on the ground or in a rigid "meditation position" – causes bodily pain or discomfort. If you are physically uncomfortable during meditation, you are putting yourself through unnecessary obstacles and making the meditation unnecessarily challenging. As we know from the above truths, meditation is challenging enough *without* dealing with physical discomfort.

Comfort should be Queen. So when you meditate, we invite you to ensure your physical comfort. If that means sitting in a chair, or stacking pillows under your knees, or making any number of physical adjustments, make sure your body is happy. We do recommend sitting up (rather than lying down) and keeping a generally upright spine (rather than folding forward or leaning back), as these positions will make it easier to control your attention. But beyond that, ensure your bodily comfort. By putting your body into a comfortable position, you will be able to direct most of your attention to monitoring your fluctuating emotions and thoughts, rather than also having to contend with physical hardships.*

Remember that despite all of those awesome Instagram posts, meditation is not about creating the *appearance of peacefulness*, it is about turning our attention inward and meeting ourselves – and all of our imperfections – *with peace* and non-judgmental acceptance. "Meditation practice isn't about trying to throw ourselves away and become better," says Pema Chodron, an American monk of the Tibetan Buddhist tradition. "It's about befriending who we already are."

When we get caught up in sitting a certain way, or holding our body in a certain fashion, we are drifting away from the true purpose of meditation. It does not matter how we look on the outside; it matters how we navigate the inside.

Meditation Myth #4: You are bad at meditating.

Meditation Truth #4: There is no such thing as being bad at meditating!

We cannot tell you how often we hear people tell us they are "bad" at meditation. Because both of us previously thought this about ourselves, we can empathize. Our hope is that the above truths about the inability to quiet the mind and the often-

---

* Of course, if you have a physical limitation that prevents you from sitting in this recommended posture, please just do whatever feels good and comfortable to your body.

tumultuous nature of meditation will naturally erode the illusion that you are "bad" at meditating. Once you realize that having an active mind and turbulent emotions while meditating are not indications of failure or incompetence, but rather, a standard part of the meditation experience, you can hopefully let go of some of your self-judgments.

But there is another source of our illusion that we are "bad" at meditation: we are not *accomplishing* anything tangible and measurable during meditation. Throughout our lives, we have been programmed to believe we are "good" at something if we deliver positive results and "bad" at something if we do not. The problem with – *actually, the gift of* – meditation is that there are no results or outcomes to achieve. So when we complete the meditation, we are unable to point to anything tangible and say, "*That* is what I accomplished during my meditation!" Which inevitably makes us feel like failures. *In every other sector of our life,* when we spend time and effort on an activity, we are able to identify the tangible result that flows from success. We either sent out the email or we did not, we either completed the reading or we did not, we either dropped the package off at the post office or we did not, we either knew the answer to the professor's cold-call question or we did not, we either enjoyed our study break or we did not, we either made it to the gym or we did not, we either got the grade we wanted or we did not, and we either got the summer job we wanted or we did not.

Virtually all of our activities in life involve active doing. They are called "activities," after all, so they are generally "active" in nature. As such, we spend most of the day "doing" – doing one thing, then doing another, then doing another. When we "do" effectively and get the result we want, we feel successful. We determine we are "good" at that activity. But, as an old meditation cliché states, "We are human beings, not human *doings.*" We are not meant to "do" all day, we are also meant to "be." And meditation is the purest form of "being." During meditation, we are not producing anything, we are not delivering anything, and we are not accomplishing anything in the world. We are simply "being." We are being with our thoughts, we are being with our emotions, and we are being with ourselves.

This practice of "being" can trigger our social conditioning that we always must be "productive," and it can therefore make us feel like we are failing when we are meditating. But we are not failing and we are not "bad" at meditating. Meditation, by definition, involves inaction and the absence of tangible results.* "The only 'bad' meditation is the one you did not do," Deepak Chopra likes to say.

So we invite you to notice if part of the reason you struggle to meditate is an unconscious belief that you are not being productive and not accomplishing anything tangible. If that belief is present, we invite you to exchange it for the belief that meditation is not about "doing" or about "accomplishing," but about unconditionally "being." When you give yourself permission to take a pause from your life of perpetual "doing," and allow yourself just to "be" for a short window, it will likely become much easier to build a meditation practice.

Meditation Myth #5: I didn't get much from meditation so I stopped.

Meditation Truth #5: You won't receive the rich benefits of meditation until you commit to it for a few weeks.

A meditation and spiritual master, Swami Mukundananda, says that meditation is like taking a train from Delhi to Agra. The passenger arrives at the Delhi train station and asks the booking agent for a train ticket to Agra. The booking agent says (in Hindi), "That will be 800 rupees" (approximately $10). The passenger says, "I will pay when I arrive safely in Agra." The agent responds, "No, you must pay now if you want to board the train." The passenger says, "That's absurd! If I pay you now, I have no guarantee I will be taken to Agra. You may take me to some other city and then I will have lost my money! I don't want to pay until I have arrived in Agra." The agent explains, "You

---

* One clarification on this theme: Meditation of course leads to rich results over the course of our practice, as confirmed by the scientific research outlined above, and as further discussed in Myth/Truth #5 below. But each time we complete a meditation, it can be difficult to identify a tangible "outcome" in that moment. For this reason, it can feel as if we are not "succeeding" or "accomplishing" anything when we are initially building a practice, and this impression can deter us from continuing. Of course, by noting that each meditation does not produce the sort of direct and tangible results generated by most other activities in life, we are not implying that meditation does not eventually lead to profound results.

MEDITATION: IT'S SUPER ANNOYING! (YET LIFE-CHANGING)

have to pay now and then trust that the train will take you to Agra. If you don't pay now, you cannot get on board and you have no chance of ever arriving in Agra." The passenger refuses to pay the fare under these conditions, so he decides to return to his home in Delhi.

Swami Mukundananda explains that most new meditators are like this train passenger. If they were to receive the rich benefits of meditation at the outset, then they would happily commit to meditation. But getting them to commit to meditation before they have received the benefits is very challenging. Yet without making the commitment in advance – *before the benefits accrue* – they will never receive the very benefits they seek. They want to do a couple of meditations and feel completely different. If this occurred, they would be motivated to dedicate themselves to a daily meditation going forward.

But that is not how it works. We have to be willing to pay the ticket fare by committing to meditation *before* we arrive at the destination. If we fully commit for several weeks, we will begin to experience the multifaceted benefits, and at that point, continuing to commit going forward will be much easier. However, most new meditators quit before the benefits accrue, and thereby deprive themselves of the vast benefits of this life-altering tool.

Are you willing to commit to one minute of meditation each day for the next 28 days? Consistent with the "small victory" tip of habit formation (see Tool #10, page 260),* you can slowly increase your meditations beyond one minute once that length feels habitual. Over time, you can slowly increase your meditations to five minutes, and eventually to 10 minutes. Once you are meditating 5–10 minutes per day for a couple of weeks, we will be shocked if you are not experiencing obvious benefits.†

In order to assess the benefits, Deepak Chopra suggests we compare the internal states we experience in response to life challenges both before and after meditating consistently. For

---

* If you desire to build a daily meditation practice, implementing the various other habit formation tips from Tool #10 at page 255 ("Goals & Habits: Achieve What You Seek") will make it much easier to succeed in doing so.

† We've even had people tell us that building a 2-minute per day meditation practice led to palpable benefits for them over time.

example, after building a daily meditation practice, you may notice less anxiety when you are thinking about final exams, or you may be less reactive when your roommate or sibling says something triggering, or you may notice yourself feeling less distracted while doing homework, or you may get less upset when you are stuck in traffic, or you may feel that you are absorbing your law school material more easily, or you may feel less fatigued during the average day, or you may feel closer to your best friend, or you may feel less self-judgmental after you say something misguided in class, or you may sleep a bit better at night, or you may feel more positive about law school. These are just examples, but after you have built a daily meditation practice, you can evaluate how the practice is affecting your life.

The fundamental question, of course, is: Are willing to pay for the meditation ticket before you arrive at the meditation destination?

CLOSING

We hope our attempt to shed light on these meditation myths and truths will support you in building a daily meditation practice. A wonderful app we recommend is Insight Timer, which has over 130,000 free meditations. (That should be enough to get you through the next few weeks!) You can filter by level (e.g., "beginner"), by subject matter (e.g., stress, focus, energy, mindfulness, breathing, depression, body scan, compassion, sleep, happiness, etc.), and by duration (you can pick super short ones). Compared to just sitting in complete silence with your eyes shut, receiving verbal guidance from meditation teachers through this or other apps can make meditation slightly less painful as you build the habit.

Although meditation is often boring, irritating, and turbulent, these experiences are ultimately small costs to pay for the multifaced and transformative benefits it provides to our heart, mind and brain. To temporarily pull away from your constant barrage of law school stressors and obligations and instead turn inward for your daily meditation is no easy task. However, that is the path to clarity and awakening. "Your vision will become clear only when you look into your heart," wrote Carl

MEDITATION: IT'S SUPER ANNOYING! (YET LIFE-CHANGING)

Jung in 1916. "Who looks outside, dreams; who looks inside, awakes."

TOOL 12

VISUALIZATION: TRICK YOUR BRAIN INTO RESILIENT GREATNESS

"Everything you can imagine is real."

— Pablo Picasso

Have you ever engaged in visualization while preparing for or performing a high-stakes academic assignment, whether in law school or college? While we cannot hear your answer (unfortunately books tend to be unilateral in their communication!), we believe that over 95% of you would answer this question with a "no." That is what we have found from asking this question to thousands of law students and lawyers.

If you in fact answered in the negative, we would like to respectfully disagree with you. We are quite certain you *have* engaged in visualization. Why is this? Because you *have worried* about a high-stakes academic assignment before. In fact, like all students, you have worried about countless assignments, papers, and exams. And what is occurring neuropsychologically when you are worrying? You are thinking of that assignment unfolding *in the future* in an unsuccessful way. Your brain is actually seeing it go badly: you are envisioning yourself struggle as you complete it or you are envisioning yourself performing poorly on it. You are experiencing a split-second image in your mind of the fear manifesting into reality (which feels like it is happening), which triggers you into a state of stress or anxiety. This visualization occurs rapidly and unconsciously (System 1 thinking), but make no mistake about it, it is happening. If you don't believe us, go ahead and worry about something right now, but do not allow any images to pop into your mind. See how that's impossible?

The truth is that we are all visualizing constantly; *we are just visualizing negative outcomes.* And then we call it "worrying." Our mind generates images of the bad thing occurring and our emotions fire into stress, which as we know, also induces cognitive impairment.

Since you are already visualizing undesirable outcomes, we would like to invite you to continue to visualize – except with desirable outcomes. Don't worry, it's nothing new: Just do the same thing you do when you worry, except see yourself succeeding rather than failing. When you engage in positive visualization, you will induce feelings of resilience, rather than stress, and you will enhance your cognition, rather than impair it.

When we worry, we are visualizing a poor outcome
and flooding our system with additional stress.

Virtually all of the greatest professional athletes of the last couple of decades have one thing in common: they all swear by visualization. Rather than waiting until the actual championship game, or the Super Bowl, or the NBA Finals, or the Wimbledon Finals to mentally and emotionally navigate the

VISUALIZATION: TRICK YOUR BRAIN INTO RESILIENT GREATNESS

high-stakes pressure and overwhelming stress, they begin doing it in advance. They use their mind to *pre-experience* the event in great detail and see themselves flourishing and succeeding. Then, when the actual game arrives, their brain responds with a level of confidence, resiliency, and poise that primes them for maximal success.

Here are some of the greatest athletes in history who have relied on visualization: Michael Jordan, Serena Williams, Lebron James, Lionel Messi, Ronda Rousey, Kobe Bryant, Tom Brady, Simone Biles, Stephen Curry, Mia Hamm, Aaron Rodgers, Alex Rodriguez, Diana Taurasi, Michael Phelps, Muhammad Ali, Mike Trout, Misty May-Treanor, Patrick Mahomes, Carli Lloyd, Cristiano Ronaldo, Billie Jean King, Usain Bolt, and countless others whose addition would make this lengthy sentence far longer.

As stressful as law school is, imagine if you were taking that final exam with 50 million people watching every sentence you write in real time, and then tweeting about every error you make. "OMG, she wrote that damage to the plaintiff is an element of trespass to chattels but it is NOT! LOL!! #loser." That is a whole new level of pressure. We have much to learn about stress resiliency and peak performance from the world's greatest athletes – who have decoded how to mentally, emotionally, cognitively, and physically excel under the most stressful circumstances. Unsurprisingly, visualization is probably the most common non-physical tool that superstar athletes rely upon. Following in the footsteps of these masters of peak performance would be a prudent decision for any law student (and lawyer).

Modern science reveals that the human brain struggles to differentiate between visualized experience and actual experience – which is why visualization yields such potent results. One study, for example, used brain scans to measure the brain activation of individuals when they performed an activity and when they visualized performing the activity.[222] The study found that visualization produced regional brain activation that was similar to, and highly overlapped with, actually performing the activity.

This is why picturing yourself getting called on in class causes so much stress. You haven't even entered class yet, but your brain's visualization mechanism is replicating the experience. It's also why even a split-second thought of yourself taking the final exam without knowing any of the answers causes a jolt of dread. The exam is still weeks away, but your brain doesn't seem to know that in the moment. These are examples of your brain engaging in System 1 (unconscious) visualization by spontaneously forming an image of some bad outcome that you desperately want to avoid. Which, of course, triggers an unpleasant emotional reaction.

Since, as we mentioned above, all law students (and humans) are *already* engaging in visualization throughout the week, we might as well begin using visualization to optimize, rather than undercut, our well-being, resilience, and cognition. Instead of allowing *automatic, negative* visualizations to monopolize our visualization experience, we would be wise to add *deliberate, positive* visualizations to the mix.

The science shows that this sort of visualization can yield major benefits. Perhaps our favorite visualization study was conducted by the Cleveland Clinic, one of the most prestigious medical institutions in the country. The researchers sought to determine whether visualization can build muscle strength – without any associated muscle movement. You read that correctly: they wanted to see if visualization, alone, could strengthen our muscles.

The researchers intentionally selected a muscle that was underdeveloped in most people because this approach would yield the clearest scientific results across the research population. So they chose the pinky abductor muscle, which connects the first joint of the pinky with the edge of the palm. (Nobody walks around the most dangerous part of town late at night flashing their pinky abductor muscle, shouting out, "Don't mess with me, my pinky abductor muscles are yoked!")

The participants were broken into three groups: (i) a group that would perform 15 minutes of pinky abductor exercises five days per week for twelve weeks, (ii) a group that would perform 15 minutes of pinky abductor visualizations (but no actual pinky exercises) five days per week for twelve weeks, and (iii) a control

VISUALIZATION: TRICK YOUR BRAIN INTO RESILIENT GREATNESS

group that did neither. The exercise group, using rubber bands, did a variety of pinky strength exercises each day, such as pinky curls, pinky squats, pinky raises, and of course, pinkie lunges. The visualization group sat in a chair for those same 15 minutes while visualizing themselves performing those same exercises. All of the participants' pinky abductor strength was measured before and after the twelve-week period.

We will now point you to the results. (Sorry, *terrible* finger pun.) The actual exercise group experienced a whopping 53% increase in muscle strength in the pinky abductor muscle over the twelve weeks. But even more startling, the visualization group experienced a 35% increase in muscle strength. That's correct, from *pure visualization*, they increased their muscle strength by 35%. And they didn't even lift a finger! (Another *awful* finger pun, sorry about that.) The control group, unsurprisingly, experienced no change in their muscle strength across the twelve-week period. This study demonstrates the remarkable power of visualization – that we can build physical strength without even contracting or using our muscle. That is how potent the human mind is, and how potent the technique of visualization is.

More importantly for your purposes, visualization is effective at building mental and emotional muscle. According to Johns Hopkins, "[S]tudies have shown that imagery [aka visualization] can help the mind and body relax" and "can also help . . . manage anxiety, stress, and depression."[223] Moreover, it can help "reduce pain," "lower blood pressure," and "give you a better sense of control and well-being." One study found that people who practice positive visualization about a future goal are far more optimistic and confident both in the present and as they approach that goal: "We found a robust relationship between vividness of positive imagery and optimism, indicating that the more vividly someone could imagine a future achievement, for example, the more optimistic the individual was."[224] Another study asked half of the participants to visualize a positive future event that was described to them and asked the other half to think about the verbal meaning of the same description that was provided to them.[225] Both groups experienced an improvement in their emotional state, but the visualization group's boost was even higher. Moreover, the visualization group had more positive interpretations of unrelated events that were subsequently described to them.

Visualization has even been shown to decrease exam anxiety among graduate and undergraduate students. One study found that first-year graduate students in nursing school experienced "significantly reduced" test anxiety after just one week of daily visualization, unlike the control group, who experienced no reduction in test anxiety over the same period.[226] Another study assessed whether a less-than-one-minute guided visualization practiced by undergraduate students right before taking an extra credit math test could affect their test anxiety.[227] It did. Their test anxiety levels after the visualization were approximately half the levels of the control group, who were tested after completing an informed consent form that took about the same amount of time as the visualization.

A separate study found that individuals with moderate public speaking anxiety experienced reductions in their anxiety and distress about public speaking after practicing visualization, unlike the control group, which did not engage in visualization.[228] Another study found that employees in Denmark suffering from intense stress and burnout experienced large reductions in stress levels and major improvements in well-being and overall mood as a result of visualization.[229]

What we know is that visualization is a powerful yet underused tool for improving our emotions and mood. We invite you to make visualization a standard part of your law school experience by doing a 30–60 second visualization every 2–3 days. You can take out your phone right now and create a calendar reminder for every two days (or three days, if you prefer). When your reminder pops up, finish whatever you are doing, and then close your eyes and imagine yourself thriving in law school and excelling in your exams. The ideal visualization contains two components: (1) imagery; and (2) emotion. Create rich and detailed images in your mind of you flourishing in your learning, studying, memorizing, and exam-taking, and then conjure up the palpable emotions that such flourishing brings.

Truly allow (or force) yourself to feel the emotions you would feel if this were really happening. You may be surprised at how

VISUALIZATION: TRICK YOUR BRAIN INTO RESILIENT GREATNESS

easy it is to evoke a specific emotion on command. Just suspend disbelief and pretend to feel the vivid emotion. See yourself grinding out your success. See the challenges you fear – and then see yourself overcoming those challenges. Feel your mental strength, feel your courage in the face of fear, and feel your inner power. See yourself performing with greatness. See yourself triumphing. See yourself smiling brightly – glowing from head to toe. Feel the exuberance from all of your efforts paying off. Feel the glory.

And then open your eyes and continue on with your life. If you do this 30–60 second practice every 2–3 days between now and your final exams, you can expect tangible benefits. Through this simple practice, you will be consistently priming your mind to feel confidence, positivity, and resilience. This practice can reap benefits not only on final exam "game day," but also for your mindset and mood between now and then. If visualization helped Michael Jordan, Serena Williams and Tom Brady achieve greatness and manage their stress along the way, it can certainly help us do the same.*

---

* Visualization is also a wonderful thing to do in those nerve-racking last moments before a final exam, when you are sitting at your desk waiting for the proctor to pass out the exam. Rather than stewing in stress, or obsessively cycling through the material you memorized, you can visualize yourself thriving and excelling on the exam. This activity puts your brain in prime condition for the exam. You can do the same thing right before any high-stakes event, such as your moot court argument, a summer job interview, or an important meeting with a professor. You can even do it in your personal life, such as before a first date or stressful social event.

Tool 13

Verbalization: Neither Vent Nor Suppress

"To share your weakness is to make yourself vulnerable; to make yourself vulnerable is to show your strength."

— Criss Jami

As we enumerated in detail at the outset of the "Judgment to Compassion" mindset shift in Section II, law school involves a healthy dose of frustrating realities. Notwithstanding that attending law school is undoubtedly a great privilege that offers invaluable education and long-term career opportunities, let's be real: law school also presents a veritable cornucopia of irritants on a daily basis. Although having regular triggers and frustrations during your law school experience is completely natural and predictable, how you choose to verbalize them plays an important role in your stress, anger, and emotional well-being.

It turns out that most of us fall into one of two primary verbal coping mechanisms when a circumstance outside our control upsets us: we either *vent* or *suppress*. Although we all dabble in both methods at different times, each one of us has one *primary* mechanism that is our "pet" coping mechanism. See if you recognize yourself in the following descriptions of these two go-to coping archetypes (you likely have fallen into one of these categories since your early childhood).

Venters take the frustrations and injustices of life (and law school) and spend their energy venting and complaining about the situation and the people who brought about the situation. Their verbal expression is blame-focused: They identify the cause of the unacceptable situation and then direct their energy and attention to vilifying that cause. When something stressful or upsetting occurs in life, venters tend to hop from person to person in their life, recycling the same set of complaints to each person. Venters operate under the illusion that vehemently complaining about the cause of their stressful circumstance will make them feel better about the circumstance. "OMG, Professor Watkins is the worst! His lectures are a snooze-fest and his explanations only make things more confusing. He's so awful with questions from students – he doesn't ever address what is being asked, and he's so arrogant whenever anyone challenges him. What he said last class about law school grades was so tone deaf. The guy is a dinosaur."

Suppressors take the opposite approach. When something stressful or upsetting occurs in life (or law school), suppressors push their emotional reaction down so no one can see how stressed or upset they are. Regardless of how emotional they are feeling inside, suppressors attempt to convey the appearance of being "cool, calm and collected." Suppressors operate under an illusion, too: they believe their intense emotions are a sign of weakness or lack of resiliency, and they fear that other people would lose respect for them if those people saw how stressed or upset they really feel. Suppressors assume that if they ignore and hide their difficult emotions, the emotions will go away or become a non-factor.*

There is one small problem with both suppressing and venting: *they do not work*. In fact, they generally *exacerbate* the existing problem. Although we suppress or vent to cope with stress and anger, the science shows that both of these behaviors actually increase the very stress and anger we are struggling with. Talk about a backfire.

When we suppress our stress, without honestly acknowledging its existence to ourselves (or others), we are not taking action to process it in a healthy way. So it inevitably metastasizes and snowballs within us. The science is clear that when we pretend – to ourselves or others – that we are not

---

* I [*your co-author Jarrett*] have been a life-long suppressor. When my law school girlfriend would notice how stressed and overwhelmed I looked, and would gently comment, "You look stressed, are you ok?" I would snap back with ferocious intensity, "I'm *not* stressed! I'm just ... *focused*!!!" Many years later I began studying the science of suppression, which led me to begin changing my suppressor ways – which, in turn, led to enhanced resiliency, mental strength, and happiness in my career and life.

VERBALIZATION: NEITHER VENT NOR SUPPRESS 307

experiencing the unpleasant emotions that are present, our emotional state worsens.[230] Indeed, pretending we don't have unpleasant emotions does not make those emotions disappear any more than pretending we don't have homework for our Contracts class makes that assignment disappear. When we ignore and refuse to process those emotions, however, the emotions surreptitiously take greater hold of us.

Studies have even found, as noted in Section II, that when we suppress physical pain, rather than acknowledge it, the level of pain increases in the future, and we tend to interpret unrelated, non-painful events as painful.[231] This is due to the "rebound effect," whereby the suppressed pain "rebounds" into inappropriate situations because it was never healthily processed, creating the false perception that the unrelated event is more painful than it actually is. Studies show that the rebound effect applies to painful emotions, too. If you have ever bottled up your law school stress only to find yourself melting down upon learning the law school café ran out of blueberry muffins, you know all about the rebound effect.

Venting is just as counterproductive as suppressing. When we vent our stress, it can feel cathartic in that moment – as if we are expelling our frustrations and upset from our body. But within minutes (or moments) after venting, we typically feel more stressed and more upset than we did before we vented. Venting is akin to throwing a bucket of fuel on a small fire: It appears to extinguish the fire in the moment, but the fire soon comes raging back with redoubled potency.

Unsurprisingly, the science confirms that venting our stress or anger makes those emotions more intense and more unmanageable.[232] According to the late Dr. Jeffrey M. Lohr, a psychology professor at the University of Arkansas and a leading researcher on venting, "If venting really does get anger 'out of your system,' then venting should result in a reduction of both anger and aggression. Unfortunately for catharsis theory, the results [of many studies] showed precisely the opposite effect."[233] Dr. Lohr continued, "What people fail to realize is that the anger would have dissipated had they not vented. Moreover, it would have dissipated more quickly had they not vented and tried to control their anger instead."

So are you a venter or a suppressor? It should be pretty easy to identify your primary coping mechanism. You probably have been a venter or suppressor most of your life – it was just your default method of dealing with the trials and tribulations of life. Having this self-awareness is important, as it is the starting point of breaking your old pattern. Most of us engage in both venting and suppressing at different times, but nevertheless we typically have one "go-to" verbal coping mechanism. Once you are clear on your primary coping mechanism, you may be wondering what you are supposed to do as an alternative. "If I can't vent *or* suppress when I am stressed out, what am I supposed to do . . . ?!"

The answer can be summed up in one word: *vulnerability*. Expressing your emotions vulnerably is the antidote to both suppressing and venting. Vulnerability breaks the denial of suppression, and it evaporates the judgment of venting. Although "vulnerability" and "venting" may sound similar at first glance, they differ in a subtle but critical way. Venting consists of talking about the stressor through the lens of blame or judgment, while vulnerability consists of talking about the same stressor through the lens of one's own emotional experience – without focusing on blame or judgment (although some may incidentally arise).

> **Venting:** "Ryan is such a gunner! He has to raise his hand and express his opinion on every single issue! He dominates the class discussion as if the whole class is all about him, which is super egotistical. Doesn't he realize there are other students in the class?! And that obnoxious position he took yesterday in our Con Law class was so unjust and shows what a jerk he is."
>
> **Vulnerability:** "It's really challenging having Ryan in class. When he dominates the class discussion, I feel super frustrated that we are wasting valuable class time and I feel deprived of the learning that I am paying for. I start feeling more stressed that I am not going to do well in this class. So my own fears get magnified by Ryan's behaviors. And the position he took yesterday in our Con Law class filled me with rage. Probably half of

VERBALIZATION: NEITHER VENT NOR SUPPRESS 309

America agrees with that position, but I could feel myself boiling up inside as he was talking."

It may not seem like there is much of a difference between these two verbal expressions, but there is. The first one was primarily focused on attacking Ryan as a person; the second one was primarily focused on disclosing the uncomfortable emotions *the speaker is experiencing* as a result of Ryan's behaviors.

Here's another example involving the stress arising from the fast-approaching final exams (with all three verbal coping mechanisms displayed):

Suppressing: "I'm fine, just studying a lot. It is what it is. Stressing out isn't going to help anything. I'm fine."*

Venting: "Our final exam schedule is ridiculous! How can we be expected to memorize all of this stuff in so little time?! My best friend from college goes to another law school and her final exam schedule is far more spaced out. Our administration doesn't care about us as people – they just want to cash our tuition checks while demonstrating zero intelligent leadership. If our administration had any sense of ethics, they would modify the schedule rather than force us to suffer unnecessarily like this. They are heartless."

Vulnerability: "Our final exam schedule is ridiculous! With how compressed it is, and the mountain of information we have to memorize, I am super stressed that I am going to underperform. I feel shaky and overwhelmed when I think about it. My best friend from college goes to another law school and her final exam schedule is far more spaced out. That messes with my brain even more, because I feel like I'm more likely to fail because of our administration's policies. I feel small and irrelevant to them. It hurts my heart."

Rather than just venting anger at the administration (which bypasses our own emotional experience and only further

---

* If this sort of statement is made while actually feeling stressed or overwhelmed inside, then it constitutes suppressing. However, if this statement is an accurate reflection of the person's underlying emotional state, then it does not constitute suppressing and is a perfectly healthy expression.

inflames our anger and stress), vulnerability directly and courageously honors the fears, anxieties, and self-doubt that reside within, rather than projecting these emotions onto the administration in the form of judgment. Vulnerability acknowledges the role of the administration in triggering these emotions, without allowing blame to be the focal point of the expression.

Importantly, the science shows that vulnerability – unlike venting and suppressing – actually *increases* our resiliency and stress tolerance. A 2019 study reviewed the existing research on verbal expression style and concluded that "the free and uninterrupted expression of emotion possesses clear and sustainable benefits for physical and mental health and general well-being," while further finding that "concealing and repressing emotions can give rise to stress-related physiological reactions."[234] Vulnerable and authentic expression of difficult emotions has been shown to improve mood and joy, reduce stress and sadness, decrease activation of the amygdala, increase self-confidence and autonomy, reduce symptoms of depression, deepen trust and connection in interpersonal relationships, and improve overall well-being and mental health.[235]

Expressing ourselves vulnerably does not eliminate the stressor, but it makes the stressor less overwhelming and less damaging to our well-being. You can think of vulnerability like an anchor used by a ship at sea. When an intense storm arises, the captain drops the anchor, which protects the ship from total destruction. Of course, the anchor does not eliminate the storm; it merely prevents the storm from having such a destructive effect. Similarly, when we practice vulnerability in response to our law school stressors, we do not eliminate the stressors, but those same stressors have less of a destructive effect on our mental health and emotional well-being.

The world's foremost expert on vulnerability is Dr. Brené Brown, a research professor at University of Houston who has spent the last two decades researching, analyzing, and writing about vulnerability, authenticity, shame, courage, and empathy. In her viral TED Talk, *The Power of Vulnerability*, and her related book, *The Gifts of Imperfection*, Brown provides a compelling, science-based explanation for why simple acts of

VERBALIZATION: NEITHER VENT NOR SUPPRESS

vulnerability reduce our stress and increase our well-being: When we open up to a trusted friend or family member about the stress we are experiencing (without complaining about or attacking others), we are courageously accepting ourselves as we *truly are*, while undercutting the shame and self-judgment that typically accompanies that stress. Indeed, speaking our stress to another guts much of the power that stress has over us. When we are not judging ourselves for feeling stressed, or judging others for causing us stress, we begin to feel happier, more resilient, and more authentic. "Authenticity is the daily practice of letting go of who we think we're supposed to be and embracing who we are," says Brown. When we practice vulnerability, we step into a more authentic and more empowered version of self.

As the inevitable stressors of law school (and life) percolate, we encourage you to resist the urge to either vent or suppress the stress. Instead, we invite you to openly acknowledge it and practice vulnerability in response to it. In so doing, you will be enhancing your resiliency, your happiness, and your sense of self.

Tool 14

EMOTIONAL GRANULARITY: SPECIFICALLY LABEL YOUR EMOTIONS

"Let's not forget that the little emotions are the great captains of our lives and we obey them without realizing it."

— Vincent Van Gogh

If something occurs that induces you into an unpleasant emotion like stress, sadness, or anger, does the way you label that unpleasant emotion in your own mind affect the intensity and disruptiveness of that emotion? Assuming you choose not to vulnerably verbalize it, and assuming you choose not to reframe your emotional reaction using the techniques from Section II (*or do not yet feel ready to do so for the reasons outlined in footnote * on page 87*), does the way you internally label that emotion alter your resiliency, well-being, and decision making in response to the emotion? The science says it does.

In 2001, Dr. Lisa Feldman Barrett, an acclaimed neuroscientist and psychologist at Northeastern University and the Chief Science Officer for the Center for Law, Brain & Behavior at Harvard Medical School and Massachusetts General Hospital, coined the term "emotional granularity" (aka "emotional differentiation"). Emotional granularity is the ability to put our feelings or emotions into words (internally or otherwise) with a high degree of specificity and precision. For example, low granularity would be identifying ourselves as feeling "bad" or "upset," while high granularity would be identifying ourselves as "sad," "demoralized," "lethargic," "lonely," "ashamed," "anxious," "furious," "jealous," "underappreciated," "disrespected," "self-conscious," or "disempowered." Emotions can often be conceived of in more general, broad terms, or in more specific, narrow terms.

Fascinatingly, the research shows that when we self-identify our unpleasant emotional state in precise and narrow terms, we improve our emotional intelligence, our overall well-being and resilience to the emotion at issue, and our consequent behavior in response to the emotion. Emotional granularity serves as a sort of buffer to the emotion, or an internal anchor that prevents the emotion from taking such a hold over us. In this way, the negative emotional reaction we have can be regulated and tempered based on our ability to specifically label it in our mind as the reaction is unfolding.

To better understand how this works, Dr. Barrett has used the following analogy. Imagine an artist and a normal person looking at two slightly different shades of blue.[236] The non-artist may just see them both as "blue," while the artist may see one as "azure" and the other as "royal." The artist's specific label positions her to better understand how each color was originally generated and how best to complement each color with surrounding colors going forward. By labeling the color with specificity, the artist's ability to process, comprehend, and project implications from the color is superior. Similarly, an individual who is able to label her emotions with specificity is better able to process, comprehend, and project implications from the emotion. By identifying the emotion (or color) with particularity, her relationship to the emotion (or color) fundamentally changes.

An August 2021 study published in *Frontiers of Psychology* tracked 313 participants' emotional states from morning to evening for 21 straight days, as well their emotional granularity levels in response to stressful events during the day and their calmness levels and sleep quality each night.[237] The researchers controlled for pre-existing mental health issues, such as depression, as well as the mean levels of negative emotion each participant experienced throughout the day. The study found that the participants' emotional granularity levels "moderated the within-person relation between daily stress and calmness in the evening." The study further concluded that the "effect of daily stress on sleep quality through calmness in the evening

EMOTIONAL GRANULARITY: SPECIFICALLY LABEL YOUR EMOTIONS

was found to be conditional on an individual's standing on [emotional granularity]." In other words, the study found that participants who practiced emotional granularity in response to stressors throughout the day were calmer and more resilient in the evening, and they slept better than participants who did not. Consequently, emotional granularity was determined to be a "protective factor that helps to explain why some individuals remain more resilient during times of stress than others."

Another study found that individuals' level of emotional granularity predicted their level of unhealthy rumination in response to stressors and depression symptoms for a six-month period. The study found that higher emotional granularity is "associated with long-term psychological outcomes" and confirmed that it serves as an important "resilience factor" in navigating the stressors of life.[238] Another study found that people who are better at differentiating their negative feelings are better at impulse control and are also 20% to 50% less likely to retaliate aggressively (i.e., with a verbal or physical assault) against someone who has hurt them.[239] In another study, participants who were instructed to describe their emotions in more detail (i.e., emotional granularity) were more effective at resisting the biasing effects of emotion on judgments.[240] The participants were primed into the emotion of disgust before making moral assessments, and the group of participants who briefly performed emotional granularity, as compared to the control group, made more moral decisions that were less impaired by their unrelated emotional reaction. Moreover, another study found that individuals who engage in greater emotional granularity are less likely to drink excessively when they are stressed immediately prior to an upcoming drinking episode, consuming approximately 40% less alcohol than individuals who are lower in emotional granularity.[241]

In a study assessing emotional granularity's effects on anxiety, people who were afraid of spiders but were trained to differentiate their emotions when observing a spider (e.g., "In front of me is an ugly spider and it is disgusting, nerve-racking, and yet intriguing.") experienced less anxiety and showed a greater willingness to approach spiders (i.e., reduced behavioral avoidance) compared with people who were given other strategies, such as cognitive reappraisal (e.g., "Sitting in front of me is a little spider, and it is safe.") or distraction (e.g., "Decide on the best time to floss your teeth and make this a habit.").[242] Moreover, at a follow-up assessment one week later, the spider-fearing individuals who were trained to differentiate their emotions experienced less sympathetic nervous system arousal (i.e., the fight-or-flight response) when confronted with spiders, compared with individuals in the other groups.

Neuroscientists from the University of Wisconsin and the University of North Carolina wanted to determine what is occurring within the brain when individuals engage in emotional granularity.[243] So they conducted live EEG brain scans on participants while the participants were shown 50 separate images designed to elicit an array of emotions, including fear, anger, and disgust. The participants' level of emotional granularity directly influenced their neural patterns in the periods after seeing the evocative images. The study found, "Individuals who were high vs. low in granularity showed different neural patterns during the experience of emotions at multiple time frames." Low granularity participants experienced more negative and more volatile brain wave amplitudes. "A person's level of granularity," continued the study, "is influencing how their brain represents emotional experiences, starting from the very initial moments of stimulus presentation." The researchers observed that "this could explain why low granular individuals are ultimately worse at emotion regulation, because they have early reactivity to evocative stimuli but then do not engage resources to help make meaning of and subsequently regulate their affective responses." So not only has emotional granularity been shown to induce greater resiliency and emotional regulation in response to challenging stimuli, but brain scans also validate these findings.

In another neuroscientific study, it was found that people who were adept at describing and differentiating their feelings showed less activity in the insula and anterior cingulate cortex when rejected by a stranger during a computer-simulated ball-toss game.[244] As interpreted by a later study led by Dr. Barrett,[245] "While there might be many ways to interpret these brain findings, they are consistent with the view that emotion

EMOTIONAL GRANULARITY: SPECIFICALLY LABEL YOUR EMOTIONS

differentiation is associated with downregulating activity in regions of the brain that form part of the neural substrates for negative feeling. In a sense, people with greater emotion-differentiation skills appear to show greater equanimity when confronted with the pain of rejection."

In a study by UCLA neuroscientists and psychologists, it was found that when participants were shown images of an angry or fearful face, their amygdala (the fear and fight-or-flight center of the brain) activates.[246] However, when participants were asked to attach a one-word label to the emotion they felt (referred to as *affect labeling*, which is the most superficial form of emotional granularity), their amygdala activation reduced considerably. So when shown an evocative image, the simple act of putting their emotion into a single word materially altered their brain's fight-or-flight response.

The science shows that when the world triggers us into unpleasant emotions, the simple act of putting those emotions into specific words in our own mind fundamentally affects how our brain responds, how overwhelming that emotion feels to us, and how prudent we are in our subsequent actions. As Dr. Barrett and her colleagues remarked in a study analyzing the various benefits of emotional granularity established by this wide collection of studies, "[T]hese findings are impressive because emotion differentiation [granularity] is a simple, easily trainable skill that is frequently overlooked."[247]

We'd like to provide you with a very simple process for engaging in emotional granularity when you get triggered into a difficult emotion. *First*, label the emotion (or emotions) with the highest degree of specificity that you can. In the figure below, you will find a wheel of unpleasant emotions. Reviewing this can assist you in clarifying the nuanced distinctions between the various emotions.

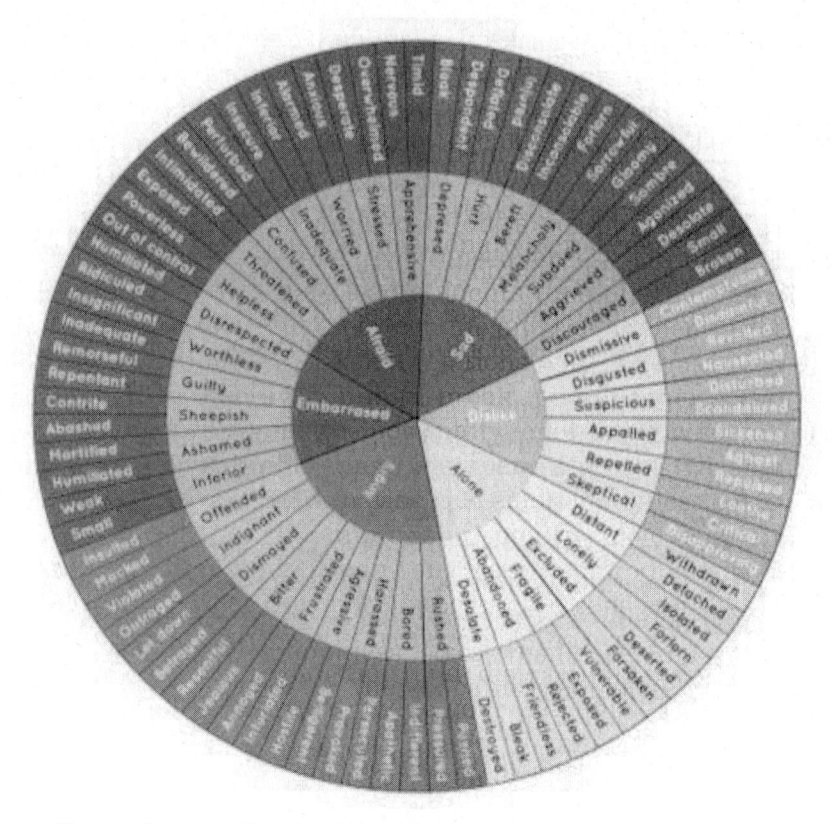

Human Systems Emotion Wheel System: Uncomfortable Emotions/
Negative Affect, https://humansystems.co/emotionwheels/.

***Second*, fill in the blanks in the following sentence in your** head:

I feel [*specific emotion*] **because/that** [*specific reason*].

For example, "I feel demoralized because it seems that no matter how hard I try in my Property class, I am not going to absorb the material." Or "I feel embarrassed and ashamed by the answers I gave when I was called on in class." Or "I feel grief and guilt that I have not been very responsive lately to my best friend from college." Or "I feel inadequate compared to some of my classmates." Or "I feel betrayed because my friend didn't include me in the weekend get together."

EMOTIONAL GRANULARITY: SPECIFICALLY LABEL YOUR EMOTIONS

Once you have identified the specific emotion and the specific reason you are feeling that emotion, move to the third and *final step* (*the bonus step*): Rate the intensity of that emotion on a scale of 1–10, with ten being the most intense and most overwhelming, and one being the least intense and least overwhelming. (You can skip this bonus step if you'd like, as the first two steps constitute the level of emotional granularity encompassed by most of the research. But this third step is an easy way of adding one last notch of specificity.)

This simple 3-part practice can be a powerful tool to use in response to the emotional triggers that occur in law school and life. So when you feel a rush of challenging emotions, remember you have this tool in your back pocket. It only takes 10–20 seconds to perform, and the research reveals that your brain, your overall well-being, and your subsequent behaviors will all benefit.

TOOL 15

SECOND-HAND STRESS: STRENGTHEN YOUR "NO NINJA"

"When you say 'yes' to others, make sure you are not saying 'no' to yourself."

— Paulo Coelho

Just as second-hand smoke has been shown to cause respiratory problems to non-smokers, exposing yourself to second-hand stress can elevate your stress levels. This means that an important aspect of optimizing your well-being and stress resiliency is to intelligently navigate the sources of second-hand stress in your life. To better understand this issue, let's look at a groundbreaking neuroscientific study involving monkeys and gelato. Yes, we said, "monkeys and gelato."

It was 1991 in a neuroscience lab at the University of Parma in Italy. A neuroscientist named Giacomo Rizzolatti, with the help of some graduate students, was studying the brain of a macaque monkey. Dr. Rizzolatti wanted to better understand the functioning of the premotor cortex, which was known at the time to be involved in the planning and initiation of movement. In the study, needle-thin electrodes were inserted into the monkey's premotor cortex to measure electrical activity from the neurons in that region based on various actions the monkey performed. The electrodes revealed that whenever the monkey began a physical movement, such as reaching its hand for something, the neurons in the premotor cortex fired vigorously.

And then something fascinating occurred. Dr. Rizzolatti and his graduate students took a lunch break but neglected to turn off their equipment. One of the graduate students began enjoying a gelato for dessert in plain sight of the monkey. To everyone's astonishment, neurons in the monkey's premotor cortex began firing every time the student took a spoonful of gelato, as if the monkey's own hand were feeding the gelato to itself. The monkey's brain was mirroring the activity of the student's brain each time the student took a bite of gelato.

As a result of this serendipitous experience, Dr. Rizzolatti discovered a major breakthrough in neuroscience – the existence of "mirror neurons," brain cells that simultaneously replicate the neural activity of the brain of beings with whom we interact. The discovery of mirror neurons is considered one the biggest breakthroughs in neuroscience in the last half century, and perhaps the greatest neuroscientific breakthrough in the history of Italy. That's right, Italy's most groundbreaking neuroscientific discovery was the result of *gelato*. It is almost a cliché, akin to the greatest neuroscientific discovery in the history of France resulting from a croissant.

Mirror neurons are often referred to as "empathy neurons" because they cause our brains to mirror the neurological and emotional reactions that others are experiencing. For example, a study in the *Journal of Psychoneuroendocrinology* (now that's a mouthful!) found that merely witnessing another person stress out can cause a material increase in our own stress and cortisol levels.[248] In the words of a lead author of the study, Veronika Engert, a social neuroscientist, "The fact that we could actually measure this empathic stress in the form of a significant hormone release was astonishing."[249] Even watching a video of a stranger having a stress response can spike our cortisol and stress levels, according to the study. "Stress has enormous contagion potential," concludes Dr. Engert.*

In another study,[251] university students were recruited to do public speaking – an activity that is consistently ranked as one of the most stressful in life. The level of stress each student was under, however, differed based on which of three conditions they were subjected to: low stress, high stress, or stress recovery. These conditions were manipulated based on the difficulty of the subject matter, as well as the facial expressions and verbal feedback of the planted audience, who were part of the study.

---

* This physiological reaction even occurs for mice. Researchers in one study exposed a mouse to stress in an isolated environment and then brought the mouse back to its partner. When the brains of both mice were evaluated, both brains experienced similar stress-related brain changes, compared to their brain functioning before the isolated exposure.[250]

SECOND-HAND STRESS: STRENGTHEN YOUR "NO NINJA"

Imagine giving a speech to a bunch of strangers who just stare blankly at you, regardless of what you say or how you say it. It is unnerving.*

A second group of students was then recruited to watch the video recordings of the first students. The stress levels of both groups of students were monitored by electrocardiogram – the first group when they spoke and the second group when they observed. The results showed that the stress levels of the observers mirrored the stress levels of the speakers.[†/‡]

"We naturally catch other peoples' emotions unconsciously, just like we might a cold," explains Laurie Santos, Ph.D., a cognitive scientist and psychology professor at Yale University who hosts *The Happiness Lab* podcast. This emotional contagion is wired into our neurobiology as a survival mechanism, explains Tony Buchanan, Co-Director of the Neuroscience Program at Saint Louis University and one of the world's leading experts on stress contagion (aka second-hand stress): "In animals who live in groups, such as humans, your chances of survival are greater if you pay attention to others' stress, as a warning sign of danger, and mobilize internal resources to get your muscles working to flee that situation."[§]

In light of all that you now know about mirror neurons and stress contagion, it is critical to your happiness and stress resiliency that you protect yourself from people in your life – including your law school colleagues – whose negative emotional state can be unconsciously transferred to you. Our great mentor

---

* Trust us, we know from experience. At a couple of law firms where we presented, we wondered mid-way through the presentation whether the attendees had fallen into some sort of spontaneous coma.

† This stress contagion was even greater when the observers had high empathy quotients, which were assessed in each observer before they watched the videos.

‡ Stress has also been shown to be transferred from teachers to students. In a study entitled "Stress contagion in the classroom? The link between classroom teacher burnout and morning cortisol in elementary school students," researchers found that the stress and burnout levels of teachers created a "significant" contagion effect in their students.[252] This finding was based on the students' exposure to different teachers during each interval of the school day, as measured by the students' varying cortisol levels, which were collected by saliva sample three times per day. The students' cortisol levels fluctuated throughout the day commensurate with the levels of stress and burnout of each teacher to whom they were exposed.

§ Another classic example of the brain's contagion effect is yawning, where it has been found that even if an individual is not tired, observing the yawning of another person can induce their brain to generate a "contagious yawn."[253]

whom we mentioned previously, Victoria Allen, creatively refers to this concept as deploying one's "No Ninja": Drawing firm boundaries around whom you spend your time with and what you say "yes" to. We all have a tendency to say "yes" (expressly or tacitly) to events, people, and casual interactions that actually stress us out or drain our energy, when we would be benefitted by simply saying "no." Allen lovingly urges people to strengthen their No Ninja in life by saying "no" more frequently. We can and should communicate the "no" boundary with kindness to the person, but it is important that we not acquiesce to or allow, due to fear of hurting the person's feelings, interactions that harm us. As we more frequently and more purposefully deploy our No Ninja in our lives, explains Allen, we experience noticeable improvements to our emotions, energy levels, and overall happiness. So we encourage you to begin strengthening your No Ninja by becoming more intentional about whom you spend time with and interact with – even whom you casually chat with outside the library during a study break.

SECOND-HAND STRESS: STRENGTHEN YOUR "NO NINJA"

You should specifically try to minimize your interactions with three personality archetypes that abundantly roam the halls of every law school: (1) stress balls (i.e., law students who are visibly stressed out at all times, from morning to evening); (2) venters (i.e., law students who like to corner you so they can launch into a long venting session about how horrible their day or week is); and (3) conspiracy theorists (i.e., law students who love to spread conspiracy theories that tend to scare the pants off people – "I heard that every few years, Professor Karoli's final exam only asks questions pertinent to the 28th Amendment and everyone fails!")*

After a few minutes, these people walk away from you, yet you notice yourself feeling more stressed, worried, and irritable than you felt before they arrived. That is a sign that they are passing their stress onto – *and into* – you. But you have the ability (and right) to prevent your precious emotional state from becoming crippled by them.

We are not suggesting that you coldly reject your friends or loved ones if they are overwhelmed by stress, or only spend time with happy, cheerful people. Rather, we are suggesting that you not allow yourself to get swept into conversations throughout the day with people you are not close to who are going to unintentionally contaminate you with their stress. Try to consciously anticipate this risk and then actively exert yourself to prevent this risk from manifesting. When you see one of those individuals approaching you on campus, instead of just silently acquiescing to their emotional barrage, you can deliver a firm but kind boundary to protect your emotional state: "Hey, I'm heading off to the library but I hope you're having a wonderful day!" (Then make a run for it.)

Regarding your friends and family members who seem to be constantly stressed out or emotionally venting, perhaps just notice over time which ones tend to leave you feeling more stressed. It is possible you experience different levels of stress contagion from each of them. Then, based on your findings, take *some* action. Whether you make a decision to reduce the total

---

* Did that cause you to look up the 28th Amendment? If so, you will have noticed the 28th Amendment does not exist! The 27th Amendment is the final one. Behold, you just learned something about Constitutional Law from this book!

amount of time you spend connecting with them, or you strategically plan the circumstances or timing of when you connect with them (e.g., you make sure you don't hang out with them right before you start a big study push), there is very likely *some* tangible action you can take to protect your emotions. An important part of optimizing your resiliency and happiness in law school is taking radical responsibility over whom you allow to occupy your attention and influence your emotional state.

Tool 16

Nature: Purposefully Connect to Nature and Awe

"One touch of nature makes the whole world kin."

— William Shakespeare

According to a 2-year study sponsored by the U.S. Environmental Protection Agency, the average American spends 93% of their life indoors.[254] Although this statistic is alarming, we sense the average law student spends as much, if not more, time indoors. Think of all of your classes, much of the time between classes, your library study sessions, your study sessions in coffee shops, your campus extracurriculars, the restaurants and other indoor locations where you socialize, and of course all of that time in your home. If you were to estimate, how much time do you spend outdoors each day and each week? And perhaps more importantly, as we will explain below, how much time do you spend in nature? Not just outdoors amidst the paved streets, rushing cars, and buildings, but outdoors where these things are absent, or at least minimal?

In his book *The Comfort Crisis: Embrace Discomfort To Reclaim Your Wild, Happy, Healthy Self*,[255] Michael Easter outlines the biological and evolutionary basis for why spending time in nature is essential to our mental and emotional well-being. "Famed biologist E. O. Wilson developed a theory, called the biophilia hypothesis, which says we have an ingrained call to be in nature[,]" explains Easter. "The thinking goes like this: we evolved in nature, and therefore have programmed within our genes a need to be in and connect with nature and living things. If we don't, we go a little haywire, as if we're missing a necessary nutrient for our body, mind, and sense of self."

As elaborated by a 2009 study titled, "Why is Nature Beneficial? The Role of Connectedness to Nature,"[256]

> [H]umans have lived the vast majority of their lives embedded in nature, belonging to the natural world in very real ways. In geological time, it is only a tick of the clock that we have spent in highly urban settings, working in concrete buildings, driving in climate-controlled cars, and living in relatively densely populated areas, shut off from nature. As [prior research] estimated, for 350,000 generations humans have lived close to the land as hunter-gatherers; a sense of belonging, place, and feeling embedded within the broader natural world characterized these cultures. In some ways, then, it would be surprising if the modern life of being divorced from nature did not have some negative consequences associated with it and that being in nature had positive benefits.

Unsurprisingly, the science reveals a vast collection of mental, emotional, and even cognitive benefits from spending brief periods in nature. A 2019 study conducted by 26 different researchers from a host of universities in the U.S., such as Stanford, the University of Chicago, and the University of Washington, as well as several universities across Europe, sought to review the history of scientific research on the effects, if any, of time spent in nature on mental and emotional health.[257] The study arrived at a clear conclusion:

> A wealth of studies has demonstrated that nature experience is associated with psychological well-being. These include investigations of single as well as cumulative occasions of nature contact, and range from experimental to observational designs. The forms of association include evidence that links nature experience with increased positive affect [i.e., positive mood and positive emotions]; happiness and subjective wellbeing; positive social interactions, cohesion, and engagement; a sense of meaning and purpose in life; improved manageability of life tasks; and decreases in mental distress, such as negative affect [i.e., negative mood and negative emotions]. In addition, with longitudinal studies, as well as natural and controlled experiments, nature experience has been shown to

positively affect various aspects of cognitive function, memory and attention, impulse inhibition, and children's school performance, as well as imagination and creativity.

So what are some ways you can connect to nature to reap some of these mental, emotional, and cognitive benefits? One thing you can do is periodically sit or walk in a park or other "green space." Scientists use the term "green space" to mean an area of grass, trees, or other vegetation set apart for recreational or aesthetic purposes in an otherwise urban environment. In other words, not just your walk from your apartment to your law school building, even if you happen to pass trees and vegetation, but rather a park, arboretum, garden, or other area that is specifically set apart for the enjoyment of nature.

In one study, researchers tracked the cortisol levels of individuals living in downtown Ann Arbor, Michigan who agreed to spend 20–30 minutes in a park or other green space of their choosing three days per week for eight weeks.[258] The researchers regularly tested the participants' cortisol levels immediately before and after spending time in the green space. The participants' cortisol levels dropped, on average, by a whopping 21% after each 20–30 minute period they spent in the green space. "We know that spending time in nature reduces stress, but until now it was unclear how much is enough, how often to do it, or even what kind of nature experience will benefit us," explained Mary Carol Hunter, the study's lead author.[259] "Our study shows that for the greatest payoff, in terms of efficiently lowering levels of the stress hormone cortisol, you should spend 20 to 30 minutes sitting or walking in a place that provides you with a sense of nature."

Another study found that a brief session in a green space reduces blood pressure, stress levels, and anger, and increases positive emotions and mood.[260] Another study found that walking in a green space both reduces anxiety and induces attention restoration.[261] Another study found that outdoor walks reduce symptoms of depression and increase memory for individuals struggling with depression.[262] In yet another study, it was found that a 15-minute walk in a green space increases positive emotions, overall mood, attentional capacity, and the ability to effectively process life problems.[263] Additionally, another study found that when college students were taken to a part of campus with towering eucalyptus trees and asked to gaze up at the trees for just one minute, as compared to when they looked up at campus buildings of similar height on a different part of campus, they experienced a material increase in feelings of humbleness and altruism, which are two well-known markers of emotional well-being.[264]

In addition to the improved well-being and lower stress, time in a green space has also been shown to improve cognition. Two of the above studies found an increase in attention and memory from brief periods in a green space. Moreover, a study conducted by a team of psychologists and neuroscientists at University of Michigan found that a walk of 50–55 minutes in a park improved memory and attention by 20%.[265] "Imagine a therapy that had no known side effects, was readily available, and could improve your cognitive functioning at zero cost," noted the study. "Such a therapy has been known to philosophers, writers, and laypeople alike: interacting with nature. Many have suspected that nature can promote improved cognitive functioning and overall well-being, and these effects have recently been documented." Another study found brief periods in nature induce "improvements in executive-functioning performance and self-regulation effectiveness."[266]

In a study from July 2021, researchers assessed the neurological effects of time spent in green spaces by young professionals aged 24–32 who lived in a city. The participants received MRI brain scans twice per week, on average, for 6–8 months. In addition to tracking the participants' time in green spaces, the researchers also tracked and controlled for a wide variety of other factors that could contribute to neurological changes over the duration of the study period, such as exercise, down time, caffeine intake, and fluid and alcohol intake.

The study reached "remarkable" findings, using the word of the study, namely, that participants' intermittent times in green spaces led to a 3% growth in gray matter in the dorsolateral prefrontal cortex, which is an epicenter of executive functioning that is critical to working memory, cognitive flexibility, attention control, planning, processing abstract rules, and impulse inhibition. These "[r]esults indicate remarkable and potentially behaviorally relevant plasticity [i.e., changes] of cerebral structure within a short time frame driven by the daily time spent outdoors." As noted in the study, this level of brain plasticity had previously only been shown for cognitive training programs or rigorous exercise over a lengthy period of time. The study concluded: "It is therefore remarkable that we find effects of a similar size in this more naturalistic study design assessing daily variations." That is, the researchers found it surprising that spending relaxing periods in nature led to the same vast neurological growth that was previously believed to be possible only from cognitive training or exercise.

Importantly, several of these studies have found that the benefits from walking or sitting in a park or other green space do not arise from walking or sitting outside in an "urban area," such as the tree-lined street you stroll along to go to class, or the patio of the coffee shop at the corner of campus. Scientists in this field use the term "urban" to mean any area that is not a green space, including small towns as well as larger cities. As one study explained, "Unlike natural environments [i.e., green spaces], urban environments are filled with stimulation that captures attention *dramatically* and additionally requires directed attention (e.g., to avoid being hit by a car), making them less restorative."[267] (Emphasis in original.) In *The Comfort Crisis*, Easter offers an illustration of why we don't receive the scientific benefits from being outdoors if that outdoor location is not a green space: "Imagine crossing a busy street: our involuntary attention is being pulled one way then the other by all sorts of stimuli. There are other people on a collision course, crossing signals to decipher, police sirens in the distance – not to mention the cars, buses and motorcycles whizzing past on the road. All this buzz means we continually have to decide where our attention should be directed. This is tiring."

Although walking to class is better than driving to class, and although sitting on the outdoor patio of the coffee shop is better than sitting inside, spending time in a green space causes a different mental, emotional, and cognitive restoration to occur. Even if you are relaxing on that outdoor patio, your attention is being continually pulled to the influx of modern buildings, cars, horns, and other stimuli that are surrounding you, rather than to a vast backdrop of nature. Only the latter induces the maximal benefits for your well-being, emotions, and cognition.

For these reasons, in order to enhance well-being and overall thriving, Easter and other experts in the field recommend that people spend 2–3 separate sessions in a green space per week for 20 minutes per session. We know what you are thinking: *"I don't have time for that!"* Perhaps you can think of it not as a loss of time, but as an investment of time to free up more time, more energy, and more academic success throughout the week. If you spend this 40–60 minutes per week in a green space, imagine how much more energized and productive you will be for the remaining 167 hours of the week. Remember, there are 168 hours in week, so if you dedicate one hour maximum to this practice, you will likely accomplish more and experience greater happiness in the remaining 167 hours than you would in the 168 hours without any green space.

CAN I RECEIVE SOME OF THE BENEFITS OF NATURE FROM THE COMFORTS OF MY DESK?

"If the mountain will not come to Muhammad, then Muhammad must go the mountain," says the great proverb. After reading the above section, you may be wondering if the opposite can be arranged: "If I cannot go the mountain, can I bring the mountain to me?" Perhaps you don't feel like you can get to a green space 2–3 days per week, or maybe you are contemplating the days in-between your green space sessions. Either way, a *natural* question (no pun intended, we promise!) is whether there are any "shortcuts" to receiving some of the benefits of a green space without having to lug yourself all the way over there.

The good news is that there are some shortcuts. They may not be as beneficial as the real thing, but the science shows you can still derive clear mental, emotional, and cognitive benefits from them. We are going to share three such shortcuts: (1) viewing pictures and videos of nature; (2) listening to sounds of nature; and (3) placing plants and other nature around you. You can do all of these from the comfort of your living room couch or

NATURE: PURPOSEFULLY CONNECT TO NATURE AND AWE

even the law library (minus the plants, perhaps), and the science shows that you will *transplant* some of the rich benefits of nature to your working environment without having to leave it. (Okay, that pun was intended.)

Regarding the first short cut, the science shows that viewing images or videos of nature can deliver some highly beneficial returns. In two of the studies above that involved walking in green spaces,[268] the researchers also tested whether showing the participants images and videos of green spaces would produce effects similar to those from visiting a green space. Benefits were found in both studies from viewing nature images and videos in the lab, as compared to viewing images and videos of an urban area in the lab. For example, in one of the studies, just 10 minutes of images and videos of nature improved the participants' performance on an executive attention test, as well as on a memory test, although not as much as did walking in the green space.

Several other studies have shown that the emotion of awe can be induced from one's computer screen by viewing photos or videos of nature, without having to go outdoors. Some of the well-established effects of awe include feeling a deeper connection to the universe and other people, increased well-being, lower stress, increased feelings of being in the moment, and improved mental clarity. Although these are common effects of awe, let's briefly discuss how researchers describe the actual experience of awe. We will then turn to identifying ways of activating awe from your library or office chair.

"A majestic waterfall, the Taj Mahal, towering redwoods, the Grand Canyon, a tornado, Beethoven's Symphony Number 9, Monet's Water Lilies, a fractal, a spiritual experience, a performance by Prince, a child being born, a speech by Martin Luther King, Jr., the view of Earth from space," listed a White Paper titled *The Science of Awe*, issued by the UC Berkeley Greater Science Center.[269] "What do all these things have in common? They're likely to induce one of the most mysterious and mystifying of emotions: awe."

"Awe is a positive emotion triggered by awareness of something vastly larger than the self and not immediately understandable – such as nature, art, music, or being caught up in a collective act such as a ceremony, concert or political march," says Dr. Dacher Keltner, a UC Berkeley Psychology professor, the Founding Director of the Greater Good Sciences Center, and one the world's preeminent researchers of awe.[270] In a landmark 1999 study on awe, Keltner and colleagues described it this way: "Awe is the feeling of wonder and astonishment experienced in the presence of something novel and difficult to grasp – a stimulus that cannot be accounted for by one's current understanding of the world."[271] Keltner has further stated that "experiencing awe can contribute to a host of benefits including an expanded sense of time and enhanced feelings of generosity, well-being and humility."[272]

Although actually being immersed in nature is one of the most powerful ways of experiencing awe, the science shows we can also experience it from our desk by briefly viewing images and videos depicting the majesty of nature. In one study, participants were shown 90 seconds of slides of impressive nature images (six different images each displaying for 15 seconds).[273] The researchers hypothesized that this brief exposure to awe-inspiring images "would be accompanied by signs of parasympathetic activation and/or sympathetic withdrawal" – meaning the participants' sense of calm and safety would increase (parasympathetic activation) and their sense of fight-or-flight would reduce (sympathetic withdrawal). This dual hypothesis was, in fact, confirmed by the study, with one interesting caveat: the participants' respiratory rates increased while triggered into awe. This result was interesting because respiratory rates typically map sympathetic nervous system activation (i.e., when you're stressed, you breath faster.) So these 90 seconds of images triggered participants into an overall calmer and less anxious state, yet they were simultaneously more invigorated.

Another study involved participants viewing 14 images of mundane items (e.g., a desk, chair, ladder, bucket, etc.) before viewing 14 images of grandiose nature images the researchers collected from the Internet (e.g., sunsets, rainbows, oceans, mountains, etc.).[274] The researchers performed emotion and behavior assessments of the participants at the outset and after each set of images. The mundane images had no effect on the participants' baseline states, but the expansive nature images induced improvements in their overall mood and their willingness to engage in prosocial behavior. As noted by the study, "[A]s our results show, brief exposure to relatively small images of awesome nature (under the form of, say, landscape posters or screensavers) may have significant positive effects on people's emotions and behavior."

Participants in another study were shown a 60-second video from a commercial for an LCD television that featured a series of towering nature clips in order to induce them into a state of awe.[275] They were also shown a 60-second video of joyful people celebrating at a joyous event in order to induce them into a state of happiness. Before the inductions, the scientists primed the participants to feel a sense of time pressure about the experiment – in order to later assess the effect of the videos on this priming. Both inductions succeeded in eliciting the desired emotion (awe v. happiness), but interestingly, the study found that only the awe video generated a perception of having more available time and a feeling of being less time constrained.

In other portions of the study, the researchers induced the participants into a state of awe by having them briefly reflect upon a moment in their life when they were overcome by the beauty of nature, as well as by having them read a brief story about ascending the Eiffel tower and seeing all of Paris from that perspective. After each of the three brief awe inductions (the video, the memory, and the story), the participants' relationship to time altered and their collective life satisfaction increased.

The study found, "[E]xperiences of awe bring people into the present moment, and being in the present moment underlies awe's capacity to adjust time perception, influence decisions, and make life feel more satisfying than it would otherwise." The study also found that "a small dose of awe even gave participants a momentary boost in life satisfaction," which is noteworthy considering that momentary experiences rarely alter a person's overall life satisfaction. Importantly, the study emphasized that tapping into the powerful emotion of awe does not require much effort or time, remarking that the study "demonstrated that awe can be elicited by reliving a memory, reading a brief story, or even watching a 60-second commercial."

Considering that the feeling of time scarcity is one of the major complaints of law students (and lawyers), and a major driver of stress, awe's apparent ability to alter the experience of time can be particularly valuable to you. As the study concluded, "awe-eliciting experiences might offer one effective way of alleviating the feeling of time starvation that plagues so many people in modern life."

Another awe study that may have direct implications for your law school experience is one that found that brief feelings of awe increase one's critical thinking capacities and decrease one's susceptibility to being persuaded by poor arguments.[276] The researchers primed the participants into several different positive emotions while attempting to persuade them with various levels of logical messages while they were experiencing each emotion. As found by the study, "[W]e showed that the positive emotions of anticipatory enthusiasm, amusement, and attachment love tended to facilitate greater acceptance of weak persuasive messages (consistent with previous research), whereas the positive emotions of awe and nurturant love reduced persuasion by weak messages." Relatedly, another study found that participants induced into the emotion of awe by a short video, in contrast to those induced into neutral emotions or standard happy emotions, were more likely to accurately assess the factual events that subsequently unfolded and less likely to be improperly influenced by the cognitive bias of confirming one's prior expectations.

Even the mere sounds of nature (e.g., streams, birds chirping, etc.) in audio recordings without video footage or images have been shown to have substantial emotional and cognitive benefits. One study found that participants managed and recovered from stress better when they listened to nature sounds as compared to urban sounds,[277] another study found that participants experienced faster stress recovery and higher perceived attention restoration when they listened to nature sounds,[278] another study found that cognitively fatigued individuals felt more restored after listening to nature sounds versus office sounds,[279] another study found that nature sounds led office workers to be more productive and report better moods than individuals in the sound-masking control group,[280] and yet another study found that nature sounds improved the participants' working memory and attention control in comparison to recorded urban sounds, noting that "relative to participants who were exposed to urban soundscapes, we observed significant improvements in cognitive performance for individuals who listened to nature soundscapes."[281] So when you are feeling stressed, fatigued, or motivated to enhance your cognitive performance, you may consider listening to a recording of nature sounds.

Finally, the science shows that you can bring some of the benefits of nature to you in a slightly more literal way: by placing plants and other vegetation around your home environment, especially in the areas where you do your homework and studying. In one study, researchers broke similarly situated participants into two groups, with one group going to a windowless computer lab with no plants and the other group going to a windowless computer lab with some plants adorning some of the wall space.[282] The participants in both groups then took computer tests under time pressure, and the researchers assessed their productivity levels, stress levels based on blood pressure, and perceived attention levels. The participants in the plant room had better scores in every category assessed: "When plants were added to this interior space, the participants were more productive (12% quicker reaction time on the computer task) and less stressed (systolic blood pressure readings lowered by one to four units). Immediately after completing the task, participants in the room with plants present reported feeling more attentive (an increase of 0.5 on a self-reported scale from one to five) than people in the room with no plants."

In another study, psychologists at the University of Essex in England and Cardiff University in Wales conducted an experiment at two large offices of international companies, one in England and one in Holland, in which plants were added to the previously "lean" and "modern" offices to assess employee well-being and productivity.[283] Not only did employee job satisfaction rates increase as a result of the "greening" of the offices, but employee productivity rates also increased by 15% in the weeks that followed. "Simply enriching a previously Spartan space with plants served to increase productivity by 15% – a figure that aligns closely with findings in previously conducted laboratory studies," found the study, noting that this outcome "identifies a pathway to a more enjoyable, more comfortable and a more profitable form of office-based working." Dr. Chris Knight, one of the lead researchers, explained that the trend towards "lean" space décor focuses only on what looks good without accounting for the emotional or productivity effects of depriving people of natural vegetation: "If you put an ant into a 'lean' jam jar, or a gorilla in a zoo into a 'lean' cage – they're miserable beasties," he said.[284] "People in 'lean' offices are no different," he added.

Another study analyzed the mental health, organizational loyalty, and job satisfaction of 444 Amazon workers in India and the U.S.[285] The study found the happiest and healthiest employees were employed at Amazon branches that had plants and natural sunlight, as opposed to the branches that lacked these items. The study concluded that "natural elements [i.e., visible plants] and sunlight exposure related positively to job satisfaction and organizational commitment, and negatively to depressed mood and anxiety," and that these natural elements "buffered the relationship between role stressors and job satisfaction, depressed mood, and anxiety." The researchers concluded by recommending that workspaces incorporate plants and natural light to support the mental health and job satisfaction of employees.

Even looking at green vegetation for a mere 40 seconds in the middle of an exhausting cognitive task can improve university students' subsequent cognition.[286] As summarized in the study: "Experimental findings show how impressive nature's healing powers can be – just a few moments of green can perk up a tired brain. In one example, Australian researchers asked students to engage in a dull, attention-draining task in which they pressed a computer key when certain numbers flashed on a screen. Students who looked out at a flowering green roof for 40 seconds midway through the task made significantly fewer mistakes than students who paused for 40 seconds to gaze at a concrete rooftop."

GREEN IS THE NEW BLACK

Based on all of this wide-ranging research, we strongly recommend making nature a pivotal part of your emotional well-being and cognitive optimization strategy. Here are some tangible takeaways you can apply:

- spending 2–3 sessions per week in a green space, for 20–30 minutes each session
- regularly viewing videos and images of nature that inspire and uplift you (especially if you are not able to visit the "real thing")
- periodically listening to the sounds of nature via your smart phone apps
- placing plants and other vegetation in your home work environment

We are not saying you need to do all of these things every week. What we are suggesting is that you engage in a paradigm shift where you begin consciously thinking of "green time" (in any of the above four manners) as a concrete tool for advancing your emotional state and cognitive performance in law school. Do not just think of engaging with nature as something that is lovely but frivolous; think of it as an aspect of your thriving and peak performance.

Tool 17

Time Boxing: A Crest Jewel of Time Management

"I must govern the clock, not be governed by it."

— Golda Meir

A very simple yet potent time management technique you can use to optimize your focus, productivity, and efficiency in your law school work is called "time boxing." Before we discuss how to timebox, let's discuss why time boxing is needed.

The reason can be boiled down to two words: Parkinson's Law. The opening sentence of an article published in *The Economist* in 1955 by British naval historian and author, Cyril Northcote Parkinson, read: "It is a commonplace observation that work expands so as to fill the time available for its completion." Parkinson went on to share a story of an old woman whose only task in the day is to send a postcard – a task that would take a busy person about 3–5 minutes. But the woman spent an hour finding the card, another half hour looking for her glasses, 90 minutes writing the card, 20 minutes deciding whether to take an umbrella with her on her walk to the mailbox, and a litany of other small inefficiencies that ended up filling the entire day. (Does that sound like you trying to get to your Torts reading on the weekend?)

Although Parkinson spent much of the article evaluating the inefficient bureaucratization of the British Civil Service, his story of the old lady later led to the coining of a new term, "Parkinson's Law," which today refers to that time management (*or mismanagement*) phenomenon we have all experienced: work expands to fill the available time to complete it. Have you ever noticed that if you have four hours and 15 minutes to finish your reading, it takes you four hours and 15 minutes, but if you only have one hour and 45 minutes to complete the same reading, it takes you one hour and 45 minutes? When space exists to complete our work, the work expands like a metastasizing cancer – filling up all of the available space.

Time limitation, on the other hand, intensifies the brain's ability to focus. For this reason, long-term assignments or projects, such as outlining or a writing assignment, are particularly susceptible to Parkinson's Law. But our homework on any given evening can also be plagued by Parkinson's Law.

Studies have confirmed the human tendency to become inefficient when there is space to be so. For example, when participants were given anagrams to solve and a five-minute time limit, they solved an average of 4.7 per minute (for an average of 23.4 total anagrams during the 5-minute period).[287] But when they had a 20-minute time limit, they only solved 2.2 anagrams per minute (for a total of 44.4 anagrams on average across the 20-minute period). So the extra time caused them to become less than 50% as efficient. Another example involved the amount of time given to participants to prepare a speech on a particular topic.[288] Regardless of how long the participants were given (e.g., 5 minutes, 15 minutes, etc.), they used the full time. In addition, those participants given 15 minutes on the first trial took much longer to prepare another speech when they were told they could take as long as they wished.

So what is the solution to Parkinson's Law? Time boxing. Huh? Time boxing is the technique of setting a clear time limitation (i.e., a time box) for every task throughout the day. We create false interim deadlines for ourselves for each and every task. You may be thinking, "More deadlines? My whole life *is* deadlines. The last thing I want to do is add *more* deadlines to my life. That would just create more stress and anxiety. Isn't this book supposed to make me less stressed, not more?" Fair question. We actually expected the same result when we initially heard of this technique, but when we researched it and began applying it ourselves, we learned that "looks can be deceiving," as they say. It is counterintuitive, but erecting these microdeadlines throughout the day tricks our brain into becoming more productive and efficient, causing us to accomplish a lot more in less time, which actually leads to a greater sense of ease and relaxation throughout the day. As a result of this technique,

TIME BOXING: A CREST JEWEL
OF TIME MANAGEMENT

space opens up during the day, which makes life less stressful and less frenetic. This act of creating micro-deadlines is therefore an act of self-care and a catalyst to well-being.

Two of the most legendary time boxers, Bill Gates and Elon Musk, are uncoincidentally two of the most productive humans in the history of business. Both purportedly time box in five-minute increments throughout the day, meaning they break the entire business day into tiny five-minute segments that are each filled with a specific task or sub-task. We refer to this as "time boxing on steroids" – and we do not recommend it for normal humans. Although it would probably catapult anyone's productivity, it also feels like an overly intense and stressful way to live each day, and we believe this extreme form of time boxing would unavoidably lead to impairments in well-being.*

What we recommend is what we call "*ad hoc* time boxing," meaning to set a specific internal deadline for every task you are about to begin. You can think of it as time boxing *on the fly*. Right before you are about to begin any task or project, briefly pause and assign a targeted time deadline to it. And then start working. That's it. Because you have set a specific time limitation, your brain will intensify its focus, and you will likely resist some of the tempting distractions you would otherwise succumb to. We have shared this technique with countless law students and legal professionals and have received extremely positive feedback. People regularly inform us that it elevated their efficiency and productivity.

Let's take some examples. Say you are a few minutes from finishing the case you are reading for Property, and you tell yourself you are going to reply to some emails when you finish the case, before starting your Contracts reading. A few minutes later, you complete the case and then turn to emails to start replying to some. *Red Flag!* You are about to get pummeled by Parkinson's Law! You have no clarity on how many emails you are going to reply to, which specific emails will be selected, or how much time you intend to spend on this "email detour." Now

---

   *   Just to clarify, although we believe it would be prudent to replicate these two individuals' penchant for time boxing in order to improve your time management and productivity, we are not intending to suggest that other aspects of their lives, decision making, or behavior should be replicated.

you are virtually guaranteed to be swept up by Parkinson's Law: the email session is going to be inefficient and laden with poor micro-decisions that waste valuable time (and you are likely to impulsively – rather than purposefully – reach for another distraction after sending these emails). We say this from lived experience, not from judgment.

In contrast, this is what time boxing would look like: Instead of mindlessly diving into email and figuring out the game-plan as it unfolds, you first pre-select the four (or whatever number of) emails you would like to respond to, and then you select a targeted time goal. So you say, "I'm going to try to complete these four emails in 20 minutes – about five minutes each." This simple structure and target you have established will likely cause you to be more focused and to complete the email session in less time and with more prudent micro-decisions (e.g., the level of detail and perfectionism will likely be positively influenced by your time box).

Now, perhaps 20 minutes into the session, you are still working on email number three, despite doing your best. Not a problem! Just continue through this email efficiently and then attempt to complete email number four within the same five-minute intention. It ultimately may take you 27 minutes to send these mails, but had you not time boxed, it might have taken you 42 minutes. Additionally, you might have irrationally ended up replying to two additional emails that were not important enough to warrant a reply at this time, and consequently postponed one of the four emails that you otherwise pre-selected. So you might have spent an additional five minutes on the fifth email, causing the session to run 47 minutes. So in this hypothetical, time boxing converted a 47-minute detour into a 27-minute detour. These 20-minute "savings" start to add up over the course of the day and generate major spaciousness (not to mention the significant decision fatigue benefits that are outlined in Tool #7 at page 219, which arguably provide even greater benefits to your daily productivity and well-being than the large blocks of time you have saved).*

---

* For this reason, time boxing provides two separate yet interdependent productivity benefits: (1) it leads to the completion of tasks in a shorter period of time, which frees up new windows of time for the remainder of the day; (2) it reduces the

TIME BOXING: A CREST JEWEL
OF TIME MANAGEMENT

Another example. You are in the reading period of final exams and have been painstakingly pushing forward on your Civil Procedure outline, among many other things. You wake up one morning and decide to start on your Civ Pro outline as your first project of the day. You open the document and start working on the next available section. *Red Flag!* Again, there is no structure or timeframe identified, so you are likely going to have a very inefficient and distraction-heavy session. The vast, boundary-less space in which you are about to outline will almost certainly lead you toward frequent distractions and task-switches as you sluggishly advance the outline.

If, instead, you identify the section you want to start and complete (i.e., the subject matter and underlying cases), and then establish a targeted timeframe, you will likely have a very different experience. So you say, "During this next block, I am going to outline Rule 11 of the FRCP, its constituent parts, and the *Mohammed v. Union Carbide Corp.* case. Then I am going to take a break by checking my phone. My goal is to complete this block in 45 minutes." Take a look at the clock and get to it! While you may not be distraction-proof, you will likely be far less distracted and impulsive than you would have been without this simple time box.

You can also set time boxes on your reading assignments, rather than just opening the case and entering the black hole of time. We recognize that you may not have a basis for accurately predicting the amount of time to be allotted to a particular case or section of the outline, but that is not an issue because time boxing is not about hitting your time target *per se*, it is about increasing your focus, efficiency, and productivity in completing the task. Regardless of the task or project, assigning a structure and timeframe to it before commencing will likely change your brain's reaction to it.

Another example: If you are about to resume working on your brief for Legal Research & Writing, do not just start on the next part lackadaisically. Instead, break the remaining portion of the brief into constituent parts and then determine the time

---

amount of fatigue our brain experiences in completing those initial tasks, which causes our brain to perform more efficiently (and proficiently) on tasks for the remainder of the day, which also frees up additional windows of time.

target for the part you are about to start and finish. Between now and your next break, aim to accomplish that one part in the identified time. If that part will take longer than you would like before your next break, then divide that part into smaller pieces. This time-bound "divide and conquer" approach can convert an otherwise impenetrable behemoth into digestible parts that you are extremely capable of attacking.

By the way, phone calls with family or friends back home are a wonderful thing to time box. Bonus points if you announce your timeframe at the outset of the call or at the mid-way point. It's a firm and kind way of expressing your needs and ensuring that the call's duration does not spiral out of control. A pre-communicated time box prevents the ultimate disaster from manifesting: You have been talking for 55 minutes and are now five minutes away from wrapping up the call at your internal 60-minute time box, when the person suddenly brings up a major problem they are having in life. What?! Because you did not pre-disclose your time boundary, you now find yourself in the ultimate Catch-22: If you tell them you are not able to talk about this issue because you need to finish up in five minutes, it's not a good look. And if you instead bite your tongue and choose to support them with their problem (while wondering why it took them 55 minutes to raise this critical issue), you are now on the hook for another 45 minutes minimum – which will further fatigue you and derail your next study window.

So establishing – *and pre-disclosing* – a time box for certain phone calls and social obligations that you want to contain can be a very effective way of honoring your own needs and protecting the other person's feelings when you bow out. Of course, you want to do this in a gentle and kind way. "Hey, I'm so excited to get to connect with you today! Just so you know, I have set aside 60 minutes for our chat – which is going to be so fun, and then I'm going to pop back to my law school homework. So tell me what's been going on in your life!" Boom. You have erected a kind yet firm boundary.* It can be a little awkward to execute this, but when you start to wrap up the call at about the

---

* This does not mean you have to rigidly end the call at exactly the 60-minute mark. It is your choice whether you want to enforce that boundary tightly or loosely. Either way, the pre-boundary will make it far easier and less controversial to execute at the operative moment.

TIME BOXING: A CREST JEWEL
OF TIME MANAGEMENT

60-minute mark and notice how much easier it is to close it out, you will be immensely grateful for your pre-disclosure. Obviously, there is no need to time box social encounters that you are genuinely excited about and have no time concerns about, just the ones that have the potential of going down a rabbit hole.

So start time boxing as many of your law school and non-law school tasks as possible. You will very likely experience greater focus, efficiency, and productivity – as well as emotional ease and spaciousness – as a result. If you end up having any struggles in following through on some of your targeted time boxes, know that you will get more and more effective at it as you practice it more and more. You will slowly wire your brain to fire up when a time box is set, and it will become easier and easier over time. And remember, the purpose of the time box is *not* to "succeed" in completing the task in the exact time allotted, but to optimize your efficiency in completing that task. The question is not whether you hit the specific time allotted, but rather, whether you were more efficient, focused, and productive as a result of that time allotment. You can even use an internal mantra as a reminder, such as, "I time box in order to induce focus and productivity, not as a litmus test of my success."

We will leave you with a final thought on this technique. If you have enjoyed this book, then we invite you to thank the technique of time boxing. We can confidently say that this book would not have gotten written without this technique.

TOOL 18

TIME OF DAY DISCERNMENT: WHEN DOES *YOUR* BRAIN EXCEL ON WHICH TASKS?

"The key is in not spending time, but in investing it."

— Stephen Covey

"The early bird catches the worm." One of the most repeated proverbs in our society. It reminds us that if we start our day early, we will be more successful. If, on the other hand, we get a late start, we will likely miss out on the precious opportunity at hand. During my [*your co-author Jarrett's*] childhood, however, I was alerted to a poignant counterquestion: "What happened to the early *worm*??" The answer is: He got *eaten*. If that worm had only slept in a bit later that day, he would have been safely tucked away in the moist soil, and the early bird would never have found him. The early bird would have found some other early-rising, wandering worm to eat for breakfast.

So is it better to get a jump on the day or to sleep in a bit later? Relatedly, when is the human brain designed to function best throughout the day? And are there differences between people on these questions, and if so, what are these differences? Understanding the relationship between time and your cognitive performance is an important aspect of personal optimization in law school.

Chronobiology is the science and study of biological rhythms and the effects of time on living beings. In short, it is the biology of time. Chronobiology has found that as a general matter, there are two windows of time each day when the human brain is most receptive to acquiring and processing information: 10:00 a.m. to 2:00 p.m., and 4:00 p.m. to 10:00 p.m. However, research has found that adolescents and young adults (ages 14 to 24) are often a bit of an exception to this rule, with their peak times being up to 2–3 hours later than these ranges before slowly reverting to the mean in their 30s.[289] So if you often feel like you have brain fog during your first class of the day, it could be a consequence of a normally functioning biological system.

In addition to these statistical norms, the research further shows that there are individual differences in circadian rhythms (the body's internal clock that regulates the sleep-wake cycle) based on a unique set of genetic, physiological, hormonal, and lifestyle factors that influence each of us. For example, the science uses the term "larks" to refer to people whose circadian rhythms run on an earlier timeframe than the statistical norm and "owls" to refer to people whose circadian rhythms run on a later timeframe than the norm. Moreover, some people's circadian rhythms run 24 hours, while others' run slightly shorter or slightly longer than 24 hours.

How our brain functions throughout the day – and how our brain functions at specific times each day – is also highly variable. As a result of the wide variability in our relationship to time, the science "suggests a need to be more conscious about how to manage time on an individual basis in order to maximize productivity and minimize health risks."[290]

Moreover, "[a]ll times of day are not created equal," explains Daniel Pink, author of *When: The Scientific Secrets of Perfect Timing*.[291] "Our performance varies considerably over the course of the day, and what task to do at a certain time really depends on the nature of the task." Have you noticed how you tend to perform certain cognitive and law school tasks more effectively at different times of the day? For example, your brain may be super-efficient at reading your cases first thing in the morning, but late at night you feel foggy and your reading becomes distracted. Yet your law school friend may have foggier and more distracted reading comprehension first thing in the morning but is laser-like later in the evening. Moreover, whatever time of day your brain is most effective at reading case law may not be the same time that you are most disciplined with writing assignments. Or, whenever you tend to be best at outlining may be different from when you are best at creative brainstorming. And all of these times may be different from the time of day when

TIME OF DAY DISCERNMENT: WHEN DOES YOUR BRAIN EXCEL ON WHICH TASKS?

you are most effective at executing administrative paperwork or paying your bills.

A critical aspect of performance optimization is what we call "Time of Day Discernment": knowing what time of day your brain functions best on which cognitive tasks. In other words, pairing each type of cognitive task with a particular time of day. "Know thyself," the legendary aphorism of Ancient Greece, has never been more applicable. When we know how our brain functions on specific tasks during the various periods of the day, we make very different – *and much more prudent* – decisions about when we execute which tasks, causing our overall productivity to skyrocket.

Here is a simple exercise for clarifying this consideration for yourself: On the left side of a piece of paper, write a vertical list of the four approximate periods of the day that you are awake. You can use a standard 16-hour day, broken into four periods of four hours each. For example, 8 a.m. to 12 p.m., 12 p.m. to 4 p.m., 4 p.m. to 8 p.m., and 8 p.m. to 12 a.m. (Adjust this based on your standard wake and sleep schedule.) You can use the following labels for these four periods of day: Morning, Afternoon, Evening, Night. On the right side of the page, write a vertical list of the 8–10 cognitive tasks that you most frequently perform in a typical law school week. For example, reading, briefing, reviewing/updating your class notes, creative brainstorming, group studying/collaborations, outlining, writing, memorization, practice tests, administrative tasks, etc. Any activities you regularly perform in furtherance of your law school success should be included in this list. So you should now have two separate lists on the page, separated by some space. See the figure below for a sample of the setup.

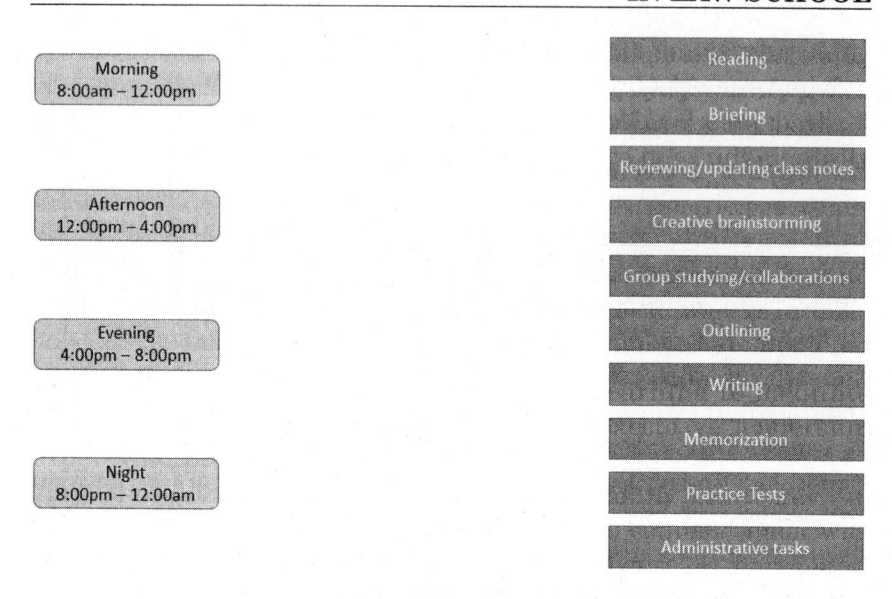

HAPPINESS AND PEAK PERFORMANCE IN LAW SCHOOL

Periods:
- Morning 8:00am – 12:00pm
- Afternoon 12:00pm – 4:00pm
- Evening 4:00pm – 8:00pm
- Night 8:00pm – 12:00am

Cognitive Tasks:
- Reading
- Briefing
- Reviewing/updating class notes
- Creative brainstorming
- Group studying/collaborations
- Outlining
- Writing
- Memorization
- Practice Tests
- Administrative tasks

Once you have completed this setup, we invite you to take a pen or pencil and draw a line from each cognitive task to each of the periods of day that *your brain* functions most effectively. In other words, for each cognitive task, determine which period or periods of the day you tend to have more natural energy, focus, and productivity for that particular cognitive task. You will likely notice some interesting findings. See the next figure for a sample of this step.

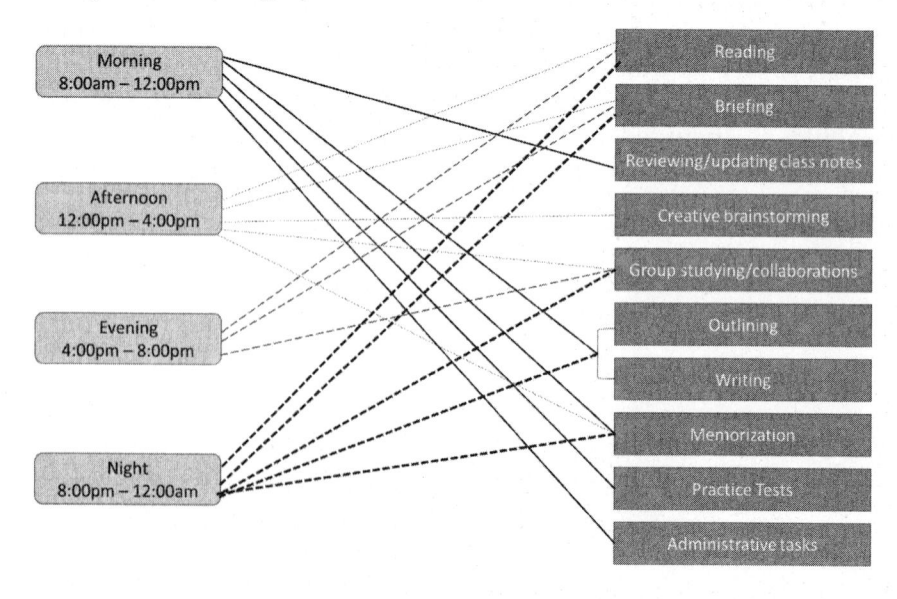

TIME OF DAY DISCERNMENT: WHEN DOES YOUR BRAIN EXCEL ON WHICH TASKS?

Now you have arrived at the final step: convert the prior list into a collated chart that enumerates each cognitive task and then provides the time or times when you excel most on each cognitive task. This chart incorporates the data from the prior list into an easily usable document. See the next figure for a sample of this chart, which we will call "Jarrett's Time of Day Discernment Chart." We are providing three different versions of the chart (Versions A, B, and C) – each of which organizes the data in a different way. You can choose the version that is most usable and preferable to you and your brain.

Version A: Jarrett's Time of Day Discernment Chart

Morning (8:00am to 12:00pm)
Reviewing/updating class notes
Outlining
Writing
Memorization
Practice tests
Administrative tasks
Afternoon (12:00pm to 4:00pm)
Reading
Briefing
Creative brainstorming
Group studying & collaborations
Memorization
Evening (4:00pm to 8:00pm)
Reading
Briefing
Group studying & collaborations
Night (8:00pm to 12:00am)
Reading
Briefing

Group studying & collaborations
Outlining
Writing
Memorization

Version B: Jarrett's Time of Day Discernment Chart

Activity	Time of Day
Reading/briefing	Afternoon, evening, night
Reviewing/updating notes	Morning
Creative brainstorming	Afternoon
Group studying & collaborations	Evening
Outlining/writing	Morning, night
Memorization	Afternoon, night
Practice tests	Morning
Administrative tasks	Morning

Version C: Jarrett's Time of Day Discernment Chart

Activity	Morning	Afternoon	Evening	Night
Reading/briefing		X	X	X
Reviewing/updating notes	X			
Creative brainstorming		X		
Group studying & collaborations			X	
Outlining/writing	X			X
Memorization		X		X
Practice tests	X			
Administrative tasks	X			

Let's do a brief summary of Jarrett's "T.O.D.D. Chart" in order to provide additional guidance on your process. This is a

TIME OF DAY DISCERNMENT: WHEN DOES YOUR BRAIN EXCEL ON WHICH TASKS?

hypothetical chart of how my [*your co-author Jarrett's*] brain would function on law school tasks if I were in law school today.

- **Reading/briefing:** I am aware that I am generally less effective and more distracted while reading first thing in the morning. My brain feels foggy and has a hard time "locking in" its attention for information acquisition at this time of day. I therefore attempt to do my reading in the afternoon, evening, and night – when my brain seems to attack reading much more effectively. Same goes for briefing.

- **Reviewing/updating notes:** I am aware that when I finally finish classes for the day/evening, the last thing on planet earth I am motivated to do is to review or update my notes from that *same day*. However, I am much more likely to do this task if I target it for the next morning – after taking some space from the material. Unlike reading brand new material first thing in the morning, my brain is much more adept at reviewing previously learned information first thing in the morning. It feels less overwhelming and requires less willpower for me.

  However, many other students' brains function differently. They would much prefer to review and update their class notes the same day as class – when the information and lecture are most fresh in their minds. Moreover, to them it may feel more burdensome to "revisit" the class notes the next morning, as they would rather have "closure" on those notes the same day they are originally produced. Again, "Know thyself."

- **Creative brainstorming:** I have a lot of natural energy for creative brainstorming, so I deliberately pair this task with periods when I am otherwise more fatigued, such as during the post-lunch lull. (We typically experience drowsiness and a willpower reduction about 60–90 minutes after eating lunch. It's a dangerous time of the day for distractions and inefficiency because we are already fatigued from several hours of work earlier in the day, yet we are not close enough to the end of the day to receive that precious "second wind.") If I attempt to perform many of the other tasks during the post-lunch lull, I will find ways to distract myself and derail any productivity, i.e., this is the perfect time to go down a social media or web-browsing rabbit hole!

We recommend that you determine which tasks you do best when you are fatigued or exhausted – and then deliberately pair those tasks with your typical low-energy periods. You may not perform those tasks as effectively as possible when you are depleted, but the key question is whether you perform those tasks *better than other tasks* when you are depleted. This allows you to generate at least marginal productivity in a time period when you would otherwise possibly generate zero productivity.

- **Group studying/collaborations:** Because I am an introvert who gets highly depleted from group interactions and collaborative studying, I attempt to do these sessions later in the day – ideally during energy lulls or in the late afternoon or after. I have noticed that when I engage in these group interactions in the morning, I feel completely exhausted afterwards, and this exhaustion derails my efficiency and productivity for the rest of the day. So I ideally attempt to pair this task with the post-lunch lull or later lulls. Then, the presence of the group prevents me from succumbing to the distractions I otherwise might succumb to if I were working alone during that time period. I may be extremely fatigued afterwards, but there is now less time left in the day, so this energy depletion will have a smaller net effect on my overall productivity for the day. In other words, I am mitigating the harm.

Being mindful of whether you gather or lose energy from social interactions (extrovert v. introvert tendencies) can help you intelligently pair socializing and group studying with the particular times of the day that will best advance your vitality and overall productivity.

- **Outlining/writing:** I am aware that my outlining and writing need prolonged uninterrupted periods more than any other task, so I attempt to match these tasks with the most open spaces in my day – which typically end up being the morning window and night window (as well as the evening window, to a lesser extent). If I pair these tasks during the "choppier" part of the day, I know I will make very little, if any, progress on them. This is in contrast, for example, to reading for class – which I can effectively perform through short and efficient periods that are separated by class and other interruptions.

- **Memorization:** When studying for final exams (in my real life), I used to structure my schedule so that my memorization periods were paired with the time of day that I assumed was my most rejuvenated time: first thing in the morning. When I was a bit tired at the end of the night, I would prefer to go to sleep and wake up earlier to start on the memorization task, rather than dedicate any depleted nighttime performance to it, and then sleep a bit later to compensate for it.

But many years later, I learned that the human brain does its highest level of memory consolidation during sleep.* When memorizing for final exams,

---

* During sleep, the brain consolidates long-term memories at a much higher rate than during wakefulness. Sleeping before learning new information helps prepare the brain to comprehend that new information, according to Dr. Matthew Walker, a neuroscientist and sleep expert at UC Berkeley, "and then, sleep after learning is essential to help save and cement that new information into the architecture of the brain, meaning that you're less likely to forget it."[292]

In one study in this area, researchers provided participants with photos of 20 different faces and the names of each person in the photos. After the participants attempted to memorize which names went with which faces, the researchers provided a one has to first engage in memory acquisition (the process of reviewing information and consciously attempting to commit it to memory) and then one has to engage in memory consolidation (the process by which the hippocampus, the long-term memory center of the brain, integrates or stabilizes that information into a long-term memory). I found, consistent with this research, that when I performed memory acquisition before going to sleep, and then allowed my brain to consolidate those memories during sleep, my ability to memorize information shot up. So I try to do key memorization stretches (i.e., memory acquisition) before naps and before going to bed at night.

Obviously during the finals period, we have to spend much of the day doing memory acquisition, but it would be prudent for you to experiment with how your brain absorbs memories based on when you conduct the memorization. You can then structure your biggest or most challenging memorization pushes around that time of day.

- **Practice tests:** Because I find practice tests to be so distasteful, I know that if I target them for later in the day, developments will occur during the day that I will use to justify postponing the practice test. For example, a few minutes before my targeted afternoon practice test for Property, I think to myself, "I am not through nearly as much of my Contracts outlining as I had hoped for at this point in the day, so I am going to postpone my Property practice test and spend the next couple of hours working on the Contracts outline." And then the Property practice test gets bumped to the next day,

---

12-hour break and then tested their memorization. However, half of the participants performed their initial memorization in the morning after waking up, while the second half of the participants performed their initial memorization in the evening before going to sleep. The participants whose memorization session was followed by sleep significantly outperformed the participants whose memorization session followed sleep, confirming the researchers' hypothesis that the participants' post-memorization sleep would enhance their memorization due to the heightened memory consolidation that occurs during sleep.[293]

TIME OF DAY DISCERNMENT: WHEN DOES YOUR BRAIN EXCEL ON WHICH TASKS?

and then something similar occurs the following day. This pattern repeats itself until the *real* Property exam is over, with no practice test ever having occurred.

So to prevent this chain-reaction from occurring, I schedule my practice tests for the morning, when I am more likely to muster up the discipline to execute this painful task and less likely to come up with a viable excuse to postpone it.

- **Administrative tasks:** Dealing with my archnemesis – administrative tasks and paperwork of any kind – involves a delicate discernment. Like disarming a bomb. If I intend to do an administrative task first thing in the morning in order to "knock it out," I wake up and instead commence "Operation Avoidance," which includes engaging in every possible distraction while the administrative task sits there untouched. Starting the day with this torture is simply too demoralizing to achieve overall success for the day. Yet if I target the administrative task for later in the day, say 3:00 p.m., I will inevitably come up with an excuse not to do it at that time, such as this gem: "I've accomplished so much today and I'm understandably fatigued now that it's 3 p.m., so I'm going to go to ESPN.com instead and will do the administrative task tomorrow at this time!" I will keep bumping this annoying task in this same manner one day at a time, until three years have suddenly passed.

  So to avoid this, I target the window of 10:00 a.m. to 12 p.m. as my "administrative task window." I have found that if I knock out a couple of hours of work from 8 a.m. to 10 a.m., I feel a sense of momentum and energy from my morning productivity that I can use to capitalize on the administrative task, before my energy depletes throughout the day and thwarts my ability to execute the administrative task. It's my administrative task "sweet spot."

This is the level of thought we invite you to give to each of the cognitive tasks as you complete your chart.

Once you complete your Time of Day Discernment Chart, we are confident that you will have newfound levels of self-awareness and will make different micro-decisions throughout the day on what tasks you do *when*. As a result, you will begin accomplishing a great deal more in the same amount of time.

TOOL 19

LAUGHTER: THE UNDERRATED SUPERPOWER FOR BOOSTING WELL-BEING AND COGNITION

"We don't laugh because we're happy, we are happy because we laugh."

— William James

Do you know how many times the typical four-year-old child laughs per day? 300 times, on average. Do you know how many times the typical adult laughs per day? 17 times.[294] That's just sad. (We're talking about real laughs, not the polite chuckle you do when someone says something marginally funny.)

How did we become so serious about life? How did we lose 94% of our laughter over the course of our life? And most importantly, should we allow ourselves to be so serious during law school – and as lawyers? These are the questions to consider as you read about this tool and as you proceed through law school.

Our profession is rooted in a history of solemn formality. American lawyers at the beginning of the republic wore powdered white wigs and proudly presented themselves as dignified, erudite, and highbrow at all times. These norms can be traced back to British nobility and the royal courts of England, where lawyers and other distinguished professionals were expected to carry themselves in a formal, stately, and sophisticated manner. Indeed, the word "courtly," itself, which appears to have first been used in England in the 15th century, means "a quality befitting the court," or "polite or formal in behavior," or "polite, refined and elegant."[295] So the epicenter of our legal system – the court – was so synonymous with formality that a new word, "courtly," was created to capture that reality. Our American legal system ultimately arose from the British royal courts and adopted many of the legal principles, doctrines, and cultural norms of those courts, including the air of formality and seriousness.

A noteworthy example of a distinguished British nobleman who revered formality and detested humor was Lord Philip Dormer Stanhope, who lived from 1694 through 1773. He was a highly respected statesman and diplomat, and he became the 4th Earl of Chesterfield. In a letter he wrote his son on March 9, 1748, Lord Stanhope explained his disdain for laughter and implored his son to never engage in it.[296] His letter expresses the misguided notion – still prevalent today – that laughter is a sign of frivolity and triviality. (The irony, of course, is that his anti-laughter letter can only be described as *hilarious*. If it doesn't make you laugh, then perhaps you should send a friend request to Lord Stanhope and become friends!) Here is Lord Stanhope's heartfelt advice to his son:

> Having mentioned laughing, I must particularly warn you against it: and I could heartily wish, that you may often be seen to smile, but never heard to laugh while you live. Frequent and loud laughter is the characteristic of folly and in manners; it is the manner in which the mob express their silly joy at silly things; and they call it being merry. In my mind, there is nothing so illiberal, and so ill-bred, as audible laughter. True wit, or sense, never yet made anybody laugh; they are above it: They please the mind, and give a cheerfulness to the countenance.
>
> But it is low buffoonery, or silly accidents, that always excite laughter; and that is what people of sense and breeding should show themselves above. A man's going to sit down, in the supposition that he has a chair behind him, and falling down upon his breech for want of one, sets a whole company a laughing, when all the wit in the world would not do it; a plain proof, in my mind, how low and unbecoming a thing laughter is: not to mention the disagreeable noise that it makes, and the shocking distortion of the face that it occasions. Laughter is easily restrained, by a very little reflection;

LAUGHTER: THE UNDERRATED SUPERPOWER FOR BOOSTING WELL-BEING AND COGNITION

but as it is generally connected with the idea of gaiety, people do not enough attend to its absurdity.

I am neither of a melancholy nor a cynical disposition, and am as willing and as apt to be pleased as anybody; but I am sure that, since I have had the full use of my reason, nobody has ever heard me laugh.

Awesome fatherly advice.

Portrait of Philip Stanhope, 4th Earl of Chesterfield (1694–1773), National Portrait Gallery: NPG 533

He looks like a blast!

The legal industry today suffers from this same distorted reasoning, and it trickles down to law school: the belief that laughter is a sign of frivolity and triviality. In other words, if we are laughing, we are not taking things seriously. Laughter is a dishonoring of the importance of the matter at issue. This belief can lead law students (and lawyers) to become overly serious and to refrain from embracing (and chasing) laughter in law school – in order to ensure they are treating the experience at issue with "appropriate reverence." But this path can lead to impairments in one's mental health, emotional well-being, stress resiliency, and cognitive performance.

This is because laughter has been shown to be a mental, emotional, and cognitive **superpower**. Its benefits are multifaceted and wide-ranging. For example, laughter has been shown in several studies to reduce our levels of cortisol and other stress hormones.[297] Moreover, one study attempted to test whether a brief experience of humor would affect participants' subsequent stress levels when subjected to an intentionally stressful experience.[298] Participants were shown either a 9-minute humorous video or a 9-minute neutral video, before performing unexpected math subtractions while being exposed to electric shocks. Ya, that sounds stressful. (Prior to this stress test, the intensity of the shocks was adjusted to match each individual's level of pain tolerance, so each participant experienced the same relative amount of pain from the shocks.)

The participants' stress levels were measured before the video, before the stress test, and after the stress test. The results showed that the participants who watched the 9-minute humorous video not only reported much lower levels of stress after both watching the video and taking the stress test, but their cortisol levels also materially dropped after watching the humorous video. In contrast, the cortisol levels of the participants who watched the neutral video remained constant. Most interestingly, however, the participants who watched the humorous video had a much smaller increase in cortisol levels during the subsequent electric shock math experience, compared to the other participants whose cortisol levels spiked during the stressful task. So a short experience of humor not only reduces our cortisol and stress levels, but also can prime us to respond to subsequent stressors with greater resilience.

Moreover, even the anticipation of *future laughter* has been shown to decrease stress hormones and improve mood. In one study,[299] the participants' baseline stress hormone levels and moods were assessed, and then half of the participants were told they would be shown a humorous video in the future, while the other half were told they would be shown an informational video. In response to this information, the humorous video group experienced a material decrease in stress hormones and increase in positive mood, while the other group experienced no change in either stress hormones or mood as a result of the information they received. So the mere *anticipation* of humor changed the participants' stress levels and mood.

In addition to reducing stress hormones, laughter has been shown to increase a wide variety of happy hormones. For instance, even a short instance of laughter releases endorphins (and other endogenous opioids) that are "feel good" hormones that serve as natural pain killers and stress reducers.[300] Laughter also causes the release of serotonin, the natural mood stabilizer that produces feelings of calm and that is induced by many anti-depressant medications (selective serotonin reuptake inhibitors).[301] In addition, laughter triggers the release of dopamine, the pleasure hormone.[302] In this vein, laughter interventions have been shown to reduce symptoms of depression and anxiety.[303] From a biochemical perspective, laughter is probably the single best thing we can do to quickly and simultaneously reduce cortisol and increase endorphins, serotonin, and dopamine. Talk about a happiness cocktail!

Laughter is not just good for your happiness, mood, mental health, and stress resilience, it is also good for your learning and memorization, as revealed by several studies. For example, in a study testing memorization and retention of political information, researchers provided participants with the same political information, but one group received the information through a political comedy program (e.g., the Daily Show), while the other group received the same information through a traditional news program (the evening news).[304] The group that received the information through a comedy program significantly outperformed the other group in tests of memory and retention of the underlying political information.

Similar results occurred in the university context when researchers picked an intentionally "dry" subject – Statistics – to test the impact of humor on learning.[305] Students listened to statistics lectures with and without statistics-related humor interjected into the lectures, and then were given surveys at the end of each class regarding their enjoyment of the lectures and tests measuring their learning and retention of the material. The results revealed that students enjoyed the lectures that included some content-related humor much more than the other lectures, and they performed far better on the tests of learning and retention after the humor-sprinkled lectures. In another study, participants were shown either a 20-minute comedic video intended to induce laughter or a 20-minute neutral video before taking a set of memory tests.[306] The participants who watched the short comedic video substantially outperformed the participants who watched the more serious video.

We believe this research is hysterical! We mean, "noteworthy"! In light of the many benefits of laughter, we recommend that you resist the social conditioning of law school (and the legal industry) that will attempt to make you a more serious, less playful version of yourself. You get to choose whether you want to conform your behavior to the illusion that laughter is frivolity or to the truth that laughter is prosperity. If you do not actively rebut this social conditioning, then you face the risk that millions of law students before you have succumbed to, which is to slowly become a more serious, less playful version of yourself whose laughter slowly dries up.*

In addition to actively resisting the laughter-reducing effects of the legal industry, we invite you to begin engaging in *deliberate acts of laughter* each day, especially if you feel you are not laughing as much as you used to. Perhaps you can have two dedicated "Laughter Sessions" every day – one during the first half of the day and the other during the second half of the day. During your "Laughter Sessions," pause your law school work and watch something online that is designed to make you laugh, whether it is a short clip from a stand-up comedy routine, a two-minute scene from one of your favorite comedy shows, or one of the countless hilarious clips on YouTube or TikTok. Or read an article from the Onion.com or some other comedic website. Or just close your eyes and think about a hilarious moment from your week (or month) for one full minute. Deliberately conjure up an experience of laughter to enhance your internal state.

---

* In an attempt to prevent this from occurring to business school students, Stanford Business School professors Jennifer Aaker and Naomi Bagdonas created and teach a wildly popular class at the business school called "Humor: Serious Business," where they explore the widespread benefits of humor and laughter in business and life. They recently published an insightful book on the topic called, *Humor, Seriously: Why humor is a secret weapon in business and life: And how anyone can harness it. Even you.*[307]

LAUGHTER: THE UNDERRATED SUPERPOWER
FOR BOOSTING WELL-BEING AND COGNITION

When you do this, we encourage you to really allow yourself to bask in the experience of laughter. Do not "hold in" your laughter or otherwise attempt to prevent yourself from appearing silly to onlookers. If you can induce even a short session of belly laughing (*really let 'er rip!*), you are going to reduce your stress hormones, diminish your perceived stress, flood your brain with happy hormones, improve your overall mood, and enhance your learning and memorization capacity. That is an eminently intelligent thing to do if you want to be happier and more successful in law school. Over time, as you make laughter a more regular component of your typical day, you will likely experience a reduction in your baseline stress levels and an increase in your overall well-being, happiness, learning, and memorization.

"If you can laugh in the face of adversity," says comedian Ricky Gervais, "you're bullet-proof." We know how much adversity there is in law school; the least you can do for yourself is to laugh regularly and heartily. Unlike Lord Stanhope, who proclaimed nearly 300 years ago that "there is nothing so illiberal, and so ill-bred, as audible laughter," modern science proves there is nothing so illiberal, and so ill-bred, as the absence of audible laughter.

Supreme Court Justice Alfred Hemmington II

In 1842, Supreme Court Justice Alfred Hemmington II keenly observed: "Law without laughter is like fishing without a hook." His astute words are as true, if not truer, today as they were nearly two centuries ago.* †

* For purposes of full transparency: Justice Hemmington II did not really say this.

† One more thing: Justice Hemmington II is not a real person. We made him up.

TOOL 20

KINDNESS: SMALL ALTRUISTIC ACTS INCREASE *YOUR OWN* HAPPINESS

"Kindness is never wasted. It always makes a difference. It blesses the one who receives it, and it blesses you, the giver."

— Barbara De Angelis

In Section II, we discussed the rich mental and emotional benefits we receive from reframing unfair actions of others through the lens of compassion rather than judgment. While that mindset shift is critical to our own happiness and well-being, that shift relates to situations where another person has acted unfairly, selfishly, or otherwise undesirably (which, unfortunately, is not a rarity in life). So what about the many situations where the people in your life are *not* currently acting in an undesirable way? They are behaving positively or neutrally – simply minding their own business. We would now like to share a tangible tool for increasing your happiness in those situations: purposeful acts of kindness.*

The science shows that when we commit small altruistic acts for others, our own happiness and emotional well-being get a boost. This is counterintuitive because we assume that if we are feeling sad or upset about something, or just feeling somewhat "lukewarm" about life in that moment, we need to

---

* We are not attempting to suggest that you should withhold purposeful acts of kindness from people who act unfairly and only extend them to people who act positively or neutrally. We are simply acknowledging that engaging in the Judgment-to-Compassion reframing discussed in Section II is challenging enough when someone acts unfairly towards us, so also committing a purposeful act of kindness towards that person may be a longshot. However, to the extent you are able to internally find compassion for the person <u>and</u> externally commit a purposeful act of kindness towards them, it would be a grand slam on your part. But if this feels like too much, then you can focus on extending purposeful acts of kindness to neutral and positive individuals only.

focus 100% of our attention and energy on ourselves so we can begin feeling better. So our focus turns inward to our own needs, desires, and preferences, and we may unintentionally ignore, downplay, or deprioritize the needs, desires, and preferences of others. To be clear, this is not a mean-spirited act or conscious self-centeredness, it is just a natural reaction to not feeling good inside. We understandably want to focus on improving that state.

But the irony is that if we over-focus on our own interests in those situations, and under-focus on the interests of others, we can worsen our own internal state, or at least dampen our ability to improve it. So when we are overwhelmed with stress or just not feeling particularly happy inside, one of the most self-loving things we can do is to commit a small act of kindness for another person – whether it's a friend, family member, law school colleague, or stranger.

It can be any small act that takes very little time to perform, such as giving a compliment to a stranger, helping a neighbor carry their grocery bags in, picking up an extra cup of coffee while at the coffee shop and bringing it your friend who has been studying non-stop, telling the manager of a restaurant or store that the employee who helped you did a fantastic job, helping an elderly person cross the street safely, sending a "checking-in" text message to your family member who has been struggling, letting someone merge into your line while you are driving, writing a positive Yelp review for a local business, sending a thank you note or email to someone, paying a few bucks towards the meal of the car behind you in line at a drive-through restaurant, doing a chore or house task for your roommate or family member that they typically do, having a two minute conversation with an unhoused person about how they are doing, sending a "thinking of you" text to a friend from college you haven't reached out to in a while, cleaning up the leftover food and trays left on another table at a self-service restaurant, holding the elevator door open for a stranger when the door would otherwise close long before they approached, bringing a meal to a grieving or sick friend, letting someone who looks rushed move ahead of you in line at the coffee shop or restaurant,

KINDNESS: SMALL ALTRUISTIC ACTS INCREASE YOUR OWN HAPPINESS

offering food to a hungry person on the street, or helping the law librarian by stacking the strewn books on the cart.

Pretty much all of these acts of kindness can be done in about two minutes or less, and the science shows these sorts of small acts of kindness can enlarge our happiness. "When it comes to the pursuit of happiness, popular culture encourages a focus on oneself," explains a major study on happiness and altruism published in 2016 by several renowned happiness researchers.[308] "By contrast, substantial evidence suggests that what consistently makes people happy is focusing pro-socially on others." Indeed, study after study shows that small acts of kindness or altruism improve our well-being and happiness. This is often referred to as "helper's high" – because helping others or doing kind things for others so potently elevates our own state. According to the Mayo Clinic, committing acts of kindness releases a variety of happy hormones: "Physiologically, kindness can positively change your brain. Being kind boosts serotonin and dopamine, which are neurotransmitters in the brain that give you feelings of satisfaction and well-being, and cause the pleasure/reward centers in your brain to light up. Endorphins, which are your body's natural pain killer, also can be released."[309]

One study tested whether doing one small act of kindness every day for 10 straight days would improve life satisfaction scores.[310] The individuals who did the kindness practice experienced substantial improvements in their life satisfaction scores in that 10-day stretch, in contrast to the control group, whose scores remained stable. A more recent study tested whether similar results would occur from a seven-day kindness practice.[311] The researchers broke the 683 participants into two groups and asked the kindness group to do at least one small act of kindness per day. Several interesting outcomes were revealed. First, the participants who did one small act of kindness per day, unlike the control group, had higher happiness scores at the end of the week. Second, the participants who did more than one small act of kindness per day on average experienced even larger improvements in their happiness scores than the participants who did only one such act per day. And finally, these positive effects on happiness occurred equally irrespective of whether the small acts of kindness were performed towards close contacts (e.g., friends and family) or strangers.

Another study inquired whether one day of kindness per week could improve people's happiness.[312] The researchers asked the kindness group to perform five small acts of kindness one day per week for a six-week stretch. This allowed the participants to "compress" their kind acts into a single day per week, while not performing any acts of kindness for the other six days of the week. At the end of the six-week period, however, the kindness group enjoyed significantly higher happiness scores than they had at the outset of the study (again, unlike the control group). So if you'd rather have a "kindness day" once per week, and take the other six days off, this study suggests you should nevertheless reap rich rewards.

Other studies have revealed that happiness can improve even without establishing a quota of kind acts. For example, one study found that simply counting one's acts of kindness each night for a one-week stretch led to improved happiness scores.[313] Another study found that merely recalling one's past kind acts once per day for three straight days increased happiness, unlike for the control group.[314]

Would you expect kindness towards oneself or kindness towards others to lead to a greater bump in happiness? The research says it's the latter. In one study, researchers asked participants to perform three acts of kindness for others in a day, one day per week, for four straight weeks, while another group of participants performed three acts of kindness for themselves according to the same schedule.[315] All participants' happiness scores were recorded at baseline before the intervention and then two weeks after the four-week intervention ended. The self-kindness group's happiness levels at the six-week follow-up matched their levels at the baseline reading, yet the kindness towards others group experienced a material increase in happiness during the six-week period.

Another study provided 1,700 undergraduate students with a $2.50 stipend and encouraged them to use that money to buy a goodie bag with chocolate, juice, etc.[316] Half of the students, however, were told to take the goodie bag home with them, while the other half were told to gift it to sick children at the local

KINDNESS: SMALL ALTRUISTIC ACTS INCREASE YOUR OWN HAPPINESS

children's hospital. Happiness levels of all participants were assessed both at arrival and later that evening. The students who donated their goodie bag to the sick children had materially higher happiness scores compared to earlier in the day, while the students who took the goodie bag home for themselves did not.

In another study, participants were given either $5 or $20 in the morning and, depending on the group to which they were randomly assigned, told to either spend the money on themselves or on others by 5 p.m. that day.[317] The researchers called the participants later that evening and reassessed their happiness levels, finding that the participants who had spent the money on others were measurably happier than the participants who had spent the money on themselves, even though there was no difference in their happiness levels at the beginning of the day. Intriguingly, the individuals who were given $5 to spend on others enjoyed the same amount of improved happiness as the individuals given $20 to spend on others.

So do not feel you need to spend large amounts, or even any monetary amounts, on others to reap the benefits of kindness. As they say, "It's the thought that counts." By measuring kindness through a monetary gift, this study allowed the researchers to establish a uniform and objectively measurable act of kindness. This approach was valuable for the methodology of the study, but as the plethora of above research reveals, kindness is not about spending money on others, *per se*, it's about *doing something for others*. And it is this act of doing something for others – not necessarily the *amount* that is done – that improves our happiness.

When we do small things for others, we also experience marked decreases in our stress levels. One study led by Yale and UCLA psychologists tracked 77 participants for 14 straight days by assessing the number of stressful events they experienced each day, the small acts of kindness they committed each day, and their well-being and resilience levels each evening.[318] The study found that the participants' small acts of kindness buffered the stress from the challenging events, increased their overall well-being on those days, and proved to be an "effective strategy for reducing the impact of stress on emotional functioning." The study's lead author, Dr. Emily Answell, a professor of psychiatry at Yale University School of Medicine, summarized the findings in this way: "Our research shows that when we help others we can also help ourselves. Stressful days usually lead us to have a worse mood and poorer mental health, but our findings suggest that if we do small things for others, such as holding a door open for someone, we won't feel as poorly on stressful days."[319]

Studies have also shown that doing small acts of kindness towards others can ease anxiety, even for individuals struggling with clinical social anxiety,[320] and can reduce symptoms of depression among individuals suffering from major depression disorder.[321] Moreover, small acts of kindness have been shown to improve gene expression (the process by which our genetic coding translates into observable effects) in a way that may lead to reduced susceptibility to long-term disease.[322] "Few studies have shown causal mechanisms between prosocial behavior and improvements in biological processes," said Sonja Lyubomirsky, one the authors of the study and a leading researcher on happiness.[323] "Our findings point to possible changes in the immune markers that influence disease development or resistance."

Small acts of kindness are rather easy to perform, yet they yield expansive benefits. They improve our happiness, reduce our stress, and enhance our mental health. In the words of the Chief Psychiatrist of Cedars Sinai Medical Center and Professor of Psychiatry at UCLA School of Medicine, Waguih William IsHak, "kindness ... has a profound impact on one's well-being."[324]

If you begin spending just two minutes each day – or every couple of days – performing a purposeful act of kindness, you will slowly turn this practice into a way of life. This small time commitment can make a difference in the lives of others, and as the science conclusively shows, can make a major difference in yours. The ancient Greek philosopher, Aesop, put it well: "No act of kindness, no matter how small, is ever wasted." Indeed, each small act of kindness you commit is contributing valuably to others' lives and to your own happiness.

FINAL THOUGHTS

Law school is a truly unique life experience. It will provide you with an elite education and ongoing opportunities in life that few people on the planet are lucky enough to receive. Yet, it is also an intensely stressful and overwhelming journey. An ancient Indian proverb states, "Thriving is the continual growth of a being under circumstances tending to press it down." Law school can at times feel like a heavy burden pressing you down – with its perpetual barrage of assignments, deadlines, and seeming long-term ramifications for everything you do. But if you can view your law school experience as an opportunity to continually grow – *mentally, emotionally, intellectually, and academically* – amidst the onerous circumstances, you can nevertheless thrive.

We are hopeful that the tools we have provided in this book can support you in maximizing your thriving, happiness, resilience, cognition, and academic success throughout this exhilarating yet turbulent journey. In closing, we want to share a poem that can serve as a reminder of what truly matters in life. When I [*your co-author Rebecca*] was a full-time law professor, I had a copy of this poem on my office door so all of my students and passersby could experience a piece of inspiration. But I did not know who wrote the poem, and the internet often attributed it to "anonymous," so at the bottom of the copy on my door, it stated "Anonymous."

Many students over the years commented that they were touched and inspired by the poem, and then one day, a new 1L attended my office hours. She was an amazing student – brilliant, incisive and creative in class, and full of positive energy. She mentioned how she loved the poem on my door and then added, "One thing though, it's not 'anonymous.'" I eagerly replied, "Really?! This is one of my all-time favorite poems. You actually know who wrote it?" She nodded and calmly replied, "Yes, my dad wrote it."

Chills ran up and down my spine. One of my most cherished poems was written by my student's father – who, to my additional surprise – was a lawyer. His name is Michael

Josephson, a former law professor and now thought leader in legal ethics (whom we quoted earlier in the book in our discussion on gratitude). Josephson is proof that with your law degree, you can become *anything* – even a poet. So without further ado, here is his poem, titled "What Will Matter."

Ready or not, some day it will all come to an end.

There will be no more sunrises, no minutes, hours, or days.

All the things you collected, whether treasured or forgotten, will pass to someone else.

Your wealth, fame, and temporal power will shrivel to irrelevance.

It will not matter what you owned or what you were owed.

Your grudges, resentments, frustrations, and jealousies will finally disappear.

So, too, your hopes, ambitions, plans, and to-do lists will expire.

The wins and losses that once seemed so important will fade away.

It won't matter where you came from or what side of the tracks you lived on at the end.

It won't matter whether you were beautiful or brilliant.

Even your gender and skin color will be irrelevant.

So what will matter? How will the value of your days be measured?

What will matter is not what you bought but what you built; not what you got but what you gave.

What will matter is not your success but your significance.

What will matter is not what you learned but what you taught.

FINAL THOUGHTS 377

What will matter is every act of integrity, compassion, courage, or sacrifice that enriched, empowered, or encouraged others to emulate your example.

What will matter is not your competence but your character.

What will matter is not how many people you knew but how many will feel a lasting loss when you're gone.

What will matter is not your memories but the memories of those who loved you.

What will matter is how long you will be remembered, by whom, and for what.

Living a life that matters doesn't happen by accident.

It's not a matter of circumstance but of choice.

Choose to live a life that matters.

We humbly hope that some of the techniques we have shared in this book can help you live a life that matters. If you make the important threshold choice to live a life that matters, and also choose to apply some of the techniques we have provided to help you succeed in living such a life, we believe you are destined for greatness. And what is more, you will be fully exercising your inalienable constitutional right to the pursuit of happiness.

ENDNOTES

[1] Achor, S. (2010). *The happiness advantage: The seven principles of positive psychology that fuel success and performance at work*. Crown Publishing.

[2] Maguire, E., Gadian, D., Johnsrude, I., Good, C., Ashburner, J., Frackowiak, R., & Frith, C. (2000). Navigation-related structural change in the hippocampi of cab drivers. *Proceedings of the National Academy of Sciences of the United States of America*, *97*(8), 4398–4403. DOI: 10.1073/pnas. 070039597.

[3] Hölzel, B. K., Carmody, J., Vangel, M., Congleton, C., Yerramsetti, S. M., Gard, T., & Lazar, S. W. (2011). Mindfulness practice leads to increases in regional brain gray matter density. *Psychiatry Research*, *191*(1), 36–43. DOI: 10.1016/j.pscychresns. 2010.08.006.

[4] Eagleman, D. M., & Vaughn, D. A. (2021). The defensive activation theory: REM sleep as a mechanism to prevent takeover of the visual cortex. *Frontiers in Neuroscience*, *15*, Article 632853. DOI: 10.3389/fnins.2021.632853.

[5] Saunders, T., Driskell, J. E., Johnston, J. H., & Salas, E. (1996). The effect of stress inoculation training on anxiety and performance. *Journal of Occupational Health Psychology*, *1*(2), 170–186. DOI: 10.1037//1076-8998.1.2.170.

[6] Kahneman, D. (2011). *Thinking, fast and slow*. Farrar, Straus and Giroux.

[7] Dibble, D. (2002). *The new agreements in the workplace: Releasing the human spirit*, New Dream Team Publishing.

[8] Gilboa, A., & Marlatte, H. (2017). Neurobiology of schemas and schema-mediated memory. *Trends in Cognitive Sciences*, *21*(8), 618–631. DOI: 10.1016/j.tics.2017.04.013.

[9] Crum, A. J. & Langer, E. J. (2007). Mind-set matters: Exercise and the placebo effect. *Psychological Science*, *18*(2), 165–71. DOI: 10.1111/j.1467-9280.2007.01867.x.

[10] Walton, G., & Cohen, G. (2011). A brief social-belonging intervention improves academic and health outcomes of minority students. *Science, 331*(6023), 1447–1451. DOI: 10.1126/science.1198364.

[11] DeWitte, M. (2018, November 5). Changing the way people perceive problems in their lives will help society too, Stanford scholar says. *Stanford News*. https://news.stanford.edu/2018/11/05/changing-people-perceive-problems.

[12] Dostoyevsky, F. (2016). *Winter Notes on Summer Impressions*. (K. Zinovieff, Trans.) Alma Classics. (Original work published 1863).

[13] Wegner, D. M., Schneider, D. J., Carter, S. R., & White, T. L. (1987). Paradoxical effects of thought suppression. *Journal of Personality and Social Psychology, 53*(1), 5–13. DOI: 10.1037/0022-3514.53.1.5.

[14] See, e.g., Ruan, Y., Reis, H., Zareba, W., & Lane, R. (2020). Does suppressing negative emotion impair subsequent emotions? Two experience sampling studies. *Motivation and Emotion, 44*(3), 427–435. DOI: 10.1007/S11031-019-09774-W. See also Campbell-Sills, L., Barlow, D. H., Brown, T. A., & Hofmann, S. G. (2006). Effects of suppression and acceptance on emotional responses of individuals with anxiety and mood disorders. *Behavior Research and Therapy, 44*(9), 1251–1263. DOI: 10.1016/j.brat.2005.10.001; see also Cameron, L. & Overall, N. (2017). Suppression and expression as distinct emotion-regulation processes in daily interactions: Longitudinal and meta-analyses. *Emotion, 18*(4), 465–480. DOI: 10.1037/emo0000334; see also Gross, J. J. (1998). The emerging field of emotion regulation: An integrative review. *Review of General Psychology, 2*(3), 271–299. DOI: 10.1037/1089-2680.2.3.271; see also Laws, B. (2019). The return of the suppressed: Exploring how emotional suppression reappears as violence and pain among male and female prisoners. *Punishment & Society, 21*(5), 560–577. DOI: 10.1177/1462474518805071; see also Nam, Y., Kim, Y.-H., & Tam, K. K.-P. (2018). Effects of emotion suppression on life satisfaction in Americans and Chinese. *Journal of Cross-Cultural Psychology, 49*(1), 149–160. DOI: 10.1177/0022022117736525; see also Richards, J. M., & Gross, J. J. (1999). Composure at any cost? The cognitive consequences of

ENDNOTES

emotion suppression. *Personality and Social Psychology Bulletin, 25*(8), 1033–1044. DOI: 10.1177/01461672992511010; see also Richards, J. M. (2004). The cognitive consequences of concealing feelings. *Current Directions in Psychological Science, 13*(4), 131–134. DOI: 10.1111/j.0963-7214.2004.00291.x; see also Srivastava, S., Tamir, M., McGonigal, K. M., John, O. P., & Gross, J. J. (2009). The social costs of emotional suppression: A prospective study of the transition to college. *Journal of Personality & Social Psychology, 96*(4), 883–897. DOI: 10.1037/a0014755; see also Roberts, N., Levenson, R., & Gross, J. (2008). Cardiovascular costs of emotion suppression cross ethnic lines. *International Journal of Psychophysiology: Official Journal of the International Organization of Psychophysiology, 70*(1), 82–87. DOI: 10.1016/j.ijpsycho.2008.06.003; see also Llewellyn, N., Dolcos, S., Iordan, A. D., Rudolph, K. D., & Dolcos, F. (2013). Reappraisal and suppression mediate the contribution of regulatory focus to anxiety in healthy adults. *Emotion, 13*(4), 610–615. DOI: 10.1037/a0032568; see also Patel, J. & Patel, P. (2019). Consequences of repression of emotion: Physical health, mental health and general well being. *International Journal of Psychotherapy Practice and Research, 1*(3), 16–21. DOI: 10.14302/issn.2574-612X.ijpr-18-2564.

[15] See Chapman B. P., Fiscella, K., Kawachi, I., Duberstein, P., & Muennig, P. (2013). Emotion suppression and mortality risk over a 12-year follow-up. *Journal of Psychosomatic Research, 75*(4), 381–385. DOI: 10.1016/j.jpsychores.2013.07.014.

[16] Vallerand, R. J. (2012). The role of passion in sustainable psychological well-being. *Psychology of Well-Being 2*, Article 1. DOI: 10.1186/2211-1522-2-1.

[17] Chen, L., & Qu, L. (2021). Opportunity or risk? Appraisal and affect mediate the effect of task framing on working memory performance in university students. *Frontiers in Psychology, 12*, Article 615329. DOI: 10.3389/fpsyg.2021.615329.

[18] Drach-Zahavy, A., & Erez, M. (2002). Challenge versus threat effects on the goal-performance relationship. *Organizational Behavior and Human Decision Processes, 88*(2), 667–682. DOI: 10.1016/S0749-5978(02)00004-3.

[19] Shih, M., Pittinsky, T. L., & Ambady, N. (1999). Stereotype susceptibility: Identity salience and shifts in quantitative performance. *Psychological Science, 10*(1), 80–83. DOI: 10.1111/1467-9280.00111.

[20] See Steele, C. (2010). *Whistling Vivaldi: And other clues to how stereotypes affect us.* W.W. Norton & Company.

[21] McGonigal, K. (2015). *The upside of stress: Why stress is good for you, and how to get good at it.* Avery.

[22] Brooks, A. W. (2014). Get excited: Reappraising pre-performance anxiety as excitement. *Journal of Experimental Psychology: General, 143*(3), 1144–1158. DOI: 10.1037/a0035325.

[23] Jamieson, J. P., Peters, B. J., Greenwood, E. J., & Altose, A. J. (2016). Reappraising stress arousal improves performance and reduces evaluation anxiety in classroom exam situations. *Social Psychological and Personality Science, 7*(6), 579–587. DOI: 10.1177/1948550616644656. See also Jamieson, J. P., Black, A. E., Pelaia, L. E., Gravelding, H., Gordils, J., & Reis, H. T. (2022). Reappraising stress arousal improves affective, neuroendocrine, and academic performance outcomes in community college classrooms. *Journal of Experimental Psychology: General, 151*(1), 197–212. DOI: 10.1037/xge0000893.

[24] Both-Nwabuwe, J., Dijkstra, M., & Beersma, B. (2017). Sweeping the floor or putting a man on the moon: How to define and measure meaningful work. *Frontiers in Psychology, 8*, Article 1658. DOI: 10.3389/fpsyg.2017.01658. See also Hassan, S., & Ansari, N., & Rehman, A., & Moazzam, A. (2021). Understanding public service motivation, workplace spirituality and employee well-being in the public sector Public service motivation. *International Journal of Ethics and Systems.* Ahead-of-print. DOI: 10.1108/IJOES-06-2021-0135; see also Steger, M. F., Dik, B. J., & Duffy, R. D. (2012). Measuring meaningful work: The Work and Meaning Inventory (WAMI). *Journal of Career Assessment, 20*(3), 322–337. DOI: 10.1177/1069072711436160; see also Rego, A., Cunha, M. P. (2008). Workplace spirituality and organizational commitment. *Journal of Organizational Change Management, 21*(1), 53–75. DOI: 10.1108/095348

ENDNOTES 383

10810847039; see also Grant, A. M., & Campbell, E. M. (2007). Doing good, doing harm, being well and burning out: The interactions of perceived prosocial and antisocial impact in service work. *Journal of Occupational and Organizational Psychology, 80,* 665–691. DOI: 10.1348/096317906X169553; see also Grant, A. M., & Sonnentag, S. (2010). Doing good buffers against feeling bad: Prosocial impact compensates for negative task and self-evaluations. *Organizational Behavior and Human Decision Processes, 111*(1), 13–22. DOI: 10.1016/j.obhdp.2009.07.003; see also May, D. R., Gilson, R. L., Harter, L. M. (2004). The psychological conditions of meaningfulness, safety and availability and the engagement of the human spirit at work. *Journal of Occupational and Organizational Psychology,* 77(1), 11–37. DOI: 10.1348/096317904322915892; see also Chalofsky, N. (2003). An emerging construct of meaningful work. *Human Resource Development International, 6*(1), 69–83. DOI: 10.1080/1367886022000016785; see also Hill, P. L., Sin, N. L., Turiano, N. A., Burrow, A. L., & Almeida, D. M. (2018). Sense of purpose moderates the associations between daily stressors and daily well-being. *Annals of Behavioral Medicine, 52*(8), 724–729. DOI: 10.1093/abm/kax039; see also Polman, E., & Vohs, K. D. (2016). Decision fatigue, choosing for others, and self-construal. *Social Psychological and Personality Science, 7*(5), 471–478. DOI: 10.1177/1948550616639648; see also PwC Charitable Foundation. (2016). Putting purpose to work: a study of purpose in the workplace. https://www.pwc.com/us/en/about-us/corporate-responsibility/assets/pwc-putting-purpose-to-work-purpose-survey-report.pdf; see also Schaefer, S. M., Morozink Boylan, J., van Reekum, C. M., Lapate, R. C., Norris, C. J., Ryff, C. D., & Davidson, R. J. (2013). Purpose in life predicts better emotional recovery from negative stimuli. *PloS one, 8*(11), e80329. DOI: 10.1371/journal.pone.0080329.

[25] Turner, Y., & Hadas-Halpern, I. (2008). The Effects of Including a Patient's Photograph to the Radiographic Examination. Abstract. *Radiological Society of North America 2008 Scientific Assembly and Annual Meeting.* http://archive.rsna.org/2008/6008880.html.

[26] Sinek, S. (2011). *Start with why.* Penguin Books.

[27] Witvliet, C. V. O., DeYoung, N., Hofelich, A. J., & DeYoung, P. (2011). Compassionate reappraisal and emotion suppression as alternatives to offense-focused rumination: Implications for forgiveness and psychophysiological well-being. *The Journal of Positive Psychology, 6*(4), 286–299. DOI: 10.1080/17439760.2011.577091.

[28] Ray, R. D., Wilhelm, F. H., & Gross, J. J. (2008). All in the mind's eye? Anger rumination and reappraisal. *Journal of Personality and Social Psychology, 94*(1), 133–145. DOI: 10.1037/0022-3514.94.1.133.

[29] Witvliet, C. V. O., Ludwig, T., & Vander Laan, K. (2001). Granting forgiveness or harboring grudges: Implications for emotions, physiology, and health. *Psychological Science, 12*(2), 117–123. DOI: 10.1111/1467-9280.00320.

[30] Friedberg, J. P., Suchday, S., & Shelov, D. V. (2007). The impact of forgiveness on cardiovascular reactivity and recovery. *International Journal of Psychophysiology, 65*(2), 87–94. DOI: 10.1016/j.ijpsycho.2007.03.006.

[31] Powell, Philip. (2018). Individual differences in emotion regulation moderate the associations between empathy and affective distress. *Motivation and Emotion, 42*(4), 602–613. DOI: 10.1007/s11031-018-9684-4.

[32] Mojrian, F., Homayouni, A., Rahmedani, Z., & Alizadeh, M. (2020). Correlation between resilience with aggression and hostility in university students. *European Psychiatry, 41*(S1), S611. DOI: 10.1016/j.eurpsy.2017.01.969.

[33] Witvliet, C. V. O., Knoll, R., Hinman, N. & Deyoung, P. (2010). Compassion-focused reappraisal, benefit-focused reappraisal, and rumination after an interpersonal offense: Emotion-regulation implications for subjective emotion, linguistic responses, and physiology. *The Journal of Positive Psychology, 5*(3). 226–242. DOI: 10.1080/17439761003790997.

[34] *See* Hinchliffe, E., & Mcglaufin, P. (2022, October 20). Indra Nooyi shares the best business advice she learned from her decade running PepsiCo. *Fortune.* https://fortune.com/2022/10/20/indra-nooyi-best-business-advice-learned-from-her-decade-running-pepsico.

ENDNOTES

[35] *See* Reynolds-Tylus, T. (2019). Psychological reactance and persuasive health communication: A review of the literature. *Frontiers in Communication. 4*, Article 56. DOI: 10.3389/fcomm.2019.00056.

[36] *See* Gino, F. (2020, November 16) Disagreement doesn't have to be divisive. *Harvard Business Review.* https://hbr.org/2020/11/disagreement-doesnt-have-to-be-divisive. *See also* Brooks, A. W. (2015, December). Emotion and the art of negotiation. *Harvard Business Review.* https://hbr.org/2015/12/emotion-and-the-art-of-negotiation; Jenkins, M. & Dragojevic, M. (2013). Explaining the process of resistance to persuasion: A politeness theory-based approach. *Communication Research, 40*(4), 559–590. DOI: 10.1177/0093650211420136.

[37] Peterson, T. D., & Peterson, E. W. (2009 Summer). Stemming the tide of law student depression: what law schools need to learn from the science of positive psychology. *Yale Journal of Health Policy, Law & Ethics, 9*(2), 357–434. PMID: 19725388.

[38] Sharot, T. (2011). The optimism bias. *Current Biology, 21*(23), R941–945. DOI: 10.1016/j.cub.2011.10.030. *See also* Maheshwari, A., & Jutta, V. (2020). Study of relationship between optimism and resilience in the times of COVID-19 among university students. DOI: 10.25215/0803.157; see also Iwanaga, M., Yokoyama, H., & Seiwa, Hidetoshi. (2004). Coping availability and stress reduction for optimistic and pessimistic individuals. *Personality and Individual Differences, 36*(1), 11–22. DOI: 10.1016/S0191–8869(03)00047–3.

[39] Chang, E. (2002). Optimism-pessimism and stress appraisal: Testing a cognitive interactive model of psychological adjustment in adults. *Cognitive Therapy and Research, 26*, 675–690. DOI: 10.1023/A:1020313427884. *See also* Conversano, C., Rotondo, A., Lensi, E., Della Vista, O., Arpone, F., & Reda, M. A. (2010). Optimism and its impact on mental and physical well-being. *Clinical Practice and Epidemiology in Mental Health: CP & EMH, 6*, 25–29. DOI: 10.2174/1745017901006010025; see also Maheshwari, A., & Jutta, V. (2020). Study of relationship between optimism and resilience in the times of COVID-19 among university students. DOI: 10.25215/0803.157; Iwanaga, M., Yokoyama, H., & Seiwa, H. (2004). Coping availability and

stress reduction for optimistic and pessimistic individuals. *Personality and Individual Differences, 36,* 11–22. DOI: 10.1016/ S0191-8869(03)00047-3; see also Puig-Perez, S., Villada, C., Pulopulos, M. M., Almela, M., Hidalgo, V., & Salvador, A. (2015). Optimism and pessimism are related to different components of the stress response in healthy older people. *International Journal of Psychophysiology. 98*(2 Pt 1), 213–21. DOI: 10.1016/ j.ijpsycho.2015.09.002.

[40] Conversano, C., Rotondo, A., Lensi, E., Della Vista, O., Arpone, F., & Reda, M. A. (2010). Optimism and its impact on mental and physical well-being. *Clinical Practice and Epidemiology in Mental Health: CP & EMH, 6,* 25–29. DOI: 10. 2174/1745017901006010025. See also Lee, L. O., Grodstein, F., Trudel-Fitzgerald, C., James, P., Okuzono, S. S., Koga, H. K., Schwartz, J., Spiro, III, A., Mroczek, D. K., & Kubzansky, L. D. (2022). Optimism, daily stressors, and emotional well-being over two decades in a cohort of aging men, *The Journals of Gerontology: Series B, 77*(8), 1373–1383. DOI: 10.1093/geronb/ gbac025.

[41] Srivastava, S., McGonigal, K. M., Richards, J. M., Butler, E. A., & Gross, J. J. (2006). Optimism in close relationships: How seeing things in a positive light makes them so. *Journal of Personality and Social Psychology, 91*(1), 143–153. DOI: 10.1037/0022-3514.91.1.143. See also Hardy, K., Donnellan, M., & Conger, R. (2007). Optimism: An enduring resource for romantic relationships. *Journal of Personality and Social Psychology, 93*(2), 285–297. DOI: 10.1037/0022-3514.93. 2.285; see also Srivastava, S., & Angelo, K. M. (2009). Optimism, effects on relationships. In H. T. Reis & S. K. Sprecher (Eds.), *Encyclopedia of Human Relationships.* Sage Publications. DOI: 10.4135/9781412958479; see also Brissette, I., Scheier, M. F., & Carver, C. S. (2002). The role of optimism in social network development, coping, and psychological adjustment during a life transition. *Journal of Personality and Social Psychology, 82*(1), 102–111. DOI: 10.1037/0022-3514.82.1.102; see also Carver, C. S., Scheier, M. F., & Segerstrom, S. C. (2010). Optimism. *Clinical Psychology Review, 30*(7), 879–889. DOI: 10.1016/j.cpr. 2010.01.006.

ENDNOTES

[42] Sharot, T. (2011). The optimism bias. *Current Biology, 21*(23), R941–945. DOI: 10.1016/j.cub.2011.10.030.

[43] Chemers, M. M., Hu, L., & Garcia, B.F. (2001). Academic self-efficacy and first year college student performance and adjustment. *Journal of Educational Psychology, 93*(1), 55–64. DOI: 10.1037/0022-0663.93.1.55. See also Maleva, V., Westcott, K., McKellop, M., McLaughlin, R., Widman, D., & College, J. (2014). Optimism and college grades: Predicting GPA from explanatory style. *Psi Chi Journal of Psychological Research, 19*(3), 129–135. https://cdn.ymaws.com/www.psichi.org/resource/resmgr/journal_2014/Fall14JNMaleva.pdf.

[44] Segerstrom, S. C. (2007). Optimism and resources: Effects on each other and on health over 10 years. *Journal of Research in Personality, 41*(4), 772–786. DOI: 10.1016/j.jrp.2006.09.004

[45] Malouff, J. M., & Schutte, N. S. (2017). Can psychological interventions increase optimism? A meta-analysis. *The Journal of Positive Psychology, 12*(6), 594–604. DOI: 10.1080/17439760.2016.1221122.

[46] Steinhilber, B. (2017, August 24). How to Train Your Brain to Be More Optimistic. https://www.nbcnews.com/better/health/how-train-your-brain-be-more-optimistic-ncna795231.

[47] Kyeong, S., Kim, J., Kim, D. J., Kim, H. E., & Kim, J. J. (2017). Effects of gratitude meditation on neural network functional connectivity and brain-heart coupling. *Scientific Reports, 7*, Article 5058. DOI: 10.1038/s41598-017-05520-9.

[48] Emmons, R. A., & McCullough, M. E. (2003). Counting blessings versus burdens: An experimental investigation of gratitude and subjective well-being in daily life. *Journal of Personality and Social Psychology, 84*(2), 377–389. DOI: 10.1037/0022-3514.84.2.377

[49] Burton, C. M., & King, L. A. (2009). The health benefits of writing about positive experiences: The role of broadened cognition. *Psychology and Health, 24*(8), 867–879. DOI: 10.1080/08870440801989946.

[50] Wilson, J. T. (2016). Brightening the mind: The impact of practicing gratitude on focus and resilience in learning. *Journal of the Scholarship of Teaching and Learning, 16*(4), 1–13. DOI: 10.14434/josotl.v16i4.19998.

[51] Wong, Y. J., Owen, J., Gabana, N., Brown, J., Mcinnis, S., Toth, P., & Gilman, L. (2018). Does gratitude writing improve the mental health of psychotherapy clients? Evidence from a randomized controlled trial. *Psychotherapy Research, 28*(2), 192–202. DOI: 10.1080/10503307.2016.1169332.

[52] See Emmons, R. A., & McCullough, M. E. (2003). Counting blessings versus burdens: An experimental investigation of gratitude and subjective well-being in daily life. *Journal of Personality and Social Psychology, 84*(2), 377–389. DOI: 10.1037/0022-3514.84.2.377.

[53] Sergeant, S. & Mongrain, M. (2014). An online optimism intervention reduces depression in pessimistic individuals. *Journal of Consulting and Clinical Psychology, 82*(2), 263–274. DOI: 10.1037/a0035536.

[54] Seligman, M., Steen, T., Park, N., & Peterson, Christopher. (2005). Positive psychology progress: Empirical validation of interventions. *The American Psychologist 60*(5), 410–421. DOI: 10.1037/0003–066X.60.5.410.

[55] Peters, R. (2017, November 23). Giving Thanks Beyond Thanksgiving. https://medium.com/@standardoftrust/giving-thanks-beyond-thanksgiving-5a60d2680d86.

[56] Yeager, D. S., Lee, H. Y., & Jamieson, J. P. (2016). How to improve adolescent stress responses: Insights from integrating implicit theories of personality and biopsychosocial models. *Psychological Science, 27*(8), 1078–1091. DOI: 10.1177/0956797616649604.

[57] Miller, H., & Srougi, M. (2021). Growth mindset interventions improve academic performance but not mindset in biochemistry. *Biochemistry and Molecular Biology Education, 49*(5), 748–757. DOI: 10.1002/bmb.21556.

[58] Yeager, D. S., Hanselman, P., Walton, G. M., Murray, J. S., Crosnoe, R., Muller, C., Tipton, E., Schneider, B., Hulleman, C. S., Hinojosa, C. P., Paunesku, D., Romero, C., Flint, K.,

Roberts, A., Trott, J., Iachan, R., Buontempo, J., Yang, S. M., Carvalho, C. M., Hahn, P.R., Gopalan, M., Mhatre, P., Ferguson, R., Duckworth, A. L., & Dweck, C. S. (2019). A national experiment reveals where a growth mindset improves achievement. *Nature. 573*(7774), 364–369. DOI: 10.1038/s41586-019-1466-y.

59   Yeager, D. S., & Dweck, C. (2012). Mindsets that promote resilience: When students believe that personal characteristics can be developed. *Educational Psychologist, 47*, 302–314. DOI: 10.1080/00461520.2012.722805.

60   Montagna, M., Marksteiner, T., & Dickhäuser, O. (2021). The effect of a computerized growth-mindset intervention on teaching students' mindset and cognitive stress appraisal. *Frontiers in Education, 6*, Article 634684. DOI: 10.3389/feduc.2021.634684.

61   Zeng, G., Hou, H., & Peng, K. (2016). Effect of growth mindset on school engagement and psychological well-being of Chinese primary and middle school students: The mediating role of resilience. *Frontiers in Psychology, 7*, Article 1873. DOI: 10.3389/fpsyg.2016.01873.

62   Fink, A., Cahill, M. J., McDaniel, M. A., Hoffman, A., & Frey, R.F. (2018). Improving general chemistry performance through a growth mindset intervention: Selective effects on underrepresented minorities. *Chemistry Education Research and Practice, 19*, 783–806. DOI: 10.1039/C7RP00244K.

63   Jiang, J. (n.d.) What I learned from 100 days of rejection. *YouTube.* https://www.youtube.com/watch?v=-vZXgApsPCQ.

64   Jiang, J. (2015). *Rejection proof: How I beat fear and became invincible through 100 days of rejection.* Harmony Press.

65   de Berker, A. O., Rutledge, R. B., Mathys, C., Marshall, L., Cross, G. F., Dolan, R. J., & Bestmann, S. (2016). Computations of uncertainty mediate acute stress responses in humans. *Nature Communications, 7*, Article 10996. DOI: 10.1038/ncomms10996.

66   Monde, C. (2014, January 15). Amy Robach debuts short haircut on 'Good Morning America' amid cancer battle.

New York Daily News. https://www.nydailynews.com/entertainment/tv-movies/amy-robach-debuts-short-haircut-good-morning-america-article-1.1580361.

[67] Sales, S. M. (1972). Economic threat as a determinant of conversion rates in authoritarian and nonauthoritarian churches. *Journal of Personality and Social Psychology, 23*(3), 420–428. DOI: 10.1037/h0033157.

[68] Sales, S.M. (1973). Threat as a factor in authoritarianism: an analysis of archival data. *Journal of Personality and Social Psychology, 28*(1): 44–57. DOI: 10.1037/h0035588.

[69] Schulz, R. (1976). Effects of control and predictability on the physical and psychological well-being of the institutionalized aged. *Journal of Personality and Social Psychology, 33*(5): 563–573. DOI: 10.1037/0022-3514.33.5.563. See also Lachman, M. E., & Weaver, S.L. (1998). The Sense of Control as a Moderator of Social Class Differences in Health and Well-Being. *Journal of Personality and Social Psychology,* 74(3), 763–73. DOI: 10.1037//0022-3514.74.3.763.

[70] Whitson, J. & Galinsky, A. (2008). Lacking control increases illusory patter perception. *Science, 322*(5898), 115–117. DOI: 10.1126/science.1159845.

[71] Farnier, J., Shankland, R., Kotsou, I., Marion, I., Rosset, E., & Leys, C. (2021). Empowering well-being: Validation of a locus of control scale specific to well-being. *Journal of Happiness Studies, 22*(6), 3513–3542. DOI: 10.1007/s10902-021-00380-7.

[72] Pannells, T., & Claxton, A. (2008). Happiness, creative ideation, and locus of control. *Creativity Research Journal, 20*(1), 67–71. DOI: 10.1080/10400410701842029.

[73] Alloy, L. B., & Clements, C. M. (1992). Illusion of control: Invulnerability to negative affect and depressive symptoms after laboratory and natural stressors. *Journal of Abnormal Psychology, 101*(2), 234–245. DOI: 10.1037/0021-843X.101.2.234.

[74] Berglund, E., Lytsy, P., & Westerling, R. (2014). The influence of locus of control on self-rated health in context of

chronic disease: A structural equation modeling approach in a cross sectional study. *BioMed Central (BMC) Public Health, 14*, Article 492. DOI: 10.1186/1471-2458-14-492.

[75] Fardaza, F. E., Heidari, H., Solhi, M. (2017). Effect of educational intervention based on locus of control structure of attribution theory on self-care behavior of patients with type II diabetes. *Medical Journal of the Islamic Republic of Iran (MJIRI), 31*(116), 774–779. DOI: 10.14196/mjiri.31.116.

[76] Ng, T., Sorensen, K., & Eby, L. (2006). Locus of control at work: A meta-analysis. *Journal of Organizational Behavior, 27*(8), 1057–1087. DOI: 10.1002/job.416.

[77] Salminen, S., Andreou, E., Holma, J., Pekkonen, M., & Mäkikangas, A. (2017). Narratives of burnout and recovery from an agency perspective: A two-year longitudinal study. *Burnout Research, 7*, 1–9. DOI: 10.1016/j.burn.2017.08.001.

[78] Abid, M. A., Kanwal, S., Nasir, M. A. T., Iqbal, S. & Noor-Ul-Huda. (2016). The effect of locus of control on academic performance of the students at tertiary level. *International Review of Management and Business Research, 5*(3), 860–869. https://www.irmbrjournal.com/papers/1467437110.pdf.

[79] Khir, A. M., Redzuan, M., Hamsan, H., & Shahrimin, M. I. (2015). Locus of control and academic achievement among Orang Asli students in Malaysia. https://www.researchgate.net/publication/319346344_Locus_of_Control_and_Academic_Achievement_among_Orang_Asli_Students_in_Malaysia.

[80] Gifford, D., Briceno-Perriott, J., & Mianzo, F. (2006). Locus of control: Academic achievement and retention in a sample of university first-year students. *Journal of College Admission, 191*, 18–25. https://files.eric.ed.gov/fulltext/EJ741521.pdf.

[81] Kader, A. (2014). Locus of control, student motivation, and achievement in principles of microeconomics. *SSRN Electronic Journal.* DOI: 10.2139/ssrn.2404768. See also Hrbáčková, K., Hladik, J., & Vávrová, Soňa. (2012). The relationship between locus of control, metacognition, and academic success. *Procedia – Social and Behavioral Sciences, 69*, 1805–1811. DOI: 10.1016/j.sbspro.2012.12.130; see also

Mohamed, A. A., Mohamed, A. M., & Ahmed, H. A.-E. (2019). Relation between locus of control and academic achievement of nursing students at Damanhour University. *Journal of Integrated Health Science, 7*(5), 1–13. DOI: 10.9790/1959-07 05120113; see also Ghasemzadeh, A., & saadat, M. (2011). Locus of control in Iranian university student and its relationship with academic achievement. *Procedia – Social and Behavioral Sciences, 30,* 2491–2496. DOI: 10.1016/j.sbspro.2011.10.486; see also Uzun, K., & Karataş, Z. (2020). Predictors of academic self efficacy: Intolerance of uncertainty, positive beliefs about worry and academic locus of control. *International Education Studies, 13*(6), 104–116. DOI: 10.5539/ies.v13n6p104.

[82] Katie, B., & Mitchell, S. (2002). *Loving what is: Four questions that can change your life.* Harmony Books.

[83] Seligman, M. E. P. (2006). *Learned optimism: How to change your mind and your life.* Vintage Books.

[84] Sahranc, Ü. (2011). An investigation of the relationships between self-handicapping and depression, anxiety, and stress. *International Online Journal of Educational Sciences, 3*(2), 526–540. https://iojes.net/?mod=tammetin&makaleadi=&makaleurl=IOJES_566.pdf&key=41287.

[85] McCrea, S. M. (2008). Self-handicapping, excuse making, and counterfactual thinking: Consequences for self-esteem and future motivation. *Journal of Personality and Social Psychology, 95*(2), 274–292. DOI: 10.1037/0022-3514.95.2.274.

[86] Figen, A. (2012). An investigation into the self-handicapping behaviors of undergraduates in terms of academic procrastination, the locus of control and academic success. *Journal of Education and Learning, 1*(2), 288–297. DOI: 10.55 39/jel.v1n2p288 (citing the prior studies).

[87] Beck, B. L., Koons, S. R., & Milgrim, D. L. (2000). Correlates and consequences of behavioral procrastination: The effects of academic procrastination, self-consciousness, self-esteem and self-handicapping. *Journal of Social Behavior and Personality, 15*(5), 3–13. https://www.proquest.com/openview/8486f2240d3fb230c16e89b309993850 (Document Preview).

ENDNOTES

[88] UF study: Excuses hurt job productivity when performing simple tasks. (2006, February 21). *University of Florida News.* https://news.ufl.edu/archive/2006/02/uf-study-excuses-hurt-job-productivity-when-performing-simple-tasks.html.

[89] Crocker, J., & Park, L. (2004). The Costly Pursuit of Self-Esteem. *Psychological Bulletin, 130*(3), 392–414. DOI: 10.1037/0033-2909.130.3.392.

[90] David., S. (2016). *Emotional agility: Get unstuck, embrace change, and thrive in work and life.* Avery.

[91] Kraft, T., & Pressman, S. (2012). Grin and bear it: The influence of manipulated facial expression on the stress response. *Psychological Science, 23*(11), 1372–1378. DOI: 10.1177/0956797612445312.

[92] Marmolejo-ramos, F., Murata, A., Sasaki, K., Yamada, Y., Ikeda, A., Hinojosa, J. A., Watanabe, K., Parzuchowski, M., Tirado, C., & Ospina, R. (2020). Your face and moves seem happier when I smile. *Experimental Psychology, 67*(1), 14–22. DOI: 10.1027/1618-3169/a000470.

[93] Mori, H., & Mori, K. (2013). An implicit assessment of the effect of artificial cheek raising: When your face smiles, the world looks nicer. *Perceptual and Motor Skills, 116*(2), 466–471. DOI: 10.2466/24.50.PMS.116.2.466-471.

[94] Mori, K. & Mori, H. (2010). Examination of the passive facial feedback hypothesis using an implicit measure: With a furrowed brow, neutral objects with pleasant primes look less appealing. *Perceptual and Motor Skills, 111*(3), 785–789. DOI: 10.2466/02.07.24.PMS.111.6.785-789.

[95] Strack, F., Martin, L., & Stepper, S. (1988). Inhibiting and facilitating conditions of the human smile: A nonobtrusive test of the facial feedback hypothesis. *Journal of Personality and Social Psychology, 54*(5), 768–77. DOI: 10.1037/0022–3514.54.5.768.

[96] Wollmer, M. A., de Boer, C., Kalak, N., Beck, J., Götz, T., Schmidt, T., Hodzic, M., Bayer, U., Kollmann, T., Kollewe, K., Sönmez, D., Duntsch, K., Haug, M. D., Schedlowski, M., Hatzinger, M., Dressler, D., Brand, S., Holsboer-Trachsler, E., &

Kruger, T. H. (2012). Facing depression with botulinum toxin: A randomized controlled trial. *Journal of Psychiatric Research, 46*(5), 574–581. DOI: 10.1016/j.jpsychires.2012.01.027.

[97] Finzi, E., & Rosenthal, N.E. (2014). Treatment of depression with onabotulinumtoxinA: A randomized, double-blind, placebo controlled trial. *Journal of Psychiatric Research, 52*, 1–6. DOI: 10.1016/j.jpsychires.2013.11.006.

[98] Wollmer, M., Makunts, T., Kruger, T. & Abagyan, R. (2021). Postmarketing safety surveillance data reveals protective effects of botulinum toxin injections against incident anxiety. *Scientific Reports, 11*, Article 24173. DOI: 10.1038/s41598-021-03713-x.

[99] Salomons, T. V., Coan, J. A., Hunt, S. M., Backonja, M. M., Davidson, R. J. (2008). Voluntary facial displays of pain increase suffering in response to nociceptive stimulation. *Journal of Pain, 9*(5), 443–448. DOI: 10.1016/j.jpain.2008.01.330.

[100] Reicherts, P., Gerdes, A., Pauli, P. & Wieser, M. (2013). On the mutual effects of pain and emotion: Facial pain expressions enhance pain perception and vice versa are perceived as more arousing when feeling pain. *Journal of Pain, 154*(6), 793–800. DOI: 10.1016/j.pain.2013.02.012.

[101] Pressman, S. D., Acevedo, A. M., Hammond, K. V., & Kraft-Feil, T. L. (2021). Smile (or grimace) through the pain? The effects of experimentally manipulated facial expressions on needle-injection responses. *Emotion, 21*(6), 1188–1203. DOI: 10.1037/emo0000913.

[102] Cuddy, A. J. C, Schultz, S. J., & Fosse, N. E. (2018). P-Curving a more comprehensive body of research on postural feedback reveals clear evidential value for power-posing effects: Reply to Simmons and Simonsohn (2017). *Psychological Science, 29*(4), 656–666. DOI: 10.1177/0956797617746749. See also Singal, J., & Dahl, M. (2016, September 30). Here is Amy Cuddy's response to critiques of her power-posing research. *New York.* https://www.thecut.com/2016/09/read-amy-cuddys-response-to-power-posing-critiques.html.

ENDNOTES

[103] Nair, S., Sagar, M., Sollers, J. III, Consedine, N., & Broadbent, E. (2015). Do slumped and upright postures affect stress responses? A randomized trial. *Health Psychology, 34*(6), 632–641. DOI: 10.1037/hea0000146.

[104] Awad, S., Debatin, T., & Albert Ziegler. (2021). Embodiment: I sat, I felt, I performed – Posture effects on mood and cognitive performance. *Acta Psychologica, 218*, Article 103353. DOI: 10.1016/j.actpsy.2021.103353.

[105] Veenstra, L., Schneider, I. K., & Koole, S. L. (2017). Embodied mood regulation: The impact of body posture on mood recovery, negative thoughts, and mood-congruent recall. *Cognition and Emotion, 31*(7), 1361–1376. DOI: 10.1080/02699931.2016.1225003.

[106] Peper, E., Harvey, R., & Hamiel, D. (2019). Transforming thoughts with postural awareness to increase therapeutic and teaching efficacy. *NeuroRegulation, 6*(3), 153–160. DOI: 10.15540/nr.6.3.153.

[107] Noda, W., & Tanaka-Matsumi, J. (2009). Effect of a classroom-based behavioral intervention package on the improvement of children's sitting posture in Japan. *Behavior Modification, 33*(2), 263–273. DOI: 10.1177/0145445508321324.

[108] Carney, D. R., Cuddy, A. J., Yap, A.J. (2010). Power posing: Brief nonverbal displays affect neuroendocrine levels and risk tolerance. *Psychological Science, 21*(10), 1363–8. DOI: 10.1177/0956797610383437.

[109] See Cuddy, A. J. C., Schultz, S. J., & Fosse, N. E. (2018). *P*-Curving a more comprehensive body of research on postural feedback reveals clear evidential value for power-posing effects: Reply to Simmons and Simonsohn (2017). *Psychological Science, 29*(4), 656–666. DOI: 10.1177/0956797617746749.

[110] Peper, E., Lin, I-M., Harvey, R., & Perez, J. (2017). How posture affects memory recall and mood. *Biofeedback, 45*(2), 36–41. DOI: 10.5298/1081-5937-45.2.01.

[111] Kasap, S. & Tanhan, F. (2019). The effect of body posture on foreign language anxiety. *Sakarya University Journal of Education Faculty, 37*, 46–65. Retrieved from https://dergipark.org.tr/en/pub/sakaefd/issue/46709/577919.

[112] Zabetipour, M., Pishghadam, R., & Ghonsooly, B. (2015). The impacts of open/closed body positions and postures on learners' moods. *Mediterranean Journal of Social Sciences, 6*(2), 643–655. DOI: 10.5901/mjss.2015.v6n2s1p643.

[113] Wilkes, C., Kydd, R., Sagar, M., & Broadbent, E. (2017). Upright posture improves affect and fatigue in people with depressive symptoms. *Journal of Behavior Therapy and Experimental Psychiatry, 54,* 143–149. DOI: 10.1016/j.jbtep.2016.07.015.

[114] Michalak, J., Mischnat, J., & Teismann T. (2014). Sitting posture makes a difference-embodiment effects on depressive memory bias. *Clinical Psychology and Psychotherapy, 21*(6), 519–524. DOI: 10.1002/cpp.1890.

[115] See Berceli, D., Salmon, M., Bonifas, R., & Ndefo, N. (2014). Effects of self-induced unclassified therapeutic tremors on quality of life among non-professional caregivers: A pilot study. global advances in health and medicine, *3*(5), 45–48. DOI: 10.7453/gahmj.2014.032. See also Lynning, M., Svane, C., Westergaard, K., Bergien, S. O., Gunnersen, S. R., & Skovgaard, L. (2021). Tension and trauma releasing exercises for people with multiple sclerosis – An exploratory pilot study. *Journal of Traditional and Complementary Medicine, 11*(5), 383–389. DOI: 10.1016/j.jtcme.2021.02.003; see also Heath, R., & Beattie, J. (2019). Case report of a former soldier using TRE (Tension/Trauma Releasing Exercises) for Post-Traumatic Stress Disorder self-care. *Journal of Military and Veterans' Health, 27*(3), 35–40. DOI: 05.2021-79147868.

[116] Puetz, T., O'Connor, P., & Dishman, Rod. (2006). Effects of chronic exercise on feelings of energy and fatigue: A quantitative synthesis. *Psychological Bulletin, 132*(6), 866–876. DOI: 10.1037/0033-2909.132.6.866. See also Hu, S., Tucker, L., Wu, C., & Yang, L. (2020). Beneficial effects of exercise on depression and anxiety during the Covid-19 pandemic: A narrative review. *Frontiers in Psychiatry, 11,* Article 587557. DOI: 10.3389/fpsyt.2020.587557; see also Sharon-David, H., & Tenenbaum, G. (2017). The effectiveness of exercise interventions on coping with stress: Research synthesis. *Studies in Sport Humanities, 22,* 19–29. DOI: 10.5604/01.3001.0012.6520; see also Bartholomew, J. B., Morrison, D., & Ciccolo, J. T.

ENDNOTES

(2005). Effects of acute exercise on mood and well-being in patients with major depressive disorder. *Medicine and Science in Sports and Exercise (MSSE)*, *37*(12), 2032–2037. DOI: 10.12 49/01.mss.0000178101.78322.dd; see also Hackney, A. C. (2006). Stress and the neuroendocrine system: The role of exercise as a stressor and modifier of stress. *Expert Review of Endocrinology & Metabolism*, *1*(6), 783–792. DOI: 10.1586/17446651.1.6.783; see also Greenwood, B. N., Kennedy, S., Smith, T. P., Campeau, S., Day, H. E., & Fleshner, M. (2003). Voluntary freewheel running selectively modulates catecholamine content in peripheral tissue and c-Fos expression in the central sympathetic circuit following exposure to uncontrollable stress in rats. *Neuroscience*, *120*(1), 269–281. DOI: 10.1016/s0306-45 22(03)00047–2; see also Nyberg, J., Henriksson, M., åberg, N. D., Wall, A., Eggertsen, R., Westerlund, M., Danielsson, L., Kuhn, H. G., Waern, M., & åberg, M. (2019). Effects of exercise on symptoms of anxiety, cognitive ability and sick leave in patients with anxiety disorders in primary care: Study protocol for PHYSBI, a randomized controlled trial. *BMC Psychiatry*, *19*, Article 172. DOI: 10.1186/s12888-019-2169-5; see also Henriksson, M., Wall, A., & Nyberg, J. (2022). Effects of exercise on symptoms of anxiety in primary care patients: A randomized controlled trial, *Journal of Affective Disorders*, *297*, 26–34, DOI: 10.1016/j.jad.2021.10.006; see also Mandolesi, L., Polverino, A., Montuori, S., Foti, F., Ferraioli, G., Sorrentino, P., & Sorrentino, G. (2018). Effects of physical exercise on cognitive functioning and wellbeing: Biological and psychological benefits. *Frontiers in Psychology*, *9*, Article 509. DOI: 10.3389/fpsyg.2018.00509; see also Guadagni, V., Drogos, L. L., Tyndall, A. V., Davenport, M. H., Anderson, T. J., Eskes, G. A., Longman, R. S., Hill, M. D., Hogan, D. B., & Poulin, M. J. (2020). Aerobic exercise improves cognition and cerebrovascular regulation in older adults. *Neurology*, *94*(21), e2245–e2257. DOI: 10.1212/WNL.000000000 0009478. 2020 Erratum in: *Neurology*, *95*(19), 890. DOI: 10.12 12/WNL.0000000000010637.

[117] Basso, J. C., & Suzuki, W.A. (2017). The effects of acute exercise on mood, cognition, neurophysiology, and neurochemical pathways: A review. *Brain Plasticity*, *2*(2), 127–152. DOI: 10.3233/BPL-160040. See also Reed, J., & Ones, D. S. (2006). The effect of acute aerobic exercise on positive activated

affect: A meta-analysis. *Psychology of Sport and Exercise*, 7(5), 477–514. DOI: 10.1016/j.psychsport.2005.11.003; see also Liao, Y., Shonkoff, E. T., & Dunton, G. F. (2015). The acute relationships between affect, physical feeling states, and physical activity in daily life: A review of current evidence. *Frontiers in Psychology*, 6, Article 1975. DOI: 10.3389/fpsyg.2015.01975; see also Yeung, R. R. (1996). The acute effects of exercise on mood state. *Journal of Psychosomatic Research*, 40(2), 123–141. DOI: 10.1016/0022-3999(95)00554-4; see also Lambourne, K. & Tomporowski, P. (2010). The effect of exercise-induced arousal on cognitive task performance: A meta-regression analysis. *Brain Research, 1341*(3), 12–24. DOI: 10.10 16/j.brainres.2010.03.091.

[118] Hogan, C. L., Mata, J., & Carstensen, L. L. (2013). Exercise holds immediate benefits for affect and cognition in younger and older adults. *Psychology and Aging, 28*(2), 587–594. DOI: 10.1037/a0032634.

[119] Ekkekakis, P., Hall, E. E., VanLanduyt, L. M., Petruzzello, S. J. (2000). Walking in (affective) circles: Can short walks enhance affect? *Journal of Behavioral Medicine, 23*(3), 245–275. DOI: 10.1023/a:1005558025163.

[120] Blomstrand, P., & Engvall, J. (2020). Effects of a single exercise workout on memory and learning functions in young adults – A systematic review. *Translational Sports Medicine, 4*, 115–127. DOI: 10.1002/tsm2.190.

[121] Mann, S. & Cadman, R. (2014). Does being bored make us more creative?. *Creativity Research Journal, 26*(2), 165–173. DOI: 10.1080/10400419.2014.901073.

[122] Id.

[123] Park, G., Lim, B.-C., & Oh, H. (2019). Why boredom might not be a bad thing after all. *Academy of Management Discoveries, 5*(1), DOI: 10.5465/amd.2017.0033.

[124] Walf, A. (2020, September 16). Dr. Alicia Walf on the science of boredom and your brain, *YouTube*. https://www.youtube.com/watch?v=X5xc5cwyBgs. See also Gornall, L. (n.d.). Why the boredom of long distance treadmill running is so good

ENDNOTES

for my mental health. *Stylist.* https://www.stylist.co.uk/fitness-health/workouts/treadmill-running-for-mental-health/621306.

[125] Madore, K. P., & Wagner, A. D. (2019, April 1). Multicosts of multitasking. *Cerebrum, 2019,* cer-04-19. PMID: 32206165; PMCID: PMC7075496.

[126] Ophir, E., Nass, C., & Wagner AD. (2009). Cognitive control in media multitaskers. *Proceedings of the National Academy of Sciences (PNAS) of the United States of America, 106*(37), 15583–15587. DOI: 10.1073/pnas.0903620106.

[127] Stothart, C., Mitchum, A., & Yehnert, C. (2015). The attentional cost of receiving a cell phone notification. *Journal of Experimental Psychology: Human Perception and Performance, 41*(4), 893–897. DOI: 10.1037/xhp0000100.

[128] Shelton, J. T., Elliott, E. M., Lynn, S. D., & Exner, A. L. (2009). The distracting effects of a ringing cell phone: An investigation of the laboratory and the classroom setting. *Journal of Environmental Psychology, 29*(4), 513–521. DOI: 10.1016/j.jenvp.2009.03.001.

[129] Ward, A. F., Duke, K., Gneezy, A., & Bos, M. W. (2017). Brain drain: The mere presence of one's own smartphone reduces available cognitive capacity. *Journal of the Association for Consumer Research, 2*(2), 140–154. DOI: 10.1086/691462.

[130] The mere presence of your smartphone reduces brain power, study shows. (2017, June 26). *UT News.* https://news.utexas.edu/2017/06/26/the-mere-presence-of-your-smartphone-reduces-brain-power.

[131] See Thomée, S., Eklöf, M., Gustafsson, E., Nilsson, R., & Hagberg, M. (2007). Prevalence of perceived stress, symptoms of depression and sleep disturbances in relation to information and communication technology (ICT) use among young adults – An explorative prospective study. *Computers in Human Behavior, 23*(3), 1300–1321. DOI: 10.1016/j.chb.2004.12.007. See also Sohn, S. Y., Rees, P., Wildridge, B., Kalk, N.J., & Carter, B. (2019). Prevalence of problematic smartphone usage and associated mental health outcomes amongst children and young people: A systematic review, meta-analysis and GRADE of the evidence. *BMC Psychiatry, 19,* Article 356. DOI: 10.1186/s12888-

019-2350-x. 2019 Erratum in: *BMC Psychiatry, 19,* Article 397. 2021 Erratum in: *BMC Psychiatry, 21,* Article 52. DOI: 10.1186/s12888-020-02986-2; see also Yang, H., Liu, B., & Fang, J. (2021). Stress and problematic smartphone use severity: Smartphone use frequency and fear of missing out as mediators. *Frontiers of Psychiatry, 12,* Article 659288. DOI: 10.3389/fpsyt.2021.659288; see also Haynes, T. (2018, May 1). Dopamine, smartphones & you: A battle for your time. *Science in the News.* https://sitn.hms.harvard.edu/flash/2018/dopamine-smartphones-battle-time; see also Kushlev, K. & Dunn, E. W. (2015). Checking email less frequently reduces stress. *Computers in Human Behavior, 43,* 220–228. DOI: 10.1016/j.chb.2014.11.005; see also Armstrong, M. J. (2017). Improving email strategies to target stress and productivity in clinical practice. *Neurology Clinical Practice, 7*(6), 512–517. DOI: 10.1212/CPJ.0000000000000395; see also Mark, G. Voida, S., & Cardello, A. (2012, May). "A pace not dictated by electrons": An empirical study of work without email. *Proceedings of the SIGCHI Conference on Human Factors in Computing Systems,* 555–564. DOI: 10.1145/2207676.2207754; see also RSNA, Press Release. (2017, November 30). Smartphone addiction creates imbalance in brain. *Radiological Society of America.* https://press.rsna.org/timssnet/media/pressreleases/PDF/pressreleasePDF.cfm?ID=1989; see also Clarke-Billings, L. (2016, January 4). Smartphone email notifications 'a toxic source of stress', psychologists say. *The Sydney Morning Herald,* https://www.smh.com.au/technology/smartphone-email-notifications-a-toxic-source-of-stress-psychologists-say-20160103-glya2e.html.

[132] Always connected: How smartphones and social keep us engaged. (2013). *International Data Corporation Research Report, sponsored by Facebook,* Document Number 240435. https://www.nu.nl/files/IDC-Facebook%20Always%20Connected%20(1).pdf.

[133] Stinson, A. (2018, March 8). This one thing you do as soon as you wake up may be sabotaging your whole day. *Elite Daily.* https://www.elitedaily.com/p/is-it-bad-to-look-at-your-phone-right-when-you-wake-up-it-might-be-sabotaging-your-day-8437383.

ENDNOTES

134 Garfield, L. (2016, May 25). Checking your phone first thing in the morning could be making you unhappy. *Business Insider.* https://www.businessinsider.com/why-you-I-check-your-phone-first-thing-in-the-morning-2016-5.

135 Rafique, N., Al-Asoom, L. I., Alsunni, A. A., Saudagar, F. N., Almulhim, L., & Alkaltham, G. (2020). Effects of mobile use on subjective sleep quality. *Nature and Science of Sleep, 12,* 357–364. DOI: 10.2147/NSS.S253375.

136 See Fossum, I. N., Nordnes, L. T., Storemark, S. S., Bjorvatn, B., & Pallesen, S. (2014). The association between use of electronic media in bed before going to sleep and insomnia symptoms, daytime sleepiness, morningness, and chronotype. *Behavioral Sleep Medicine, 12*(5), 343–357. DOI: 10.1080/1540 2002.2013.819468.

137 Exelmans, L., & Van den Bulck, J. (2016). Bedtime mobile phone use and sleep in adults. *Social Science & Medicine, 148,* 93–101. DOI: 10.1016/j.socscimed.2015.11.037.

138 Exelmans, L., & Van den Bulck J. (2017). Bedtime, shuteye time and electronic media: Sleep displacement is a two-step process. *Journal of Sleep Research, 26*(3), 364–370. DOI: 10.1111/jsr.12510.

139 Munezawa, T., Kaneita, Y., Osaki, Y., Kanda, H., Minowa, M., Suzuki, K., Higuchi, S., Mori, J., Yamamoto, R., Ohida, T. (2011). The association between use of mobile phones after lights out and sleep disturbances among Japanese adolescents: A nationwide cross-sectional survey. *Sleep, 34*(8), 1013–20.10.5665%2FSLEEP.1152.

140 See Rafique, N., Al-Asoom, L. I., Alsunni, A. A., Saudagar, F. N., Almulhim, L., & Alkaltham, G. (2020). Effects of mobile use on subjective sleep quality. *Nature and Science of Sleep, 12,* 357–364. DOI: 10.2147/NSS.S253375.

141 Baumeister, R. F., Braslavsky, E., Muraven, M., & Tice, D. M. (1998). Ego depletion: is the active self a limited resource? *Journal of Personality and Social Psychology, 74*(5), 1252–1265. DOI: 10.1037//0022-3514.74.5.1252.

142 Iyengar, S. S., & Lepper, M. R. (2000). When choice is demotivating: Can one desire too much of a good thing? *Journal*

of Personality and Social Psychology, 79(6), 995–1006. DOI: 10.1037//0022-3514.79.6.995.

[143] Sjåstad, H., & Baumeister, R. F. (2018). The future and the will: Planning requires self-control, and ego depletion leads to planning aversion. *Journal of Experimental Social Psychology, 76,* 127–141. DOI: 10.1016/j.jesp.2018.01.005.

[144] Vohs, K. D., Baumeister, R. F., Schmeichel, B. J., Twenge, J. M., Nelson, N. M., & Tice, D. M. (2008). Making choices impairs subsequent self-control: A limited-resource account of decision making, self-regulation, and active initiative. *Journal of Personality and Social Psychology, 94*(5), 883–898. DOI: 10.1037/0022-3514.94.5.883.

[145] Baumeister, R. F., DeWall, C. N., Ciarocco, N. J., & Twenge, J. M. (2005). Social exclusion impairs self-regulation. *Journal of Personality and Social Psychology, 88*(4), 589–604. DOI: 10.1037/0022-3514.88.4.589.

[146] Englert, C., & Bertrams, A. (2017). Ego depletion negatively affects knowledge retrieval in secondary school students. *Educational Psychology, 37*(9), 1057–1066. DOI: 10.1080/01443410.2017.1313963.

[147] Fischer, P., Greitemeyer, T., & Frey, D. (2008). Self-regulation and selective exposure: the impact of depleted self-regulation resources on confirmatory information processing. *Journal of Personality and Social Psychology, 94*(3) 382–395. DOI: 10.1037/0022–3514.94.3.382.

[148] Englert, C., Zavery, A., Bertrams, A. (2017). Too exhausted to perform at the highest level? On the importance of self-control strength in educational settings. *Frontiers in Psychology, 8,* Article 1290. DOI: 10.3389/fpsyg.2017.01290.

[149] Wiehler, A., Branzoli, F., Adanyeguh, I., Mochel, F., & Pessiglione, M. (2022). A neuro-metabolic account of why daylong cognitive work alters the control of economic decisions. *Current Biology, 32*(16), 3564–3575.e5. DOI: 10.1016/j.cub.2022.07.010.

[150] See Danziger, S., Lvav, J., & Avnaim-Pesso, L. (2011). Extraneous factors in judicial decisions. *Proceedings of the*

ENDNOTES

National Academy of Sciences (PNAS) of the United States of America, *108*(17), 6889–6892. DOI: 10.1073/pnas.1018033108.

[151] Corbyn, Z., (2011, April 11). Hungry judges dispense rough justice. *Nature.* https://www.nature.com/articles/news.2011.227.

[152] Linder, J. A., Doctor, J. N., & Friedberg, N. W. (2014). Time of day and the decision to prescribe antibiotics. *Journal of the American Medical Association (JAMA) Internal Medicine, 174*(12), 2029–31. DOI: 10.1001/jamainternmed.2014.5225.

[153] Persson, E., Barrafrem, K., Meunier, A., & Tinghög, G. (2019). The effect of decision fatigue on surgeons' clinical decision making. *Health Economics, 28*(10), 1194–1203. DOI: 10.1002/hec.3933.

[154] Baer, D. (2014, February 12). Always wear the same suit: Obama's presidential productivity secrets. *FAST COMPANY.* https://www.fastcompany.com/3026265/always-wear-the-same-suit-obamas-presidential-productivity-secrets.

[155] Smith, S. (2014, November 7). Zuckerberg: I wear same shirt daily for a reason. *CNBC.* https://www.cnbc.com/2014/11/07/5-things-we-learned-in-mark-zuckerbergs-facebook-qa.html.

[156] Hargroves, C. (2019, March 6). What was Elizabeth Holmes trying to prove with those black turtlenecks? *REFINERY29.* https://www.refinery29.com/en-us/2019/03/226213/elizabeth-holmes-black-turtleneck-suit-steve-jobs-style.

[157] Kahl, M. (2015, April 3). Why I wear the exact same thing to work every day. *Harper's Bazaar.* https://www.harpersbazaar.com/culture/features/a10441/why-i-wear-the-same-thing-to-work-everday.

[158] Mikel, B. (2017, November 13). Arianna Huffington's ingenious life hack to make mornings way less anxiety-inducing: Huffington takes a page out of Steve Jobs' book. *Inc.* https://www.inc.com/betsy-mikel/arianna-huffingtons-ingenious-life-hack-to-make-mornings-way-less-anxiety-inducing.html.

[159] Huffington, A. [@ariannahuff]. (2019, May 28). While decision fatigue is real, there's another reason why I'm a big proponent of style #repeats [Tweet]. *Twitter.* https://twitter.com/ariannahuff/status/1133392451165708288.

[160] Wansink, B., & Sobal, J. (2007). Mindless eating: The 200 daily food decisions we overlook. *Environment and Behavior, 39*(1), 106–123. DOI: 10.1177/0013916506295573.

[161] Steel, P. (2007). The nature of procrastination: A meta-analytic and theoretical review of quintessential self-regulatory failure. *Psychological Bulletin, 133*(1), 65–94. DOI: 10.1037/0033-2909.133.1.65.

[162] Id.

[163] Lieberman, C. (2019, March 25). Why you procrastinate (it has nothing to do with self-control). *The New York Times.* https://www.nytimes.com/2019/03/25/smarter-living/why-you-procrastinate-it-has-nothing-to-do-with-self-control.html.

[164] Sirois, F., & Pychyl, T. (2013). Procrastination and the priority of short-term mood regulation: Consequences for future self. *Social and Personality Psychology Compass, 7*(2), 115–127. DOI: 10.1111/spc3.12011.

[165] Steel, P. (2007). The nature of procrastination: A meta-analytic and theoretical review of quintessential self-regulatory failure. *Psychological Bulletin, 133*(1), 65–94. DOI: 10.1037/0033-2909.133.1.65. See also Flett, G., Stainton, M., Hewitt, P., Sherry, S. B., & Lay, C. (2012). Procrastination automatic thoughts as a personality construct: An analysis of the procrastinatory cognitions inventory. *Journal of Rational-Emotive and Cognitive-Behavior Therapy, 30,* 233–236. DOI: 10.1007/s10942-012-0150-z; see also Stainton, M., & Lay, C. H., & Flett, G. L. (2000). Trait procrastinators and behavior/trait-specific cognitions. *Journal of Social Behavior and Personality, 15*(5), 297–312. https://psycnet.apa.org/record/2002-10572-023; see also Eckert, M., Ebert, D., Lehr, D., Sieland, B., & Berking, M. (2016). Overcome procrastination: Enhancing emotion regulation skills reduce procrastination. *Learning and Individual Differences, 52,* 10–18. DOI: 10.1016/j.lindif.2016.10.001; see also Eerde, W. (2003). A meta-analytically derived nomological network of procrastination. *Personality and Individual Differences, 35,* 1401–1418. DOI: 10.1016/S0191-8869(02)00358-6.

[166] See Blunt, A. K., & Pychyl, T. (2000). Task aversiveness and procrastination: A multi-dimensional approach to task

aversiveness across stages of personal projects. *Personality and Individual Differences, 28*(1), 153–167. DOI: 10.1016/S0191-8869(99)00091-4.

[167] Milne, S., Orbell, S., & Sheeran, P. (2002). Combining motivational and volitional interventions to promote exercise participation: Protection motivation theory and implementation intentions. *British Journal of Health Psychology, 7*(2), 163–184. DOI: 10.1348/135910702169420.

[168] Gollwitzer, P. M., & Sheeran, P. (2006). Implementation intentions and goal achievement: A meta-analysis of effects and processes. *Advances in Experimental Social Psychology, 38*, 69–119. DOI: 10.1016/S0065-2601(06)38002-1.

[169] Achor, S. (2010). *The happiness advantage: The seven principles of positive psychology that fuel success and performance at work.* Crown Publishing.

[170] Id.

[171] See Clear, J. (2019). *Atomic habits: An easy & proven way to build good habits and break bad ones.* Penguin Random House USA.

[172] Szalavitz, M. (2012, March 2). Q&A: Charles DuHigg on changing your habits. *Time.* https://healthland.time.com/2012/03/02/mind-reading-qa-with-charles-duhigg-on-changing-your-habits. See also Duhigg, C., (2016, October 18). How to form healthy habits in your 20s. *The New York Times.* https://www.nytimes.com/2016/10/19/well/mind/how-to-form-healthy-habits-in-your-20s.html.

[173] Ingels, J. S., Misra, R., Stewart, J., Lucke-Wold, B., & Shawley-Brzoska, S. (2017). The effect of adherence to dietary tracking on weight loss: Using HLM to model weight loss over time. *Journal of Diabetes Research, 2017,* Article 6951495. DOI: 10.1155/2017/6951495. See also Wohn, D., & Lee, M. (2020). The effect of tracking and reflecting on study habits on study behavior and grades. *2020 IEEE International Symposium on Technology and Society (ISTAS),* 433–441. DOI: 10.1109/ISTAS50296.2020.9462241; see also Stojanovic, M., Grund, A., & Fries, S. (2020). App-based habit building reduces motivational impairments during studying – An event sampling study.

Frontiers in Psychology, 11, Article167. DOI: 10.3389/fpsyg.2020.00167; see also Compernolle, S., DeSmet, A., Poppe, L., Crombez, G., De Bourdeaudhuij, I., Cardon, G., van der Ploeg, H. P., & Van Dyck, D. (2019). Effectiveness of interventions using self-monitoring to reduce sedentary behavior in adults: A systematic review and meta-analysis. *The International Journal of Behavioral Nutrition and Physical Activity, 16*(1), Article 63. DOI: 10.1186/s12966-019-0824-3; see also Gardner, B., Smith, L., Lorencatto, F., Hamer, M., & Biddle, S. J. (2016). How to reduce sitting time? A review of behaviour change strategies used in sedentary behaviour reduction interventions among adults. *Health Psychology Rev*iew, *10*(1), 89–112. DOI: 10.1080/17437199.2015.1082146; see also Ellingson, L. D., Lansing, J. E., DeShaw, K. J., Peyer, K. L., Bai, Y., Perez, M., Phillips, L. A., & Welk, G. J. (2019). Evaluating motivational interviewing and habit formation to enhance the effect of activity trackers on healthy adults' activity levels: Randomized intervention. *Journal of Medical Internet Research (JMIR) mHealth and uHealth, 7*(2), e10988. DOI: 10.2196/10988.

[174] Hollis, J., Gullion, C., Stevens, V., Brantley, P., Appel, L., Ard, J., Champagne, C., Dalcin, A., Erlinger, T., Funk, K., Laferriere, D., Lin, P.-H., & Loria, C., Samuel-Hodge, C., Vollmer, W., & Svetkey, L. (2008). Weight loss during the intensive intervention phase of the weight-loss maintenance trial. *American Journal of Preventive Medicine, 35,* 118–26. DOI: 10.1016/j.amepre.2008.04.013. See also Duhigg, C. (2012). *The Power of Habit*: *Why We Do What We Do in Life and Business.* Random House.

[175] Zeidan, F., Johnson, S. K., Diamond, B. J., David, Z., & Goolkasian, P. (2010). Mindfulness meditation improves cognition: evidence of brief mental training. *Consciousness and Cognition: An International Journal, 19*(2), 597–605. DOI: 10.1016/j.concog.2010.03.014.

[176] Brewer, J. A., Worhunsky, P. D., Gray, J. R., & Kober, H. (2011). Meditation experience is associated with differences in default mode network activity and connectivity. *Biological Sciences, 108*(50), 20254–20259. DOI: 10.1073/pnas.1112029108.

ENDNOTES

[177] Levy, D. M., Wobbrock, J. O., Kaszniak, A. W., & Ostergren, M. (2012). The effects of mindfulness meditation training on multitasking in a high-stress information environment. *Proceedings – 38th Graphics Interface Conference*, 45–52. https://faculty.washington.edu/wobbrock/pubs/gi-12.02.pdf.

[178] Hölzel, B. K., Carmody, J., Vangel, M., Congleton, C., Yerramsetti, S. M., Gard, T., & Lazar, S. W. (2011). Mindfulness practice leads to increases in regional brain gray matter density. *Psychiatry Research, 191*(1), 36–43. DOI: 10.1016/j.pscychresns.2010.08.006.

[179] Mrazek, M. D., Franklin, M. S., Phillips, D. T., Baird, B., & Schooler, J. W. (2013). Mindfulness training improves working memory capacity and GRE performance while reducing mind wandering. *Psychological Science, 24*(5), 776–81. DOI: 10.1177/0956797612459659.

[180] Hafenbrack, A. C., Kinias, Z., & Barsade, S. G. (2013). Debiasing the mind through meditation: Mindfulness and the sunk-cost bias. *Psychological Science, 25*(2), 369–376. DOI: 10.1177/0956797613503853.

[181] Tanga, Y.-Y., Lu, Q., Fan, M., Yang, Y., & Posner, M. I. (2012). Mechanisms of white matter changes induced by meditation. *Proceedings of the National Academy of Sciences (PNAS) of the United States of America, 109*(26), 10570–10574. DOI: 10.1073/pnas.1207817109.

[182] Luders, Eileen, Kurth, F., Mayer, E. A., Toga, A. W., Narr, K. L., & Gaser, C. (2012). The unique brain anatomy of meditation practitioners: Alterations in cortical gyrification. *Frontiers in Human Neuroscience, 6*, Article 34. DOI: 10.3389/fnhum.2012.00034.

[183] Slagter, H. A., Lutz, A., Greischar, L. L., Francis, A. D., Nieuwenhuis, S., Davis, J. M., & Davidson, R. J. (2007). Mental training affects distribution of limited brain resources. *Journal of Public Library of Science (PLoS) Biology, 5*(6), e138, 1228–1235. DOI: 10.1371/journal.pbio.0050138.

[184] Zeidan, F., Martucci, K. T., Kraft, R. A., Gordon, N. S., McHaffie, J. G., & Coghill, R. C. (2011). Brain mechanisms

supporting modulation of pain by mindfulness meditation. *Journal of Neuroscience, 31*(14), 5540–5548. DOI: 10.1523/JNEUROSCI.5791-10.2011.

[185] Moore, A., & Malinowski, P. (2009). Meditation, mindfulness and cognitive flexibility. *Consciousness & Cognition, 18*(1), 176–186. DOI: 10.1016/j.concog.2008.12.008.

[186] Ostafin, B. D., & Kassman, K. T. (2012). Stepping out of history: Mindfulness improves insight problem solving. *Consciousness and Cognition, 21*(2), 1031–1036. DOI: 10.1016/j.concog.2012.02.014.

[187] Chambers, R., Lo, B. C. Y., & Allen, N. B. (2008). The impact of intensive mindfulness training on attentional control, cognitive style, and affect. *Cognitive Therapy and Research, 32*, 303–322. DOI: 10.1007/s10608-007-9119-0.

[188] Greenberg, J., Reiner, K., & Meiran, N. (2012). Mind the trap: Mindfulness practice reduces cognitive rigidity. *Public Library of Science (PLoS) One, 7*(5), e36206. DOI: 10.1371/journal.pone.0036206.

[189] Lazar, S. W., Kerr, C. E., Wasserman, R. H., Gray, J. R., Greve, D. N., Treadway, M. T., McGarvey, M., Quinn, B. T., Dusek, J. A., Benson, H., Rauch, S. L., Moore, C. I., & Fischl, B. (2005). Meditation experience is associated with increased cortical thickness. *Neuroreport, 16*(17), 1893–1897. DOI: 10.1097/01.wnr.0000186598.66243.19.

[190] Jazaieri, H., Lee, I. A., Mcgonigal, K., & Jinpa, T. (2015). A wandering mind is a less caring mind: Daily experience sampling during compassion meditation training. *The Journal of Positive Psychology, 11*(1), 1–14. DOI: 10.1080/17439760.2015.1025418.

[191] Kirk, U., Downar, J., & Montague, P. R. (2011). Interoception drives increased rational decision making in meditators playing the ultimatum game. *Frontiers in Neuroscience, 5*(49). DOI: 10.3389/fnins.2011.00049.

[192] Kaul, P., Passafiume, J., Sargent, R. C., & O'Hara, B. F. (2010). Meditation acutely improves psychomotor vigilance, and may decrease sleep need. *Behavioral and Brain Functions, 6*(47). DOI: 10.1186/1744-9081-6-47.

ENDNOTES

[193] Bhasin, M. J., Dusek, J. A., Chang, B.-H., Joseph, M. G., Denninger, J. W., Fricchione, G. L., Benson, H., & Libermann, T. A. (2013). Relaxation response induces temporal transcriptome changes in energy metabolism, insulin secretion and inflammatory pathways. *Public Library of Science (PLoS) One, 8*(5), e62817. DOI: 10.1371/journal.pone.0062817.

[194] Kerr, C. E., Jones, S. R., Wan, Q., Pritchett, D. L., Wasserman, R. H., Wexler, A., Villanueva, J. J., Shaw, J. R., Lazar, S. W., Kaptchuk, T. J., Littenberg, R., Hämäläinen, M. S., & Moore, C. I. (2011). Effects of mindfulness meditation training on anticipatory alpha modulation in primary somatosensory cortex. *Brain Research Bulletin, 85*(304), 96–103. DOI: 10.1016/j.brainresbull.2011.03.026.

[195] Weger, U. W., Hooper, N., Meier, B. P., Hopthrow, T. (2012). Mindful maths: Reducing the impact of stereotype threat through a mindfulness exercise. *Consciousness and Cognition, 21*(1), 471–475. DOI: 10.1016/j.concog.2011.10.011.

[196] Jain, S., Shapiro, S. L., Swanick, S., Roesch, S. C., Mills, P. J., Bell, I., & Schwartz, G. E. R. (2007). A randomized controlled trial of mindfulness meditation versus relaxation training: Effects on distress, positive states of mind, rumination, and distraction. *Annals of Behavioral Medicine, 33*(1), 11–21. DOI: 10.1207/s15324796abm3301_2.

[197] Oman, D., Shapiro, S. L., Thoresen, C. E., Plante, T. G., Flinders, T. (2008). Meditation lowers stress and supports forgiveness among college students: A randomized controlled trial. *Journal of American College Health, 56*(5), 569–578. DOI: 10.3200/JACH.56.5.569-578.

[198] Rosenzweig, S., Reibel, D. K., Greeson, J. M., Brainard, G. C., & Hojat, M. (2003). Mindfulness-based stress reduction lowers psychological distress in medical students. *Teaching and Learning in Medicine, 15*(2), 88–92. DOI: 10.1207/S15328015TLM1502_03.

[199] Lane, J. D., Seskevich, J. E., & Pieper, C. F. (2007). Brief meditation training can improve perceived stress and negative mood. *Alternative Therapies in Health and Medicine, 13*(1), 38–44. PMID: 17283740.

[200] Goleman, D. J., & Schwartz, G. E. (1976). Meditation as an intervention in stress reactivity. *Journal of Consulting and Clinical Psychology, 44*(3), 456–466. DOI: 10.1037/0022-006X.44.3.456.

[201] Shapiro, S., Astin, J., Bishop, S. R., & Cordova, M. (2005). Mindfulness-based stress reduction for health care professionals: Results from a randomized trial. *International Journal of Stress Management, 12*(2), 164–176. DOI: 10.1037/1072-5245.12.2.164.

[202] Ortner, C. N. M., Kilner, S. J., & Zelazo P. D. (2007). Mindfulness meditation and reduced emotional interference on a cognitive task. *Motivation and Emotion, 31*(4), 271–283. DOI: 10.1007/s11031-007-9076-7.

[203] Wu, R., Liu, L. L., Zhu, H., Su, W. J., Cao, Z. Y., Zhong, S. Y., Liu, X. H., & Jiang, C. L. (2019). Brief mindfulness meditation improves emotion processing. *Frontiers in Neuroscience, 13*, Article 1074. DOI: 10.3389/fnins.2019.01074.

[204] Kiken, L. G., & Shook, N. J. (2011). Looking up: Mindfulness increases positive judgments and reduces negativity bias. *Social Psychological and Personality Science, 2*(4), 425–431. DOI: 10.1177/1948550610396585.

[205] Chang, V., Palesh, O., Caldwell, R., Glasgow, N., Abramson, M., Luskin, F., Gill, M., Burke, A., & Koopman, C. (2004). The effects of a mindfulness-based stress reduction program on stress, mindfulness self-efficacy, and positive states of mind. *Stress and Health, 20*(3), 141–147. DOI: 10.1002/SMI.1011.

[206] J Kabat-Zinn, J., Massion, A. O., Kristeller, J., Peterson, L. G., Fletcher, K. E., Pbert, L., Lenderking, W. R., & Santorelli, S. F. (1992). Effectiveness of a meditation-based stress reduction program in the treatment of anxiety disorders. *American Journal of Psychiatry, 149*(7), 936–943. DOI: 10.1176/ajp.149.7.936.

[207] Manikonda, J. P., Störk, S., Tögel, S., Lobmüller, A., Grünberg, I., Bedel, S., Schardt, F., Angermann, C. E., Jahns, R., & Voelker, W. (2008). Contemplative meditation reduces ambulatory blood pressure and stress-induced hypertension: A

ENDNOTES

randomized pilot trial. *Journal of Human Hypertension, 22*(2), 138–140. DOI: 10.1038/sj.jhh.1002275.

[208] Garland, E. L., Gaylord, S. A., & Fredrickson, B. L. (2011). Positive reappraisal mediates the stress-reductive effects of mindfulness: An upward spiral process. *Mindfulness, 2*(1), 59–67. DOI: 10.1007/s12671-011-0043-8.

[209] Travis, F., Haaga, D. A. F., Hagelin, J., Tanner, M., Nidich, S., Gaylord-King, C., Grosswald, S., Rainforth, M., & Schneider, R. H. (2009). Effects of Transcendental Meditation practice on brain functioning and stress reactivity in college students. *International Journal of Psychophysiology, 71*(2), 170–176. DOI: 10.1016/j.ijpsycho.2008.09.007.

[210] Carpena, M. X., Tavares, P. S., & Menezes, C. B. (2019). The effect of a six-week focused meditation training on depression and anxiety symptoms in Brazilian university students with 6 and 12 months of follow-up. *Journal of Affective Disorders, 246*, 401–407. DOI: 10.1016/j.jad.2018.12.126.

[211] Khoury, B., Lecomte, T., Fortin, G., Masse, M., Therien, P., Bouchard, V., Chapleau, M. A., Paquin, K., & Hofmann, S. G. (2013). Mindfulness-based therapy: A comprehensive meta-analysis. *Clinical Psychology Review, 33*(6), 763–71. DOI: 10.10 16/j.cpr.2013.05.005.

[212] Goldberg, S. B., Tucker, R. P., Greene, P. A., Davidson, R. J., Wampold, B. E., Kearney, D. J., & Simpson, T. L. (2018). Mindfulness-based interventions for psychiatric disorders: A systematic review and meta-analysis. *Clinical Psychology Review, 59*, 52–60. DOI: 10.1016/j.cpr.2017.10.011.

[213] Stell, A. J., & Farsides, T. (2016). Brief loving-kindness meditation reduces racial bias, mediated by positive other-regarding emotions. *Motivation and Emotion, 40*(1), 140–147. DOI: 10.1007/s11031-015-9514-x.

[214] Lueke, Adam, & Gibson, B. (2014). Mindfulness meditation reduces implicit age and race bias: The role of reduced automaticity of responding. *Social Psychological and Personality Science, 6*(3), 284–291. DOI: 10.1177/19485506145 59651.

[215] Kang, Y., Gray, J. R., & Dovidio, J. F. (2013). The nondiscriminating heart: Lovingkindness meditation training decreases implicit intergroup bias. *Journal of Experimental Psychology General, 143*(3), 1306–13. DOI: 10.1037/a0034150.

216 Kilmartin, C., Semelsberger, R., Dye, S., Boggs, E., & Kolar, D. (2015). A behavior intervention to reduce sexism in college men. *Gender Issues, 32*(2), 97–110. DOI: 10.1007/s12147-014-9130-1.

[217] Djikic, M., Langer, E., & Stapleton, S. F. (2008). Reducing stereotyping through mindfulness: Effects on automatic stereotype-activated behaviors. *Journal of Adult Development, 15*(2), 106–111. DOI: 10.1007/s10804-008-9040-0.

[218] Kappen, G., Karremans, J. C., Burk, W. J., & Buyukcan-Tetik, A. (2018). On the association between mindfulness and romantic relationship satisfaction: The role of partner acceptance. *Mindfulness, 9*(5), 1543–1556. DOI: 10.1007/s12671-018-0902-7.

[219] Uchino, B. N., Bowen, K., Kent de Grey, R. G., Smith, T. W., Baucom, B. R., Light, K. C., & Ray, S. (2016) Lovingkindness meditation improves relationship negativity and psychological well-being: A pilot study. *Psychology, 7*(1), 6–11. DOI: 10.4236/psych.2016.71002.

[220] McGill, J., Adler-Baeder, F., & Rodriguez, P. (2016). Mindfully in love: A meta-analysis of the association between mindfulness and relationship satisfaction. *Journal of Human Sciences and Extension, 4*(1), 89–101. DOI: 10.54718/ddca4089.

[221] Farias, M., Maraldi, E. D., Wallenkampf, K. C., & Lucchetti, G. (2020). Adverse events in meditation practices and meditation-based therapies: A systematic review. *Acta Psychiatrica Scandinavica, 142*(5), 374–393. DOI: 10.1111/acps.13225.

[222] Miller, K. J., Schalk, G., Fetz, E. E., den Nijs M., Ojemann, J. G., & Rao, R. P. N. (2010). Cortical activity during motor execution, motor imagery, and imagery-based online feedback. *Proceedings of the National Academy of Science (PNAS) USA, 107*(9), 4430–4435. DOI: 10.1073/pnas.0913697107. Erratum in: *Proceedings of the National Academy of*

Science (PNAS) USA. (2010). *107*(15), 7113. DOI: 10.1073/pnas. 1002462107.

[223] What is Imagery? (n. d.). *Johns Hopkins Medicine.* https://www.hopkinsmedicine.org/health/wellness-and-prevention/imagery.

[224] Blackwell, S. E., Rius-Ottenheim, N., Schulte-van Maaren, Y. W. M., Carlier, I. V. E., Middelkoop, V. D., Zitman, F. G., Spinhoven, P., Holmes, E.A., & Giltay, E. J. (2013). Optimism and mental imagery: A possible cognitive marker to promote well-being? *Psychiatry Research, 206*(1), 56–61. DOI: 10.1016/j.psychres.2012.09.047.

[225] Holmes, E., Mathews, A., Dalgleish, T., & Mackintosh, B. (2006). Positive interpretation training: Effects of mental imagery versus verbal training on positive mood. *Behavior Therapy, 37*(3), 237–47. DOI: 10.1016/j.beth.2006.02.002.

[226] Maghaminejad, F., Adib, M., Nematian, F., & Armaki, M. A. (2020). The effects of guided imagery on test anxiety among the 1st-year nursing students: A randomized clinical trial. *Nursing and Midwifery Studies, 9*(3), 130–134. DOI: 10.41 03/nms.nms_65_18.

[227] Shobe, E., Brewin, A., & Carmack, S. (2005). A simple visualization exercise for reducing test anxiety and improving performance on difficult math tests. *Journal of Worry and Affective Experience* [merged with *Psychology* in 2007], *1*(1), 34–52. https://www.researchgate.net/profile/Elizabeth-Shobe/publication/259799625_A_simple_visualization_exercise_for_reducing_test_anxiety_and_improving_performance_on_difficult_math_tests/links/0c96052dea494e9cd6000000/A-simple-visualization-exercise-for-reducing-test-anxiety-and-improving-performance-on-difficult-math-tests.pdf.

[228] Landkroon, E., van Dis, E. A. M., Meyerbröker, K., Salemink, E., Hagenaars, M. A., & Engelhard, I. M. (2022). Future-oriented positive mental imagery reduces anxiety for exposure to public speaking. *Behavior Therapy, 53*(1), 80–91. DOI: 10.1016/j.beth.2021.06.005.

[229] Beck, B. D., Hansen, Å. M., & Gold, C. (2015). Coping with work-related stress through guided imagery and music

(GIM): Randomized controlled trial. *Journal of Music Therapy*, *52*(3), 323–52. DOI: 10.1093/jmt/thv011.

[230] Gross, J.J., & Levenson, R. W. (1997). Hiding feelings: The acute effects of inhibiting negative and positive emotion. *Journal of Abnormal Psychology*, *106*(1), 95–103. DOI: 10.1037//0021-843x.106.1.95. See also Gross, J. J., & John, O. P. (2003). Individual differences in two emotion regulation processes: Implications for affect, relationships, and wellbeing. *Journal of Personality and Social Psychology*, *85*(2), 348–362. DOI: 10.1037/0022-3514.85.2.348; see also Patel, J., & Patel, P. (2019). Consequences of repression of emotion: Physical health, mental health and general well being. *International Journal of Psychotherapy Practice and Research*, *1*(3), 16–21. DOI: 10.14302/issn.2574-612X.ijpr-18-2564; see also Lee, H. & An, S. (2019). Mediating effects of emotional venting via instant messaging (IM) and positive emotion in the relationship between negative emotion and depression. *Journal of Korean Academy of Community Health Nursing*, *30*(4), 571–580. DOI: 10.12799/jkachn.2019.30.4.571; see also John, O. P., & Gross, J. J. (2004). Healthy and unhealthy emotion regulation: Personality processes, individual differences, and lifespan development. *Journal of Personality*, *72*(6), 1301–1333. DOI: 10.1111/j.1467-6494.2004.00298.x; see also Vohs, K. D., Glass, B. D., Maddox, W. T., & Markman, A. B. (2010). Ego depletion is not just fatigue: Evidence from a total sleep deprivation experiment. *Social Psychological and Personality Science*, *2*(2), 166. DOI: 10.1177/1948550610386123; see also Chapman, B. P., Fiscella, K., Kawachi, I., Duberstein, P., & Muennig, P. (2013). Emotion suppression and mortality risk over a 12-year follow-up. *Journal of Psychosomatic Research*, *75*(4), 381–385. DOI: 10.1016/j.jpsychores.2013.07.014; see also Holahan, C. J., Moos, R. H., Holahan, C. K., Brennan, P. L., & Schutte, K. K. (2005). Stress generation, avoidance coping, and depressive symptoms: A 10-year model. *Journal of Consulting and Clinical Psychology*, *73*(4), 658–666. DOI: 10.1037/0022-006X.73.4.658; see also Chu, G. M., Goger, P., Malaktaris, A., & Lang, A. J. (2022). The role of threat appraisal and coping style in psychological response to the COVID-19 pandemic among university students. *Journal of Affective Disorders Reports*, *8*, Article 100325. DOI: 10.1016/j.jadr.2022.100325.

[231] See, e.g., Cioffi, D., & Holloway, J. (1993). Delayed costs of suppressed pain. *Journal of Personality and Social Psychology, 64*(2), 274–282. DOI: 10.1037/0022-3514.64.2.274.

[232] Liverant, G. I., Hofmann, S. G., & Litz, B. T. (2004). Coping and anxiety in college students after the September 11th terrorist attacks. *Anxiety, Stress & Coping: An International Journal, 17*(2), 127–139. DOI: 10.1080/0003379042000221412. See also Vicary, A., & Fraley, R. (2010). Student reactions to the shootings at Virginia Tech and Northern Illinois University: Does sharing grief and support over the internet affect recovery? *Personality & Social Psychology Bulletin, 36*(11), 1555–1563. DOI: 10.1177/0146167210384880; see also Bushman, B. J., Baumeister, R. F., & Stack, A. D. (1999). Catharsis, aggression, and persuasive influence: Self-fulfilling or self-defeating prophecies? *Journal of Personality and Social Psychology, 76*(3), 367–376. DOI: 10.1037/0022-3514.76.3.367; see also Olatunji, B. O., Lohr, J. M., & Bushman, B. J. (2007). The pseudopsychology of venting in the treatment of anger: Implications and alternatives for mental health practice. In T. A. Cavell & K. T. Malcolm (Eds.), *Anger, aggression and interventions for interpersonal violence* (pp. 119–141). Lawrence Erlbaum Associates Publishers; see also Lee, H. & An, S. (2019). Mediating effects of emotional venting via instant messaging (IM) and positive emotion in the relationship between negative emotion and depression. *Journal of Korean Academy of Community Health Nursing, 30*(4), 571–580. DOI: 10.12799/jkachn.2019.30.4.571.

[233] Angry? Breathing beats venting. (2007, February 28). *University of Arkansas News.* https://news.uark.edu/articles/8933/angry-breathing-beats-venting.

[234] Patel, J., & Patel, P. (2019). Consequences of repression of emotion: Physical health, mental health and general well being. *International Journal of Psychotherapy Practice and Research, 1*(3), 16–21. DOI: 10.14302/issn.2574-612X.ijpr-18-2564.

[235] Id. See also Al-Khouja, M., Weinstein, N., & Legate, N. (2022). Self-expression can be authentic or inauthentic, with differential outcomes for well-being: Development of the Authentic and Inauthentic Expression Scale (AIES). *Journal of*

Research in Personality, 97, Article 104191. DOI: 10.1016/j.jrp. 2022.104191; see also Kernis, M. H. (2003). Toward a conceptualization of optimal self-esteem. *Psychological Inquiry*, *14*(1), 1–26. DOI: 10.1207/S15327965PLI1401_01; see also Kraus, M. W., Chen, S., & Keltner, D. (2011). The power to be me: Power elevates self-concept consistency and authenticity. *Journal of Experimental Social Psychology, 47*(5), 974–980. DOI: 10.1016/j.jesp.2011.03.017; see also Rimé, B., Corsini, S., & Herbette, G. (2002). Emotion, verbal expression, and the social sharing of emotion. In S. R. Fussell (Ed.), *The Verbal Communication of Emotions: Interdisciplinary Perspectives* (pp. 185–208). Lawrence Erlbaum Associates Publishers; see also Graham, S. M., Huang, J. Y., Clark, M. S., & Helgeson, V. S. (2008). The positives of negative emotions: willingness to express negative emotions promotes relationships. *Personality and Social Psychology Bulletin, 34*(3), 394–406. DOI: 10.1177/ 0146167207311281; see also Zhang, R. (2017). The stress-buffering effect of self-disclosure on Facebook: An examination of stressful life events, social support, and mental health among college students. *Computers in Human Behavior, 75,* 527–537. DOI: 10.1016/j.chb.2017.05.043; see also Kahn, J.H. & Garrison, A.M. (2009). Emotional self-disclosure and emotional avoidance: Relations with symptoms of depression and anxiety. *Journal of Counseling Psychology,* 56(4): 573–584. DOI: 10.1037/a0016574; see also Lieberman, M. D., Eisenberger, N. I., Crockett, M. J., Tom, S. M., Pfeiffer, J. H., & Way, B. M. (2007). Putting feelings into words: Affect labeling disrupts amygdala activity in response to affective stimuli. *Psychological Science, 18*(5), 421– 428. DOI: 10.1111/j.1467-9280.2007.01916.x; see also Srivastava, S., Tamir, M., McGonigal, K. M., John, O. P., & Gross, J. J. (2009). The social costs of emotional suppression: A prospective study of the transition to college. *Journal of Personality and Social Psychology, 96*(4), 883–897. DOI: 10.10 37/a0014755; see also Côté, S. (2005). A social interaction model of the effects of emotion regulation on work strain. *The Academy of Management Review, 30*(3), 509–530. DOI: 10.2307/20159142.

[236] To manage your anger better, this Northeastern professor says to learn the difference between frustration and irritation. (2023, March 24). *Northeastern Global News.* https:// news.northeastern.edu/2019/02/21/to-manage-your-anger-

better-this-northeastern-professor-says-to-learn-the-difference-between-frustration-and-irritation.

[237] Lischetzke, T., Schemer, L., Glombiewski, J. A., In-Albon, T., Karbach, J., & Könen, T. (2021). Negative emotion differentiation attenuates the within-person indirect effect of daily stress on nightly sleep quality through calmness. *Frontiers of Psychology, 12*, Article 684117. DOI: 10.3389/fpsyg.2021.684117.

[238] Liu, D. Y., Gilbert, K. E., & Thompson, R. J. (2020). Emotion differentiation moderates the effects of rumination on depression: A longitudinal study. *Emotion, 20*(7), 1234–1243. DOI: 10.1037/emo0000627.

[239] Pond, Jr., R., Kashdan, T., DeWall, C., Farmer, A., Lambert, N., & Fincham, F. (2011). Emotion differentiation moderates aggressive tendencies in angry people: A daily diary analysis. *Emotion. 12*(2), 326–337. DOI: 10.1037/a0025762.

[240] Cameron, C. D., Payne, B. K., & Doris, J. M. (2013). Morality in high definition: Emotion differentiation calibrates the influence of incidental disgust on moral judgments. *Journal of Experimental Social Psychology, 49*(4), 719–725. DOI: 10.1016/j.jesp.2013.02.014.

[241] Kashdan, T. B., Ferssizidis, P., Collins, R. L., & Muraven, M. (2010). Emotion differentiation as resilience against excessive alcohol use: An ecological momentary assessment in underage social drinkers. *Psychological Science, 21*(9), 1341–1347. DOI: 10.1177/0956797610379863.

[242] Kircanski, K., Lieberman, M. D., & Craske, M. G. (2012). Feelings into words: Contributions of language to exposure therapy. *Psychological Science, 23*(10), 1086–1091. DOI: 10.1177/0956797612443830.

[243] Lee, J. Y., Lindquist, K. A., & Nam, C. S. (2017). Emotional granularity effects on event-related brain potentials during affective picture processing. *Frontiers in Human Neuroscience, 11*, Article 133. DOI: 10.3389/fnhum.2017.00133.

[244] Kashdan, T. B., Dewall, C. N., Masten, C. L., Pond, Jr., R. S., Powell, C., Combs, D., Schurtz, D. R., & Farmer, A. S. (2014). Who is most vulnerable to social rejection? The toxic

combination of low self-esteem and lack of negative emotion differentiation on neural responses to rejection. *Public Library of Science (PloS) One, 9*(3), e90651. DOI: 10.1371/journal.pone. 0090651.

245 Kashdan, T. B., Barrett, L. F., & McKnight, P. E. (2015). Unpacking emotion differentiation: Transforming unpleasant experience by perceiving distinctions in negativity. *Current Directions in Psychological Science, 24*(1), 10–16. DOI: 10.1177/ 0963721414550708.

246 Lieberman, M. D., Eisenberger, N. I., Crockett, M. J., Tom, S. M., Pfeifer, J. H., & Way, B. M. (2007). Putting feelings into words: Affect labeling disrupts amygdala activity in response to affective stimuli. *Psychological Science, 18*(5), 421–8. DOI: 10.1111/j.1467-9280.2007.01916.x.

247 Kashdan, T. B., Barrett, L. F., & McKnight, P. E. (2015). Unpacking emotion differentiation: Transforming unpleasant experience by perceiving distinctions in negativity. *Current Directions in Psychological Science, 24*(1), 10–16. DOI: 10.1177/ 0963721414550708.

248 Engert, V., Plessow, F., Miller, R., Kirschbaum, C., & Singer, T. (2014). Cortisol increase in empathic stress is modulated by social closeness and observation modality. *Psychoneuroendocrinology, 45,* 192–201. DOI: 10.1016/j. psyneuen.2014.04.005.

249 Your stress is my stress. (2014, May 1). *NeuroscienceNews.com.* https://neurosciencenews.com/cortisol-hpa-axis-stress-psychology-1007.

250 See Sterley, T.-L., Baimoukhametova, D., Füzesi, T., Zurek, A., Daviu, N., Rasiah, N., Rosenegger, D., & Bains, J. (2018). Social transmission and buffering of synaptic changes after stress. *Nature Neuroscience, 21,* 393–403. DOI: 10.1038/ s41593-017-0044-6.

251 Dimitroff, S. J., Omid, K., Necka, E. A., Decety, J., Berman, M. G., & Norman, G. J. (2017). Physiological dynamics of stress contagion. *Scientific Reports, 7*(1), 6168. DOI: 10.1038/ s41598-017-05811-1.

ENDNOTES

[252] Oberle, E., & Schonert-Reichl, K. A. (2016). Stress contagion in the classroom? The link between classroom teacher burnout and morning cortisol in elementary school students. *Social Science and Medicine, 159*(1), 30–37. DOI: 10.1016/j.socscimed.2016.04.031.

[253] Haker, H., Kawohl, W., Herwig, U., & Rössler, W. (2013). Mirror neuron activity during contagious yawning – an fMRI study. *Brain Imaging Behavior, 7*(1), 28–34. DOI: 10.1007/s11682-012-9189-9.

[254] Klepeis, N., Nelson, W., Ott, W., Robinson, J. P., Tsang, A. M., Switzer, P., Behar, J. V., Hern, S. C., & Engelmann, W. H. (2001). The National Human Activity Pattern Survey (NHAPS): A resource for assessing exposure to environmental pollutants. *Journal of Exposure Science & Environmental Epidemiology, 11*(3), 231–252. DOI: 10.1038/sj.jea.7500165.

[255] Easter, M. (2021). *The comfort crisis: Embrace discomfort to reclaim your wild, happy, healthy self.* Rodale Books.

[256] Mayer, F., Frantz, C., Bruehlman-Senecal, E., & Dolliver, K. (2009). Why is nature beneficial? The role of connectedness to nature. *Environment and Behavior, 41*(5), 607–643. DOI: 10.1177/0013916508319745.

[257] Bratman, G. N., Anderson, C. B., Berman, M. G., Cochran, B., de Vries, S., Flanders, J., Folke, C., Frumkin, H., Gross, J. J., Hartig, T., Kahn, P. H., Jr., Kuo, M., Lawler, J. J., Levin, P. S., Lindahl, T., Meyer-Lindenberg, A., Mitchell, R., Ouyang, Z., Roe, J., Scarlett, L., . . . Daily, G. C. (2019). Nature and mental health: An ecosystem service perspective. *Science Advances, 5*(7), eaax0903. DOI: 10.1126/sciadv.aax0903.

[258] Hunter, M. R., Gillespie, B. W., & Chen, S. Y. (2019). Urban nature experiences reduce stress in the context of daily life based on salivary biomarkers. *Frontiers in Psychology, 10*, Article 722. DOI: 10.3389/fpsyg.2019.00722.

[259] Stressed? Take a 20-minute nature pill. (2019, April 4). *EurekAlert*. https://www.eurekalert.org/news-releases/571880.

[260] Hartig, T., Evans, G. W., Jamner, L. D., Davis, D. S., & Gärling, T. (2003). Tracking restoration in natural and urban

field settings. *Journal of Environmental Psychology, 23*(2), 109–123. DOI: 10.1016/S0272-4944(02)00109-3.

[261] Roe, J., & Aspinall, P. (2010). The restorative benefits of walking in urban and rural settings in adults with good and poor mental health. *Health Place. 17*(1), 103–113. DOI: 10.1016/j.healthplace.2010.09.003.

[262] Berman, M. G., Kross, E., Krpan, K. M., Askren, M. K., Burson, A., Deldin, P. J., Kaplan, S., Sherdell, L., Gotlib, I. H., & Jonides, J. (2012). Interacting with nature improves cognition and affect for individuals with depression. *Journal of Affective Disorders, 140*(3), 300–305. DOI: 10.1016/j.jad.2012.03.012.

[263] Mayer, F., Frantz, C., Bruehlman-Senecal, E., & Dolliver, K. (2009). Why is nature beneficial? The role of connectedness to nature. *Environment and Behavior, 41*(5), 607–643. DOI: 10.1177/0013916508319745.

[264] Piff, P. K., Dietze, P., Feinberg, M., Stancato, D. M., & Keltner, D. (2015). Awe, the small self, and prosocial behavior. *Journal of Personality and Social Psychology, 108*(6), 883–899. DOI: 10.1037/pspi0000018.

[265] Berman, M., Jonides, J., & Kaplan, Stephen. (2008). The cognitive benefits of interacting with nature. *Psychological Science, 19*(12), 1207–1212. DOI: 10.1111/j.1467-9280.2008.02225.x.

[266] Kaplan, S., & Berman, M. (2010). Directed attention as a common resource for executive functioning and self-regulation. *Perspectives on Psychological Science, 5*(1), 43–57. DOI: 10.1177/1745691609356784.

[267] Berman, M., Jonides, J., & Kaplan, Stephen. (2008). The cognitive benefits of interacting with nature. *Psychological Science, 19*(12), 1207–1212. DOI: 10.1111/j.1467-9280.2008.02225.x.

[268] Id. See also Mayer, F., Frantz, C., Bruehlman-Senecal, E., & Dolliver, K. (2009). Why is nature beneficial? The role of connectedness to nature. *Environment and Behavior, 41*(5), 607–643. DOI: 10.1177/0013916508319745.

[269] Allen, S. (2018, September). The science of awe. *John Templeton Foundation, Greater Good Science Center, UC*

ENDNOTES 421

Berkeley. https://ggsc.berkeley.edu/images/uploads/GGSC-JTF_White_Paper-Awe_FINAL.pdf.

[270] Weiler, N. (2020, September 21). 'Awe walks' boost emotional well-being. *University of California San Francisco (UCSF).* https://www.ucsf.edu/news/2020/09/418551/awe-walks-boost-emotional-well-being.

[271] Keltner, D., & Haidt, J. (1999). Social functions of emotions at four levels of analysis. *Cognition and Emotion, 13*(5), 505–521. DOI: 10.1080/026999399379168.

[272] Weiler, N. (2020, September 21). 'Awe walks' boost emotional well-being. *University of California San Francisco (UCSF).* https://www.ucsf.edu/news/2020/09/418551/awe-walks-boost-emotional-well-being.

[273] Shiota, M. N., Neufeld, S. L., Yeung, W. H., Moser, S. E., & Perea E. F. (2011). Feeling good: Autonomic nervous system responding in five positive emotions. *Emotion, 11*(6), 1368–1378. DOI: 10.1037/a0024278.

[274] Joye, Y., & Bolderdijk, J. W. (2015). An exploratory study into the effects of extraordinary nature on emotions, mood, and prosociality. *Frontiers in Psychology, 5,* Article 1577. DOI: 10.3389/fpsyg.2014.01577.

[275] Rudd, M., Vohs, K. D., & Aaker, J. (2012). Awe expands people's perception of time, alters decision making, and enhances well-being. *Psychological Science, 23*(10), 1130–1136. DOI: 10.1177/0956797612438731.

[276] Griskevicius, V., Shiota, M. N., & Neufeld, S. L. (2010. Influence of different positive emotions on persuasion processing: A functional evolutionary approach. *Emotion, 10*(2), 190–206. DOI: 10.1037/a0018421.

[277] Alvarsson, J. J., Wiens, S., & Nilsson, M. E. (2010). Stress recovery during exposure to nature sound and environmental noise. *International Journal of Environmental Research and Public Health, 7*(3), 1036–1046. DOI: 10.3390/ijerph7031036.

[278] Ratcliffe, E., Gatersleben, B., & Sowden, P. (2013). Bird sounds and their contributions to perceived attention

restoration and stress recovery. *Journal of Environmental Psychology, 36,* 221–228. DOI: 10.1016/j.jenvp.2013.08.004.

[279] Jahncke, H., Eriksson, K., & Naula, Sanna. (2015). The effects of auditive and visual settings on perceived restoration likelihood. *Noise & Health, 17*(74), 1–10. DOI: 10.4103/1463-1741.149559.

[280] DeLoach, A. G., Carter, J. P., & Braasch, J. (2015). Tuning the cognitive environment: Sound masking with 'natural' sounds in open-plan offices. *Journal of the Acoustical Society of America, 137*(4), 2291–2291. DOI: 10.1121/1.4920363.

[281] Van Hedger, S., Nusbaum, H., Clohisy, L., Jaeggi, S., Buschkuehl, M., & Berman, M. (2018, February 27). Of cricket chirps and car horns: The effect of nature sounds on cognitive performance. *PsyArXiv Preprints.* DOI: 10.31234/osf.io/f5hcz.

[282] Lohr, V. I., Pearson-Mims, C. H., & Goodwin, G. K. (1996). Interior plants may improve worker productivity and reduce stress in a windowless environment. *Journal of Environmental Horticulture, 14*(2), 97–100. DOI: 10.24266/0738-2898-14.2.97.

[283] Nieuwenhuis, M., Knight, C., Postmes, T., & Haslam, S. A. (2014). The relative benefits of green versus lean office space: Three field experiments. *Journal of Experimental Psychology: Applied, 20*(3), 199–214. DOI: 10.1037/xap0000024.

[284] Malik, S. (2014, September 3). Office plants make workers more productive. *Business Insider.* https://www.business insider.com/office-plants-make-workers-more-productive-2014-9.

[285] An, M., Colarelli, S. M., O'Brien, K., & Boyajian, M. E. (2016). Why we need more nature at work: Effects of natural elements and sunlight on employee mental health and work attitudes. *Public Library of Science (PloS) One, 11*(5), e0155614. DOS: 10.1371/journal.pone.0155614.

[286] Lee, K., Williams, K., Sargent, L., Williams, N., & Johnson, K. (2015). 40-second green roof views sustain attention: The role of micro-breaks in attention restoration. *Journal of Environmental Psychology, 42,* 182–189. DOI: 10.10 16/j.jenvp.2015.04.003.

[287] Kelly, J. R. (1988). Entrainment in individual and group behavior. In J. E. McGrath (Ed.), *The social psychology of time: New perspectives* (pp. 89–110). Sage Publications, Inc.

[288] Aronson, E., & Gerard, E. (1966). Beyond Parkinson's law: The effect of excess time on subsequent performance. *Journal of Personality and Social Psychology, 3*(3), 336–339. DOI: 10.1037/h0023000.

[289] Evans, M. D. R., Kelley, P., & Kelley, J. (2017). Identifying the best times for cognitive functioning using new methods: Matching university times to undergraduate chronotypes. *Frontiers in Human Neuroscience, 11*, Article 188. DOI: 10.3389/fnhum.2017.00188.

[290] Facer-Childs, E. R., Campos, B. M., Middleton, B., Skene, D. J., & Bagshaw, A. P. (2019). Circadian phenotype impacts the brain's resting-state functional connectivity, attentional performance, and sleepiness. *Sleep, 42*(5), zsz033. DOI: 10.1093/sleep/zsz033.

[291] Berger, S. (2019, February 15). Early birds vs. night owls: How one has an advantage at work, according to science. *CNBC: Make It.* https://www.cnbc.com/2019/02/15/study-reveals-if-night-or-morning-people-have-brain-function-advantage.html.

[292] Sleep on it: How snoozing strengthens memories. (2013, April). *National Institutes of Health (NIH) News in Health.* https://newsinhealth.nih.gov/2013/04/sleep-it.

[293] See Maurer, L., Zitting, K. M., Elliott, K., Czeisler, C. A., Ronda, J. M., & Duffy, J. F. (2015). A new face of sleep: The impact of post-learning sleep on recognition memory for face-name associations. *Neurobiology of Learning and Memory, 126*, 31–38. DOI: 10.1016/j.nlm.2015.10.012.

[294] Martin, R. A., & Kuiper, N. A. (1999). Daily occurrence of laughter: Relationships with age, gender, and Type A personality. *Humor: International Journal of Humor Research, 12*(4), 355–384. DOI: 10.1515/humr.1999.12.4.355.

[295] "Courtly." *Online Etymology Dictionary.* https://www.etymonline.com/word/courtly#etymonline_v_28992. See also "Courtly." *Merriam Webster Dictionary.* https://www.merriam-webster.com/dictionary/courtly; see also "Courtly." *Oxford*

Learner's Dictionaries. https://www.oxfordlearnersdictionaries.com/us/definition/english/courtly?q=courtly; see also "Courtly." *Dictionary.com.* https://www.dictionary.com/browse/courtly.

[296] Gertz, S. J. (2014, March 28). The man who refused to laugh (and the book that laughed at him). *Booktryst.* http://www.booktryst.com/2014/03/the-man-who-refused-to-laugh-and-book.html.

[297] Berk, L. S., Tan, S. A., Fry, W. F., Napier, B. J., Lee, J. W., Hubbard, R. W., Lewis, J. E., & Eby, W. C. (1989). Neuroendocrine and stress hormone changes during mirthful laughter. *The American Journal of the Medical Sciences, 298*(6), 390–396. DOI: 10.1097/00000441-198912000-00006. See also Louie, D., Brook, K., & Frates, E. (2016). The laughter prescription: A tool for lifestyle medicine. *American Journal of Lifestyle Medicine, 10*(4), 262–267. DOI: 10.1177/1559827614550279.

[298] Froehlich, E., Madipakkam, A. R., Craffonara, B., Bolte, C., Muth, A. K., & Park, S. Q. (2021). A short humorous intervention protects against subsequent psychological stress and attenuates cortisol levels without affecting attention. *Scientific Reports, 11*(1), Article 7284. DOI: 10.1038/s41598-021-86527-1.

[299] Berk, L., Tan, S., & Berk, D. (2008). Cortisol and Catecholamine stress hormone decrease is associated with the behavior of perceptual anticipation of mirthful laughter. *The FASEB Journal, 22*(S1). DOI: 10.1096/fasebj.22.1_supplement.946.11.

[300] Manninen, S., Tuominen, L., Dunbar, R., Karjalainen, T., Hirvonen, J., Arponen, E., Hari, R., Jääskeläinen, I., Sams, M., & Nummenmaa, L. (2017). Social laughter triggers endogenous opioid release in humans. *The Journal of Neuroscience, 37*(25), 6125–6131. DOI: 10.1523/JNEUROSCI.0688-16.2017.

[301] Cha, M. Y., & Hong, H. S. (2015). Effect and path analysis of laughter therapy on serotonin, depression and quality of life in middle-aged women. *Journal of Korean Academy of Nursing, 45*(2), 221–230. DOI: 10.4040/jkan.2015.45.2.221.

ENDNOTES

[302] Yim, J. (2016). Therapeutic benefits of laughter in mental health: A theoretical review. *The Tohoku Journal of Experimental Medicine, 239*(3), 243–249. DOI: 10.1620/tjem.239.243.

[303] Zhao, J., Yin, H., Zhang, G., Li, G., Shang, B., Wang, C., & Chen, L. (2019). A meta-analysis of randomized controlled trials of laughter and humour interventions on depression, anxiety and sleep quality in adults. *Journal of Advanced Nursing, 75*(11), 2435–2448. DOI: 10.1111/jan.14000. See also How does humor affect mental health? (2021, March 29). *WebMD.* https://www.webmd.com/mental-health/how-does-humor-affect-mental-health.

[304] Coronel, J. C., O'Donnell, M. B., Pandey, P., Delli Carpini, M. X., & Falk, E. B. (2021). Political humor, sharing, and remembering: Insights from neuroimaging. *Journal of Communication, 71*(1), 129–161. DOI: 10.1093/joc/jqaa041.

[305] Garner, R. (2006). Humor in pedagogy: How ha-ha can lead to aha!. *College Teaching, 54*(1), 177–180. DOI: 10.3200/CTCH.54.1.177-180.

[306] Bains, G. S., Berk, L. S., Daher, N., Lohman, E., Schwab, E., Petrofsky, J., & Deshpande, P. (2014). The effect of humor on short-term memory in older adults: A new component for whole-person wellness. *Advances in Mind-Body Medicine, 28*(2):16–24. PMID: 24682001.

[307] Aaker, J. L., & Bagdonas, N. (2021). *Humor, seriously: Why humor is a secret weapon in business and life (And how anyone can harness it. Even you.)* Currency.

[308] Nelson, S. K., Layous, K., Cole, S. W., & Lyubomirsky, S. (2016). Do unto others or treat yourself? The effects of prosocial and self-focused behavior on psychological flourishing. *Emotion, 16*(6), 850–861. DOI: 10.1037/emo0000178.

[309] The art of kindness. (2020, May 29). *Mayo Clinic Health System.* https://www.mayoclinichealthsystem.org/hometown-health/speaking-of-health/the-art-of-kindness.

[310] Buchanan, K., & Bardi, A. (2010). Acts of kindness and acts of novelty affect life satisfaction. *The Journal of Social Psychology, 150*(3), 235–237. DOI: 10.1080/00224540903365554.

[311] Rowland, L., & Curry, O. S. (2019). A range of kindness activities boost happiness. *The Journal of Social Psychology, 159*(3), 340–343. DOI: 10.1080/00224545.2018.1469461.

[312] Lyubomirsky, S., Sheldon, K. M., & Schkade, D. (2005). Pursuing happiness: The architecture of sustainable change. *Review of General Psychology, 9*(2), 111–131. DOI: 10.1037/1089-2680.9.2.111.

[313] Otake, K., Shimai, S., Tanaka-Matsumi, J., Otsui, K., & Fredrickson, B. L. (2006). Happy people become happier through kindness: A counting kindnesses intervention. *Journal of Happiness Studies, 7*(3), 361–375. DOI: 10.1007/s10902-005-3650-z.

[314] Ko, K., Margolis, S., Revord, J., & Lyubomirsky, S. (2019). Comparing the effects of performing and recalling acts of kindness. *The Journal of Positive Psychology, 16*(1), 1–9. DOI: 10.1080/17439760.2019.1663252.

[315] Nelson, S. K., Layous, K., Cole, S. W., & Lyubomirsky, S. (2016). Do unto others or treat yourself? The effects of prosocial and self-focused behavior on psychological flourishing. *Emotion, 16*(6), 850–861. DOI: 10.1037/emo0000178.

[316] Aknin, L. B., Dunn, E. W., Proulx, J., Lok, I., & Norton, M. I. (2020). Does spending money on others promote happiness?: A registered replication report. *Journal of Personality and Social Psychology, 119*(2), e15–e26. DOI: 10.1037/pspa0000191.

[317] Dunn, E., Aknin, L., & Norton, M. (2014). Prosocial spending and happiness: Using money to benefit others pays off. *Current Directions in Psychological Science, 23*(1), 41–47. DOI: 10.1177/0963721413512503.

[318] Raposa, E. B., Laws, H. B., & Ansell, E. B. (2016). Prosocial behavior mitigates the negative effects of stress in everyday life. *Clinical Psychological Science, 4*(4), 691–698. DOI: 10.1177/2167702615611073.

[319] Ansell: Helping others dampens the effects of everyday stress. (2012, December 14). *Yale School of Medicine.* https://medicine.yale.edu/news-article/ansell-helping-others-dampens-the-effects-of-everyday-stress.

[320] Alden, L. E., & Trew, J. L. (2013). If it makes you happy: Engaging in kind acts increases positive affect in socially anxious individuals. *Emotion, 13*(1), 64–75. DOI: 10.1037/a0027761.

[321] Schacter, H. L. & Margolin, G. (2019). When it feels good to give: Depressive symptoms, daily prosocial behavior, and adolescent mood. *Emotion, 19*(5), 923–927. DOI: 10.1037/emo0000494.

[322] Nelson-Coffey, S. K., Fritz, M. M., Lyubomirsky, S., & Cole, S. W. (2017). Kindness in the blood: A randomized controlled trial of the gene regulatory impact of prosocial behavior. *Psychoneuroendocrinology, 81*, 8–13. DOI: 10.1016/j.psyneuen.2017.03.025.

[323] Williams, C. S. (2022, February 15). Does kindness equal happiness and health? *Medical Xpress.* https://medicalxpress.com/news/2022-02-kindness-equal-happiness-health.html.

[324] Id.